Do They Make
a Difference?

Do They Make a Difference?

The Policy Influence of Radical Right Populist Parties in Western Europe

Edited by Benjamin Biard,
Laurent Bernhard and Hans-Georg Betz

ecpr PRESS

Published by the European Consortium for Political Research, Harbour House, 6–8 Hythe Quay, Colchester, CO2 8JF, United Kingdom

British Library Cataloguing-in-Publication Data
A catalogue record for this book is available from the British Library

ISBN: HB 978-1-78552-329-8

Library of Congress Cataloging-in-Publication Data Available

ISBN 978-1-78552-329-8 (cloth)
ISBN 978-1-5381-5685-8 (pbk)
ISBN 978-1-78552-330-4 (electronic)

ecpr.eu/shop

Contents

Figures

CHAPTER 11

CHAPTER 12

Tables

Acknowledgements

This book started with a workshop organized at the University of Nottingham during the ECPR Joint Sessions of Workshops in 2017. During the editing process, another workshop was organized in Mons, at the Catholic University of Louvain (UCLouvain), in order to improve the quality of the chapters. Many people contributed to the smooth running of these workshops. We warmly thank them. Our gratitude also goes to the editors at ECPR Press for giving us the opportunity to write this book. Special thanks go to Madeleine Hatfield for her support throughout the entire process. Finally, we would like to thank Prof. Min Reuchamps (UCLouvain) for his valuable contribution from the beginning of the project.

Chapter 1

Introduction

Benjamin Biard and Laurent Bernhard

In the last decades, a new type of political party has emerged, which developed and strengthened its electoral weight in Europe (Taggart, 2000): radical right populist parties (RRPP). Three core elements are usually part of their basic definition (Mudde, 2007). In addition to authoritarianism (i.e. the belief in a strictly ordered society, in which infringements of authority are to be punished severely), the current literature puts much emphasis on populism and nativism. Populism, considered as an ideology, regards society as being ultimately separated into two homogeneous and antagonistic groups – the people and the elite, postulating that the will of the former has to prevail in any case (Mudde, 2004). Nativism, for its part, refers to the view that the sensibilities and needs of the 'native-born' should be given absolute priority over those of newcomers. It also reflects a conscious attempt by the former to defend, maintain and revive the cherished heritage of their culture (Betz, 2017).

While the emergence and development of RRPP has been particularly salient since the end of the 1990s (Widfeldt, 2010), the rise of this party family has been highly questioned. Apart from many journalists, citizens and policy-makers researchers also indeed consider populism as a threat to democracy (e.g. Urbinati, 2014; Rummens, 2017). Even though RRPPs increasingly abide by the basic rules of democracy, they are often considered a danger for the liberal principles of democracy such as the balance of power or minority rights (Urbinati, 2014). Albertazzi and Mueller (2013) have analysed policies championed by different populist parties in four European countries and have shown to what extent they are a threat to the liberal principles of democracy:

> The challenge posed by populists to liberal democracy has become most apparent in the anti-judiciary and anti-minorities policies approved in Italy,

as well as the threats to freedom of expression that have been waged in that country by the populist alliance. Polish initiatives against homosexuality, the independence of the judiciary and freedom of speech have also gone in the same direction. In Switzerland, the most anti-liberal policies (automatic expulsion of criminal foreigners and an outright ban on minarets) came about via referendums (through which the collegial government and parliament could be circumvented), while in Austria populist rule, at least at the provincial level, was marked by a willingness to openly challenge the rule of law. (Albertazzi and Mueller, 2013: 364)

Despite the difficult relationship between RRPP and liberal democracy and despite the fact that, as a reaction, many mainstream parties tend to rely on disengagement strategies towards RRPP, such as by adopting a *cordon sanitaire* (Meguid, 2005), they tend to be well integrated into the European political landscape. Several RRPP have indeed managed to formally participate in a government coalition (such as in Italy, Finland, Norway, Greece, Austria, or Switzerland) or to informally support a minority government (such as in Denmark or in The Netherlands).

To be sure, the populist phenomenon has already been extensively studied by scholars through different angles. Theoretical and empirical work mainly deals with the origins of populism (e.g. Kriesi and Pappas, 2015; Moffitt, 2016), their leaders (e.g. Vossen, 2013; McDonnell, 2016; Pappas, 2016), voters (e.g. Norris, 2005), activists (e.g. Gottraux and Péchu, 2011), citizens' voting behaviour (e.g. Bakker et al., 2015), party institutionalization (e.g. Arter and Kestilä-Kekkonen, 2014), party history (e.g. Betz, 2013), discourses (e.g. Wodak, 2015) and communication (e.g. Bernhard and Kriesi, 2019).

Despite this richness, there is an obvious need to go beyond the knowledge of these parties themselves and to explore the link between politics and policy, that is, to better understand the *policy influence* of RRPP. This need is explained by the electoral strength of RRPP, by the fact that they are often perceived as a threat to democracy and, consequently, by the fact mainstream parties tend to adopt specific strategies towards RRPP (Heinze, 2018). The aim of this book is to advance theoretical and empirical research in political science by bringing together a variety of contributions about the influence of RRPP in terms of policies. To that end, we ask under which conditions these parties are able to do so in contemporary Western Europe. This book proposes to examine the role played by *party status*. Are RRPP better able to leave their imprints on policies when they are in power than when they are not? This book focuses on the core issues of RRPP, that is, immigration, law and order issues and European integration. This choice is based on the well-established fact that parties generally give priority to the issues they own when it comes to influencing policies (e.g. Mansergh and Thomson, 2007).

DO RADICAL RIGHT POPULIST PARTIES MATTER?

The 'do parties matter' literature has explored the influence of political parties on politics, but also on policies (e.g. Schmidt, 1996; Hampshire and Bale, 2015). Analysing the policy influence of mainstream parties, these studies have adopted three main approaches: the study of the evolution of electoral pledges, the study of the correspondence between the issues defended by RRPP and policy agendas and the study of the effects of a government change (Wenzelburger, 2015; Guinaudeau and Persico, 2018). These approaches mostly indicate that political parties matter and can influence policy-making, even if their influence may vary in intensity according to a set of conditions. Because they are perceived as threatening liberal democracy, it is essential to also question if RRPP – as a specific party family – matter, and how.

The policy influence of RRPP has long been neglected by scholars. As a consequence of the spectacular rise of this party family throughout Europe, several researchers have investigated this question in recent years. It is beyond question that these studies are significant contributions to the scientific literature. Nevertheless it is obvious that the state of the art is still in its infancy (Han, 2014; Van Ostaijen and Scholten 2014).

To begin with, scholars have focused on a limited number of countries. Given that RRPP proved to be electorally successful in a wide range of West European countries, it seems appropriate to compare a large range of contexts. This book gathers several systematic comparisons as well as some more focused case studies. As to the latter, it addresses some well-documented cases such as Italy, Austria and Denmark, but also some rather understudied countries such as Switzerland, France or Germany.

In addition, the RRPP that have already been investigated in the literature refer to periods when such parties were in office (e.g. Albertazzi and McDonnell, 2015). Yet there are RRPP which support minority governments. Though the latest developments in Western Europe have made such a distinction relevant, this distinction should be taken into account. Moreover, opposition parties and parties without any parliamentary representation can also be influential actors in the policy-making process (Williams, 2006). There is thus the necessity to study these different kinds of party statuses in order to get a comprehensive overview of the influence of RRPP on policies.

Perhaps most strikingly, the state of the art suffers from a lack of coherence in terms of results. As stated by Carvalho (2016, 665), 'a frequent incongruence of this type of research concerns the contradictory character of its conclusions on similar time frames and identical case studies'. Several studies conclude that RRPP manage to shape public policy and, therefore, that they exercise a great influence on them (e.g. Minkenberg, 2001; Zaslove, 2004; Akkerman and de Lange, 2012; Afonso and Papadopoulos, 2015). At the same time, others found that their influence is strongly limited (Bouillaud, 2007; Heinisch, 2008; Tarchi, 2008).

In light of these two opposite conclusions that are available in the literature, some recently published pieces of research assert that their influence is more nuanced and may vary across policy domains (Verbeek and Zaslove, 2015) and country contexts (Carvalho, 2016). These studies bring particularly interesting insights to the literature, since they argue that the influence follows a context-dependent logic. In addition, other studies (Williams, 2006; Carvalho, 2014; Biard, 2019) draw attention to the fact that the influence exercised by RRPP can be *direct* or *indirect* in nature. In the former case, parties exert their influence based on their policy-making capacities because they hold enough seats in Parliament or because they are part of a cabinet. In the latter case, parties are able to obtain their preferred policies through the party system or via other actors (see Schain, 2006). For instance, Biro-Nagy and Boros (2016) have shown that the Hungarian Jobbik influences public policy in opposition through mainstream parties (mostly the Fidesz) since the latter one systematically implement the Jobbik pledges. Such a 'radicalization' of the legislation thus results from an indirect influence by RRPP, i.e. 'a shift in the policy preferences of mainstream parties because of perceived electoral pressure from [RRPP]' (Mudde, 2013: 10). According to this line of reasoning, RRPP would exercise an indirect influence only when they are electorally significant, that is, when they are considered as an electoral threat. Therefore, the role of mainstream parties towards RRPP is of primary importance, since these strategies affect the electoral performances of RRPP (Downs, 2001).

These burgeoning studies are of importance because they lay the ground for the understanding of the influence of RRPP on policy-making and offer keys to develop this knowledge. Given that the literature offers contradictory conclusions, we aim to clarify the understanding of the policy influence of RRPP. This edited volume is interested in the circumstances under which RRPP are able to influence policies in Western Europe. We generally hypothesize that the influence positively depends on the formal power of RRPP. Therefore, a RRPP in power – alone, with coalition partners or supporting a minority government – would exercise a greater policy influence than a RRPP in opposition or outside parliament. Ultimately, this edited volume contributes to better understand if being in power also means exercising power or influence. This is of primary importance, since many RRPP do not exercise power and since most RRPP exercising power in Western Europe are minor coalition partners, contrary to East European cases (such as Poland or Hungary, for instance). In addition, we will deal with the question of how RRPP are able to exert an indirect influence on policies. When they lack decision-making capacities, RRPP are dependent on mainstream parties.

Because they are often considered as threatening democracy, RRPP face different types of strategies adopted by mainstream parties (Meguid, 2005), which may have an impact on the policy influence of RRPP. The literature draws a distinction between inclusive and exclusive strategies (Goodwin, 2011). An inclusive strategy aims at collaborating with RRPP – legislatively or executively – while an exclusive strategy aims at excluding them from power, for instance by adopting a *cordon sanitaire* (Downs, 2001). In addition, mainstream parties may choose to accommodate when they perceive RRPP as a serious electoral threat (Meguid, 2005; Carvalho, 2016; Mudde, 2013). Costs of incumbency may indeed be high for RRPP because of their anti-establishment position (Luther, 2011). Once in power, they have to find policy compromises. Consequently, they may lose significant electoral shares. While a direct influence is expected to be found in cases where RRPP are in power, indirect effects are likely to occur when RRPP outside power do not face any exclusive strategy by mainstream parties and are considered as a serious electoral threat (Akkerman, 2012; Mudde, 2006; Schain, 2006).

To empirically study these claims, it appears appropriate to select RRPP with varying power status across time and space and facing a wide variety of strategies adopted by mainstream parties towards them. More specifically, this edited volume studies instances of RRPP in power (Swiss People's Party; Northern League in Italy; Austrian Freedom Party; The Finns), in support of minority government (the Danish People's Party), in opposition (the National Front in France; the Flemish Interest in Belgium), and without any parliamentary representation (the Alternative for Germany before 2017 in Germany). The main interest of this book is to consider the role played by formal party status as well as by the mechanisms that lead to indirect policy influence. While formal or informal government participation does not necessarily guarantee an influence on policies, being in opposition or even outside Parliament does not necessarily mean exerting no influence at all. Yet parties outside power have to exploit alternative ways in order to achieve their policy-related objectives. This book thus aims to advance our understanding of the conditions that enable RRPP to have an influence. All contributions are studied based on a same definition of influence – that is, 'a relation among actors in which one actor induces other actors to act in some way they would not otherwise act' (Dahl, 1973, 40).

All empirical chapters that constitute the main body of this volume show that RRPP exert a certain influence, be it directly or indirectly. Hence, RRPP are found to leave some imprints on their core issues. However, we need to stress that – in light of the radical demands made by RRPP – their influence proves to be usually rather limited in scope. While we are somewhat reluctant to conclude that RRPP in power are clearly more successful than those outside power when it comes to shifting policies in their desired direction, we find a consistent issue-specific pattern. In the domain of immigration, RRPP appear to have been very successful regarding the tightening of integration measures. By contrast, it turns out that the influence has been very modest as to questions related to the European Union. Another important and coherent finding pertains to the disproportionate power of parties that tolerate minority governments. As is exemplified by the intriguing case of the Danish People's Party (DPP), several chapters suggest that exploiting the blackmail potential pays off much better than being part of government coalitions. Regarding the indirect influence of RRPP, this edited volume suggests that the causal mechanisms are rather diverse.

THE STRUCTURE OF THE BOOK

The book contains eleven empirical chapters. To pursue the research question, the book is divided into three sections. The first section deals with RRPP outside power. The second section analyses RRPP in power. Finally, contrasted cases are compared in the third section.

Chapters 2 and 3 investigate RRPP outside power. In chapter 2, Malisa Zobel and Michael Minkenberg focus on the influence of the radical right in Germany, which has long played a marginal role at least when it comes to party politics. In order to contextualize the German case, the authors draw a comparison with Denmark. They find that established parties react to the growing organizational strength of RRPP by adopting their positions but also by contributing to adopt policies reflecting these positions. Their influence is thus exercised both at the agenda-setting stage of policy-making and during the adoption of decisions. The evidence for German case is particularly instructive, since it suggests that even an electorally weak radical right is able to exert a decisive influence on immigration policies.

Chapter 3 focuses on France. João Carvalho examines the influence of the French *Front national* (FN) on policies during President Hollande's term (2012–2017). This study is particularly relevant for this book, since it deals with a case of an institutionally marginalized RRPP. During the investigated period, the FN only had two seats in each of the Houses of the Parliament. Yet, the FN is found to have had an indirect influence on immigration policies, an influence that can indeed be considered disproportional in light to FN's electoral support within the French party system.

Chapter 4 by Nathalie Blanc-Noël investigates the Danish context from a comparative perspective. In order to provide some insights regarding the influence exercised by a RRPP that supported minority governments, she carefully compares the DPP to the Finns (PS). To assess and explain the influence of these two RRPP, she relies on their manifestoes as well as on the legislative acts on two major issues: immigration and culture policies. She finds that both parties are able to influence public policy but she also underlines the fact that reaching a governing position does not necessarily raise the chances for them to exert a policy influence. The author indeed concludes that the DPP exercised a much stronger influence than PS.

Chapter 5 deals with the context of Denmark. Flemming Juul Christiansen, Mikkel Bjerregaard and Jens Peter Frølund Thomsen analyse whether, and if so, how a RRPP that tolerates a government from outside is able to influence policies. This contribution is particularly interesting, given that the Danish People's Party (DPP) used to be a support party for a Liberal-Conservative minority government for ten years (2001–2011). The chapter looks at policy changes as to the party's core issues, that is, immigration, law and order and EU. The authors show that the DPP several times successfully pressurized governments to enact some policies the centre-right cabinet would not have opted for otherwise.

Chapter 6 takes a closer look at the Northern League. As a starting point, Christophe Bouillaud observes that while the Northern League had the greatest institutional opportunities to influence public policy because it often formally participated in the Italian government, most research concludes that the Northern League only exercised a marginal influence. The contribution reconsiders this claim by looking at four issue domains – immigration, European integration, federalism and the so-called Southern question. The overall policy influence proved to be inexistent with respect to Europe and only feeble as to federalism. However, the Northern League had some impact when it comes to introducing more restrictive immigration and law and order policies and managed to consolidate the structural North-South divide.

Chapter 7 – written by Fred Paxton – deals with the influence exercised by RRPP in power at the local level in Italy and Austria. In Padua and Wels, the Northern League and the FPÖ have recently been in the power by holding the position of mayor. Applying a qualitative content analysis of policy documents, this chapter demonstrates the importance of decision-making autonomy at the local level. More specifically, the government of Padua was able to make use of its greater degree of autonomy to introduce measures that exclude migrants from urban space and society, while the government of Wels put higher emphasis on rhetoric due to its lack of institutional competences.

Chapter 8 is devoted to Austria. Farid Hafez and Reinhard Heinisch focus on the FPÖ, one of the most successful RRPP in Western Europe. They convincingly show that the influence of the FPÖ has been substantial particularly with respect to questions of identity, culture, religion and immigration. The authors insist that the FPÖ has been very influential, even in times when the party was out of power. However, the party proved to be far less successful when it comes to EU-related questions.

The last section of the volume proposes comparisons between contrasted RRPP. In chapter 9, Benjamin Biard compares three dissimilar cases (the

French FN, the Swiss SVP and the Belgian VB) based on the process-tracing method. He finds that RRPP influence policy-making despite various relationships with power. Yet, their influence is also severely limited and mostly indirect, that is, exercised through other parties. The findings suggest a reflection regarding strategies adopted by mainstream parties towards RRPP but also regarding direct democracy since mainstream parties are able to prevent RRPP from exercising policy influence and since direct-democratic tools can increase the capacity of influence of RRPP.

In chapter 10, Juliana Chueri proposes to study an underdeveloped topic – welfare chauvinism. RRPP classically consider that welfare chauvinism is the solution to problems created by immigration. As underlined by Schumacher and van Kersbergen (2016, 300–301), 'their view is that immigrants make excessive use of the welfare state, which makes it unaffordable. [It is] the view that access to welfare should be restricted to the "deserving" natives'. Therefore, this chapter is also directly related to the immigration issue. Based on a large-N quantitative analysis of legislation changes in seventeen Western European countries from 1990 to 2014 the empirical analysis provides evidence for substantial direct effects. Indeed, government participation of RRPP is found to significantly reduce the immigrants' access to social policies. Strikingly enough, the statistical investigation further reveals that the influence of informal RRPP government participation on welfare chauvinism is greater than when RRPP formally participate in government coalitions.

Chapter 11 also relies on a quantitative study. Georg Wenzelburger and Pascal König investigate whether and how the strength of RRPP translates into the adoption of harsher law-and-order policies by the government. They assess this influence by comparing sixteen European countries from the 1980s to 2014 and show that centre-right or conservative mainstream parties that own law and order issues not only talk more about law and order in their manifestos but also spend more on this policy when they are in government. The policy influence of RRPP thus proves to be foremost indirect in nature and varies according to the parties in power.

Chapter 12 by Philipp Lutz focuses on the direct policy influence of RRPP on sub-domains of immigration policies. Based on a comparison of eighteen West European countries between 1990 and 2014, the author shows that RRPP in office does lead to material policy change. The empirical analysis shows that integration policies become more restrictive when RRPP are in power. By contrast, no significant effects are reported for admission and control policies. Lutz argues that restrictive policies are more likely to occur in the field of immigrant integration than in admission where governments have limited leeway for discretionary policies. In addition, the quantitative analysis shows that the influence of RRPP is stronger in the case of informal coalitions compared to formal coalitions as far as integration issues are concerned.

Finally, the conclusion by Hans-Georg Betz and Laurent Bernhard assesses the influence of RRPP in terms of policies by putting the book's main findings in a larger frame. It concludes that the Danish People's Party has been the RRPP in Western Europe that has been most effective in translating nativist rhetoric into concrete policies. It thus appears that supporting centre-right minority governments from the outside is a promising strategy. The radical right is able to exploit its 'blackmail' potential, given that government parties vitally depend on its goodwill.

BIBLIOGRAPHY

Abou-Chadi, Tarik. 2016. Niche party success and mainstream party policy shifts – how green and radical right parties differ in their impact. *British Journal of Political Science* 46, no. 2: 417–438.

Afonso, Alexandre and Yannis Papadopoulos. 2015. How the populist radical right transformed Swiss welfare politics: from compromises to polarization. *Swiss Political Science Review* 21, no. 4: 617–635.

Akkerman, Tjitske and Sarah de Lange. 2012. Radical right parties in office: incumbency records and the electoral cost of governing. *Government and Opposition* 47, no. 4: 574–596.

Albertazzi, Daniele and Duncan McDonnell. 2015. *Populists in Power*. New York: Routledge.

Albertazzi, Daniele and Sean Mueller. 2013. Populism and liberal democracy: populists in government in Austria, Italy, Poland and Switzerland. *Government and Opposition* 48: 343–371.

Arter, D. and Elina Kestilä-Kekkonen. 2014. Measuring the extent of party institutionalisation: the case of a populist entrepreneur party. *West European Politics* 37, no. 5: 932–956.

Bakker, Bert, Matthijs Rooduijn and Gijs Schumacher. 2015. The psychological roots of populist voting: evidence from the United States, the Netherlands and Germany. *European Journal of Political Research*, Online First.

Bernhard, Laurent and Hanspeter Kriesi. 2019. Populism in election times: a comparative analysis of eleven countries in Western Europe. *West European Politics* 42, no. 6: 1188–1208.

Betz, Hand-Georg. 2013. A distant mirror. Nineteenth-century populism, nativism, and contemporary right-wing radical politics. *Democracy and Security* 9, no. 3: 200–220.

Betz, Hans-Georg. 2017. Nativism across time and space. *Swiss Political Science Review* 23, no. 4: 335–353.

Biard, Benjamin. 2019. The influence of radical right populist parties on law and order policy-making. *Policy Studies*, 1: 40–57.

Biro-Nagy, Andras and Tamas Boros. 2016. Jobbik going mainstream ; strategy shift of the far right in Hungary. In *L'extrême droite en Europe*, edited by Jérôme Jamin, 243–263. Brussels: Bruylant.

Bouillaud, Christophe. 2007. La législation italienne des années 2001–2005 porte-t-elle la marque des nouvelles droites?. In *Extrême droite et pouvoir en Europe,* edited by Pascal Delwit and Philippe Poirrier, 265–290. Brussels: Ed. de l'Université libre de Bruxelles.

Carvalho, Joao. 2014. *Impact of Extreme Right Parties on Immigration Policy. Comparing Britain, France and Italy.* New York: Routledge.

Carvalho, Joao. 2016. The impact of extreme right parties on immigration policy in Italy and France in the early 2000s. *Comparative European Politics* 14, no. 5: 663–685.

Dahl, Robert. 1973. *L'analyse politique contemporaine.* Paris: Laffont.

Downs, William. 2001. Pariahs in their midst: Belgian and Norwegian parties react to extremist threats. *West European Politics* 24, no. 3: 23–42.

Goodwin, Matthew. 2011 *Right response. Understanding and Countering Populist Extremism in Europe.* London: Chatham House.

Gottraux, Philippe and Cécile Péchu. 2011. *Militants de l'UDC. La diversité sociale et politique des engagés.* Lausanne: Antipodes.

Guinaudeau, Isabelle and Simon Persico. 2018. Tenir promesse. Les conditions de réalisation des programmes électoraux. *Revue française de science politique* 68, no. 2: 215–237.

Hampshire, James and Tom Bale. 2015. New administration, new immigration regime: do parties matter after all? A UK case study. *West European Politics* 38, no. 1: 145–166.

Han, Kyung Joon. 2015. The impact of radical right-wing parties on the positions of mainstream parties regarding multiculturalism. *West European Politics* 38, no. 3: 557–576.

Heinisch, Reinhard. 2008. Austria: the structure and agency of Austrian populism. In *Twenty-First Century Populism: The Spectre of Western European Democracy,* edited by Daniele Albertazzi, and Duncan McDonnell, 68–83. Basingstoke: Palgrave Macmillan.

Heinze, Anna-Sophie. 2018. Strategies of mainstream parties towards their right-wing populist challengers: Denmark, Norway, Sweden and Finland in comparison. *West European Politics* 41, no. 2: 287–309.

Howlett, Michael and Sarah Giest. 2013. The policy-making process. In *Routlege Handbook of Public Policy,* edited by Eduardo Araral, Scott Fritzen, and Michael Howlett. New York: Routledge.

Kriesi, Hanspeter and Takkis Pappas. 2015. *European Populism in the Shadow of the Great Recession.* Colchester: ECPR Press.

Luther, Kurt R. 2011. Of goals and own goals: A case study of right-wing populist party strategy for and during incumbency. *Party Politics* 17, no. 4: 453–470.

Mansergh, Lucy and Robert Thomson. 2007. Election pledges, party competition, and policymaking. *Comparative Politics* 39, no. 3: 311–329.

McDonnell Duncan. 2016. Populist leaders and coterie charisma. *Political Studies* 64, no. 3: 719–733.

Meguid, Bonnie. 2005. Competition between unequals: the role of mainstream party strategy in niche party success. *American Political Science Review* 99, no. 3: 347–359.

Minkenberg, Michael. 2001. The radical right in public office: agenda-setting and policy effects. *West European Politics* 24, no. 4: 1–21.

Moffitt, Benjamin. 2016. *The Global Rise of populism. Performance, Political style, and Representation*. Stanford, CA: Stanford University Press.

Mudde, Cas. 2004. The populist zeitgeist. *Government and Opposition* 39, no. 3: 541–563.

Mudde, Cas. 2007. *Populist Radical Right Parties in Europe*. Cambridge: Cambridge University Press.

Mudde, Cas. 2013. Three decades of populist radical right parties in Western Europe: So what? *European Journal of Political Research* 52, no. 1: 1–19.

Norris, Pippa. 2005. *Radical Right: Voters and Parties in The Electoral Market*. New York: Cambridge University Press.

Pappas, Takkis. 2016. Are populist leaders 'charismatic'? The evidence from Europe. *Constellations*, Online First.

Röth, Leonce, Alexandre Afonso and Denis Spies. 2017. The impact of populist radical right parties on socio-economic policies. *European Political Science Review*, Online First.

Rummens, Stefan. 2017. Populism as a threat to liberal democracy. In *The Oxford Handbook of populism*, edited by Cristobald Rovira Kaltwasser, Paul Taggart, Paulina Ochoa Espejo, and Pierre Ostiguy, 554–570. Oxford: Oxford University Press.

Schain, Martin. 2006. The extreme-right and immigration policy-making: measuring direct and indirect effects. *West European Politics* 29, no. 2: 270–289.

Schmidt, Manfred. 1996. When parties matter: a review of the possibilities and limits of partisan influence on public policy. *European Journal of Political Research* 30, no. 2: 150–183.

Schumacher, Gijs and Kees Van Kersbergen. 2016. Do mainstream parties adapt to the welfare chauvinism of populist parties? *Party Politics* 22, no. 3: 300–312.

Taggart, Paul. 2000. *Populism*. Buckingham: Open University Press.

Taguieff, Pierre-André. 2007. *L'illusion populiste*. Paris: Flammarion.

Tarchi, Marco. 2008. Italy: a country of many populisms. In *Twenty-first century populism: The spectre of Western European democracy*, edited by Daniele Albertazzi, and Duncan McDonnell, 84–99. Basingstoke: Palgrave Macmillan.

Urbinati, Nadia. 2014. *Democracy Disfigured. Opinion, Truth, and the People*. Cambridge, MA: Harvard University Press.

Van Ostaijen, Mark and Peter Scholten. 2014. Policy populism? Political populism and migrant integration policies in Rotterdam and Amsterdam. *Comparative European Politics* 2, no. 6: 680–699.

Verbeek, Bertjan and Andrej Zaslove. 2015. The impact of populist radical right parties on foreign policy: the Northern League as a junior coalition partner in the Berlusconi Governments. *European Political Science Review* 7, no. 4: 525–546.

Vossen, Koen. 2013. *Rondom Wilders: portret van de PVV*. Amsterdam: Boom.

Wenzelburger, Georg. 2015. Parties, institutions and the politics of law and order: how political institutions and partisan ideologies shape law-and-order spending in twenty western industrialized countries. *British Journal of Political Science* 45, no. 3: 663–687.

Widfeldt, Anders. 2010. A fourth phase of the extreme right? Nordic immigration-critical parties in a comparative context. *Nordeuropa Forum* 1: 7–31.

Williams, Michele Hale. 2006. *The Impact of Radical Right-Wing Parties in West European democracies*. New York: Palgrave MacMillan.

Wodak, Ruth. 2015. *The politics of fear*. Thousand Oaks: Sage.

Wolinetz, Steven, and Andrej Zaslove. 2018. *Absorbing the blow. Populist Parties and Their Impact on Parties and Party Systems*. London: ECPR Press.

Zaslove, Andrej. 2004. Closing the door? The ideology and impact of radical right populism on immigration policy in Austria and Italy. *Journal of Political Ideologies* 9, no. 1: 99–118.

Chapter 2

From the Margins, But Not Marginal

Putting the German Radical Right's Influence on Immigration Policy in a Comparative European Context

Malisa Zobel and Michael Minkenberg

For a long time, post-war Germany was perceived as an exceptional case in the study of radical right party politics because these parties were not represented in national parliament. This picture changed dramatically in 2017 when the Alternative for Germany (Alternative für Deutschland, AfD) passed the electoral threshold for the first time and became the third largest party in the German Bundestag. Yet, this does not mean that the radical right in Germany did not play an important role in German politics before 2017, as we will show in the following. This chapter thus addresses the question of the radical right's influence on immigration policies in cases where they do not hold power in government and assesses the role of the radical right's electoral strength in relation to its influence. By doing so, it follows a growing stream of comparative research on the radical right's influence on policies and with a particular emphasis on the underlying processes at work. The chapter also attempts to advance the conceptualization of such research by providing an analytical model for further research. This is done by introducing and applying an interaction model (not to be confused with a statistical interaction model), which highlights the paths and patterns of the radical right's interaction with its political environment, most notably other parties and governments. At the level of the party system, the element of interaction and social control is of crucial importance and can be distinguished into types of demarcation, confrontation and ignoring on the one hand, the so-called *cordon sanitaire,* and co-optation and collaboration on the other. The existence of a *cordon sanitaire* is decisive as to whether a small or new party can be considered as acquiring 'coalition potential', and thereby exercising a high level of influence on agenda setting and policy-making, along with enjoying a high level of recognition, or whether it can only hope to exercise 'blackmail potential', which in turn depends on reaching a threshold in electoral mobilization (Sartori, 1976). Empirically, the chapter will outline the pathways by which radical right anti-immigrant politics has come to have important effects on the policies adopted by two West European democracies, Denmark and Germany, over the last thirty years. While Denmark figures as a paradigmatic case of radical right influence with a strong radical right populist party in parliament at times even supporting minority governments, Germany presents an intriguing case, diverging from West European 'normalcy' in many ways. Until recently, there were only very weak radical right parties which time and again failed to win seats in the national parliament, accompanied by a rather lively movement sector and subcultural milieus; yet the radical right parties were not inconsequential. Based on the German case but in a comparative logic, we argue that policy relevance of the radical right does not require parliamentary presence but rather depends on the interaction patterns between mainstream parties and the radical right. Moreover, the German case deserves particular attention because it combines a variety of factors and characteristics, which in their concurrence do not exist in other countries usually included in comparative studies of the radical right. A long period of a fragmented radical right party sector was followed by the meteoric rise of a new radical right party, the AfD; the weak party sector has always been complemented by a strong movement sector, which exhibited relatively high levels of anti-immigrant violence including right-wing terrorism; and Germany's reunification in 1990 added an element of post-Communist transition, thereby heightening the country's regional complexities, as organized and expressed in its federal system (see Minkenberg, 2009, 146–149).

CONCEPTUAL FRAMEWORK

Following the research on party families (e.g. Caramani, 2008; Lipset and Rokkan, 1967; Mair and Mudde, 1998; von Beyme, 1984), the radical right is defined here as a collective actor with a distinct political ideology, the core element of which is a romantic and populist ultra-nationalism directed against the concept of liberal and pluralistic democracy and its underlying principles of individualism and universalism (see Minkenberg, 1998, ch. 1; 2013a). This term and its use largely overlaps with Cas Mudde's concept of the 'populist radical right' (2007; for an alternative, see Betz, 1994). But it de-emphasizes the definitional criterion of 'populism', which we consider more a characteristic of style than of substance, and prioritizes the ideological core of such parties (see Minkenberg and Zobel, 2018; also Art, 2011, 10–12). In other words: the radical right is characterized primarily by its radicalizing inclusionary and exclusionary criteria of a primary 'we group', such as ethnicity, religion and/or gender (see also Heitmeyer, 2005).

In line with most research on the contemporary radical or populist right, it is differentiated ideologically into a number of variants: they range from outright anti-democratic or fascist-autocratic (here: extremist) to ethnocentrist but not explicitly anti-democratic, to religious-fundamentalist versions (see Minkenberg, 1998, 2013a, as well as Carter, 2005; Ignazi, 2003; Kitschelt and McGann, 1995). Moreover, the radical right can be distinguished by actor type, ranging from party to non-party manifestations such as movements and subcultural milieus. Even though each organizational type follows its own approach to institutional political power and public resonance, these groups often overlap in their membership and join forces on various occasions in practice.

As reminded in the introduction to the book, research on the role and influence of the radical right in Western democracies has unfolded only recently. Various studies demonstrate, for example, how the radical right changed or radicalized public opinion and discourse, altered the positions and strategic behaviour of mainstream parties, affected government policies or induced counter-activities by state actors and civil society (see e.g. Akkerman, 2012, 2015; Akkerman and de Lange, 2012; Bale et al., 2010; Capoccia, 2013; Carter, 2005; Carvalho, 2013; Downs, 2001; 2012; Meguid, 2005; Minkenberg, 2001, 2002, 2006; Mudde, 2007; Schain, 2006; van Spanje, 2010; Williams, 2006, 2013, 2015, 2018; Zobel, 2017).

A model which helps explain how the radical right shapes these processes must take into account the dynamics of interaction between the radical right and other political actors (particularly other parties and party competition) as well as the cultural and institutional context in which such interaction takes place (see McAdam 1999: xiv). Based on these considerations, which follow the rationale and findings of earlier studies by one of the authors (Minkenberg, 2002, 2009, 2013b, 2017), we pay particular attention to the interactions between established parties and the radical right. More specifically, the influence of the radical right does not occur linearly but takes place on various levels and to varying degrees, for example, agenda-setting and policy-making levels as well as the degree of activity or passivity of public response patterns (see Downs, 2012; Minkenberg, 2002, 2009, 2013, Mudde, 2007, 2014; Williams, 2006; Zobel, 2017). In line with the theoretical framework of this edited volume, a distinction will be made between direct influence, that is, changes which can be directly attributed to the radical right, such as policies or administrative acts executed by radical right parties in government or through collaboration with government parties, and indirect influence which occurs through radical right groups' influence on other actors, for example, by exercising pressures and lobbying activities on policy-makers.

Despite this complexity of the dynamic political process we propose an analytical model with a limited set of factors relevant to determine radical right influence on immigration policy. Immigration policy is defined broadly as all issues pertaining to the movement, settlement, status and rights of people who migrated from one country to another (for a similar definition see Bjerre et al., 2015). Figure 2.1 displays these patterns of interaction and resulting radical right influence across the different arenas. It shows that such influence depends on the specific strategic options of the mainstream parties, including the timing of their application. These strategic options are situated between the poles of a *cordon sanitaire* (ignoring or demarcating and confronting) on the one side and *contagion* (co-optation and collaboration) on the other (Downs, 2001, 2012; Meguid, 2005, 2008; Minkenberg, 1998, ch. 9; van Spanje, 2010). Mainstream parties will choose one of the available strategies if a radical right party is able to exercise electoral pressure. Whereas choosing to confront and demarcate the radical right will increase the salience of immigration issues, ignoring the radical right party will not. The latter, however, only works if all parties agree on ignoring the radical right challenger. The *cordon sanitaire* generally is only effective if all parties chose a strategy of disengagement or at least negative engagement. Nevertheless, while a *cordon sanitaire* is in place we do not expect the radical right

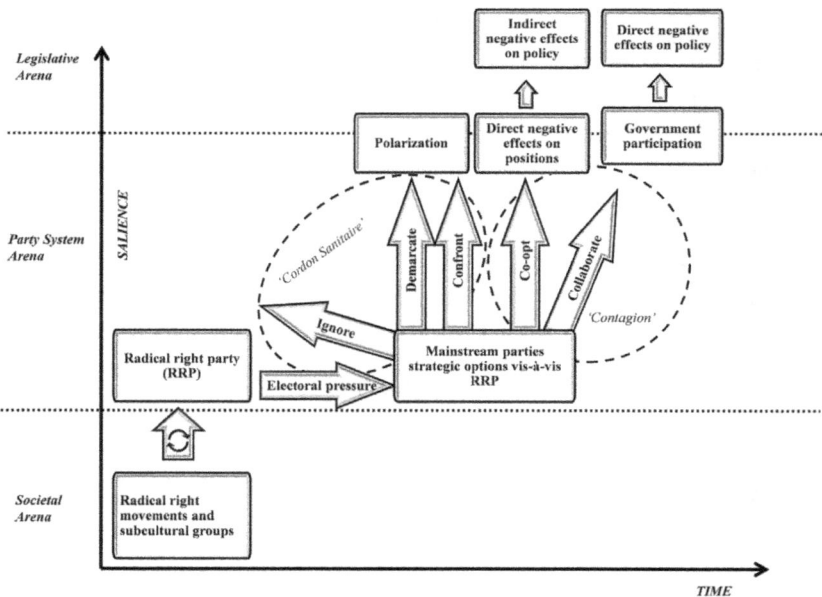

Figure 2.1.   Modelling the impact of the radical right on agenda-setting and policy-making.

to have influence on immigration policy, but party competition and discourse might become more polarized.

As time passes by (horizontal axis in figure 2.1) and the radical right party continues to be successful at the polls, it becomes harder to keep the *cordon sanitaire*. Some mainstream parties will choose to co-opt radical right positions, therefore becoming more restrictive on immigration themselves. If co-optation occurs very early, the salience of immigration issues might be reduced, but if it comes rather late and the radical right has already established ownership of the immigration issue, salience might increase instead of decreasing (see figure 2.1). Co-optation is however not limited to positions; parties might also take over the narrative framing of specific issues (see Pytlas, 2015). Moreover, depending on the timing co-optation might either lead to the demise or rise of the radical right. On the one hand, if co-optation occurs at an early point of time, it may reduce the votes for and the mobilization potential of the radical right (Downs, 2012). Yet, this short-term gain is likely to be outweighed by long-term effects, which pose risks for democracy, such as a radicalization of the mainstream and public discourse. On the other hand, the co-optation of radical right positions might also make the government participation of radical right populist parties more likely, as the ideological distance between the mainstream party and the potential coalition partner from the radical right is reduced. Once in government the radical right can directly affect immigration-related policy-making. The breakdown or the absence of a *cordon sanitaire* then feeds back into the policy-making process by increasing the radical right's credibility and room to manoeuvre vis-à-vis other parties.

The crucial element in the interaction model of figure 2.1 is the electoral pressure that the radical right puts on mainstream parties. This goes beyond a purely quantitative measure of electoral strength such as number of votes or seats won at the last national election, like it is often used in large-N studies. While electoral strength might be a good proxy, we follow Sartori's seminal work (1976) and distinguish between radical right parties that have 'blackmail potential' or 'coalition potential'. Sartori (1976) describes blackmail potential as the power of intimidation. He writes that a party with blackmail potential 'alters the direction of the competition [. . .] either leftward, rightward, or in both directions' (Sartori, 1976, 123). In order to have blackmail potential the mainstream parties need to *perceive* the RRPP as a threat. This threat can refer to the threat of losing further votes but also – and more importantly – to the threat of losing legislative majorities or being unable to form coalitions. Therefore, it is important to emphasize that radical right parties' blackmail potential is not being restricted to a presence in parliament but can also include significant levels of electoral support below the existing national electoral thresholds (see Minkenberg, 2002; also Pederson, 1982). Because even if a radical right party does not pass the national threshold, it might be threatening votes in particular electoral districts, which are more important for maintaining an electoral majority than others (see Money, 1999) or votes in regional elections, which are important in federal systems with bicameralism like Germany. Moreover, as time goes by the radical right might evolve from having blackmail potential to becoming viable coalition partners, thereby evoking a more inclusive strategy by their mainstream competitors.

Although our focus lies on radical right parties and particular spheres of interaction and influence, it does not mean that other actors and spheres are excluded from the analysis. The non-party radical right (see figure 2.1 societal arena; and Minkenberg, 2009, 2013b) may also trigger responses from the state and civil society and influence strategic choices of the radical right and mainstream political parties. These radical right groups will however only be included in the analysis to the extent that radical right parties have links to them and other actors showed a reaction to such radical right movement mobilization or racist violence, which pertains to radical right party mobilization.

From the analytical model outlined above we derive the following propositions: (i) right-ward shifts in public policy are more likely to occur if mainstream parties pursue a strategy of positive engagement (e.g. do not uphold a *cordon sanitaire*); (ii) once a right-ward shift occurs, restrictive changes are likely to prevail (policy is 'sticky'); (iii) once a right-ward shift occurs, the disappearance of the radical right from parliament or the electoral arena does not automatically lead to a 'return to the centre' (transformation of mainstream party/parties) but it might decrease the salience of immigration issues. More propositions could be derived from the analytical model in figure 2.1, but these three aforementioned propositions will be investigated in the following empirical analysis of Denmark and Germany.

Denmark presents a well-studied case (see Andersen and Bjorklund, 2000; Christiansen, 2016; Rydgren, 2004; Widfeldt, 2000, 2015, and in this edited volume chapters by Blanc-Noël and Christiansen) with a long and strong presence of radical right parties and informal government participation. In contrast, Germany has seen only sporadic episodes of radical right party support, at least until 2015 when the newly founded Alternative for Germany (Alternative für Deutschland, AfD) joined the radical right party family in Europe. Hence, the two cases provide pertinent contrasting evidence for our propositions in several regards. First, in Denmark a radical right party has been represented in national parliament for decades. Second, from 2001 until 2011 and again since 2015, the offshoot of the older radical right party has become a key supporter for a minority national governing coalition. Finally, and most importantly Denmark has not seen a *cordon sanitaire* against the radical right as Germany has. Co-optation strategies in Denmark went hand in hand with collaborating with the radical right party and the mainstream right saw in its rise an opportunity to win the prime ministerial office rather than a threat to its vote share and coalition options. In sum, Denmark is a useful starting point of our empirical analysis because it is one of the paradigmatic cases in Western Europe (the others being Austria, Italy and the Netherlands) in which radical right influence can be observed at the policy level due to the lack of a *cordon sanitaire*.

THE PARADIGMATIC CASE: DENMARK

In 1995, a group of MPs and party members around former party leader Pia Kjærsgaard split away from the older Danish Progress Party (Uafhængig Fremskridspartiet, FRP) to form the Danish People's Party (Dansk Folkepartiet, DF) (Widfeldt, 2000, 489–490). This offshoot became increasingly successful, winning 7.4 per cent of the votes in 1998. In contrast to its predecessor, the DF turned away from neoliberal policies towards welfare chauvinism. This strategic move threatened the Social Democratic led government, which had just implemented a range of welfare state cuts (Jonsson and Petersen, 2012, 124). In the run-up to the 1998 elections the DF had therefore framed immigration as the biggest threat to the welfare state, and immigrants as undeserving abusers of Danish generosity (Rydgren, 2004, 486). Fearing to lose working-class voters to the DF, the Social Democrats also adopted a sceptical position to immigration. The Social Democrat led government tried to weaken the DF's support base by introducing a two-tier welfare system with less benefits for immigrants but repealed the law in 1999 due to international pressure (see Hervik, 2011, 70; Roemer et al., 2007, 201). Yet, immigration and immigrant integration stayed on the public agenda. Within the social democratic party conflict over the right strategy towards the DF and the immigration issue erupted publicly. Abusive comments of deporting asylum-seekers to a deserted island by a prominent member of the Social Democrats (see Skou, 2006, 371) only legitimized the DF's anti-immigrant discourse and made the DF appear if not moderate, at least not very extreme.

The mainstream right party Venstre perceived the rise of the DF and the conflict within the Social Democrats over immigration issues as an opportunity to win control of government. In the period before the 1998 elections, Venstre refused to keep immigration out of the election campaign (Bjoerklund and Andersen, 1999, 26) and before the 2001 elections fully concentrated on the issue. The party promised to re-introduce the controversial two-tier welfare system (Dominelli and Moosa-Mitha, 2014, 78) and its new party leader Vogh Rasmussen published a piece in the DF's party journal, welcoming a co-operation between Venstre and DF without the DF having to give up its opposition to immigration and immigrant integration (Rydgren, 2004, 496). Among the DF campaigns during the 2001 election was a DF book listing fourteen pages of crimes by immigrants against native Danes in order to support the populist argument that immigration was leading to rising criminality (Rydgren, 2004, 485). Subsequently immigration became the most salient issue during the 2001 elections, trumping even economic issues (see Benoit and Laver, 2009).

The outcome of the 2001 election was an immense loss for the Social Democrats and large gains for both Venstre and the DF. The government changed from the centre left to the right, as Venstre entered a coalition with the conservatives (KF) supported by the DF. Together these three parties commanded an absolute majority of seats (Rytter and Pedersen, 2013, 2306). Moreover, the DF received five chairmanships and six vice-chairmanships in important parliamentary committees; this meant that they now had considerable influence on immigration and integration policy (Rydgren, 2004, 496). The Venstre-led government then significantly restricted immigration and increased conditions and requirements for already residing immigrants, and the DF was thus able to shape immigration policy according to its preferences (see also Christiansen, 2016, 104–5).[1]

These legislative restrictions, however, did not tame the DF. After one legislative period of lending support to the Venstre minority government, the 2005 DF election campaign continued to focus on immigration. DF leader Pia Kjærsgaard made many speeches against immigration, while the party enlisted Søren Krarup from the Danish Association (a far right extra-party group) to write most of the position papers on the issue (Karpantschof, 2003, 36).[2] Simultaneously, the police registered an increasing case of hate speech (EUMC, 2005, 77–78). Moreover, the DF became increasingly Islamophobic. In 2004 the DF rallied against plans for building a mosque and a Muslim cultural centre in Århus, the second largest Danish city. This only intensified after the publication of caricatures of prophet Muhammad by Danish newspaper *Jyllands-Posten* led to the so-called cartoon crisis in 2005. In the same year the DF continued its support for the re-elected Venstre–KF coalition government. Meanwhile the Social Democrats also became more immigration sceptical during their time in opposition as they elected Thorning-Schmidt, known for her outspoken criticism of immigration, as their party leader.[3] Yet, the Social Democrats were not able to win back government from the Venstre–KF minority government with DF support until 2011. Once in government, the social democratic-led coalitions further restricted asylum. In fact, the restrictions were so severe that the government was criticized by the UNHCR for it. In 2013 after two years in government and a range of unpopular economic reforms the Social Democrats fell to 17 per cent in voters' support, the party tried to regain favour by engaging very tough immigration rhetoric (see Zobel, 2017, 111). This was also a result of the Social Democrats and the DF competing over the same segment of voters. From the start, the DF mobilized even more working class voters than the Social Democrats. In 1998, it drew 49 per cent of its vote from that source, as compared to 43 per cent for the Social Democrats. This vote share increased to 56 per cent in the 2001 election, a sign that working-class alienation from the traditional working class parties has occurred in Denmark, just as it has in other West European countries (Rydgren, 2004, 490; also Rydgren, 2013). The attempts by the Social Democrats to outcompete the DF on immigration and asylum were, however, not successful as they lost governmental power in 2015. Similar to 2001 and 2005, the 2015 elections were again dominated by the immigration issue and for the first time the DF became the second largest party in the country with 21.1 per cent (see Christiansen, 2016, 95). This also meant that for the first time the right bloc was dominated not by the mainstream right but by the radical right, as the DF received more votes and seats than Venstre.

Denmark's established parties have neither tried to isolate nor adopted a *cordon sanitaire* with regard to the DF. To the contrary, populist anti-immigrant rhetoric found its way into mainstream political discourse and has transformed the established parties permanently (i.e. Venstre moved far to the right and now shares little with liberal parties in other countries). Liberal and Conservative politicians (Venstre and Det Konservative Folkepartiet) began to adopt a more right-wing rhetoric from 1997 onwards (Rasmussen, 2001, 109) and have not toned down anti-immigrant positions since then. The Social Democrats were initially more conflicted on immigration issues but have equally engaged in anti-immigrant rhetoric and implemented a range of restrictive changes in this policy field. All parties took a more or less aggressive anti-immigrant tone, favouring reductions in development aid, banning Muslim prayers at their work places, and repatriation of immigrants.

The Danish case lends support to all three propositions from the conceptual part of this chapter. The absence of a *cordon sanitaire* and the positive engagement by both the Social Democrats and the mainstream right party Venstre first moved these parties to the right on immigration issues and second made the informal government participation of the DF possible. Once the key party on which the centre right minority government had to rely on family reunification was severely restricted. Venstre never returned to moderate positions on immigration and the Social Democrats now also have very restrictive positions on these issues. Today, the DF has accomplished what other radical right parties in Europe are still hoping for: they have acquired a 'normal status' in the party system and are accepted by almost all the established parties. Even the Social Democrats do not rule out future co-operation with the DF anymore, thus pointing at the possibility that Denmark might get a Social Democratic government with support from the radical right, as happened already in several cases in Eastern Europe (see Minkenberg, 2017, 122–130).

THE INTRIGUING CASE: GERMANY

Germany provides at once a contrast to Denmark and a crucial case because here the radical right exerted significant indirect influence on the political discourse, party system and immigration policy-making despite it receiving only very limited electoral support and – until the rise of the AfD – no representation in national parliament (see also Zobel, 2017, ch. 4). To understand the German case, three factors need to be paid close attention to: First, the relevance and strength of the radical right movement sector and subcultural milieu and its disposition to the use of political violence (see Minkenberg, 1998, 288–306; Stöss, 2010, ch. 7); second, the importance of sub-national elections and coalition-building at the regional level due to the importance of the federally elected upper chamber for the legislative process (for a good overview see Rudzio, 2006); and finally, the new layer of complexity due to West and East Germany's reunification in 1990, thereby comprising an element of post-Communist transition and an internal east–west difference (see Minkenberg, 2009, 146–149; Stöss, 2010, 82–95, and below).

In this respect, it is important to note that the radical right in Germany is not one homogenous actor but a heterogeneous conglomerate of various actors with some distinct east–west differences. Especially after German reunification in the 1990s the German radical right developed along different lines in the so-called old and new *Länder*. The oldest radical right party in Germany is the National Democratic Party (Nationaldemokratsiche Partei Deutschlands, NPD), which during the 1990s was more or less stable with around 5,000 members. By contrast membership in the Eastern radical right parties was low until the mid-1990s, then grew within the NPD and later – in part due to the public debate and governmental effort to ban the NPD (see Minkenberg, 2006) – shifted to the Republicans (Republikaner, REP). During the late 1980s and 1990s the REP party achieved some notable electoral success, particularly at the regional level. During the same period the number of militant and violent right-wing extremists steadily rose since unification and reached a record level of 10,000 at the beginning of the new decade. Here, the centre of gravity has always been in the East. This trend was accompanied by a dramatic increase of right-wing violence, which also occurred disproportionately in the East (see Minkenberg, 1998, 306; Stöss, 2010, ch. 7). Since 2014 right-wing violence again increased with an alarming number of violent attacks against refugee housings.[4] Again, these occurred mainly in the new *Länder*.

The difference between East and West can also be illustrated by electoral trends: before 1998, radical right parties, in particular the REP, scored higher in *Länder* and national elections in the West than in the East. At the turn of the century, the reverse was true. By 2006, the radical right, that is, NPD and German People's Union (Deutsche Volksunion, DVU), had representatives in three of the five East German state parliaments (Brandenburg, Mecklenburg-West Pomerania, Saxony) but – contrary to the 1990s – none in their West German counterparts. This picture changed with the rise of the AfD, which subsequently gained representation in each of the *Länder* by 2018 and in 2017 in the national parliament as well. The AfD's support is concentrated in the East, but in some of the *Länder* in the West the AfD also received more than 12 per cent of the vote.

It is important to look at two time periods in which the radical right in Germany was able to exert some considerable influence on the positions of the other established parties and to some extent on policy-making as well. The first period covers the 1990s and the second important period spans the time since the rise of the AfD in 2013 until today.[5] Both periods are characterized by rising refugee inflows and right-wing violence but differ with regard to the electoral success of radical right parties. Nevertheless, both periods show that the radical right (in the form of parties and a violent movement sector) influenced the established parties and policy-making on immigration and asylum.

The First Period: 1990s until Mid-2000s

The first period starts with German reunification in 1990. At the time three main radical right parties existed: the extremist NPD (founded in 1964), the equally extremist DVU (founded in 1971 as an association and turned into a party in 1987) and most prominently the REP party (founded in 1986 as a split-off from the Christian Democrats). Among the former parties, the NPD never clearly drew strict boundaries to the violent movement sector (see Stöss, 2010, 125–25). Having mainly campaigned on the issue of German reunification and a rehabilitation of German ethno-nationalism, the REP party 'lost' its core issue after Germany was reunified in 1990 (see Thränhardt, 1995, 334). But rising numbers of asylum seekers after 1990 provided the REP party with a new political opportunity to mobilize xenophobic sentiments. They subsequently were successful in regional elections at the *Länder* level in Baden-Württemberg in 1992 where they gained 10.9 per cent of the vote and their competitor the DVU gained 6.2 per cent in Bremen and 6.3 per cent in Schleswig Holstein (ibid.).

These regional successes of the radical right concerned the governing mainstream right parties, the Christian Democratic Union/Christian Social Union (Christdemokratische Union/Christlich-Soziale Union, CDU/CSU), which feared that further increases in radical right vote shares might impede its ability to form governments at the *Länder* level. This was an important concern, because in 1991 the CDU/CSU only governed in the two southern states of Baden-Württemberg and Bavaria (Boesch, 2004, 56) and, in the German political system the partisan composition of the *Länder* governments matters to be able to pass legislation in the upper chamber called the *Bundesrat* (Federal Council). Moreover, since the mid-1980s the outspoken strategy of the CDU/CSU had always been that no party competitor on the right flank of the CDU/CSU should be allowed to form. Consequently, the CDU/CSU tried to thwart off any radical right party gains by co-opting their positions on asylum seekers and immigrants.

In an interaction, in which the mainstream right parties' strategy to move to the right outweighed by far the public responses of anti-xenophobic counter-mobilization, the CDU/CSU's competition with radical right parties and reaction to strong right-wing violence largely led to the so-called asylum crisis of 1992–1993 (see Minkenberg, 2002). Between 1991 and 1993 a rising discourse on the 'abuse of asylum' and on the alleged crime rate of foreigners emerged. The REP party campaigned fiercely against asylum seekers; already in 1990 the party used the slogan 'the boat is full' claiming that Germany (metaphorically here the boat) could not bear more refugees and was at the brink of sinking (Pagenstecher, 2008). This metaphor should subsequently dominate the German debate on asylum as it was adopted by major newspapers and magazines such as the *Spiegel* (ibid.). During the same period violent right-wing extremist activities increased. There were the riots against asylum seekers in the East German cities of Hoyerswerda and Rostock in 1991, and the murder of immigrant families in the West German towns of Mölln and Solingen in 1992–1993. Instead of adopting a confrontational approach to the radical right (the REP party as well as the violent groups), the CDU/CSU used the radical right pressure from the streets and the polls against the mainstream left opposition party, the Social Democratic Party of Germany (Sozialdemokratische Partei Deutschlands, SPD), pressuring it to support the government's restrictive approach on asylum.

The government thereby largely followed the radical right's framing of asylum-seekers as threatening German society and adopted a position to halt refugee inflows. One reason was that the CDU/CSU wanted to get rid of the radical right electoral competition, which was threatening its power in the *Länder*, by co-opting its position and changing the right to asylum as guaranteed in the German constitution. Yet, to change the constitution required a supermajority in parliament of two-thirds of the MPs, which the governing CDU/CSU-FDP coalition did not command. By instrumentalizing the fear of the SPD to lose voters to the radical right, the CDU/CSU was able to convince the SPD to support the constitutional change regarding asylum. After a long intra-party conflict within the SPD a 'grand coalition' of CDU/CSU, Free Democrats and Social Democrats agreed in late 1992 to amend the constitution's asylum article. Three newly introduced instruments were crucial: the introduction of a 'safe third country' and a 'safe country of origin'-rule and the foundation of transit zones at German airports (see Meier-Braun, 2002, 76; Zobel, 2017, 156). As Germany is a landlocked country and all neighbouring countries were declared 'safe third countries', it became virtually impossible to ask for asylum because of these new rules (see Joppke, 1999, 93–94). A central demand of the radical right was therefore fulfilled: to stop refugee flows to Germany.

The co-optation of radical right positions and discourse by the CDU/CSU and the U-turn of the SPD on the individual right to asylum in 1992 transformed these parties permanently and made any subsequent liberal reforms to asylum and immigration difficult. The hostile discourse of the early 1990s and public resentment fed a new 'subculture of resistance' to change in the politics of citizenship and immigration in Germany and posed a severe obstacle to policies attempting to tackle the country's demographic realities and economic needs by increasing migration. Large majorities in both East and West Germany favoured restricting immigration to labour migrants from EU countries, asylum seekers, and German resettlers from Eastern Europe (see Statistisches Bundesamt, 2002, 561). In 1996, half of the East Germans favoured a complete prohibition of labour migrants from non-EU-countries – a clear sign of widespread anxieties about the labour market situation in the new *Länder* and an expression of 'welfare chauvinism' (see Minkenberg, 2003, 234).

These patterns of public opinion and organizational mobilization significantly shape efforts by established political parties to control the German radical right. From the 1994 Bundestag campaign until the end of the 2000s, the CDU/CSU emphasized its opposition to immigration, its limited support for integration and its devotion to law and order; the SPD has also tried to instrumentalize these issues (see Joppke, 1999, 95–99; also Thränhardt, 1995). Hence, the issue of asylum helped de-legitimize the entire project of multiculturalism and integration; asylum seekers were linked to rising crime und unemployment. After the federal elections of 1998 the new mainstream left government coalition of the SPD and the Greens did not dare to change the restrictive policy approach regarding immigration control but wanted to liberalize German nationality law. But the CDU/CSU, now in the opposition, continued its hard-line approach against the Schröder government's reforms. In the state of Hesse, Roland Koch engineered a signature campaign against the new nationality code. The resulting compromise eliminated the option of dual citizenship for immigrants' children born in Germany, thus restricting their political incorporation as envisaged by the reforms (see Minkenberg, 2003, 231–232).

In sum – at least for the CDU/CSU – the co-optation strategy worked, as the radical right parties experienced electoral decline and never made it into national parliament during the 1990s and 2000s. The first case of the German case thus supports proposition (i) and (ii) and partly proposition (iii) as well. The positive engagement of the CDU/CSU and SPD and the failure to uphold a complete *cordon sanitaire* against the REP party moved the party system to the right on migration issues and triggered restrictive changes in the asylum legislation. Here the radical right exerted an indirect and mediated effect by influencing the position and framing of its mainstream competitors, which then implemented these restrictive positions (for a detailed conceptualization and analysis of this indirect and mediated effect see Zobel, 2017). Furthermore, the change was permanent as the German constitution ceased to grant a right to asylum. Finally, the CDU/CSU continued in its opposition to immigration but the SPD was not transformed permanently. Once in government, the SPD did not try to undo previous asylum restrictions but at least did try to liberalize the status and rights of already residing migrants.

The Second Period: 2013 until Today

The second period took place almost twenty years after the first. In 2013, the Alternative for Germany was founded and soon made headlines, because it almost made it into the German national parliament only seven months after its foundation. By 2018, it is represented in all of the German *Länder*. In the 2013 national elections, the AfD campaigned mainly on a Eurosceptic platform although nationalist and xenophobic undertones were already present (see Berbuir et al., 2015). In 2015, after a long period of party infighting, the neoliberal faction, many of which were university professors, left the party and the AfD became more clearly part of the radical right. Since then the party has campaigned against multicultural society and Islam as well as against the acceptance of refugees and asylum seekers.

During 2015 Germany experienced a large influx of refugees mainly due to the Syrian civil war. Nevertheless, one should not see the rise of the AfD as a purely functional consequence of rising refugee numbers. Instead, one can understand the AfD rather as a successful issue entrepreneur, who was able to profit from the political opportunity structure, as the high influx provided the AfD with a highly salient topic on which the other established parties were internally conflicted on. These internal conflicts made it difficult for the established parties to react with a clear and coherent position. In particular, Chancellor Merkel's decision of a temporary suspension of the Dublin rules became a central issue of contention, not only in the public but also within her own party (CDU) and sister party (CSU). As before in the 1990s, exogenous shocks such as an increase of immigration resulted in 'public response patterns', which benefited a hitherto marginal radical right party. The AfD seized this opportunity by calling the large inflow of refugees illegal and claiming that it was threatening the survival of the German people.[6]

But even before the large refugee inflows in 2015 and 2016, the AfD had already mobilized xenophobic fears of what they called 'overforeignization' (*Überfremdung*) of Germany. The early embracement of the xenophobic anti-Islam Pegida movement by core party officials is symptomatic for this. Already in December 2014 Frauke Petry and Alexander Gauland positively referred to Pegida, and Gauland (later in 2017 elected co-party leader) even joined the protesters on the streets. Moreover in the only stronghold of Pegida, the federal state of Saxony, many of the AfD party members were directly involved in the Pegida movement.[7] Pegida has since then lost significance but was central in the consolidation of the AfD between 2013 and 2017, because as a social movement it gave legitimacy to the AfD's anti-establishment and xenophobic positions. Moreover, there was large press coverage of Pegida (despite the its limited geographical reach) (see Vorländer et al., 2016, ch. 3). This large media echo also benefitted the AfD.

In early 2016 the AfD further increased its anti-refugee rhetoric. Frauke Petry, the party leader at the time, and Beatrix von Storch, the vice party leader and an MEP, demanded that German border police should be able to shoot refugees trying to cross the German border, even if these were women and children. Yet, these provocative remarks did not hurt the AfD electorally. In 2016 five *Länder* held regional elections and in all five the AfD crossed the electoral threshold easily and made it into state parliaments. In Saxony-Anhalt, the AfD even became the second largest party with 24.3 per cent of the vote, thereby trumping the Social Democrats and the Left party, which is traditionally strong in the Eastern states. These wins increasingly threatened the established parties. While all parties have lost voters to the AfD, it was particularly the CDU and the SPD, which lost many voters to the radical right competitor.[8] Moreover, in almost all of the regional states, coalition-building became more difficult due to the success of the AfD.

In several regards, the situation was thus very similar to the early 1990s. Increasing numbers of refugees coincided with strong electoral success of radical right parties in regional elections, which threatened legislative majorities in the upper chamber, the *Bundesrat*. Furthermore, right-wing violence was again on the rise. With 3500 attacks on refugees and refugee housing facilities, 2016 registered as the most violent year so far.[9] Similar to the 1990s, the CSU and a faction within the CDU wanted to contain the AfD by co-opting their profile and pressuring the SPD coalition partner to support further asylum restrictions. Yet, in the beginning the position of the CDU party leader and German chancellor Angela Merkel was a rather liberal one, namely, to welcome and integrate refugees. Her main opponent within the centre-right mainstream was the CSU party leader and regional head of state of Bavaria, Horst Seehofer. He co-opted the AfD's framing of the refugee influx as a crisis that allegedly put Germany in a state of emergency. He also publicly invited the right-wing Hungarian prime minister and strongest critic of Merkel's refugee policy Victor Orbán, who has a similar position and rhetoric on refugees like the AfD, to a party conference in Bavaria.[10] The CSU then demanded an absolute limit on the number of refugees and threatened to leave the coalition government.[11]

Pressured by increasing electoral success of the AfD and fearing further conflict with the CSU, the CDU/CSU-SPD government coalition passed several new asylum restrictions in the years 2015 and 2016. Already in July 2015 new legislation had already facilitated deportations of rejected asylum seekers. The fall of 2015 was characterized by an intense debate as the new restrictions needed approval in the upper chamber from state governments that were governed by different party coalitions than at the national level. After intense conflict the lower (*Bundestag*) and the upper chamber (*Bundesrat*) passed the so-called asylum package I (*Asylverfahrensbeschleunigungsgesetz*) in October 2015. It added three new countries to the list of safe countries of origin (Albania, Kosovo and Montenegro), prohibited to give benefits for refugees in cash and made the reception of working permits more difficult. It also extended the maximum length of obligatory stay in assigned refugee housing from three to six months. Especially, the prolonged centralized housing and restriction of movement as well as the stop to giving refugees cash allowances evoked the notions of the AfD portraying refugees as undeserving and dangerous.

Yet, these restrictions did not suffice to quiet the debate on refugees and asylum. Continuing high numbers of arriving refugees combined with the AfD being able to constantly keep the topic high on the public agenda led to further restrictions in early 2016. First, a new law on information sharing introduced a national identification card for asylum seekers and a comprehensive register with data on asylum seekers in Germany in January 2016. Followed by the so-called asylum package II (*Gesetz zur Einführung beschleunigter Asylverfahren*) in March 2016, which introduced expedited asylum procedures, further facilitations for deportations (health risks are now only impeding a deportation if they are life-threatening) and most importantly suspended family reunification for refugees receiving subsidiary protection. The latter point was primarily a result of the severe conflict between CSU party leader Horst Seehofer and chancellor and CDU party leader Angela Merkel. Nevertheless, the restrictions cannot be understood without focusing on the competitive pressure exerted by the AfD. Not only did the AfD endanger vote shares and therefore government coalitions at the regional level, but it also pushed the CSU further to the right on refugee issues. Since the

1980s the CSU's firm belief is that an organized electoral threat to its right flank cannot be permitted. Therefore the CSU co-opted many AfD frames and positions.

In 2017 the number of refugees arriving in Germany decreased, in part due to a controversial arrangement with the Turkish government to hinder people from crossing into the European Union in exchange for visa exemptions for Turkish citizens and monetary support for hosting refugees in Turkey. While the refugee issue temporarily lost some of its saliency, it again became the centre of public debate briefly before the general parliamentary elections in September 2017. This benefitted the AfD, which became the third largest party and the first radical right party represented in the Bundestag since the 1950s.[12] Just a week after the AfD had its national breakthrough at the German parliamentary elections in 2017, Andrea Nahles, the leader of the Social Democratic parliamentary group, demanded that her party should take a tougher stance on asylum and refugee policy. The second phase of the German case illustrates that the German mainstream parties again chose a strategy of positive engagement at a time when the radical right AfD was not yet represented in national parliament but only in the *Länder*. A special role takes the CSU, which wants to ostracize the AfD while at the same time co-opting its positions and framings. The restrictive changes in asylum policy cannot be explained solely by increasing numbers, but the role of the radical right needs to be taken into account. Merkel's CDU, as well as the coalition partner SPD and even the smaller Greens, changed their position after the AfD continued to increase its support from one Land election to the next. Refugee numbers of course played a role but cannot solely explain how the relevant political actors changed from a welcoming frame to a 'walling off' approach. Overall, the German case shows that asylum legislation was severely restricted not in cooperation with the radical right, but in co-optation of its agenda.

CONCLUSION

This chapter has shown how radical right parties have influenced the positions, framing and importance given to immigration issues. Moreover, the chapter also showed the pathways by which radical right parties – despite their sometimes small vote shares – have achieved significant legitimacy within mainstream debate for positions that once might have been considered on the extreme end. The major point of this chapter is that established political actors have reacted to the growing organizational strength of the radical right – its concentration around a dominant actor, its attraction to the working class and other segments of the electorate and its influence on public opinion – by adopting and legitimizing some of its elements. This represents

a major shift from earlier patterns in which established actors effectively
ostracized such positions.

Table 2.1 summarizes our findings in a synoptic way. On the agenda setting level regarding immigration politics, we observed rather similar patterns
of interaction between mainstream and radical right parties and resulting
effects in both countries, despite the striking divergence in the electoral and
parliamentary fate of the respective radical right parties. Mainstream parties in Denmark and Germany co-opted radical right positions and frames,
thereby shifting their programmatic outlook to the right. This finding corroborates proposition (i) above.

Yet, the radical right parties did not only affect positions but also effected
policy shifts in immigration and asylum issues. In line with our proposition
stated above, in both Germany and Denmark right-ward shifts regarding
minority inclusion and migrant and refugee rights occurred once mainstream
parties gave up their *cordon sanitaire* and pursued a strategy of positive
engagement, and these changes in policies and mainstream party positions
by and large prevailed even when governments changed (proposition ii)
or, as the German case suggests, the radical right disappeared from (state)
parliaments (proposition iii). Neither in Denmark nor in Germany, the mainstream right parties, or nearby competitors returned to a centrist position on
these issues. However, due to the different electoral threats, policy effects
in Germany were indirect and more moderate than those in Denmark. These
findings run against research that refutes a significant impact of radical right
parties in power (see Mudde, 2007, ch. 12; Mudde, 2013, 2014).

The German case is particularly instructive, because it demonstrates that
even – until recently – an electorally marginal radical right can exert influence on immigration policies, given favourable public response patterns.
The German case is characterized by two episodes of radical right party
influence. First, the interplay of the rise of the Republikaner in the early
1990s, the growing right-wing violence and the sensitivity ('irritability') of
the mainstream parties regarding an electoral threat from the far right contributed to a right-ward shift in immigration policies, albeit not in a linear
fashion (as witnessed by the partial liberalization under the Schröder government 1998–2005). Second, the rapid rise of the AfD coincided with large
numbers of refugees arriving in Germany, thereby providing the AfD with a
political opportunity to win voters based on their anti-immigrant positions.

Table 2.1.   Summary of radical right parties' effects on agenda-setting and policy-making

RRP Influence on	Germany	Denmark
Agenda-setting (Positions, frames)	Strong indirect influence	Strong indirect influence
Policy-making	Indirect and moderate	Direct and strong

This has put the remaining parties under pressure, not least because the AfD complicated the building of legislative majorities in state parliaments and the Bundestag. In an attempt to contain the AfD the two biggest mainstream left and right parties have passed the most extensive restrictions in asylum legislation since the 1990s.

Overall, our chapter shows that mainstream parties change their views on immigration and integration when competing with the radical right and that policy influence is not necessarily contingent upon such parties holding governmental power or even mobilizing large shares of electoral support at the polls. We have also shown that the conceptualization of policy influence should play closer attention not only to the patterns of interaction between the radical right and mainstream parties but also to the political environment in which they interact. Regarding the structure of party competition, social control is a particularly important variable, and it is of tantamount interest whether a so-called *cordon sanitaire* exists. The absence of such a *cordon* in Denmark provided an invitation to the radical right to negotiate a particular form of collaboration with a government party. The persistence of the *cordon sanitaire in* Germany so far helped cast the radical right as a pariah with no hopes for such negotiations. Nonetheless, policy influence did take place. Whether the AfD can leave the pariah role and follow the DF as a recognized political partner by part of the German mainstream (most likely at the *Land* level) remains to be seen. Its electoral successes already surpass that of any of its predecessors in the Federal Republic, and of many in other European countries. But as our chapter shows, 'coalition potential' is not always necessary to wield policy influence in sensitive and contested policy areas such as immigration.

NOTES

1. Refugees' eligibility requirements for permanent residence were increased and for UNHCR refugee resettlement quotas selection criteria were changed to accept Christian instead of Muslim refugees (see Rytter and Pedersen 2013, 2307). The most severe restriction was however the change in family reunification rules; requirements were increased, new conditions introduced, and it was generally not possible to bring family members in if under 24 years of age (see Jonsson and Petersen 2012, 133).

2. The Danish Association has supported the DF since 1997 and many of its adherents later became members of the party (Rydgren 2004, 483). For example, Søren Krarup, Pia Kjærsgaard, Søren Espersen (author for *Danskeren* and DF's man for public relations), Jesper Langballe, and others have been members of the Danish Association. Before 2001 the Danish Association often attacked the government claiming that it was hiding information about immigrants and their impact on Danish society, whereas the Danish Association aimed to "correctly" inform the population (Zølner 2000, 204).

3. Together with co-authors she had published the book "A Defense of the Community" warning that immigration was threatening the Danish welfare state (see Jonsson and Petersen, 2012, 138).

4. See *Zeit Online 24 April 2017* "Politische Straftaten auf Höchststand" http://www.zeit.de/gesellschaft/zeitgeschehen/2017-04/polizeiliche-kriminalstatistik-bundesinnenministerium-gewaltkriminalitaet-wohnungseinbrueche-jugendkriminali taet. Last accessed 4 May 2018.

5. The German literature usually distinguishes two periods in the 20 years after unification: the 1990s and developments after 2000 the latter being characterized by a shifting of weight to the East (see Stöss 2010, 109f.). In light of our chapter's focus, the breakthrough of the AfD in 2014 and accompanying developments, we treat the 1990s and 2000s as one period in which radical right parties remained electorally marginal, despite their (limited) upswing in the 1990s.

6. Common metaphors used by the AfD are 'Überfremdung' ('over-foreignization'), 'Islamization' and warnings of 'waves' of immigrants and refugees (see for example Welt "Kalkulierter Tabubruch der AfD bei der Zuwanderung", 15 September 2014. http://www.welt.de/politik/deutschland/article132278661/Kalkulierter-Tabubruch-der-AfD-bei-der-Zuwanderung.html. Regarding the AfD claims on illegal migration see their homepage: https://afdkompakt.de/tag/illegale-migration/. Last accessed: 20 April 2018.

7. *Spiegel Online* "AfD-Spitze streitet um Pegida-Kurs". 14 December 2014. http://www.spiegel.de/politik/deutschland/pegida-demonstration-afd-vize-hans-olaf-henkel-mahnt-seine-partei-a-1008429.html. Last accessed 16 December 2014.

Sueddeutsche.de "Wie die AfD den Rücktritt Bachmanns beeinflusste". 22 January 2015. http://www.sueddeutsche.de/politik/pegida-gruender-wie-die-afd-den-ruecktritt-bachmanns-beeinflusste-1.2315975. Last accessed 2 August 2015.

8. Already in the first three of the regional elections in 2016 (Saxony-Anhalt, Baden-Würtemberg and Rhineland-Palatine) the CDU lost about 272,000 voters to the AfD, whereas the SPD lost 143,000, followed by the Green party with 76,000, the LINKE with 62,000 and the FDP with 32,000. See *Welt* "CDU verliert Hunderttausende Wähler an die AfD". 13 March 2016. https://www.welt.de/politik/deutschland/article153256475/CDU-verliert-Hunderttausende-Waehler-an-die-AfD.html. Last accessed 9 April 2018.

9. See *Sueddeutsche.de* Mehr als 2200 Angriffe auf Flüchtlinge im vergangenen Jahr. 28 February 2018. www.sueddeutsche.de/politik/fremdenfeindlichkeit-mehr-als-angriffe-auf-fluechtlinge-im-vergangenen-jahr-1.3886072. Last accessed 9 April 2018.

10. See *Zeit Online* Seehofer lädt Orbán ein. 11 September 2015. www.zeit.de/politik/deutschland/2015-09/seehofer-merkel-orban-ungarn-fluechtlinge. Last accessed 9 April 2018.

11. See *N-tv.de* Seehofer droht Merkel mit der Opposition. https://www.n-tv.de/politik/Seehofer-droht-Merkel-mit-der-Opposition-article19331536.html. Last accessed 3 May 2018.

12. To be very precise: There were several small radical right parties in the first and second *Bundestag* (1949–1957), most notably the All German Bloc/League of

Expellees and Deprived of Rights (*Gesamtdeutscher Block/Bund der Heimatver-triebenen und Entrechteten, BHE*) which gained 5.9 per cent in the 1953 elections and collaborated with the CDU-led federal government under Konrad Adenauer (and with the Social Democrats in several *Länder*). This collaboration was not hindered by the fact that the BHE was filled with revanchists and ex-Nazis and pushed, among other things, for a termination of the criminal prosecution of (former) Nazis (see Salzborn 2015, 40).

BIBLIOGRAPHY

Akkerman, Tjitske. 2012. Comparing radical right parties in government: Immigration and integration policies in nine countries. *West European Politics* 35(3): 511–529.

Akkerman, Tjitske. 2015. Immigration policy and electoral competition in Western Europe: A fine-grained analysis of party positions over the past two decades. *Party Politics* 21(1): 54–67.

Akkerman, Tjitske and Sarah de Lange. 2012. Radical right parties in office: Incumbency records and the electoral cost of governing. *Government and Opposition* 47(4): 574–596.

Andersen, Jorgen Goul and Tor Bjorklund. 2000. Radical right-wing populism in Scandinavia: From tax revolt to neo-liberalism and xenophobia. In: Paul Hainsworth, ed. *The Extreme Right in Europe and the USA*. London: Pinter Publishers, pp. 193–223.

Art, David. 2011. *Inside the Radical Right*. Cambridge: Cambridge University Press.

Bale, Tim, Christoffer Green-Pedersen, Andre Krouwel, Kurt Richard Luther and Nick Sitter. 2010. If you can't beat them, join them? Explaining social democratic responses to the challenge from the populist radical right in Western Europe. *Political Studies* 58(3): 410–426.

Benoit, Kenneth and Michael Laver. 2009. *Party Policy in Modern Democracies*. London: Routledge.

Berbuir, Nicole, Marcel Lewandowsky and Jasmin Siri. 2015. The AfD and its sympathisers: Finally a right-wing populist movement in Germany? *German Politics* 24(2): 154–178.

Betz, Hans-Georg. 1994. *Radical Right-Wing Populism in Western Europe*. London: Macmillan.

Bjerre, Liv, Marc Helbling, Friederike Römer and Malisa Zobel. 2015. Conceptualizing and measuring immigration policies: A comparative perspective. *International Migration Review* 49(3): 555–600.

Boesch, Frank. 2004. Two crises, two consolidations? Christian Democracy in Germany. In: Steven van Hecke and Emmanuel Gerard, ed. *Christian Democratic Parties in Europe since the End of the Cold War*. Leuven: Leuven University Press, pp. 55–78.

Capoccia, Giovanni. 2013. Militant democracy: The institutional bases of democratic self-preservation. *Annual Review of Law and Social Science* 9 (November): 207–226.

Carvalho, Joao. 2013. *Impact of Extreme Right Parties on Immigration Policy: Comparing Britain, France and Italy*. Abingdon and New York: Routledge.

Caramani, Daniele. 2008. Party systems. In: Daniele Caramani, ed. *Comparative Politics*. Oxford: Oxford University Press, pp. 318–347.

Carter, Elisabeth. 2005. *The Extreme Right in Western Europe: Success or Failure?* Manchester: Manchester University Press.

Christiansen, Flemming Juul. 2016. The Danish People's Party: Combining cooperation and radical positions. In: Tjitske Akkerman, Sarah de Lange and Matthijs Rooduijn, eds. *Radical Right-Wing Populist Parties in Western Europe*. Abingdon and New York: Routledge, pp. 94–112.

Downs, William. 2001. Pariahs in their midst: Belgian and Norwegian parties react to extremist threats. *West European Politics* 24(3): 23–42.

Downs, William. 2012. *Political Extremism in Democracies: Combating Intolerance*. New York: Palgrave.

EUMC. 2005. *The Impact of 7 July 2005 London Bomb Attacks on Muslim Communities in the EU*. Vienna: European Monitoring Centre on Racism and Violence.

Heitmeyer, Wilhelm. 2005. Gruppenbezogene Menschenfeindlichkeit. In: Wilhelm Heitmeyer, ed. *Deutsche Zustände*. Vol. 3. Frankfurt am Main: Suhrkamp, pp. 13–36.

Ignazi, Piero. 2003. *Extreme Right Parties in Western Europe*. Oxford: Oxford University Press.

Joppke, Christian. 1999. *Immigration and the Nation State*. Oxford: Oxford University Press.

Karpantschof, Rene. 2003. Højreradikalismen i Danmark – en politik model på historisk-sociologisk grund. *Dansk Sociologi* 14(3): 25–41.

Kitschelt, Herbert and Anthony McGann. 1995. *The Radical Right in Western Europe: A Comparative Analysis*. Michigan, MI: University of Michigan Press.

Lipset, Seymour M. and Stein Rokkan, eds. 1967. *Party Systems and Voter Alignments: Cross-National Perspectives*. New York: Free Press.

Mair, Peter and Cas Mudde. 1998. The party family and its study. *Annual Review of Political Science* 1: 211–229.

McAdam, Doug. 1999. *Political Process and the Development of Black Insurgency, 1930–1970*. 2nd ed. Chicago, IL: University of Chicago Press.

Meguid, Bonnie M. 2005. Competition between unequals: The role of mainstream party strategy in niche party success. *American Political Science Review* 99(3): 347–359.

Meguid, Bonnie M. 2008. *Party Competition between Unequals: Strategies and Electoral Fortunes in Western Europe*. Cambridge: Cambridge University Press.

Minkenberg, Michael. 1998. *Die neue radikale Rechte im Vergleich. USA, Frankreich, Deutschland*. Opladen/Wiesbaden: Westdeutscher Verlag.

Minkenberg, Michael. 2001. The radical right in public office: Agenda-setting and policy effects. *West European Politics* 24(4): 1–21.

Minkenberg, Michael. 2002. The new radical right in political process: Interaction effects in France and Germany. In: Martin Schain, Aristide R. Zolberg and Patrick Hossay, eds. *Shadows over Europe: The Development and Impact of the Extreme Right in Western Europe*. New York: Palgrave Macmillan, pp. 245–269.

Minkenberg, Michael. 2003. The politics of citizenship in the new republic. *West European Politics* 26(4): 219–240.

Minkenberg, Michael. 2006. Repression and reaction: Militant democracy and the radical right in Germany and France. *Patterns of Prejudice* 40(2): 25–44.

Minkenberg, Michael. 2009. Anti-immigrant politics in Europe: The radical right, xenophobic tendencies, and their political environment. In: Jennifer Hochschild and John Mollenkopf, eds. *Bringing Outsiders In: Transatlantic Perspectives on Immigrant Political Incorporation.* Ithaca, NY: Cornell University Press, pp. 140–157.

Minkenberg, Michael. 2013a. From pariah to policy-maker? The radical right in Europe, West and East: Between margin and mainstream. *Journal of Contemporary European Studies* 21(1): 5–24.

Minkenberg, Michael. 2013b. Political opportunity structures and the mobilization of anti-immigration actors: Modeling effects on immigrant political incorporation. In: Jennifer Hochschild, Jacqueline Chattopadhyay, Claudine Gay and Michael Jones-Correa, eds. *Outsiders No More? Models of Immigrant Political Incorporation.* Oxford: Oxford University Press, pp. 241–253.

Minkenberg, Michael. 2017. *The Radical Right in Eastern Europe: Democracy under Siege?* New York: Palgrave Macmillan.

Minkenberg, Michael and Malisa Zobel. 2018. Populism – A new – ism and a new schism in the study of the far right? Paper presented at the *ECPR General Conference* in Hamburg, August 22–25, 2018.

Mudde, Cas. 2007. *Populist Radical Right Parties in Europe.* Cambridge: Cambridge University Press.

Mudde, Cas. 2013. Three decades of populist radical right parties in Western Europe: So what? *European Journal of Political Research* 52: 1–19.

Mudde, Cas. 2014. Fighting the system? Populist radical right parties and party system change. *Party Politics* 20(2): 217–226.

Pagenstecher, Cord. 2008. Das Boot ist voll – Schreckensvision des vereinten Deutschland. In: Gerhard Paul, ed. *Das Jahrhundert der Bilder.* Göttingen: pp. 606–613.

Pederson, Mogens. 1982. Towards a new typology of party lifespan and minor parties. *Scandinavian Political Studies* 5(1): 1–16.

Pytlas, Bartek. 2015. *Radical Right Parties in Central and Eastern Europe: Mainstream Party Competition and Electoral Fortune.* London: Routledge.

Rasmussen, Søren Hein. 2001. Modstanden og det nationale. In: Den jyske Historiker, ed. *Mødet med den europæiske jungle: National strategi og identitet i dansk europapolitik 1945–2000.* Århus: Århus Universitet, pp. 96–112.

Rudzio, Wolfgang. 2006. *Das politische System der Bundesrepublik Deutschland.* Wiesbaden: VS Verlag für Sozialwissenschaften.

Rydgren, Jens. 2004. Explaining the emergence of radical right-wing populist parties: the case of Denmark. *West European Politics* 27(3): 474–502.

Rydgren, Jens. 2007. The sociology of the radical right. *Annual Review of Sociology* 33: 241–262.

Rydgren, Jens, ed. 2013. *Class Politics and the Radical Right.* London: Routledge.

Rytter, Mikkel and Marianne Holm Pedersen. 2013. A decade of suspicion: Islam and Muslims in Denmark after 9/11. *Ethnic and Racial Studies* 37(13): 2303–2321.

Salzborn, Samuel. 2015. *Rechtsextremismus. Erscheinungsformen und Erklärungsansätze.* 2nd ed. Baden-Baden: Nomos.

Sartori, Giovanni. 1976. *Parties and Party Systems.* Cambridge: Cambridge University Press.

Schain, Martin. 2006. The extreme-right and immigration policy-making: Measuring direct and indirect effects. *West European Politics* 29(2): 270–289.

Skou, Kaare R. 2006. *Dansk politik A-Å: Leksikon.* 1. udg., 2. opl ed. Copenhagen: Aschehoug.

Stöss, Richard. 2010. *Rechtsextremismus im Wandel.* 3rd ed. Berlin: Friedrich-Ebert Stiftung.

Thränhardt, Dietrich. 1995. The political uses of xenophobia in England, France and Germany. *Party Politics* 1(3): 323–345.

van Spanje, Joost. 2010. Contagious parties: Anti-immigration parties and their impact on other parties' immigration stances in contemporary Western Europe. *Party Politics* 16(5): 563–586.

Von Beyme, Klaus. 1984. *Parteien in westlichen Demokratien.* 2nd ed. München: Piper.

Vorländer, Hans, Maik Herold and Steven Schäller. 2016. *Pegida: Entwicklung, Zusammensetzung und Deutung einer Empörungsbewegung.* Wiesbaden: VS Verlag.

Widfeldt, Anders. 2000. Scandinavia: Mixed success for the populist right. *Parliamentary Affairs* 53: 486–500.

Widfeldt, Anders. 2015. *Extreme Right Parties in Scandinavia.* London and New York: Routledge.

Williams, Michelle Hale. 2006. *The Impact of Radical Right-Wing Parties in West European Democracies.* New York: Palgrave.

Williams, Michelle Hale. 2013. Tipping the balance scale? Rightward momentum, party agency and Austrian party politics. *Journal of Contemporary European Studies* 21(1): 68–86.

Williams, Michelle Hale. 2015. Are radical right-wing parties the blackholes in party space? Implications and limitations in impact assessment of radical right-wing parties. *Ethnic and Racial Studies* 38(8): 1329–1338.

Williams, Michelle H. 2018. The political impact of the radical right. In: Jens Rydgren, ed. *The Oxford Handbook of the Radical Right.* Oxford: Oxford University Press, pp. 305–326.

Zobel, Malisa. 2017. *A Race to the Right? The Impact of Radical Right Parties on Immigration in Liberal Democracies from 1980–2013.* Unpublished dissertation manuscript. European-University Viadrina, Frankfurt Oder.

Zølner, Mette. 2000. *Re-imagining the Nation. Debates on Immigrants, Identities and Memories.* Bruxelles; Bern; Berlin; Frankfurt/M.; New York; Oxford; Wien: PIE Lang.

Chapter 3

The Front National's Influence on Immigration during President François Hollande's Term

João Carvalho

Fifteen years after the victory in the 1997 legislative elections, the French centre-left Parti Socialiste (PS) celebrated its return to power with the 2012 presidential elections. As widely expected, the PS candidate François Hollande was elected president of the French Fifth Republic after beating the incumbent centre-right President Nicolas Sarkozy, albeit with a mere 51.64 per cent of the vote in the second round (Gaffney, 2015). At the same time, the 2012 presidential elections represented the first national ballot contested by the French radical right populist party (RRPP) – Front National (FN) – under Marine Le Pen's leadership, who managed to achieve a historical new electoral record for this party. Driven by Marine's 'de-demonization' project, the FN's electoral inroads progressed throughout the cycle of second-order ballots taking place during the presidential term, whereas the PS's electoral support observed a continuous and severe nationwide decline. The pressure posed by the FN over the French Socialist presidency intensified, especially after the polls started to forecast Marine's participation in the second round of the 2017 presidential ballot (Feltesse, 2017). Given this context, this research explores what the FN's influence was on the French policies of immigration control and immigrant integration during President Hollande's term.

Research on the RRPPs' influence on their domestic political systems mostly focuses on immigration given that xenophobia/racism is a distinctive trait of most members of this party family (Carter, 2005). Furthermore, the member states of the European Union (EU) benefit from broad discretionary powers on this topic, unlike what happens in other areas, such as macroeconomic management. However, most researchers focusing on RRPP influence on immigration failed to acknowledge that immigration control is typically the outcome of a bargaining process between distinct stakeholders rather than being driven solely by political parties' preferences (Mudde, 2013; see Carvalho, 2014). Another shortcoming reflects the disregard for the interdependence between immigration policies and other policy areas, such as the labour market or foreign policy (Czaica and Haas, 2013). By contrast, this research will highlight the broadening of the FN's influence from domestic policy into French foreign policy in the context of the European asylum crisis.

Most of the research available on RRPPs' influence focuses on the terms led by centre-right parties or right-wing coalitions that integrated these extremist parties (Minkenberg, 2001; Schain, 2006; Akkerman, 2012; Carvalho, 2014). With a few exceptions (see Bale et al., 2010; Alonso and Fonseca, 2011; Odmalm and Hepburn, 2017; Carvalho and Ruedin, 2018), the political interaction between RRPPs and centre-left parties or executives remains overlooked in the literature. Thus, President Hollande's term constitutes a crucial case to study the influence of one of the most successful RRPPs in Western Europe over a centre-left executive. Recent comparative analysis drawing on Austria, Belgium, Netherlands and Switzerland suggested that RRPPs' influence on the mainstream left's political claims regarding immigration between 1995 and 2009 was negligible. Furthermore, the liberal tone of the mainstream left's political claims on immigration control and immigrant integration was closely aligned with their left-wing ideological preferences in seven European nations (excluding France; Carvalho and Ruedin, 2018). In parallel to the assessment of the FN's influence, this research will assess the potential alignment between the Socialist executive's discourse on immigration and its centre-left's positioning or if in alternative, an ideological 'aggiornamento' was observed.

Past investigations asserted that the FN's electoral entrenchment had moderate or intense repercussions at the electoral and policy level since the 1990s (Schain, 2006; Williams, 2006; Hainsworth, 2008). Further research identified a significant level of influence on immigration control by the FN during President Jacques Chirac's term (2002–2007). This political process was closely associated with Nicolas Sarkozy's tenures at the Interior Ministry, where he announced a new policy paradigm of 'selected immigration against unwanted inflows'. However, the intensity of this political process expanded to a very significant level throughout the first two years of President Sarkozy's term (2007–2009). This trend reflected for example in the creation of the ephemeral Ministry of Immigration and National Identity in 2007 (Carvalho, 2014). This comparative investigation suggested that the RRPP's impact in Italy and France on immigration policy was contingent upon two premises: the RRPP's salient electoral threat to mainstream parties and the formal or informal engagement of mainstream political elites with the RRPPs (Carvalho, 2014). Through the employment of process tracing, this research will evaluate the potential FN's influence on immigration during

President Hollande's term and assess the observation of the suggested causal mechanism.

This chapter is divided into two main parts. The first part of this research lays down the theoretical background for this analysis. This starts by exploring the proposed definition of RRPP's influence and the methodology employed to identify this political process. The subsequent section examines the French republican paradigm that supports the French immigration model and the Socialists' approaches towards immigration in the past tenures in office. The final section of the first part appraises the FN's electoral development under Marine's leadership, as well as the contents of her 'de-demonization strategy'. The second part examines the FN's influence on the PS executive approaches towards immigration control and immigrant integration. The first section of the second part investigates the French government's policy towards EU citizens of Roma origin led by the interior minister Manuel Valls, who was promoted to Prime Minister by President Hollande in 2014. The second section explores the French president's single speech on immigration, and the third section investigates the centre-left executive's response to the European asylum crisis. Lastly, this chapter reviews the government's relationship with Islam after the 2015 terrorist attacks.

DEFINITION OF RRPP INFLUENCE

RRPP influence has been frequently associated with the observation of the 'co-option of radical-right issues', a political process that produces a modification of the political agenda and the terms of conflict between political parties (Schain, 2006). Drawing on past research, an RRPP's political influence is conceived as the ability to promote a policy outcome that would not have been otherwise observed if not for the agency of the selected party (Carvalho, 2014; 2016a). This past research suggests that the political influence of these parties on immigration politics and policy should encompass the dissemination of their xenophobic framing of immigration and the formal/informal co-option of their anti-immigration proposals by mainstream parties (van Spanje, 2010; Carvalho, 2014). Nonetheless, this investigation seeks to expand the scope of this definition to include the promotion of policy inaction. This political process is interpreted as the executive's covert unwillingness to deploy the necessary resources to attain their proposed policy objectives throughout the implementation stage of the policy process. While it can be conceived as a conventional form of policy making at the theoretical level, the problem consists of tracing the causal factor that propels the undisclosed inaction (Page, 2008).

The FN's influence will be classified as proportional/disproportional at relative level, considering the selected RRPP's relevance and electoral support within the domestic party system. Second, RRPP's influence can also be dis-aggregated as direct or indirect depending on these parties' representation in government and their access to the policy-making process. Nonetheless, this research also acknowledges the potential observation of several constraints on the scope of RRPP's influence derived from France's EU membership, the liberal character of the political system and the presence of domestic veto players (Carvalho, 2016). EU membership presupposes recognition of the right of free movement of EU citizens and respect of the directives set at the supranational level. In parallel, the French political executive and legislature must abide by their national legal framework and constitutional rights were extended to foreign citizens. This legal entitlement forced French centre-right governments to reverse the halt to family reunion in the past (Hollifield, 2014). Lastly, this investigation highlights that domestic veto players either of partisan or institutional character can overturn government's decisions and water down RRPP's influence on policy developments (Tsebelis, 2002).

This analysis develops a single-case analysis of the FN's influence on immigration control and immigrant integration during President Hollande's term supported by the employment of process tracing. Process tracing seeks to trace the causal mechanism behind the selected political phenomena by exploring causal process observations to assess the proposed causal relation-ships (George and Bennet, 2004; Collier, 2011). Building on past research, this study will employ a theory test-based approach to evaluate the presence of the aforementioned casual mechanism related with the RRPP's electoral threat and the agency of mainstream parties (Beach and Pedersen, 2013). Remarkably, President Hollande was distinct from his predecessors due to the publication of a controversial tell-all book based on private conversations with two journalists from Le Monde before the end of his term (Davet and Lhomme, 2016). This source alongside two of his close collaborators' autobi-ographies enhances access to the French president's state of mind throughout his tenure in power providing indispensable empirical evidence to support the argument presented in this investigation alongside the analysis of political discourse and policy developments. The next section reviews the influence of the French republican heritage on contemporary management of immigration.

THE FRENCH REPUBLICAN PARADIGM AND THE PS'S PAST APPROACHES TOWARDS IMMIGRATION

France's founding myth is based upon the French Revolution of 1789, which preceded the development of large-scale immigration into the country. France, as a republic, depicts itself according to the Jacobin slogan of 'one and indivisible', presuming the ethnic homogeneity of its population. Since the French Revolution was driven by a mass rejection of feudalism, the Declaration of the Rights of Man and Citizen expresses a violent rejection of any privilege or stigmatization based on origin (Noiriel, 2011). Thereby, the French republican paradigm inhibits the employment of concepts like ethnicity or race and imposes strict colour blindness, preventing the collection of ethnic statistics (Simon, 2013). On the other hand, the Revolution also represented an intense struggle against the clerical power of the Catholic Church. This trend was reflected on the importance attributed to laicity and the confinement of religion to the private sphere, strictly separated from the public sphere. Access to the French citizenship became determined by nationality, and foreigners were welcomed as citizens if they assimilated the French republicanism and relinquished their native cultures (Hollifield, 2014). As it is widely recognized in the literature, the French republican heritage entails important repercussions on the contemporary management of immigration.

In the post–Second World War period, labour immigration increased steeply, until it was halted after the oil shocks of the mid-1970s, with this topic rising to the forefront of the French political agenda thereafter. The election of PS President François Mitterrand in 1981 led to the regularization of 143,000 irregular immigrants and the reinstatement of the right to family reunion, alongside the maintenance of the halt to labour immigration. The centre-left's approach was labelled the 'grand bargain', which involved strict control of inflows to promote immigrants' integration in France (Hollifield, 2014). Subsequently, President Mitterrand sought to split the centre-right electorate in favour of the FN by supporting anti-racist policies and the immigrants' right to vote in local elections. The 'grand bargain' strategy was recovered after the PS victory in the 1997 legislative elections, as Prime Minister Lionel Jospin announced a 'new republican pact'. The centre-left government deployed the 1997 regularization programme, which benefited 90,000 irregular immigrants, while the 1998 law on immigration control aimed to combine 'toughness with humanitarian flexibility' (Schain, 2008). After this brief review of the French republican paradigm and the PS's legacy on immigration control, the next section reviews the FN's evolution within the French political system throughout the 2010s.

THE FN'S ELECTORAL EXPANSION UNDER MARINE'S LEADERSHIP

The FN is considered one of the most successful RRPPs in Western European political systems. Under the leadership of Jean-Marie Le Pen, the FN attained its electoral peak in the 2002 presidential elections, after collecting 16.8 per cent of the vote in the first round. Le Pen's progression to the second round, to the detriment of the socialist candidate, Lionel Jospin, fostered a 'political earthquake' in French politics. However, the FN's candidate was unable to increase his electoral share in the second round and was defeated by the centre-right candidate Jacques Chirac, who obtained 82.2 per cent of the vote (Carvalho, 2014). In the 2007 presidential elections, many of the FN's voters shifted their support in favour of Sarkozy, and Le Pen observed his lowest score at the polls since the early 1980s with just 10.4 per cent of the vote. In the aftermath of the election, Le Pen (2007) commented: 'paradoxically winners on ideological grounds, we have temporarily lost in the electoral arena', indicating the increasing hegemony of the 'Lepenisation of minds' across the French political elite. In 2011, the FN's leadership was transferred to Le Pen's daughter, Marine Le Pen, after she won an internal poll.

The new leader intensified a 'de-demonization' strategy, which involved the de-radicalization of the FN's electoral programme and the suppression of anti-Semitic references to enhance this RRPP's credibility and respectability. Consequently, the FN intensified its opposition to the EU and its Islamophobia by presenting itself as the defender of the French republic against the Islamic threat and subsequent communitarisation of French society under religious beliefs. This trend was evident in Marine's claim that 100 per cent of the meat sold around Paris was halal or a comparison of Muslim street prayers to Nazi occupation (Mondon, 2014). Research on the FN's electoral manifestos presented between 2002 and 2012 associates this strategy with the acknowledgement of abortion and civil union contracts, the inclusion of a larger set of socio-economic topics and the downgrading of anti-immigration rhetoric (Ivaldi, 2016). The FN's de-demonization strategy was boosted by Le Pen's expulsion in August 2015 due to his anti-Semitic rhetoric. Effectively, the FN's electoral support observed a steady expansion since Marine took over the leadership. In the 2012 presidential election, the FN candidate amassed 18 per cent of the vote in the first round, which represented 2.7 million more votes than the 4.5 million obtained by her father in 2002 (Carvalho, 2014).

Notwithstanding Marine's success at the presidential ballot, the FN only obtained two parliamentary seats after collecting 13.6 per cent of the vote in the first round of the 2012 legislative elections. In the 2014 elections for the European parliament (EP), the FN was, for the first time ever, the most voted-for party at the national level with 24.9 per cent of the vote (Ivaldi, 2016). A new historical peak was observed in the 2015 departmental elections, as the FN obtained 22.23 per cent of the vote.[1] In the 2015 regional elections, the FN achieved 27.73 per cent of the vote, against the 23.4 per cent obtained by President Hollande's party, and was the most voted-for party in six of the twelve regions. However, the FN's electoral share in the second ballot expanded by a meagre two points, following an increase in turnout and a lack of mobilization of centrist voters, which prevented the FN from winning a single regional presidency (Jaffré, 2017). In face of the FN's successes in 2015, President Hollande ranked Marine as his major political challenge in acknowledgement of the FN's salient electoral threat (Davet and Lhomme, 2016). The next sections examine the FN's influence during President Hollande's term.

PRESIDENT HOLLANDE'S U-TURN ON HIS ELECTORAL PLEDGE

After President Hollande's victory in the presidential elections, the French centre-left's success was later confirmed in the 2012 legislative elections, where the coalition between the PS and the Greens obtained 300 seats out of the 577 available in the National Assembly. Within the French semi-presidential system, this result represented a lack of checks and balances on the new President's ability to implement his political programme with the support of a Prime Minister of his preference. However, Hollande was considered an accidental candidate lacking an overall plan, only considering himself a potential French president after the expected centre-left candidate Dominique Strauss-Khan was forced to retreat from the PS primaries in 2011 (Gaffney, 2015). By his mid-term, President Hollande was considered to lack 'essential leadership skills' and was ranked as the most unpopular French President in the history of the fifth republic (Kuhn, 2014). During the 2012 electoral campaign, Hollande criticized President Sarkozy's legacy on immigration for promoting the division of the French people and proposed granting the right to vote in local elections to foreign citizens. At the same time, the PS candidate promised a strict approach to labour inflows and to reduce the number of annual inflows (Evans and Ivaldi, 2013).

Under pressure from Marine's result, Hollande adopted a more restrictive tone in the electoral campaign in between rounds and claimed 'there are too many irregular immigrants in France', an unusual remark for the leader of a centre-left party (Le Monde, 2012). President Hollande's management of immigration became intrinsically linked to the agency of Manuel Valls (initially appointed as the Interior Minister in 2012 and then Prime Minister after the PS's disastrous results in the 2014 local elections). Valls' appointment to the cabinet sought to appease right-wing voters, since this member of parliament (MP) was nicknamed the 'Sarkozy of the left' after he was part of the fourteen socialist MPs who supported the Burqa ban proposed by President Sarkozy in 2010 (Kuhn, 2014). During the PS's presidential primary,[2] Valls proposed the deployment of a strict quota system according to immigrants' origins, which challenged the absolute equality imposed by the French Republican paradigm as well as the right of any individual to have a normal family life (Nouveau Observateur, 2011).[3] At the Interior Ministry, Valls supervised the abolition of the Gueant *circulaire* (administrative act) concerning the settlement and access to the labour market by foreign students in France as well as the law on the criminalization of solidarity towards irregular immigrants.

These policy developments initially suggested a shift from the highly restrictive approach pursued during former President Sarkozy's term (Carvalho, 2016b). A new *circulaire* was published to clarify the access criteria for the regularization of irregular immigrants on an individual basis included in the legislation. Even so, Valls ensured that a broad regularization programme was not considered by the centre-left executive, which marked a break with the PS's past approach to irregular immigration (Hollifield, 2014). While an expansion of the number of regularized immigrants was observed from 2013 onwards,[4] the interior minister preferred to emphasize the increase in forced removals of irregular immigrants in comparison to 2012 (Proteau, 2013). Against a public letter signed by 75 socialist MPs demanding the fulfilment of the President's electoral pledge, the Interior Minister dropped the concession of right to vote in local elections to foreigners because it did not constitute a mean to promote integration, which he ranked as the greatest challenge of French society. This decision appeased the FN whose rejection of this proposal was long established in the 1980s during the Presidency of François Mitterrand and restated during the 2012 electoral campaign.

VALLS' APPROACH TO THE ROMA CAMPS

Few months after the legislative elections, the French socialist executive issued a new *circulaire* on the dismantlement of Roma camps that sought to combine 'humanism' with 'firmness'. This document guaranteed abidance by the republican paradigm of absolute equality and non-discrimination during the implementation process. This action extended former President Sarkozy's repressive approach, emboldened by the Grenoble speech in 2010 (Carvalho, 2016b) and constituted another U-turn from Hollande's electoral pledge to adopt a new approach to the Roma camps. A month later, the Interior Minister boasted that the Roma's vocation was to return to Eastern Europe because 'these populations have a way of life that is extremely different from our own'. He also added that it was 'illusory' to think that the Roma could be integrated into French society (Libération, 2013). Valls' statement transgressed the republican paradigm expressed in the government's document and deepened the stigmatization and racialization of the Roma (Simon, 2013). Moreover, the Interior Minister's statements indicated the influence of the FN's cultural xenophobia while Marine highlighted the similarities between Valls and Sarkozy's tenures at the interior ministry and attacked their approaches towards the Roma due to their support of free movement within the EU (Le Parisien, 2013).

The interior minister's approach to the Roma camps opened cracks within the Socialist government, but President Hollande threw his support behind Valls and commented that 'The question that must be asked is whether France is meant to welcome all the most vulnerable' (Valerio, 2013). Whereas Hollande (2012) had publicly criticized his predecessor in the past due to the racialization of the Roma, now, the French Socialist President contributed to legitimize the cultural xenophobia inherent to Valls' discourse. The Socialists' policy of clamping down on bogus inflows was left in disarray after the Leonarda Affair, when a Kosovan Roma was detained by police during a school trip and deported with her family to Kosovo. After intense public protests, Hollande announced on TV that Leonarda could return to France to finish school but not her family, despite immigrants' right to family reunion and her being a minor (Gaffney, 2015). Unsurprisingly, the President's proposal fostered alienation among left-wing supporters, disdain from its opponents, and was publicly rejected by Leonarda and her family leading to the collapse of the French President's popularity (Kuhn, 2014). The government's approach to the Roma and the divisions within the Socialist camp suggest that the FN's influence started to attain a significant level in the first half of President Hollande's term. The next section reviews the FN's influence on the centre-left President's proposals on immigrant integration.

THE SOCIALISTS' CONSENSUS ON
THE 'INTEGRATION CRISIS'

At the official inauguration of the History of Immigration Museum in December 2014, President Hollande delivered his single speech on immigration and emphasized immigrants' past contributions to France, the low proportion of inflows in relation to France's population, defended free movement and the Schengen system and concluded that 'the success of integration will determine our national destiny'. The Socialist president announced the creation of a 'Passport for Talents' (an entry visa for highly skilled immigrants), the expansion of the duration of residence authorizations from one to two years, and the liberalization of the naturalization procedures to improve immigrants' integration (Hollande, 2014). Nonetheless, these liberal policy developments were followed by the reiteration of the supposed 'integration crisis' that became hegemonic in French politics in the aftermath of the 2002 political earthquake (Carvalho, 2014). According to President Hollande (2014), every immigrant would 'have to learn French and receive civic training on Republican values, its rules, usages, rights and duties'. This rhetoric reinforced the perception of French sovereignty as being under threat from the settlement of foreign citizens within national territory, as the FN proposed.

Moreover, the Socialist president restated the fusion between immigration control and immigrant integration deployed by the preceding centre-right president, as integration became a prerequisite for obtaining an entry visa or a residence authorization rather than being a long-term objective to be promoted through the concession of long-term residence authorizations (Simon, 2013). Unsurprisingly, the 2016 immigration law replaced the 'Contract of Welcome and Integration' introduced by Sarkozy with the 'Republican Integration Contract', which indicated a mainstream party consensus on the supposed 'integration crisis' denounced by the FN. Notwithstanding the paramount concern with immigrant integration among the French mainstream parties, polls conducted in the late 2000s suggested that French national sentiment was shared by 52 per cent of the respondents from the immigrant population (reaching around two-thirds for North African immigrants), while national affiliation increased to 79 per cent of the respondents who obtained French citizenship through naturalization (Simon, 2013, 214). By contrast, the fight against discrimination on education and on access to the labour market received a brief reference while immigrants' residential segregation was not addressed in the president's speech. The legacy of President Hollande's discourse on immigration was undermined by the publication of the tell-all book.

Five months earlier, the French president commented that 'I think there are too many arrivals, immigrants who shouldn't be there'. Hollande then added: 'we teach them to speak French and then another group arrives, and we have to start all over again. It never stops. So, what do we do? We work in one neighbour, we provide them habitation . . . and then, there are others who arrive, poorer than the other' (Davet and Lhomme, 2016). Therefore, inflows had to be stopped because they undermined immigrants' integration, while left wingers' accusations of betrayal were justified by their misunderstanding of the mutations in French society. The president's misgivings help to understand the ambiguous management of immigration by the socialist executive in the first half of his term and the subsequent political dealignment into the far-right's grounds after unexpected exogenous events like the 2015 terrorist attacks. Parallel to this, the contradiction between his private statements and public discourse the Socialist president's vulnerability to the 'Lepenisation of minds', while the restatement of the fusion of immigration control with immigrant integration indicates the FN's significant influence. References to the FN's ideological contagious effects resurfaced within the context of the asylum crisis observed in Europe in 2015 (Feltesse, 2017).

THE SOCIALIST EXECUTIVE'S INACTION
ON THE ASYLUM CRISIS

In the face of an increasing number of asylum seekers at the external EU borders arriving via the Mediterranean Sea or through south-eastern Europe, the German Chancellor Angela Merkel unilaterally opened the national borders to refugees from Syria stranded in Hungary. At the same time, the EU Commission drafted a quota system to distribute 160,000 asylum seekers stranded in Italy and Greece between all member-states. While the French Interior Minister initially suggested that the EU commission's plans were partially inspired by his government's proposals, Valls publicly disavowed his colleague and rejected any reference to a quota system (Leclerc, 2015). Moreover, Valls demanded that EU member states assumed their responsibilities to separate irregular immigrants from genuine refugees. The French government's response to the asylum crisis indicated the divisions regarding the management of inflows within the Socialist's government, the lack of solidarity at the European level and disregard for France's heritage as the birthplace of the Declaration of the Rights of Man. In parallel, Marine accused the French government of submission towards the EU plans and rejected the commission's proposal because it would enhance human trafficking into the continent (FN, 2015a).

President Hollande also initially supported the rejection of the quota system proposed by the EU commission and commented: 'people who come because they think that Europe is a prosperous continent, even when they are not hired by companies [. . .] they must be escorted back, that's the rule' (AFP, 2015). Whereas Franco-German cooperation was regarded as indispensable to overcome EU crises in the past, France abandoned Germany on asylum, and the bilateral relationship between Hollande and Merkel was strained to levels unobserved in the past (Gouzy, 2015). Furthermore, the French President failed to challenge and indirectly condoned the FN's framing of the asylum crisis as a wave of irregular immigration with economic purposes orchestrated by the EU Commission (FN, 2015a). Thereby, the association of asylum seekers and bogus irregular immigrants became hegemonic in the French political debate, providing evidence of the RRPP's ideological victory (Lemarié et al., 2015). At the FN's summer university, Marine depicted immigration as a 'burden' to the French society and directly blamed Chancellor Merkel for inciting inflows to address Germany's demographic deficit, 'reduce wages and to continue to recruit slaves through mass immigration' (Faye, 2015b).

However, a U-turn was observed on France's approach to the asylum crisis after the widespread circulation of a photo of a drowned Syrian boy lying on a Turkish beach in early September, an event interpreted by Hollande as an opportunity to resume Franco-German cooperation on this topic (Gantzer, 2017). As such, Hollande announced that 24,000 refugees would be taken in within two years, a number perceived as evidence of France's lack of generosity by both the centre-right and the left (Feltesse, 2017). After accepting to participate in a meeting with the Socialist mayors who organized a solidarity movement to welcome the asylum seekers, President Hollande failed to follow through. This action suggested a lack of commitment to his previous goal, leaving his policy adviser perplexed and questioning himself over the potential 'Lepenisation' of the French President's mind (Feltesse, 2017). In his tell-all book, Hollande justified his restrictive approach towards the refugees, stating that it was due to the diversity of the immigrants' origins and the economic purposes of the newcomers. On a different occasion, Hollande stated that his restrictive approach was a means of preventing accusations of 'exploiting refugees to boost the far right' (Davet and Lhomme, 2016).

President Hollande's initial comments suggested full agreement with the FN's framing of the asylum crisis, while this RRPP's electoral inroads that were evident at the 2014 EP elections and the 2015 departmental elections were directly associated with his restrictive approach to this European crisis. Months after the 2015 regional elections wherein the FN campaigned on a promise to deport all asylum seekers (Faye, 2015b), the embattled Franco-German cooperation on asylum was further hampered by Valls' direct critiques of Merkel's strategy on German soil in consonance with Marine's discourse.[5] The French Prime Minister added that 'Europe could not accommodate more refugees' and closed the door to the further distribution of refugees (Lemaître, 2016). Rather than disavowing his subordinate's comments, President Hollande acknowledged them as the French official position and placed further strain on the bilateral relationship with Germany (Davet and Lhomme, 2016). Therefore, the FN's significant influence on immigration control at the domestic level contained salient repercussions into the French foreign policy at the EU level and hampered France's bilateral relations. By the end of 2016, France only welcomed 7,000 Syrian asylum seekers, in a demonstration of policy inaction, which provides further evidence of the FN's significant influence on immigration control during President Hollande's term.

PRESIDENT HOLLANDE'S CHALLENGE TO THE FRENCH REPUBLICAN PARADIGM

In the aftermath of the Paris terrorist attacks in November 2015, President Hollande convened a special congress of Versailles with all members of the upper and lower houses of parliament. Three days after the attacks, the Socialist president proposed a constitutional reform to enshrine the state of emergency (including controversial special powers like detention of suspects without judicial authorization) as well as the power to revoke the French citizenship of convicted terrorists who were born in France and held dual citizenship. Convinced of a right-wing shift in public opinion after the terrorist shock (Davet and Lhomme, 2016), the Socialist President informally co-opted a long-standing proposal by the French RRPP. The FN's 2002 electoral manifesto demanded: 'the application of withdrawal of nationality included in the nationality law for crimes such as terrorism, drugs traffic, and murders' (FN, 2001, 29). Notwithstanding the inclusion of a similar mechanism in the French legislation since 1938,[6] President Hollande pushed forward with his highly symbolic constitutional reform weeks before the 2015 regional elections, in which the FN was expected to capitalize on the terrorist wave.

Moreover, President Hollande operated a U-turn from his past opposition to a similar unsuccessful initiative undertaken by his centre-right predecessor in 2010. In a televised statement, Hollande considered that Sarkozy's proposal to strip French citizenship from individuals with foreign origin that attacked French public authorities was 'detrimental to what is ultimately the republican tradition and fails to protect citizens' (Soullier, 2015). As Hollande recognized, the proposal transgressed the absolute equality imposed by French Republicanism, whilst the potential efficacy of representing a deterrent against further terrorist attacks committed by French nationals was very dubious. The French constitutional ombudsman for citizens' rights Jacques Toubon (former centre-right justice minister) warned against 'a fundamental division of French people into two categories' that enhanced the stigmatization of the 3.2 million French citizens with dual nationality. Consequently, the President's proposal fostered the perception that dual citizenship was problematic, legitimizing the FN's long-established opposition to dual nationality because it threatened national sovereignty (FN, 2001; 2012).

The President's informal engagement with the FN's proposition fostered the implosion of the Socialist Party and the opposition of members of government, leading to the resignation of the Justice Minister Christine Taubira in January 2016. Consequently, the second article of the constitutional revision's project was rejected by 40 per cent of the PS members of the lower chamber of parliament. The potential enshrinement of the FN's pledge in the national constitution would represent evidence of this RRPP's very significant influence in the French politics. By March 2016, the constitutional reform was scrapped by the Socialist President due to the lack of consensus between the National Assembly and the Senate over its contents. Therefore, institutional veto players specified by the French constitution watered down the FN's very significant influence on President Hollande's management of immigration. Subsequently, eighteen months before the presidential election, President Hollande's approval rating among the general electorate dropped to 15 per cent, a drop that was especially steep among his centre-left voters. Nevertheless, the Socialist government's approach to Islam further realigned itself away from the Republican paradigm.

THE SOCIALIST PRIME MINISTER'S DRIFT
INTO ISLAMOPHOBIA

In the aftermath of the Charlie Hebdo shootings in January 2015, Prime Minister Valls vowed on TV to tackle 'a territorial, social and ethnic apartheid [which] has imposed itself on our country', which supposedly led French citizens to feel as 'second-class citizens' (Le Monde, 2015). Valls was implicitly referring to the three attackers' residence in socially disadvantaged urban areas. However, his rhetoric was ambiguous and could be interpreted as either the implicit denunciation of religious communitarianism or a reference to the process of urban segregation of ethnic minorities. In fact, geographical segregation was a recurrent theme of the FN's electoral campaigns, where it proposed the 'dismantlement of ethnic ghettos' and the tackling of the supposedly expanding 'communitarian ghettoization' (FN, 2001). An analogous relationship was thus observed between the Socialist Prime Minister's rhetoric and the RRPP's discourse. Nevertheless, Valls still accused the FN of promoting 'division and stigmatization' that conveyed the 'germ of civil war' before the 2015 regional elections (Rovan, 2015). While the Prime Minister promoted the FN's demonization among the electorate, his own informal co-option of this RRPP's discourse increased the saliency and legitimacy of this RRPP's proposals.

The Socialist Prime Minister's drift into the cultural xenophobia that was previously observed towards the Roma resurfaced in June 2015, after framing the January shootings as evidence of a war of civilizations between France and the terrorists (Libération, 2015). In his view, the French government led the defence of French society, civilization and values from the terrorist menace, placing identity politics at the top of the political agenda, as the President's media adviser decried (Gantzer, 2017). This action legitimatized the FN's (2001) long-established framing of Islam as a 'threat to French sovereignty and civilization'. The French Prime Minister's stigmatization of Muslim citizens deepened a year later, after proposing the ban of headscarves from universities and claiming that most French people thought Islam was incompatible with the Republic. In reaction to this, the head of the Observatory on Islamophobia expressed his exasperation: 'We are fed up of being stigmatized [. . .] [and] of this populist discourse which is worse than [that of] the far-right' (*The Guardian*, 2016). For the first time during his term, President Hollande publicly expressed his direct opposition to the Prime Minister's proposal, a rejection espoused by other cabinet members in public, indicating the Socialists' disarray regarding immigrant integration (Gantzer, 2017).

The Socialist Prime Minister leaned further towards the FN's Islamophobia after Valls granted his full public support to the French right-wing mayors who banned full-body swimsuits from beaches. According to Valls, the detainment of Muslim women who dressed 'burkinis' was a 'question of law and order', while the education minister Najat Vallaud-Belkacem associated the local bans with the 'liberation of racist speech' (Le Monde, 2016). The ban was overturned by the French Council of State due to its violation of civil liberties, whilst President Hollande ruled out a national ban on burkinis due to the stigmatization of Muslim citizens in opposition to his Prime Minister's stance (Le Point, 2016). Notwithstanding the President Hollande's overt criticism of his Prime Minister, the tell-all book quotes President Hollande as saying in December 2015 that: 'It's true [that] there is a problem with Islam' and criticizing the mainstream left for not understanding that 'Islam comprises a risk' in reference to religious radicalization (Davet and Lhomme, 2016). These statements reinforced Hollande's political ambiguity while the public dismay provoked by this publication buried his chances of re-election and alienated the overwhelming support of Muslim voters obtained at the 2012 ballot. In short, the FN's influence on immigrants' integration persisted at significant levels by the second half of President Hollande's term,

CONCLUSION

This research suggested that FN's influence on immigration attained a significant level during President Hollande's term despite this RRPP being excluded from the national government or the diminished size of the FN's parliamentary representation. Therefore, this case study suggests that the intensity of RRPP's influence should not be equated with these parties' access to national office or their representation in the national parliament. Exogenous events such as the Charlie Hebdo shootings and the Paris terrorist attacks in 2015 intensified the FN's influence on immigration as the Socialist President decided to informally co-opt the RRPP's long-term proposal to strip bi-nationals of French citizenship in disrespect of the national Republican paradigm. The very significant intensity of the French RRPP's was nonetheless watered down by institutional veto players due to the lack of consensus between the chambers of parliament over the Socialist President's constitutional reform. Hence, studies on RRPP influence ought to acknowledge the observation of salient domestic constraints on the scope of this political process.

In addition to the informal co-option of the FN's discourse and proposals, this investigation associated this RRPP's influence with the observation of policy inaction over the Socialist government's management of the asylum crisis in 2015. Moreover, this investigation also highlighted the dissemination of the FN's influence on immigration control at the domestic level into the Socialist government's management of international relations, in particular towards Germany and the EU Commission. In sum, the significant intensity of the FN's influence on immigration during President Hollande's term presented an indirect character and was considered disproportional in relation to this RRPP's electoral support within the French party system. RRPP's influence on policy developments can also be observed during the terms led by centre-left parties and superseded the mere discourse or cultural levels. The observation of this political process was closely associated with the FN's growing electoral threat from 2012 to 2017 and the Socialist executive's willingness to informally engage with this RRPP's discourse and proposals, which was boosted by the exogenous events in 2015. Further analysis should explore the effects of the FN's influence over the French foreign policy during the 2015 asylum crisis to expand the scope of the available research on RRPP literature.

NOTES

1. In opposition to past depolarization, the FN imposed the triangulation of political competition in the second round (it contested 60 per cent of the cantons in the second round, while the centre-left competed on 66 per cent).

2. Valls only obtained the support of 5.63 per cent of the PS voters in the first round of the 2011 primary elections, which indicated his unpopularity across the centre-left party's members.

3. Effectively, similar proposals were presented by Sarkozy in 2005 and 2008 but were vetoed on Republican grounds by President Chirac and a Senate's commission chaired by Pierre Mazeaud (Carvalho, 2014).

4. Overall, this reform expanded the rate of regularized immigrants by 30 per cent between 2012 and 2017.

5. Remarkably, Valls commented: 'A few months ago, the French media questioned: "where is the French Merkel?" Or those who wanted to give the Chancellor the Nobel Prize. Today, I see the results'. These statements followed the aftermath of the Cologne sexual attacks during the New Year's Eve that were erroneously associated with asylum seekers (Lemaître, 2016).

6. Article 23-7 of French civil code states: 'The Frenchman that behaves in fact as the national of a foreign nation can, if he holds the nationality of this country, be declared, after obtaining the opinion of the Council of State, to have lost the French status' (Weil and Lepoutre, 2015). Effectively, President Hollande deprived five individuals of French citizenship in 2015 without public outcry (Davet and Lhomme, 2016).

BIBLIOGRAPHY

AFP 2015. Hollande rejects EU migrant quotas but backs better distribution. *The Guardian*, 19 May.

Alonso, Sonia and Sara Fonseca. 2011. Immigration, left and right. *Party Politics*, 18, no. 6: 865–884.

Akkerman, Tjitske 2012. Comparing radical right parties in government: Immigration and integration policies in nine countries 1996–2010. *West European Politics*, 35, no. 3: 511–529.

Akkerman, Tjitske, Sarah de Lange, and Matthijs Rooduijn. 2016. *Radical Right-wing Populist Parties in Western Europe: Into the mainstream?* Oxon: Routledge.

Bale, Tim, Christoffer Green-Pedersen, André Krouwel, Kurt R. Luther, and Nick Sitter. 2010. If you can't beat them, join them? Explaining social democratic responses to the challenge from the populist radical right in Western Europe. *Political Studies*, 58, no. 3: 410–426.

Carvalho, João. 2014. *Impact of Extreme-Right Parties on Immigration Policy: Comparing Britain, France and Italy*. Oxon: Routledge.

Carvalho, João. 2016a. The influence of extreme-right parties on immigration policy in Italy and France in the early 2000s. *Comparative European Politics*, 14, no. 5: 663–685.

Carvalho, João. 2016b. The effectiveness of French immigration policy under President Nicolas Sarkozy. *Parliamentary Affairs*, 69, no. 1: 53–72.

Carvalho, João, and Didier Ruedin. 2018. The positions mainstream left parties adopt on immigration: A cross-cutting cleavage? *Party Politics*, published online on 15 June, available at: http://journals.sagepub.com/doi/full/10.1177/1354068818780533.

Carter, Elizabeth. 2005. *The Extreme Right in Western Europe. Success or Failure?* Manchester: Manchester University Press.

Czaika, Mathias and Hein De Haas. 2013. The effectiveness of immigration policies. *Population and Development Review*, 39, no. 3: 487–508.

Chrisafis, Angelique. 2016. French PM calls for ban on Islamic headscarves at universities. *The Guardian*, 13 April.

Cole, Alistair, Sophie Meunier and Vincent Tiberj. 2013. *Developments in French Politics*. Basingstoke: Palgrave.

Davet, Gérard and Fabrice Lhomme. 2016. *'Un président ne devrait pas dire ça . . .'. Les secrets d'un quinquenat*. Paris: Stock.

Evans, Jocelyn and Gilles Ivaldi. 2013. *The 2012 French Presidential Elections: The Inevitable Alternation*. Palgrave Macmillan.

Faye, Oliver. 2015. Face à la crise migratoire, Marine Le Pen martele son intransigeance. *Le Monde*, 7 September.

Feltesse, Vincent. 2017. *Et si tout s'était passé autrement*. Paris: Plon.

Front National. 2001. *300 Mesures Pour La Renaissance De La France*.

Front National. 2012. Droit de vote des étrangers: PS et UMP main dans la main. *Communiqués FN*, 18 September.

Front National. 2015a. Quotas de migrants: l'Union européenne plus criminelle que les passeurs. *Communiqués FN*, 13 May.

Front National. 2015b. Quotas de migrants voulus par l'UE: derrière leur agitation médiatique, Valls et Sarkozy soumis à la politique d'immigration massive. *Communiqués FN*, 17 May.

Gaffney, Jaffney. 2015. *France in the Hollande Presidency: The Unhappy Republic*. Basingstoke: Palgrave Macmillan.

Gantzer, Gaspard. 2017. *La politique est un sport de combat*. Paris: Fayard.

Gouzy, Jean-Pierre. 2015. La vie politique en Europe et dans le monde. *L'Europe en Formation*, 2015/3 no. 377: 151–172.

Hainsworth, Paul. 2008. *The Extreme Right in Western Europe*. Oxon: Routledge.

Hollifield, James. 2014. Immigration and the Republican tradition in France in controlling immigration: A global perspective, edited by James Hollifield, Phillip Martin, and Pirra Orrenius, 225–250. Stanford, CA: Stanford University Press.

Hollande, François. 2012. Letter to Collectif National Droits de l'Homme Romeurope. Paris, 27 March.

Ivaldi, Gilles. 2016. A new course for the French radical right? The Front National and 'de-demonization'. In *Radical Right-wing Populist Parties in Western Europe. Into the Mainstream?* edited by Tjitske Akkerman, Sarah de Lange and Matthijs Rooduijn, 225–246. Oxon: Routledge.

Jaffré, Jérome. 2017. *Le Front National face à l'obstacle du second tour*. Paris: Foundation pour l'innovation politique.

Kuhn, Raymond. 2014. Mister unpopular: François Hollande and the exercise of presidential leadership, 2012–14. *Modern and Contemporary France*, 22, no. 4: 435–457.

Leclerc, Jean-Marques. 2015. Les ambiguïtés du gouvernement sur les quotas de migrants. *Le Figaro*, 18 May.

Lemaître, Frédéric. 2016. 'Nous ne pouvons pas accueillir plus de réfugiés', selon Manuel Valls. *Le Monde*, 13 February.

Le Monde. 2015. Manuel Valls évoque 'un apartheid territorial, social, ethnique' en France. 20 January.

Le Monde. 2016. 'Burkini': Manuel Valls désavoue Najat Vallaud – Belkacem. 25 August.

Le Nouvel Observateur. 2011. Primaire PS. Comparez les projets des candidats sur l'Immigration. 20 October.

Le Pen, Jean-Marie. 2007. La revanche des legislatives. Saint – Cloud. 24 April 2007. http://www.frontnational.com/doc_interventions_detail.php?id_inter=78.

Le Point. 2016. Burkini: Hollande ne veut 'ni provocation ni stigmatisation. 25 August.

Libération. 2013. Pour Valls, 'les Roms ont vocation à rentrer en Roumanie ou en Bulgarie. 24 September.

Libération. 2015. Le jour où Manuel Valls parla de 'guerre de civilisation'. 28 June.

Le Parisien. 2013. Manuel Valls: Les Roms ont vocation à revenir en Roumanie ou en Bulgarie. 24 September.

Minkenberg, Michael. 2001. The radical right in public office: Agenda-setting and policy effects. *West European Politics* 24, no. 4: 1–21.

Mondon, Aurelien. 2014. The Front National in the twenty-first century: From pariah to Republican Democratic contender? *Modern and Contemporary France*, 22, no. 3: 301–320.

Mudde, Cas. 2013. Three decades of populist radical right parties in Western Europe: So what? *European Journal of Political Research*, 52: 1–19.

Noiriel, Gérard. 2011. Immigration, collective memory and national identity in France. University of Coimbra, 12 April.

Nouvel Observateur. 2011. Primaire PS: comparez les projets des candidats sur l'Immigration. 20 November.

Page, Edward. 2008. The origins of policy in *The Oxford Handbook of Public Policy*, edited by Michael Moran, Martin Rein and Robert Goodin, 207–227. Oxford: Oxford University Press.

Rovan, Anne. 2015. Valls agite le spectre de la guerre civil. *Le Figaro*, 12 December.

Schain, Martin A. 2006. The extreme right and immigration policy-making: Measuring direct and indirect effects. *West European Politics*, 29, no. 2: 270–289.

Schain, Martin. 2008b. *The Politics of Immigration in France, Britain, and the United States: A Comparative Study*. Basingstoke: Palgrave Macmillan.

Simon, Patrick. 2013. Contested citizenship. In *France: The Republican Politics of Identity and Integration, Developments in French Politics*, edited by Alistair Cole, Sophie Meunier and Vincent Tiberj, 203–217. Basingstoke: Palgrave.

Soullier, Lucie. 2015. Quand Hollande et Valls conspuaient la déchéance de nationalité au nom de grandes valeurs. Le Monde, 4 January.

Tsebelis, George. 2002. *Veto Players: How Political Institutions Work*. Princeton, PA: Princeton University Press.

Valerio, Ivan. 2013. François Hollande en soutien à Manuel Valls sur les Roms: 'Est-ce que la France a vocation à accueillir tous les plus vulnérables?'. *Europe 1*, 26 September.

van Spanje, Joost. 2010. Contagious parties: Anti-immigration parties and their impact on other parties' immigration stances in contemporary Western Europe. *Party Politics*, 16, no. 5: 563–586.

Vincent, Elise. 2012. La circulaire sur les évacuations de campements roms publiée. *Le Monde*, 29 August.

Weil, Patrick and Jules Dupoutre. 2015. Refusons l'extension de la déchéance de la nationalité! *Le Monde*, 3 December.

Williams, Michelle. 2006. *The Influence of Radical Right-wing Parties in West European Democracies*. New York: Palgrave Macmillan.

Chapter 4

When Governing Is Losing Advantage

Denmark and Finland, Two Opposite Cases of Radical Right Populist Parties' Influence on Policy Making

Nathalie Blanc-Noël

In the twentieth century, Nordic countries have often been equaled to triumphant social democracy. By contrast, the beginning of the twenty-first century offers a very different picture: four of the five Nordic countries have radical right populist parties (RRPP) in governing positions. In Norway, the Progress Party (Fremskrittspartiet, FrP) has been a member of two government coalitions since 2013. In Finland, The Finns party (Perussuomalaiset, PS) had refused to enter the ruling coalition in 2011 but has been part of the Sipilä cabinet since the 2015 election. The position of Denmark's Progress Party (Dansk Folkeparti, DF) is a special case: since 2001, it has refused to take part in coalitions, but as the third-largest party from 2001 to 2015 and the second since this date, it is a needed supporter of minority governments. In Iceland, the Progressive Party (Framsóknarflokkurinn, PP), having originated as an agrarian party, has recently developed a nationalist, anti-Muslim rhetoric; it now forms a coalition with the Independence Party and the Left-green movement (it obtained 10.7 per cent in the 2017 parliamentary election). Lastly, the Sweden Democrats (Sverigedemokraterna, SD) entered the *Riksdag* in 2010. At the last general elections in 2018, they obtained almost 18 per cent of the vote (third party after the Social Democrats and the Moderates), which caused a political crisis: other parties having deployed a *cordon sanitaire* against them, they faced the greatest difficulty to form a government.

The Nordic RRPP differ by their histories and status on the political scene of their respective countries but they also have strong similarities, so they can be put in the same category of RRPP (Jungar and Jupskås, 2014). In the present chapter, we will refer to the definition established by Jens Rydgren: 'The radical right-wing parties share a core of ethno-nationalist xenophobia and anti-establishment populism. In their political platforms this ideological core is often embedded in a general socio-cultural authoritarianism that stresses themes such as law and order and family values' (Rydgren, 2012). According to the general problematic of this book regarding the policy influence of RRPP, we will compare two opposite cases. Despite its electoral success and its ascending trajectory, the Danish People's Party (DPP) has chosen to stay outside cabinets but plays a key role of government supporter from the *Folketing*. This position has allowed it to develop major policy influence and to enforce large portions of its program. The Finns Party (PS) equally chose to stay outside the cabinet after the 2011 election but took part in the governing coalition in 2015. The result is the party relatively failed to put its ideas in practice and ended up with a shrunk electoral support and a split. To assess and explain the policy influence of DF and FP, I will study their historical trajectories, and then will compare their programs with the evolution of legislation on two major subjects: immigration and culture policies. Lastly, I will compare my findings with the supply/demand side theory (Mudde, 2007, Kitschelt and Mc Gann, 1997) to isolate factors that can explain the chances for RRPP to exert a policy influence.

HISTORICAL TRAJECTORIES OF RRPP IN DENMARK AND FINLAND

Both the Finns Party and the Danish People's Party have roots in protest parties that have been on the political scene for several decades. Four waves can be identified in their development. The first one began in the 1950s. In Finland, Veikko Vennamo founded a small rural holder's party from the Center Party (an agrarian party). In 1966, it became the Finnish rural party (SMP). A typical populist party, its success was linked to Vennamo's personality, who exploited the fact that small rural holders felt threatened by industrialization and modernization of the economy. He opposed peasant, traditional values to urban elites formed of 'rotten gentlemen', as he said. A second wave of rising popularity occurred in the 1970s. SMP made its best score in 1970 (10 per cent at the legislative election). The same trend repeated in 1973 in Denmark (and in Norway[1]). Mogens Glistrup's newly founded Progress Party (Fremkridtspartiet, FP) obtained 15.9 per cent of the vote at the so-called earthquake election and became the second party in the *Folketing*. FP was more liberal than the Finnish SMP, as it was positioned against taxes and the welfare state, whereas Venammo defended modest people and solidarity between urban and rural areas. FP also benefited from the first EU referendum in Denmark, attracting voters disapproving of other parties' support to the membership.

The third and fourth waves corresponded to the development of anti-immigrant rhetoric Europe in the 1980s and the accession of RRPP to governing positions from the 1990s. In Denmark, The Progress Party collapsed in 1983 when Mogens Glistrup was sentenced for tax fraud. In 1991, he was replaced by his second in command, Pia Kjærsgaard, who in 1995 founded the Danish People's Party (Dansk Folkeparti, DF). In 2012, Christian Thulesen Dahl became the new leader of the party. DF is an ethno-nationalist, xenophobe party, aiming at drastically diminishing immigration and fighting multiculturalism. As its predecessor, it is anti-elitist, but it has given up neoliberal stances and now supports the welfare state. In 2001, it obtained 12 per cent of the vote. Whereas DF has always refused to take part to governing coalitions, it has been in a position of participating in governmental policies as minority governments need its support. In 2011, it still obtained 12.3 per cent of the vote but a Social Democratic/Social Liberal/Socialist People's coalition captured power. In 2005, DF gained 21.1 per cent of the vote and became the second largest party after the Social Democrats, still refusing to enter governments formed of centre-liberal-conservative coalitions.

In 1995, after Vennamo's party collapsed, its former secretary Timo Soini founded a new party, the True Finns (Perussuomalaiset, PS). (It is called this name in Finnish and Swedish, whereas the official English translation has been changed for the 'Finns Party'.) PS is an anti-Europe, anti-immigration, anti-elite welfare chauvinist party. It entered in *Eduskunta* in 2003. At the 'big bomb' election in 2011, it obtained 19.05 per cent of the vote (third score), but refused to enter government. In the legislative election in 2015, it became the second party by number of voices with 17.65 per cent of the vote. Then PS went into the Sipilä cabinet with the Center Party and the National Coalition Party. But in June 2017, the moderate branch of PS split off to form New Alternative, a parliamentary group, which gave birth to a new party, Blue Reform (Blue Future in Finnish, Sininen tulevaisuus). It has replaced PS in government. Its chairman is Sampo Terho. While still nationalist, this new party presents itself as more moderate. However, its discourse now seems to harden on the immigration question.

GOVERNMENT PARTICIPATION – OR NOT

DF's position consists of reigning without governing (Blanc-Noël, 2013): it refused to take part in governing coalitions even if it has obtained third and second scores at general elections since 2001. The main reason invoked for this is that DF's opinion regarding the EU is incompatible with other parties' positions. But another tactical reason could have been to avoid the responsibility for unpopular measures. Anyway, DF has made numerous deals with governments needing its support, which has allowed large areas of its program to be put in practice. However, this position is less and less defensible.

DF is now the second party in parliament and with the balance of power at 90/89 seats split between the right and left blocs, its support is crucial for the minority government. Moreover, a Gallup poll from June 2015 showed that 60 per cent of the Danes wanted it in government (*The Copenhagen Post*, 23 June 2015). But Christian Thulesen-Dahl said he did not wish to take part to government at any cost. He still asks for policies that are refused by *Venstre,* such as an increased border control and a withdrawal from the *Schengen* space, opposition to further EU integration and a 0.8 per cent growth of the public sector per year (he offered to finance welfare benefits and pensions by cuts on housing for asylum seekers).

The Finns electoral success is comparable to that of DF – the third best score in 2011 and the second at the 2015 – but in a shorter period of time. In 2011, with 19.1 per cent of the votes they refused to be part of the coalition because of the EU question (they quit the coalition talks as other parties had agreed to support the bailout for Portugal). Moreover, anti-elitism had always been a central argument in the Finns argumentation, so accepting a governing position would have deprived them of a powerful lever of influence. In Finland, given the consensual political system, political discourse is generally moderate and constructive, so 'it is relatively easy to stand out and gain public attention by simply displaying populist, adversarial rhetoric' (Niemi, 2013). So the PS chose to become the leading opposition party. This was accepted by the party's supporters and its popularity kept growing after the election.

But a few months later, in the 2012 municipal election, the Finns received a serious forewarning, obtaining only 12 per cent of the vote. In the meantime, their image had been altered by a series of scandals, revealing the extremist ideas of some of their members: for instance, MP James Hirvisaari's assistant, Helena Eronen, suggested on her blog that it should be mandatory for immigrants, as well as for Swedish Finns and homosexuals, to wear an armband enabling the police to identify them easily (*Helsinki Times*, 13 April 2012). The Finns appeared to be more and more divided, between the 'Soinites' and a faction much more critical of immigration. Moreover, Soini had developed a bad strategy, trying to turn the municipal election into another referendum on the eurozone crisis, which was not the subject of a local election.

However, the Finns managed to obtain 17.7 per cent of the vote at the parliamentary election in 2015, becoming the second largest party by votes. This success was largely due to Soini's electoral campaign. He continuously assured he was ready to govern and kept criticizing the UN's rescue package to Greece, but he toned down criticism of immigration, while refraining from condemning members of his party making xenophobe declarations. This time, Soini entered into a coalition with the Centre and the National coalition parties. He refused to become the Minister of Finance as it is the tradition for the leader of the second party; instead, he became Minister of Foreign Affairs (a position he is said he always had dreamt of).

The Finns Party's trajectory, however, seems to confirm the idea that RRPP parties do not survive the experience of power: in October 2015, a few months after the election, almost 60 per cent of the Finns electorate said they would have reconsidered their choice and would have voted for the Social Democrats if elections had taken place then (*Helsinkin Sanomat*, 23 October 2015). A poll conducted by *Yle* in January 2017 showed their support had fallen to 8.8 per cent. When the Finns had to re-elect their party chair, Soini announced that he would not be the candidate. The election was won by Jussi Halla-aho who represented the radical anti-immigration faction. The governing coalition was on the verge of dissolving because of Halla-aho's links with extreme-right movements. Then Soini, along with a group of MPs, quit the Finns. Their new party, Blue Reform, has replaced PS in government without having been elected. It had to find a way on a narrow path: it presented itself as an independent conservative party, critical of old parties, wanting to implement reforms and at the same time to respect traditions, for instance by consolidating the welfare state.

Blue Reform did not present a candidate at the presidential election held in January 2018 (it did not expect to gather enough signatures to set a candidate, being a newcomer). The Finns for their part obtained 6.9 per cent of the votes (with a very unexperienced candidate, Laura Huhtasaari); anyway, their popularity seems to be rising again. In June 2018, a poll gave them 10.3 per cent support, and they were the fifth most preferred party in Finland, while Blue Reform had a mere 1.1 per cent support (*Helsinki Times*, 5 July 2018). Blue Reform still has to find its ideological way: later in 2018, some of its members have launched a few 'Denmark-inspired' ideas on immigration. Simon Elo, their chairperson, stated that Finnish citizens should get higher social benefits than non-citizens and MP Tina Elovaara introduced a bill to the parliament suggesting that the process of granting asylum should take into consideration the education and working background of applicants.

DF AND PS: QUITE SIMILAR PROGRAMMES

Although DF and PS have different positioning on the political spectrum, their programmes are very similar. DF positions itself on the right and occupies the rightest seats in *Folketing*. PS for its part depicts itself as a centre or centre-left party and occupies middle seats in *Eduskunta* (Blue Reform is now on the right of the Finns). The claim of being a centre party made by PS is purely founded on its agrarian origins and is a question of symbolic self-representation. Content analysis, however, allows putting PS and

DF in the RRPP category, which a majority of researchers do (Betz, 1994; Mudde, 2007; Rydgren, 2013). Their ideologies have, according to the above-mentioned definition established by Jens Rydgren, a core of ethno-nationalist xenophobia. They share anti-establishment stances and defend law, order and family values. Moreover, both parties define themselves as 'populists', drawing a line between 'populism', which accepts democratic institutions, and 'extreme-right', a category concerning overtly racist, neo-Nazi or fascist movements. However, members of both parties have links with extreme-right movements. DF has links with the Danish association (Den danske forening). Its journal, *Den danskeren*, publishes papers with a clearly more racist and nativist tone than the ordinary discourse of DF, but its themes and argumentation are a direct source of inspiration for DF.[2] Several prominent DF members belong (or have belonged) to the Danske forening.[3] On many occasions, DF members pronounced harsh racist statements, often condemned by justice but less often followed by sanctions from the party.[4]

In Finland, several PS members belong to Suomen Sisu (Finnish Sisu), a nationalist, anti-immigration association.[5] Several members of the Finns also publicly expressed overtly racist ideas, such as Jussi Halla-aho (MEP and now leader of the party), whose blog, *Scripta*,[6] has a link on its front page with *Gates of Vienna*, a site hosting neo-Nazi authors and tenants of the Eurabia conspiracy theory (such as the Norwegian mass-murderer Anders Breivik). Halla-aho also regularly writes on *Hommaforum*, an anti-immigration forum whose users call themselves *'Net-zis'* (*netsis* in Finnish)[7]. He was convicted by the Finnish Supreme Court but never expelled from the party, as was the case of several other party members. Timo Soini has always had a very ambiguous attitude towards racist trash-talking. On the one hand, he personally condemned racism, but on the other one, he said he was 'not a school master' (ANTIFAxFINLAND, 2013). The party gradually became divided in two camps, one moderate and the other one more radical, led by Jussi Halla-aho, now the head of the Finns after their split.

The programmes of DF and PS are clearly ethno-nationalist. They are both focused on the defence of the Danish and Finnish peoples and models of society. The latest version of DF's programme (Dansk folkeparti, 2009) begins with the assertion that 'The aim of DF is to assert Denmark's independence (and) to guarantee the freedom of the Danish People in their own country'. The sovereignty of the Danish people is the point of departure and central argument in this programme, concerning both its inside aspect ('free citizens empowered to defend their own fate and to benefit from "free rights"') and its outside aspect ('Danish independence and freedom'). DF often refers to Danish occupation in the Second World War by the Germans and the idea that Islam is planning to invade Europe/the world, thus making implicit allusions to white supremacist theories. Moreover, its discourse gives a distorted echo to the national identity narrative that was elaborated in the nineteenth-century wave of national-romanticism, when Denmark lost its southern territories after the Duchies war and was turned into a small, more ethnically homogeneous country (Blanc-Noël, 2016). DF's definition of the people is based on two pillars: ethnicity[8] and culture, which are linked: ethnicity is menaced by the fact 'immigrants have a higher nativity rate than the Dane' (Dansk folkeparti, 2009); as a result, the Danish culture is presented as endangered, therefore the Danish heritage (The monarchy, the rule of law and the Lutheran Church) must be preserved and strengthened.

Similarly, the Finns Party programme (2011, 2015, 2015a, 2017) positions the party as the defender of the people and the Finnish culture. However the tone is less dramatic. There is no allusion to any foreign occupation. Instead, the argumentation invokes an economic justification: the Finnish model balance has to be maintained against what could alter it. In general, PS arguments are more practical than principled; they are oriented towards the Finnish people's interests in financial terms or in terms of rights (to one's own language or culture). The tone of PS is also less aggressive than DF's. DF politicians have often asserted the Danish culture is a superior one, as Denmark is one of the world's most advanced democracies. For instance, Pia Kjærsgaard declared, during the 2005 opening debate of the Folketing, 'It has been mentioned that September 11 became the beginning of a fight between civilizations. I don't agree about this, because a fight between civilizations would imply that there were two civilizations, and that is not the case. There is only one civilization, and that is ours' (Kjærgaard, 2005). PS has a milder way to refer to Finnish culture: it is 'a unique element of the world's culture. It is something to be valued as the cornerstone of Finnish society. It must be preserved'. Yet, like DF, PS condemns multiculturalism, which it called 'an artificial shoring up' that must not be financed by the Finish taxpayers: 'A generous welfare state and open borders are not compatible' (Finns Party, 2011).

While DF is overtly nativist, PS places its arguments on a down-to-earth, economic or legal ground. Some factors explain this difference, the first being that the immigration debate is something quite new in Finland. This country has one of the lowest immigration rates in Europe, even if the phenomenon has developed very fast and very recently. The total immigrant population grew from 0.8 per cent of the population in 1990 to 6.2 per cent in 2015 (Hangartner and Sarvimäki, 2017). In Denmark, an influx of refugees arrived in the 1980s, due to the 1983 liberal law on immigration and the Iraq–Iran war. According to Danmarks Statistik, immigrants now represent a bit more than 8 per cent of the population.

Another reason for the different tones used by the two parties is also linked to their respective political culture. In Finland, the Cold War imposed a very peculiar political situation made of consensus and self-censorship. Finland had to follow a realpolitik line considering its proximity to the USSR; the superior goal of national security imposed a 'disciplined' political debate, along the Paasikivi–Kekkonen line. In the 1990s, the consensual style of Finnish politics was maintained because the severe economic recession narrowed the differences between parties, and there were several 'rainbow coalition' governments. In such a context, a populist discourse, with strong, controversial arguments, risks being perceived as too extreme, and too unco-operative to be taken seriously. So, on the one hand, the Finns brought something new and seducing in the Finnish political life, liberating the expression of previously unheard feelings. But on the other hand, they have used as pragmatic argumentation as possible in accordance with the Finnish political culture and/or for tactical reasons.

Another difference is that the Finnish nationalism is language-based. Having been part of the Swedish-Finnish kingdom for more than five centuries, Finland is a bilingual country. The defence of the Finnish language is a cornerstone of the PS program that promises to suppress the obligation to learn Swedish at school, to reduce the state funding of Swedish-speaking media and to defend Finnishness: 'We feel that Finnish-speaking Finns can be constructive members of Finnish society without any knowledge or concern for the Swedish language or culture'. . . 'Swedish is a foreign language' (Finns Party, 2011). PS supports the projects of a referendum on language policy and of changing the Constitution to make teaching of the Swedish language optional. It does not seem to have the same ambition as DF to develop a heritage policy (see below); however, it promotes an educational policy based on the *Kalevala* compulsory teaching, protection of Finn-Ugric languages (especially Karelian as Karelia was taken to Finland to be incorporated into the USSR) and teaching of traditional arts and crafts (Finns Party, 2011). PS also develops very conservative values: emphasis is put on religious and physical education (a 'matter for both physical and mental health'), 'reduction of enrolment rates of universities' (PS praises ordinary people against elites); it wants the national hymn to be sung at school (Finns Party, 2017) and separate toilets for boys and girls (a criticism of 'ideological and feminist ideas' (Finns Party, 2017)). In sum, the school should 'promote and preserve Finnish culture and values' (Finns Party, 2017). Moreover, like DF, PS is opposed to the rights of homosexuals to marry or adopt children.

The ethno-cultural nationalism of DF and PS has logical consequences regarding immigration. This question has been central in DF's project from the mid-1980s, when an influx of refugees from the war between Iran and Iraq came to Denmark, and the press campaigned against immigrants (Hervik, 2011). In Finland, where immigration is recent, this argumentation has developed in the 2000s. DF's programmes state that 'Denmark is not an immigrant country and never has been. Thus we will not accept trans-formation to a multi-ethnic society'. The Finns again are more pragmatic: 'The purpose of immigration policy (. . .) is to provide beneficial, or at least neutral results from immigration and to prevent it from causing economic or other societal damage to Finland' (Finns Party, 2015). PS makes a distinction between a useful immigration that will contribute to Finland's economy, and a burden of immigration bringing a non-working population to the country, with a risk that it will not integrate and will break the solidarity on which the Finnish model is based. But this position does not prove that PS members are less nativist in their heart than DF members. Actually, PS's low tone can be explained for two practical reasons: the first one is that Finland has an ageing population and needs workforce. The second is that PS is an anti-immigrant party in a country having one of the lowest immigration rates in Europe. Therefore, instead of refusing immigration per se, PS argues that the welfare state could be put in danger due to the costs of a growing immigration (Finns Party, 2011). This line of argumentation, developed on the economic ground, presents the advantage to depoliticize and de-radicalize the Finns' discourse and to avoid accusations of xenophobia. Nevertheless, PS mentions DF as a source of inspiration for their (very strict) family reunification policies. Of course, both parties are in favour of assimilation: immigrants have to be able to support themselves, to master the national language, to contribute to the national welfare state by their work and tax-paying and to be loyal to their new country.

Another consequence of DF and PS nationalism is that these parties want to defend the Danish/Finnish model, a pillar of the Danish/Finnish culture. DF defends the welfare state, the family, an educational system 'of the high-est standard' and Danish prosperity in general. The values it emphasizes are clearly conservative, law and order being part of the picture. The Finns Party has the same views, putting an emphasis on health and help for the poorest. Both parties agree that the public sector must provide basic services, but that they can be outsourced or privatized. In this respect, they cannot be qualified as liberal or leftist, but rather, as 'neo-liberal of the lower strata' (Andersen, 1992). They are welfare chauvinists in the sense that the welfare system should benefit to Finnish/Danish citizens in the first place and that they con-sider immigration could endanger its financial balance. Immigrants are fre-quently accused of making profit on the Danish welfare state. PS adds liberal dimensions in welfare policies by underlining that citizens should be 'active participants in the reforming process' (Finns Party, 2011a) and by wanting to 'encourage the individual to take responsibility for their own well-being'.

Concerning international affairs, both parties are against the EU as they see the Union as a menace to national sovereignty. In Denmark, the 2000 refer-endum on the euro currency and the 2015 referendum on the opt-out reform ended on a no victory, although almost all parliamentary parties except DF and parties left to the Social Democrats campaigned on the 'yes' side; this boosted DF's legitimacy, the party arguing it stood on the people's side and against the interests of the establishment. Similarly, the EU question benefited PS in a different context. The Finns largely drew benefit from this topic in the 2011 political debate (Borg, 2012); just before the election, the Eurozone crisis and the bailout funds question became a major topic they took a decisive advantage from. Again they used pragmatic, down-to-earth arguments aimed at seducing simple people: why should Finnish people pay for bad management of foreign economies?

In all, DF and PS programmes are very similar. Their tone may be different, but in the public debate, politicians from both parties use rude, loathsome and provocative words, especially against immigrants and Islam. Both parties are ethno-nationalists, DF being overtly more nativist. Their economic positions may be 'leftist' on some points or 'rightist' on others, they are nationalist above all: every aspect of their programmes derive from their conception of the national culture and the national interest. Moreover, if we take into consideration the national contexts and the different timings of both parties' electoral histories, we can say that their programmes are less different than similar, belonging to the same ideological family.

POLICY INFLUENCE: THE CASES OF IMMIGRATION AND CULTURAL POLICIES

As a needed partner for minority coalition governments, DF has managed to influence Danish legislation especially in two areas: the immigration and cultural policies.[9] Regarding the first of these policies, a comprehensive immigration legislation has been adopted, aiming to limit entries on the Danish territory, to reduce the number of resident permits and to make acquisition of the Danish nationality and family reunification an incredibly difficult obstacle course. The idea is that immigrants and their families must assimilate to the Danish culture and support themselves (Blanc-Noël, 2013). This severe legislation never ceases to be completed. For instance, the famous '24-year rule' forbids a Dane younger than this age to marry a foreigner. Another famous bill conceived in 2016 (the 'jewellery law') states that asylum seekers who arrive in Denmark with more than 10,000 kroner in cash ($1,500) will have to use the surplus to pay for their stay and the authorities can seize any non-essential possession worth more than this sum. This bill also states that parents coming to Denmark without their children will have to wait for at last three years before they can apply to be reunited (*The Copenhagen Post*, 6 January 2016).

In all, these measures have been so severe and efficient that Denmark recently had to adopt a bill to make family reunification easier for Danes themselves, for the set of rules one has to apply in order to move to Denmark also applies to Danes living abroad, preventing some of them to go back home (they have to prove that their link with the nation is still sufficiently strong), but at the same time, a new plan for family reunification will place new demands on a foreign spouse. The language requirement for the applicant will be increased, and the pair applying for reunification must have savings of 100,000 Kr ($15,180) as 'economic insurance', a doubling of the sum previously necessary. Moreover, couples living in designated underprivileged areas will see their application rejected, regardless of other criteria (*The Copenhagen Post*, 16 January 2018). In 2016, the government presented a 2025 Plan with 44 measures aiming at introducing more restrictions on the immigrants already living in the country (*The Local*, 31 August 2016).

During the 2018 general election campaign, the Danish obsession for immigration laws strikes again: on 1 March, the Prime Minister announced a 'ghetto plan' (Regeringen, 2018) now mostly adopted: in 25 areas qualified as 'ghettos' (the use of this word is not innocent: DF has often compared immigration with the Second World War Nazi occupation), criminal punishments for certain crimes can be doubled; people receiving state income will see these reduced when moving to a so-called ghetto area; municipalities will be given easier access to the personal information of residents, their employees will be more severely punished if they fail to report potential poor conditions for children, etc. One adopted rule is particularly shocking: children from one year of age living will be required to attend compulsory day care institutions with an education programme for 25 hours a week – excluding sleeping times – unless their social welfare grants will be cut (*New York Times*, 1 July 2018). Moreover 're-acculturation trips' (*genopdragelsesrejser*) from the Ministry of Immigration defines as 'sending children or young people under 18 years of age – often against their will – to their parents' homeland or another country for an extended period' will be criminalized (up to four years in prison); the ground of this rule is that such trips would compromise their assimilation to Danish culture. But it is only a milder version of what DF proposed: the party suggested that ghetto children could be confined to their homes after 8 p.m., on which the Chairman of the *Folketing* Integration committee added they could be fitted with electronic ankle bracelets. The Pandora box of immigration laws has long been opened in Denmark, and the trend endlessly develops. In May 2018, a new law forbade *niqab* and *burqa*. Among subjects presently discussed are mandatory serving of pork in public institutions (some towns already practice), and the ban of circumcision. Many other ideas have flourished among DF members to reinforce Danish values, as a call for immigrants to celebrate Christmas and Easter (*The Local*, 17 February 2017).

The effect of this endless succession of reforms is a situation where the Danish law is no more equal for all citizens, some of them having lost certain liberties. Of course, Denmark has been criticized several times by international authorities, such as the UNHCR for the decision to give smaller social benefits to immigrants than to native Danes, as well as the United Nations and the Council of Europe for the twenty-four-year law. Some scandals aroused concerning the conditions of the naturalization process, applicable also to children born in Demark, and so demanding that they risk being deported. In 2009, 400 children from Palestinian refugee families, born and raised in Denmark, were refused the Danish nationality, contrary to the NU convention on the rights of stateless children (*The Copenhagen Post*, 5 October 2011), and similar cases happen regularly. So far, this legislation seems to be reaching its goals: in 2017, less than 3,500 people applied for asylum, the lowest figure since 2008 according to the Ministry of Immigration. These rules may have social consequences. For instance, in December 2017, the Confederation of Danish Employers let publicly known that the need for foreign workers is growing in the country. The number of EU citizens coming to Denmark to work has fallen by 65 per cent in the space of 15 months, and according to the Confederation, if the flow from Eastern Europe dries up, Denmark could quickly be short of qualified workers (*The Local*, 4 December 2017).

The DF-driven immigration legislation has been completed with a cultural policy destined to strengthen Danish culture against multiculturalism. The underlying idea is that immigrants who do not master Danish culture represent a menace for the fundamental values of the country. In 2002 the Danish Heritage Cultural Agency was created. It launched a program called 'the Danish canon', consisting of a listing of the greatest accomplishments of the Danish culture; the canon was intended to 'provide reference points and awareness of what is special about Danes and Denmark in an ever more globalized world' and 'to strengthen the sense of community by showing key parts of our common historical possessions' (kulturministeriet). The canon was augmented in 2016, following a poll asking people to elect the ten most fundamental Danish values.

Moreover, a political canon has also been established in 2008, destined to protect democracy against 'the risk of the cohabitation of different cultures that are not looking in the same direction' (Kulturministeriet, 2008).

The canons must serve as guides for educational curricula, TV programmes, etc. This canon policies contain an essentialist conception of culture that has nothing to do with the anthropologic concept, but is a mark of cultural racism. They reflect an idea largely developed by DF members: that the Danish culture is superior. DF also has had successes in other policy areas; for instance, higher resources for families with children and for the elderly (such as the old age check in 2003), improvements in health care and stricter sentences for criminals. But contrary to other European RRPP, they did not seem to be much concerned with the idea of reforming the Danish democracy – already a model for the world.

Comparatively, the Finns' governing position has been close to failure in terms of policy influence. PS hardly kept its promises, hence a dramatic loss of popular support. First of all, the Sipilä government arrived at a time of deep economic crisis. Juho Sipilä, a former successful businessman, intended to impose drastic cuts on the budget, focusing on health, education, culture and public pensions. All these measures were very unpopular for the 'forgotten people' that PS said it represented against the elites (Jungar, 2011). Another major question for PS was the United European policy that Finns had campaigned on. In spite of PS 2011 position on this matter, Finland accepted the third Greek bailout in 2015, while Minister of Foreign affairs Soini's discourse on Europe was curiously toned down. After the British referendum on the Brexit, he even seemed to have changed his mind, saying 'I have said lots of things about the EU along the way but I am not in favour of an uncontrollable collapse that would not be good for anybody' (Reuters, 2016) and refused to support the idea of a similar Finnish referendum. Actually, his choice to become the Minister of Foreign Affairs instead of becoming Minister of Finances was not popular either; it made him appear as wanting to escape responsibilities in a time of heavy reforms and as belonging to the establishment he so often criticized, because he sojourned abroad and met foreign heads of states.

On the question of immigration, the Finns obtained mitigated results. In September 2015, the government announced plans for tightening the immigration policy, but many measures that were proposed were in opposition to the Finnish Constitution and to several human rights conventions. Some measures were taken, yet; for instance, Soini's Foreign Ministry launched a campaign on the social media to discourage candidates to come to Finland (*Sputnik News*, 2015). Moreover, this period coincided with the European refugee crisis so Finland had to welcome lot of refugees. The Finnish government first wanted the country to be an example, willing to welcome 15,000 refugees in 2015 and to double this figure the next year. Prime Minister Sipilä himself offered his second home for free. But faced with a tremendous number of applications (163,000 in 2015, the highest rate of applications per capita in Europe), the government tried to reverse the trend and announced about 20,000 asylum seekers would be expelled (BBC News, 2016). Finally, the government tightened the immigration policy, following a deal that was made between the three governing parties (Soini accepted reforms of the health and social services in exchange of a hardened family reunification law, which made him loose on the area of welfare chauvinism).

In January 2017, new rules on family reunification were adopted that seem to derive inspiration from the Danish law. For instance, refugees have to prove they have sufficient means of subsistence to exert their right to family reunification. There is a lower income limit of €1,700, but for a spouse with two children, it will be of €2,600 net (of course, such requirements are almost impossible to meet as there is less than 50 per cent of people in Finland having such net income). In spite of the fact PS has had a relative influence on the adoption of these measures, in the eyes of many voters, it seems that globally the immigration policy was another promise PS did not manage to keep. Moreover, there were other questions on which the Finns equally failed. They firmly campaigned against the law on same-sex marriage, but it was adopted in 2016. They organized a petition against Swedish compulsory teaching, gathering 50,000 signatures necessary in order to put the question on the *Eduskunta*'s agenda. The result was another failure: in 2015, the MP massively voted to maintain Swedish teaching (134/48).

So far, PS has not succeeded in exerting a strong policy influence as their Danish counterparts did. Major parts of the Finnish opinion are still opposed to xenophobic ideas (there were anti-racist marches (*The Guardian*, 2016)), even if hate speech has developed (as well as racist actions by ultra-nationalist groups such as the Soldiers of Odin). Moreover, some of Soini's conservative ideas are controversial: in September 2018, he faced a no-confidence vote initiated by the Swedish People's Party, the Social Democrats, the Left Alliance and the Green League because he had taken part in an anti-abortion rally in Canada. Had the vote passed, it could have broken the ruling coalition but finally it was rejected. PS successor in government, Blue Reform, seems to do worse, with very bad opinion polls. And now PS seems to be more and more isolated on the political scene: with the next general election approaching (April 2019), the Social Democrats, the National Coalition Party and the Centre Party let know they did not wish to go into a government with it again. So the Finnish governing position was a double failure: they did not exert much policy influence, *and* they did not manage to appear as a responsible party.

PASSING THE GOVERNMENT TEST?

Denmark and Finland offer an interesting case of two RRPP Nordic parties with comparable programmes having reached very similar electoral turnouts. Having chosen opposite tactics, staying outside government for DF, entering coalition for PS, they ended up with very contrasting results: large success for DF in terms of policy influence, failure and split for PS, whose popularity seems to be growing again now it is in opposition (and radicalized). However, endorsing the general idea that RRPP parties do not pass the government test may be too expeditious a conclusion. As an abundant literature has shown, there are many demand- and supply-side factors governing the fate of RRPP parties and determining their capacity of influence (Mudde, 2007). If we consider these factors, we can say that whether or not they chose to enter government, DF and PS did not exactly have the same cards in hands to become policy influencers able to enforce their program.

Concerning the demand-side factors, the Finns had an advantage in the sense their country experienced several economic crisis periods since the end of the Cold War. That was exploited by the Finns willing to represent those left aside. The Danish economy on the contrary is flourishing, the 'Danish model' being praised worldwide (Blanc-Noël, 2018); so DF's discourse had to develop welfare-chauvinist arguments, defending the most modest people against forces that could alter the Danish welfare (globalization and immigration). Another advantage for PS is the general loss of political trust due to a consensual political culture and rainbow coalition governments (Karvonen, 2014), so it was easy to appear as the only different party (what DF also did during the EU-referendum campaigns). But another important difference on demand-side factors is what Mudde called 'ethnic backlash': in Finland, immigration is a very new phenomenon and even if it has grown fast, it is still comparatively very moderate. In Denmark, however, the story of immigration is older, and the phenomenon is more important.

Moreover, DF has benefited from several supply-side factors such as media, that is to say events related to immigration such as the 2005 cartoon crisis (Larsen, 2008) and 9/11. The result was DF has managed to durably politicize the immigration question. Doing so, DF has also beneficiated another external supply-side factor: the political culture context. The Danish national identity narrative that was elaborated in the nineteenth century and since then has been taught in schools. It depicted 'little Denmark' (*lille Danmark*) as a small but homogeneous and strongly united country, having lost many territories in history (Blanc-Noël, 1991). This narrative is easily referred to by DF, albeit in a simplistic, distorting way omitting values such as modernity and tolerance, and promoting a society where universalist, egalitarian values are turned into selectiveness between good and bad citizens. Echoes of the ancient narrative can also be found in the cultural policy DF has inspired. Finland on the contrary has very different story of bilingual country, and PS's project of 'finnishisation' of the country is not popular.

Another supply-side factor, the other parties' attitude towards RRPP, has been very important. In Denmark, where the 2001 electoral success of DF was a big shock, other parties soon promised stricter immigration policies as well. Actually, even if DF has passed many deals with liberal governments between 2002 and 2011, some immigration laws were also supported by the Social Democrats (who lost many voters in favour of DF). As DF made more and more electoral gains, other parties went on cooperating. In 2011, the Liberal government and its main ally, DF, lost election, because of a very unpopular project of retirement pay scheme, and also because of a DF wanted to close borders with Germany and Sweden to limit immigration, which may have caused problems with EU. But during the ten years spent in opposition, DF still managed to make important policy changes such as the old age cheque (considered as a real achievement) by making deals with the left (Social Democrats and Social Liberals). In the end, it appeared more and more as a responsible and competent party. On social and economic questions, RRPP defend what can be called a leftist position. This offers them a considerable room of manoeuvres: when leftist parties realize too many of their traditional voters are attracted to RRPP, they can be tempted to make deals with them or to adopt their stances. The Social Democrats have thus supported the jewellery law, the ban on face veils, the ban on room prayers in schools and the ghetto plan. In 2018, with the perspective of the 2019 election, the Social Democrats have adopted a very detailed plan for a new immigration policy, titled 'Legitimate and realistic. An immigration policy that gathers Denmark' (Socialdemokratiet, 2018). It contains many ideas DF has repeatedly promoted, with slightly more humanitarian considerations. It is aimed at reducing the number of immigrants, with measures such as strict requirements for family reunions, border control and a 'repatriation reform' to send rejected asylum seekers back, but it also plans a kind of 'Marshall plan' to help Africa. Even the Social Liberals, a liberal, usually pro-immigration party seems to follow, as shows the book *Dansk*, published in 2018 by one or its leaders, Ida Auken, who advocates a stricter immigration policy (Auken, 2018).

The Finns' trajectory has almost been the opposite. At first, PS has been considered by other parties and by the press as a party like others, representing a portion of the electorate and thus having to be fairly treated and respected. This was facilitated by the fact there was an old tradition of hostility to immigration in Finland, so the Finns' discourse was not particularly shocking. During the period they were in government, there were no strong dissensions among the three ruling parties, which has been compared to the Paao Alto three-legged chair: if you cut one, the chair falls. But this does not seem to have benefited to PS in the end. The party hardly gained an image of competence. PS members of government (all from the moderate branch) appeared as 'betrayers' of many of their voters, especially on social benefits and EU questions. Moreover, three of them were faced with suspicions of bad governance (financial problems) and one of them, Jari Lindström, expressed shocking statements such as a desire for the return of death penalty. The result is that leaders of parties such as the National Coalition and the Social Democrats are now taking position against the idea of ruling with the Finns in the future (and Blue Reform has such poor opinion support that it is not even mentioned).

The internal supply-side factors also explain the differences between DF and PS in terms of policy influence. Whereas their respective ideologies are largely similar, the two parties have strong differences in terms of leadership and organization. DF is a well-organized, centralized party, whereas it is not the case of PS, especially on the local sections level, who attracted too inexperienced, versatile members. Moreover, Timo Soini never managed the division between the moderate and the anti-immigration factions hosted by the party. His ambiguity towards the latter may have been a strategy to get the greatest number of votes as possible but in the end, he was outflanked by the radical faction.

Another factor rarely mentioned in the demand/supply side theories is the timing factor, which could be described as belonging partly to the demand-side factors (concerning the historical events happening on a RRPP trajectory) and partly to the supply-side factors (concerning a party's longevity and its ability to stay focused on a coherent set of ideas). Here the advantage was for DF: it responded to the immigration and the EU challenges brilliantly (appearing as the only party defending the ordinary Dane against the cosmopolite, pro-European establishment); it never ceased to put the same ideas forward for a period long enough to appear as a stable, reliable and ultimately responsible party: the more policy influence a RRPP gets, the more benefits its image gains. PS in contrast had less advantages; even if it politicized the EU crisis and the immigration question so as to get excellent electoral scores, it did not manage to turn this advantage into a real policy influence, arriving in a time of economic crisis and social reform. In the end it did not appear a stable, reliable party; it remained sort of an unexperienced newcomer instead, using hazardous strategies, with a message blurred by compromises, which was fatal.

CONCLUSION

Although PS did not particularly benefit from its governing experience, from 2001 on, DF has been in position of enforcing its programme by adopting one of the strictest immigration legislation in Europe. In less than two decades, DF has turned the tolerant, welcoming and open-minded Denmark into one of the most chauvinist countries in Europe. This shows that a governing position does not necessarily raise the chances for RRPP to exert a policy influence. On the contrary, the position of supporter of a minority government seems to be ideal. It offers to parties that do not always claim to belong to the right or to the left (or which belong to the right but with acquaintances to the left on some points a large room of manoeuvres to conclude alliances. This position also has the advantage to prevent RRPP to bear the responsibility for unpopular policies and to elude the question of European membership, which seems to act as an ultimate limit to their room of manoeuvres (DF and PS did not enter governments on this ground, and when PS did, its chairman and Minister of Foreign Affairs, Timo Soini, reversed his discourse about Europe).

Another aspect this comparison shows is that the policy influence of RRPP depends on their ideological influence. To become policy influencers, RRPP must develop certain capabilities, the major one being able to stay active on the ideological ground and to be a constant force for bringing forward creative proposals – always pushing demands further, always raising the level of tolerance to questionable measures. This point is a big advantage for DF (which is a great ideological source of inspiration for other RRPP in Europe). The ideology production factor is in our sense a very important factor determining the fate and influence capacity of RRPP, even if RRPP ideologies look simplistic and have been called 'thin' by academics: the important thing is that they address to (bad) feelings, not to intellect. As a matter of fact, these parties appear to be ideologically different from other mainstream parties. They constantly flirt with moral and legal limits, acting as provokers and aiming at fending off these limits. They seem to be incapacity to achieve a major change on the political scene of democracies by freeing the bad genies of parochialism, xenophobia and racism from the bottle, by gradually making the public debate accustomed to hate speech, to provocation and by pushing the trend always further.

In spite of many provocations and scandals, the Finns were provided access to government very fast; their ideas, of course, still have many opponents in the Finnish society, but nonetheless they were not considered as incompatible with democracy – as if their most radical branch was a youthful mistake (and with mainstream parties betting they would not pass the government test). Now racism, hate speech and violence are present in the Finnish society in a way that was unthinkable a few years ago. Moreover, and *despite its position outside government*, it is their most radical branch that is growing again, not Blue Reform (obliged to raise its tone to stay in the game). Two decades ago, DF appeared as an extremist party. It is now a mainstream one, considered as a banal element of democratic pluralism. More than that, the xenophobic rhetoric it has initiated is now commonplace in the Danish society; it has given way to an extensive legislation and is used by other parties. Regarding the ghetto plan for instance, one interesting development is that the opposition parties hardly discussed it on the ground of equality between citizens or human rights (not even on compatibility with European law), but on the ways the plan should be implemented. A few years ago, in conversations with Danes, a sentence often came: 'DF just says what people think quietly'. Now almost everything can be said aloud. This is the point when RRPP parties have become real influencers.

NOTES

1. In Norway, a party with similar views, 'Ander's Lange party for a drastic reduction in taxes, fees and public intervention' also appeared on the political scene and entered in parliament. It later became the Progress Party.

2. Jens Rydgren (2004) identified three themes developed by the Danish association that directly inspired DF: immigration as threat to Danish culture and identity, as a cause of crime and as a burden on the welfare state, all arguments being subordinate to ethnicity.

3. Such as MP Søren Karup (who wants Denmark to take back its former Swedish provinces and the Duchies lost to Germany) and MP Jesper Langballe (who supports the thesis of Islam planning to invade Europe).

4. For instance, MEP Morten Messerschmidt, one of the party's brains, was condemned for having sung Nazi songs in Tivoli Park, while he was drunk. Messerschmidt vandt over B.T. i nazi-sag. Berlingske. 26 February 2009. https://www.b.dk/danmark/messerschmidt-vandt-over-b.t.-i-nazi-sag.

5. *Sisu* is a Finnish word frequently used in national-romantic literature. Difficult to translate, it refers to courage, integrity and stubbornness. PS elected members of *Suomen Sisu* are for example Jussi Halla-aho, Olli Immonen, James Hirvisaari and Juho Eerola. See: Jutila, Karina, Sundell, Björn. The populism of the Finns Party, fun or ugly? e2 Think tank, www.e2.fi.

6. http://www.halla-aho.com/scripta/.

7. Interestingly, Matias Turkkila, the co-founder of *Hommaforum* (founded when *Scripta*'s guest book was overwhelmed by messages), is also the editor of the Finns party newspaper, *Perussuomalainen* and the webmaster of the Finns party website.

8. The *Riksfaellskab* (the fact Denmark is constituted of continental Denmark, plus the Faroese islands and Greenland) is never mentioned in DF's programmes or argumentations. The Danish culture is presented as homogeneous, which is not historically and anthropologically exact. See: Østergaard (2000).

9. Another main concern of DF is law and order; it is dealt with in another chapter of this book.

BIBLIOGRAPHY

Andersen, Goul. 1992. Denmark: The Progress Party. Populist neo-liberalism and welfare state chauvinism. In *The Extreme Right in Europe and the USA*, edited by Paul Hainsworth. London: Pinter: 193–205.

ANTIFAxFINLAND, BBC Hard Talk grills Timo Soini on racism. February 2013, https://www.youtube.com/watch?v=2tqn9BrpEkA&t=57s.

Auken, Ida. 2018. *Dansk*. Køpenhaven: People's Press.
BBC News. 1 February 2016. Migrant Crisis: Prime Minister Sipilä halts plan to host refugees. http://www.bbc.com/news/world-europe-35458641.
Betz, Hans-Georg. 1994. *Radical Right-Wing Populism in Western Europe*. Basingstoke: Palgrave Macmillan.
Blanc-Noël, Nathalie. 1991. Populisme et détournement du récit identitaire national. In *The Land of the Living, the Danish Folk High Schools and Denmark's Non-violent Path to Modernization*, edited by Steven Borish. Nevada City: Blue Dolphin.
Blanc-Noël, Nathalie. 2013. Régner sans gouverner – ou presque: le cas du Parti populaire danois, un populisme établi. *Politeïa* 24: 323–336.
Blanc-Noël, Nathalie. 2016. Populisme et détournement du récit identitaire national: le cas du Parti du peuple danois. In *L'extrême droite en Europe*, edited by Jérôme Jamin. Bruxelles: Bruylant.
Blanc-Noël, Nathalie. June 2018. A recurring mantra in French political debate: Reference to the Nordic model. *French Politics*. https://doi.org/10.1057/s41253-018-0057-x.
Borg, Sami. 2012. *Muutosvaalit 2011*. Helsinki: Oikeusministeriö, 2012: 29–42.
Dansk folkeparti. 2002. *Principprogram*.
Dansk folkeparti. 2009. *Arbejdsprogram. Dit land – dit valg*.
Finns Party. 2011. *Fitt for the Finns – The Finns party's election programme for the parliamentary election platform*.
Finns Party. 2011a. *The Finns party manifesto*.
Finns Party. 2015. *The Finns party immigration policy*.
Finns Party. 2017. *The Finnish Workday is the Starting Point, The Finns party platform, Municipal Elections*.
Hangartner, Dominik and Matti Sarvimäki. 2017. Dealing with the refugee crisis: Policy lessons from economics and political science. https://www.talouspolitiika narviointineuvosto.fi/wordpress/wp-content/uploads/2017/04/dealing-with-the-refugee-crisis-policy-lessons-from-economics-and-political-science.pdf.
Helsinki Times. 13 April 2012. Finns Party MP's assistant suggests armbands for immigrants.
Helsinki Times. 5 July 2018. Yle: Finns party gains popularity, Blue reform slides further down in poll.
Helsinkin Sanomat. 23 October 2015. Fewer than half voters would recast their vote for Finns party.
Hervik, Peter. 2011. *The Annoying Difference: The Emergence of Danish Neo-nationalism, Neo-racism and Populism in the Post-1989 World*. Oxford: Berghahn Books.
Jungar, Ann-Catherine. 2011. *Populism på finska*. https://www.dixikon.se/populism-pa-finska-1/.
Jungar, Ann-Cathrine, Anders Ravik Jupskås. 2014. Populist radical right parties in the Nordic region: A new and distinct party family? *Scandinavian Political Studies* 37, no. 3: 215–238.
Karvonen, Lauri. 2014. *Parties, Government and Voters in Finland*. Harbour House: ECPR Press.

Kitschelt, Herbert and Anthony Mc Gann. 1997. *The Radical Right in Western Europe: A Comparative Analysis.* Ann Arbor, MI: The University of Michigan Press.

Kjærgaard, Pia. 2005. *Folketing speech*, 4 October.

Kulturministeriet. The Cultural Canon. https://kulturkanon.kum.dk/english/. Accessed 9 April 2019.

Kulturministeriet. 2008. *Report on the Democracy canon.*

Larsen, Henrik. 2008. L'affaire des icatures: un nouvel équilibre Europe-États-Unis dans la politique étrangère danoise. *Nordiques* 16: 87–103.

Mudde, Cas. 2007. *Populist Radical Right Parties in Europe.* Cambridge: Cambridge University Press.

New York Times. 1 July 2018. In Denmark, harsh new laws for immigrant ghettos. https://www.nytimes.com/2018/07/01/world/europe/denmark-immigrant-ghettos.html.

Niemi, Mari. 2013. The true Finns identity politics and populist leadership on the threshold of the party's electoral triumph. *Javnost-The Public* 20, no. 3: 77–92.

Østergaard, Uffe. 2000. Danish national identity: Between multinational heritage and small state nationalism. In *Denmark's Policy Towards Europe after 1945*, edited by Hans Branner and Morten Kelstrup. Odense: Odense University Press.

Regeringen. 2018. *Et Danmark uden parallel samfund – Ingen ghettoer I 2030.* https://www.regeringen.dk/nyheder/ghettoudspil/.

Reuters. 6 October 2016. Finland's Soini tempers anti-EU rhetoric after Brexit shock. https://www.reuters.com/article/us-finland-populists/finlands-soini-tempers-anti-eu-rhetoric-after-brexit-shock-idUSKCN1260YY.

Rydgren, Jens. 2004. Explaining the emergence of radical right wing populist parties: The case of Denmark. *West European Politics* 27, no. 3: 474–502.

Rydgren, Jens, ed. 2013. Introduction. In *Class Politics and the Radical Right*, edited by Jens Rydren. London: Routledge.

Sputnik News. 2015. Don't come: Finland launches Facebook campaign to grapple with migration. https://sputniknews.com/europe/201510241029043098-finland-campaign-facebook-migrants/.

Socialdemokratiet. 2018. *Rætferdig og realistisk. Et undlændingepolitik der samler Danmark.* København.

The Copenhagen Post. 5 October 2011. 'New era' for nation's immigration debate.

The Copenhagen Post. 23 June 2015. Majority of Danes want DF in the government. http://cphpost.dk/news/majority-of-danes-want-df-in-the-government.html.

The Copenhagen Post. 26 January 2016. Danish Parliament adopts highly criticized asylum austerity measures. http://cphpost.dk/news/danish-parliament-adopts-highly-criticised-asylum-austerity-measures.html.

The Copenhagen Post. 16 January 2018. Denmark to make family reunification easier . . . for Danes. http://cphpost.dk/news/denmark-to-make-family-reunification-easier-for-danes.html.

The Guardian. 25 September 2016. Finns protests against racism after man assaulted at neo-Nazi rally dies. https://www.theguardian.com/world/2016/sep/25/finns-protest-against-racism-after-man-assaulted-at-neo-nazi-rally-dies.

The Local. 31 August 2016. Denmark is locking every door to immigration. https://www.thelocal.dk/20160831/denmark-is-locking-every-door-to-immigrants.

The Local. 17 February 2017. Immigrants must celebrate Christmas to be Danish: DF. https://www.thelocal.dk/20170217/immigrants-must-celebrate-christmas-to-be-danish-dpp.

The Local. 4 December 2017. https://www.theloal.dk/20170217/immigrants-must-celebrate-christmas-to-be-danish-dpp.

Chapter 5

From Marginalization to Political Insider

The Policy Influence of the Danish People's Party

Flemming Juul Christiansen, Mikkel Bjerregaard
and Jens Peter Frølund Thomsen

Ever since its foundation in 1995, The Danish People's Party (DPP) has been part of the radical right family. Like most other contemporary radical right parties, the DPP calls for harsh immigration policies, law and order, much less European integration and generous welfare services to deserving natives (Christiansen, 2016; Cole, 2005). Unlike its predecessor (the Progress Party), however, the DPP has always been rather pragmatic as a means to achieving political influence.

In 2001, the DPP experienced a major breakthrough in terms of winning enough seats to bring a Liberal-Conservative government to power. For ten consecutive years, The DPP remained outside the cabinet as a permanent support party (De Lange, 2012). Expanding on this feature raises an important question: Did the DPP also leave their own distinctive impression on public policy as a support party compared to other periods of its existence? This is hardly a trivial question as some scholars emphasize that minority governments often treat their support parties as 'voting cattle' (e.g. Bale and Bergman, 2006). More generally, in his influential contribution on radical right parties, Kitschelt (1997) concluded that they were politically marginalized. From the end of the Second World War until the 1990s, the establishment excluded these parties from influence on policy-making. Consistent with this view, Akkerman (2012) reported that the influence of radical right parties on immigration policies has been negligible.

In contrast, we expand previous research by showing how the DPP achieved direct influence on government policy albeit with reservations, in the period 2001–11. The DPP managed to make a policy deal that ensured important policy concessions in the immigration area at the cost of supporting the government's coalition agreements and a wider set of policies, and the party still needed to prove itself as 'responsible'. To be sure, the DPP's insider position involved the acceptance of welfare retrenchment, international commitments in the immigration area and Danish EU membership (Christiansen, 2016). Did the party also achieve indirect influence while in opposition in 2011–2015? This was not so much the case if the emphasis is on policy decisions since the government included the Social Liberal Party, which had conflicting policy goals. Since 2015, the DPP has sought a more pivotal role in the party system, achieving more influence on general economic policies than previously.

The chapter starts with a brief review of the sparse literature on the policy influence of the DPP. This generates four research questions about the preconditions for, and observations of, the DPP's direct and indirect policy influence. To address these questions, we present both existing and novel data including a short introduction to the functioning of the Danish parliament.

PREVIOUS RESEARCH ON THE DPP'S POLICY INFLUENCE

Previous research has examined various characteristics of the DPP. Ringsmose (2003) and Rydgren (2004) explained the historical emergence of the DPP without focusing on policy achievements. Green-Pedersen and Odmalm (2008) studied the party's influence on the immigration agenda. In contrast, Christiansen and Damgaard (2008) explored the influence of the DPP on legislative agreements and state budgets (also Christiansen and Pedersen 2014). Bale et al. (2010) and Meret and Siim (2013) examined how the DPP influenced strategic choices made by the Social Democrats. Interestingly, Christiansen and Pedersen (2012) found that the DPP has had almost no influence on EU policies. Christiansen (2016, 2017) concluded that the DPP has been recognized as democratically legitimate among right-wing parties and affected their policy positions.

Despite their undeniable merits, previous studies have paid scant attention to DPP's policy influence. Akkerman (2012) is the notable exception, who noted the DPP does not follow the pattern of RRPPs holding limited influence. It is important to advance knowledge on this issue more generally, however, as it concerns the extent to which radical political parties are able to initiate real changes. Accordingly, drawing on the classic decision-making approach to political power (Dahl, 1961), we believe that direct policy influence occurs when two conditions are met. First, the DPP must directly negotiate with the government over the terms and conditions of policy. And second, the final policy output (i.e. legislation) must be consistent with at least some of the DPP's key (initial) demands. This definition differs from a case of indirect influence that occurs when the DPP somehow pressurizes other political parties to make decisions (or policy positions) that are consistent with its own. According to our approach, both types of influence share a strict focus on policy that should correspond to the demands and priorities of the DPP. Obviously, both conceptions of influence entail counterfactual reasoning: legislation and policy agendas should vary when the DPP's influence is turned on and off. Indeed, we claim that the DPP demands constitute a cause of policy change. Direct influence is most likely while in office, although it may also be achieved in legislative agreements with minority governments while in opposition. We try to establish a relevant counterfactual by comparing similar events across time.

Drawing on this theoretical reasoning, the chapter addresses four questions:

1. Have the mainstream parties accepted the DPP as a legitimate negotiating partner?
2. To what extent has the DPP indirectly affected decision making while not a support party?
3. Did the legislative output change in the immigration policy area when the DPP was a support party compared to other periods?
4. Which mechanisms are conducive to the DPP's direct influence on immigration policy?

DANISH PARLIAMENTARY DEMOCRACY

In 2018, there were nine political parties in the Danish parliament, primarily due to a low electoral threshold. All of them belong to either the left-wing or right-wing bloc. Among these, The Social Liberal Party is the only one that has ever repositioned, but has refrained from doing so since 1993. Since 1994, however, Denmark has had an unbroken string of minority governments requiring support from other parties. Consequently, governments regularly introduce so-called legislative agreements, according to which the involved parties all commit to policy deals stretching over time, changes in government and elections (Christiansen and Damgaard, 2008). Strong parliamentary norms dictate that in order to qualify as 'responsible', a political party must comply with such agreements. The 'responsible' label serves as a necessary pre-condition for achieving policy influence. Legislative agreements differ from 'coalition agreements'. Since 1993, every coalition government has made such agreements. As far as minority governments are concerned, this means that the content of coalition agreements only constitutes an initial step to find support for their policy proposals. In practice, most governments also negotiate with the opposition, which is thereby able to achieve policy influence (ibid.).

The Social Democrats are the leading centre-left party, whereas the centre-right candidates for prime minister have all come from the Liberals (Venstre) since the 1990s. The DPP has consistently supported centre-right PM candidates, although it does not exclude co-operation with the Social Democrats should the left-wing bloc win the next election in 2019. Except for 2011, the DPP won more seats in every general election since its formation to the point where it became the second largest party in the *Folketing* after the 2015 election. The DPP did not start as a major success – unlike its predecessor. Until 2001 (and again 2011–2015), the DPP was in opposition to centre-left governments. In 2001–11, the party was a permanent support party for a centre-right government. Since 2015 the party has been part of the parliamentary basis for centre-right governments; but not as closely integrated as a support party as in 2001–11.

MAINSTREAM ACCEPTANCE

Direct policy influence requires acceptance from other parties in systems where the formation of coalitions is necessary. Since its foundation in 1995, the DPP has deliberately strived to avoid marginalization and has become recognized as a reliable support party. During this transition process, the Liberals and Social Democrats had to choose between accepting or rejecting the DPP as partner. After some years of hesitation, the traditional right-wing parties saw the possibility of a more or less permanent expansion of their parliamentary power base (Green-Pedersen and Krogstrup, 2008). In return for this recognition, the DPP went far to protect their image as a reliable coalition partner, consistently supporting the Liberal-Conservative minority government during the period 2001–11.

It is important to recall that the DPP has its roots in the Progress Party, which was founded in 1972. Until the early 1990s, the other parties considered the Progress Party's liberal zero-tax platform and anti-Muslim agenda as far too radical. The party's 'style' also caused controversy, and it was regarded as unreliable with respect to government formation and in the legislative process more generally. Moreover, the Progress Party found itself in almost permanent turmoil because of internal, rivalling sections. After an annual meeting in 1995 with tumultuous scenes in front of rolling cameras, Pia Kjærsgaard, Kristian Thulesen Dahl and two other MPs founded the DPP.[1] The leaders of the new party established an effective organization based on internal discipline (meant to expel internal rebels) and hierarchy (meant to delegate influence to a few experienced, reliable persons).

In its first manifesto, the DPP generally continued the radical policies of its predecessor, emphasizing outright opposition to immigration, the EU and high income taxes (Christiansen, 2016). In a much-cited speech in 1999, Kjærsgaard called for the expulsion of the relatives of criminal offenders with foreign origins, effectively arguing for collective punishment. This radical statement suggests that the difference between the sections within the Progress Party did not so much concern the objectives themselves, but rather the means with which to achieve them. To establish a more mainstream political style, the DPP promptly established strong leadership accompanied by strong internal discipline. However, this attempt to introduce a different style did not affect the Social Democrats. In a remarkable speech in 1999, the Social Democratic Prime Minister aired his view on the DDP's status in national politics. Speaking in parliament, he addressed the DPP, making particular reference to its policies towards ethnic out-group members: 'Therefore, I say to the Danish People's Party: Regardless of how hard you may try, in my eyes you will never become housebroken' (Statsministeriet, 1999).

The government acted accordingly by excluding the DPP from negotiations over the state budget, and it did not take part in any significant policy negotiations until the 2001 election (see Bille, 2001). It had no direct policy influence. Essentially, the government tried to establish a *cordon sanitaire* against the DPP (see Bale, 2003). For such a guarded line to be effective, it had to be accepted by both sides in parliament, but the Liberals declined. The campaign leaders of the major centre-right opposition party had addressed but deliberately avoided playing the 'immigration card' during the 1998 election campaign, which ended with a narrow victory to the centre-left (Mortensen, 2008, 149). This hesitation probably reflected an interest to not cut off all ties to the Social Liberals whose support might be necessary in a 'muddy' parliament (Green-Pedersen and Krogstrup, 2008). But the Liberals had a new leader after the 1998 election, and the Social Liberals remained strongly tied to the centre-left. In the 2001 election, the Liberals finally made immigration a major campaign issue, although their specific policy proposals were more moderate than those of the DPP (Green-Pedersen and Krogstrup, 2008).

The 2001 electoral outcome meant that a Liberal-Conservative government could achieve a majority by adding the DPP's seats. Both right-wing MPs and pundits initially had doubts about the DPP's 'governing capacity'. The first test was the state budget for 2002 (Bille, 2006, 23–29), which proved to be the starting point for almost ten years of close cooperation. The DPP passed the test, as it never reneged on any of the many agreements over legislation and state budgets in which it was involved – irrespective of the size of the majorities behind them (Christiansen, 2016, 103–106). Kjærsgaard openly declared that the purpose of close cooperation over so many years was not only to have policy influence but also to earn recognition as a 'normal' party (ibid.). In view of these circumstances, the DPP would actually appear to have achieved this status. Even without its support party status since 2011, the party continues to negotiate and reach agreements with other parties, now also including the Social Democrats, on many topics. The DPP also supports the final passing of the state budget each year.

The final chapter of the DPP's parliamentary maturation remains to be written as it has yet to accept formal cabinet participation. Kjærsgaard has characterized this role as the ultimate recognition (ibid.). Liberal Prime Minister Lars Løkke Rasmussen rejected the idea prior to the 2011 election, however, and opinion polls indicated that the average right-of-center voter supported his decision. At the time, some pundits saw the EU issue as the main barrier to such a project (Christiansen and Pedersen, 2012). While opinion polls had grown more positive towards the DPP in an office position prior to the 2015 election, the new party leader Thulesen Dahl explicitly refused cabinet seats, which he believed would reduce their policy influence. He defended this view even after the election made his party the second largest in parliament. Apparently, the Liberals did offer the DPP cabinet seats in 2015, which they declined. The turning point came in 2018, when Thulesen Dahl declared the DPP ready to form a government with the Liberals. Interestingly, he added that he was also ready to support a Social Democratic minority government if necessary. This move most likely reflects the fact the DPP has shifted closer to the Social Democrats as it supports the expansion of traditional welfare programmes – except for those that disproportionately benefit non-Western immigrants (e.g. social assistance, programmes benefitting families with many children). With these manoeuvres, the DPP aspires to a pivotal role in the party system, an important precondition for influence seeking in minority government formation.

INDIRECT INFLUENCE OF THE DPP IN OPPOSITION

Immigrant policy is a great concern for the DPP – probably the greatest. Hence, the party may have an impact if the decision making of other important parties becomes affected by the DPP. This influence could be achieved either while a support party or not. A precondition is that the immigration issue is salient for other parties, which has changed over time.

In 1983, a broad majority in parliament passed an exceptionally lenient immigration law granting asylum seekers extensive rights to family reunification.[2] The law essentially resulted from pressure from the Social Liberals (see Damgaard and Svensson, 1989). Most of the time from 1929 to 2001, the Social Liberals controlled the median legislator and determined the ideological leaning of the government. As the number of immigrants increased from the mid-1980s and because the Progress Party leader launched a campaign against Muslim immigrants, immigration became a more politically salient issue. Even so, due to the Social Liberals' pivotal position, the major political parties still made immigration a legislative non-issue (Green-Pedersen and Krogstrup, 2008). As mentioned above, this elite-driven attempt to organize the immigration issue out of national politics came to a halt around 2000 when the Liberals broke the peace. The DPP had previously been a minor actor, but its strengthened voter base rendered them attractive for other parties to adjust to, among these, the centre-right Liberals.

The key question is the extent to which the DPP impacts stricter immigration policies among the parties that used to reject this, even with the party in opposition. One conditional measure of such indirect influence of the DPP is how often the other parties address immigration in both negative and positive terms. Table 5.1 uses indicators from the Manifesto Data set (Volkens et al., 2015).[3] The immigration issue, which used to be of minor importance in Danish politics, has received considerably more attention from all political parties. It hit the party political agenda around 1998 and reached an all-time high in 2001 as the main focal point of national politics.

The script is not the play; nevertheless, political parties and governments may act on their intent. Christiansen (2017) has coded the immigration policies of the political parties including those of the DPP. The dataset covered policy positions in party manifestoes and coalition agreements along four dimensions of immigration: foreign labour power, asylum/refugees, family reunification and integration (for the most recent general elections i.e. 2007, 2011 and 2015). For each dimension, +1 means introducing 'stricter policies', −1 more lenient policies, and 0 indicates a neutral position. Thus actual observations were summated into an index ranging from −4 to +4 for a party in a given election year.

Table 5.2 reports the total results. Generally, the DPP has emphasized the need for stricter policies on almost all dimensions, whereas the Liberals

Table 5.1. Frequency of the immigration issue in electoral platforms of selected Danish parties and generally. 1987–2011. Percentages

	1987	*1988*	*1990*	*1994*	*1998*	*2001*	*2005*	*2007*	*2011*
Liberals	2.8	0	1.1	0	15.7	14.5	11.9	16.3	12.8
DPP	NA	NA	NA	NA	16.7	40.0	20.0	29.8	21.6
Progress Party	9.8	2.7	1.3	5.0	10.0	NA	NA	NA	NA
All mentioning	2.8	0.3	0.5	4.7	7.9	13.8	8.1	13.0	8.3

Source: Comparative Manifesto Set. Five items (Bjerregaard, 2017).

Table 5.2.   Manifesto and coalition agreement positions on immigration 2007–2015. Index

	2007	*2011*	*2015*
Social Democrats	+1	−1	+2
Liberals	+1	+2	+1
Danish People's Party	+3	+3	+4
Government	+1	−4	+2

Source: Christiansen 2017: Table 1–3.

Note: Index based on four policy dimensions. + indicate stricter policies, and − more lenient.

remained tolerant towards traditional labour immigration in line with the ideology of economic liberalism as well as organized business interests.

The Social Democrats have been more ambivalent. According to electoral research, it lost many of its voters to the DPP after 2000 due to the immigration issue (Thomsen, 2017). The party was internally divided; some members called for stricter policies, which others opposed for humanitarian reasons. Even when the party called for harsher policies, it decided to form a government with the Social Liberals during the 1990s and once more in the period 2011–2015. The Social Liberals blocked the initiation of stricter immigration policies in the late 1990s. During the negotiations over the coalition agreement in 2011, the Social Liberals even managed to reverse some of the restrictions made during the previous decade (Christiansen, 2017, 63). A −4 score for the government in 2011 thus reflects less strict policies on all dimensions. Although the changes reflects the Social Liberals' influence. Afterwards, the government did pass most of these mitigating initiatives (Christiansen, 2017). In 2015, the new centre-right government did intend to pursue stricter policies (+2) but would not go as far as the DPP (+4).

Despite the government's cooperation with the Social Liberals, the Social Democrats emphasized the need for stricter immigration policies during the 2015 election campaign. Once again, Prime Minister Thorning-Schmidt officially reassured that her party would no longer be 'soft' on immigration. The Social Democrats wanted stricter policies, and this position clearly seems influenced by the pressure on its voter base from the DPP. Nonetheless, its ability to have an impact on policies remained highly limited by its cooperation with the Social Liberals. After 2015, this may have changed. Remarkably, Mette Frederiksen, the new party leader in 2018 explicitly emphasized that the Social Democrats fully accepted the so-called firm but fair immigration policy maxim (Christiansen, 2017, 66). Indeed, the Social Democrats have made it clear that the Social Liberals will not be forming part of a left-wing government at any time in the near future. Moreover, the Social Democrats have started cooperating with the DPP on a number of issues concerning migration and not least social welfare issues. More specifically, since

2015, the two parties have cooperated on a number of occasions to prevent the right-wing government's introduction of tax cuts.

The major centre-right and centre-left parties have all been governed by office-seeking motives in their approach to immigration and the Social Liberals; however, the entry of the DPP opened a novel path to power for centre-right parties, because it remained loyal to this coalition. The DPP has also undermined the Social Democrats by attracting many of their traditional voters. In combination, the DPP's immigration policy agenda has most likely influenced other parties' agendas in the same area, albeit for the Social Democrats not as much its policies until recently.

DIRECT INFLUENCE? THE DPP AS SUPPORT PARTY, 2001–11

A Liberal-Conservative government was in office from 2001 to 2011, and it enjoyed a majority thanks to the DPP. However, a distinction can be drawn between 'holding' and 'knowing how to use' a majority. In this case, the two government parties managed to cooperate intensively with the DPP (Christiansen and Pedersen 2014). This cooperation was not based on any formal agreement between a minority government and a support party, such as the 2017 agreement between the Conservative government and the Democratic Unionist Party in the UK.[4] Even so, numerous features of the cooperation inevitably indicate the magnitude and scope of the DPP's policy influence. The essential elements are the coalition and legislative agreements, including the state budget. The DPP's political support related to almost all items of legislation except for those linked to the EU.

The Liberals and Conservatives negotiated the coalition agreements after each of the elections in 2001, 2005 and 2007. Prior to 2001, the DPP demanded influence on coalition agreements in order to support any government (Bille, 2006). However, in 2001, the DPP supported the formation of a Liberal-Conservative without this type of influence, only being promised that immigration policies would become stricter (Christiansen, 2016, 104). In both 2005 and 2007, the DPP did not influence the terms and conditions of the coalition agreement. It is distinctly possible that the government may have been preoccupied with the feasibility of specific policies. Indeed, Prime Minister Fogh Rasmussen was a proponent of a so-called contract policy (inspired by Newt Gingrich and Tony Blair) according to which the government wanted to initiate the policies it had promised the electorate (Kurrild-Klitgaard, 2011).

Christiansen and Pedersen (2014) discovered that this strategy had an extra layer of complexity. They compared the Liberal-Conservative 'formal' minority government (2005–2007) with the DPP as a permanent support party to a 'substantial' minority government (1998–2001), and to a majority government in office (1993–1994). They found that the DPP facilitated the passing of most of the coalition agreement. Compared to the substantial minority government, they found a slightly lower share of legislation mentioned in both coalition and legislative agreements. This share should have been higher if the DPP had wanted to amend the coalition agreement substantially. It indicates that the DPP did not seek to amend declared government policy before passing it. Christiansen and Pedersen (2014) also found a significantly higher share of legislation originating in a legislative agreement but not in a coalition agreement (31.0 per cent compared to 19.8 per cent). Since the DPP voted 'yes' to almost all additional legislation, the party was involved in all of these agreements. Logically, this means that almost every third law was not stipulated in the coalition agreement but followed a policy agreement with the DPP. These observations support the claim that the DPP had direct influence on matters related to legislative agreements not initially defined as government policy.

Christiansen and Pedersen (2014) also found a pattern with the relatively small share of legislation passed by the government only supported by the DPP.[5] Compared to the substantial minority government, this share of bloc politics dividing left from right was higher for legislation originating in agreements (coalitional or legislative). Alas, it was lower for bills with no relation to an agreement. Combined with the observation above, this pattern indicates that the DPP helped to pass divisive government policies from the coalition agreement without asking for amendments but likewise achieved divisive policy concessions in return in areas not covered by the coalition agreements.

This raises the logical question about which topics the government and the DPP agreed to in addition to the coalition agreement. It is where we should expect to find the direct influence of the DPP. While Christiansen and Pedersen (2014) found no difference between the formal and substantial minority governments as far as traditional distributional issues were concerned, they found that agreements on immigration and environment issues were much more common.[6] Specifically, immigration policies were obviously a major concern for the DPP. In a section below, we examine actual changes in immigration policies during this period.

Negotiations over the annual state budget became an important event meant to coordinate the wishes of the centre-right government and the DPP. State budget agreements occurred ten consecutive times, and they were made between the government and the DPP every year. The agreements covered policies on major and minor issues. Thulesen Dahl played an important role during the entire period together with three different Liberal ministers of finance. The result came in booklets laying out the agreed policies. Each year when the state budget agreement was made, the DPP endorsed the government's general economic policies. In turn, the government offered the DPP policy concessions (e.g. special assistance to needy pensioners) as well as increased funding for the preservation of national and historic monuments. In an interview, Thulesen Dahl characterized the annual state budget negotiations as 'one of the most important pathways to the DPP's policy influence' (Christiansen, 2016, 104).

These data suggest that the DPP had little influence on the coalition agreement of the Liberal-Conservative minority government in office between 2001 and 2011. The party did not directly negotiate the agreement, and it subsequently accepted most of it with few alterations. Yet, the data also show that the DPP most likely had direct influence on issues not explicitly covered by the coalition agreement. The DPP achieved its influence by negotiating legislative agreements, state budgets and immigration policies in particular. It seems likely that the DPP pressurized the government to initiate specific policies that it would not otherwise have chosen. However, international conventions limited the DPP's influence on immigration policy, the undisputed legitimacy of which was repeatedly emphasized by government officials.

DIRECT AND INDIRECT INFLUENCE AT THE SAME TIME?

To examine the direct policy influence of the DPP while a support party (2001–2011) we compare the policies implemented in this period with those implemented in the period 1998–2001 when the Social Democrats and Social Liberals were in power. While any difference might merely reflect fundamentally different policy objectives, we have shown that the immigration policy objectives of the Liberals and Social Democrats were different but not in any fundamental sense (e.g. the latter have always emphasized the importance of cultural assimilation and national cohesion). This would suggest that different alliance partners (the DPP or Social Liberals) help explain why immigration policies vary.

Table 5.3 shows the number of immigration laws and the extent to which they became stricter, more lenient, or had a neutral position. For this part of the coding, each of the 131 laws passed between 1998 and 2011 is measured

Table 5.3. Immigration legislation in Denmark 1998–2011. Absolute numbers (Percentages)

	Stricter	Lenient	Neutral	All laws	Average ann. Change
1998–2001	7 (28)	3 (12)	15 (60)	25 (100)	0.68
2001–2005	12 (29)	3 (7)	27 (64)	42 (100)	2.92
2005–2007	9 (41)	1 (4.5)	12 (54.5)	22 (100)	1.64
2007–2011	13 (31)	3 (7)	26 (62)	42 (100)	1.57

Source: Coding by the Authors, see also Bjerregaard (2017).

according to their characteristics along five dimensions: citizenship, asylum, crime, family reunification and integration. Each item allows for a score of +½ or −½, or, if very substantial or affecting children, an extra +½ or − ½ is added. Thus, a single item of legislation may vary from +5 to −5 in the most extreme cases. In most cases, this is a qualitative assessment made by one of the authors, who coded everything twice to ensure intra-coder reliability. In some cases, not only the text of the law but also the parliamentary debate, statements from experts in the field, and newspaper articles were included as context (Bjerregaard, 2017).

Table 5.3 shows how the relative share of restrictionist legislation was only slightly higher after 2001 compared to the period before, except for the electoral term 2005–2007. Yet, the coding opens for assessment not only of the direction of change but also the extent of changes. The annual average of change reveals that the laws passed after 2001 were stricter than those prior to 2001. This is particularly significant for the first term in which the government initiated major immigration policy changes in 2002. In 2002, the Liberal-Conservative coalition government rewarded the DPP for its support in general and its support for the coalition agreement including the state budget. Specifically, the actual policy changes in the immigration area were substantial; for instance, the government cancelled the right to family reunification for persons below age twenty-four. Indeed, 2002 introduced a new immigration policy paradigm in Denmark, replacing the one from 1983. The DPP thus influenced immigration policies both directly and indirectly, as its very existence and the number of seats they won changed the Liberals' office-seeking calculations.

CONCLUDING REMARKS

Most remarkably, major studies of radical right parties have not examined their influence on public policy-making (e.g. Carter, 2005; Ignazi, 2003; Kitschelt, 1997; Norris, 2005). This chapter assesses the extent to which such policy influence is dependent on the power status of such a party in a minority government setting. In its early stages, this new party was marginalized in Danish politics. Indeed, the Social Democratic PM shunned the party and deliberately excluded it from policy influence, and the right-wing bloc remained loyal towards this policy of exclusion as long as Uffe Ellemann-Jensen led the Liberals (1984–98) (see Ellemann-Jensen, 2007). Along these lines, Kitschelt's marginalization thesis about radical right parties also applies to Danish politics during the period 1973–2001.

From 2001–2011, the DPP was tested in terms of its ability to remain loyal towards its natural (right-wing) partners at the outset. They passed the test as all parties now seem to have recognised the DPP as a 'normal' and 'responsible' party. This test limited the DPP's policy influence. Yet we did demonstrate how the DPP achieved policy influence through unique legislative agreements (distinctively different from the coalition agreements), and the state budget agreements. Likewise, the DPP accepted the coalition agreements and state budgets, meaning that they became 'hostages' to some extent (Bale and Bergman, 2006). Overall, Danish immigration policy has objectively become much stricter since 2001. The DPP was also undeniably the first to call for major policy changes in the immigration area, which all other parties rejected. This changed in 2001 with the election of the new Liberal-Conservative government. By all indications, the DPP has had considerable influence on immigration policies.

After 2011, the influence of the DPP was limited in opposition until 2015 due to the renewed dependence of the Social Democrats on the Social Liberals. After 2015, as the largest party in the governing right-wing bloc, but without any cabinet seats, the DPP sought influence from outside of the government, often working together with the Social Democrats to block government initiatives; something the party had not yet been able to do in the 2001–2011 period. It seeks to break being held 'hostage' by seeking a pivotal role in the party system similar to that of the Social Liberals prior to 2001 (and again in 2011–2015). If successful, it becomes difficult for the Liberals and Social Democrats alike to govern without its support, and particularly concerning immigration. The pledge made by the Social Democrats not to work together with the Social Liberals on immigration after the 2019 election is thus a major achievement for the long-term policy influence of the DPP. Nonetheless, a coalition involving the Social Democrats and the DPP may be difficult, since it may conflict with the basic values of a radical right party, not least in light of the fact that a competing radical right party is on the ballot for the next election. Indeed, at the 2019 election in June, the DPP lost more than half of its votes.

Following the methodology of the decision-making approach, a key question remains: What made the DPP influential? First, the party promptly displayed its electoral muscle by attracting voters across the ideological divide; it became a dangerous competitor, seeking a pivotal role in the party system. Second, its effective and disciplined organization go a long way to explaining why the DDP has been able to operate as a unitary and competent actor in the legislative process. Third, right-wing governments have required DPP support to provide a coherent parliamentary majority. The DPP expanded the voter base of the right-wing coalition. Even more, the cooperative relationship between the DPP and the traditional right-wing parties has not involved unsolvable disagreements over policy. In other words, politically relevant power resources – electoral support, organizational effectivity and parliamentary seats – facilitated the party's policy influence. Ideological proximity to the traditional right-wing parties may count as an additional power resource (contrasting with the anarchism of the previous generation of radical right parties).

The Danish case points out how, in a minority government system, the influence of a radical right party may depend on which parties are able to support the government. First, the DPP had to prove itself a reliable partner. Next, it was limited in opposition, as long as the Social Democrats depended on the Social Liberals. This historical alliance prevented the Social Democrats from following a course that would enable it to win back DPP voters; and in 2015, the party has broken with it. Hence, the Danish case suggests that the influence of this RRPP has depended on its formal power status. Until now, its influence has been greatest as a support party during centre-right governments. This may change after the election due in 2019 if the Social Democrats win office and follow their electoral pledges.

NOTES

1. Ms. Kjærsgaard was party leader from 1995 until 2012; since 2015, she has served as Speaker of the Parliament. Thulesen Dahl has led the party since 2012.

2. The issue also divided public opinion (Thomsen, 2006; Jensen and Thomsen, 2013).

3. Indicators are national way of life: positive (Per601), national way of life: negative (Per602), multiculturalism: positive (Per607), multiculturalism: negative (Per608), underprivileged minority groups (Per705).

4. Or similar agreements in Sweden and New Zealand (Bale and Bergman, 2006).

5. Very little legislation was passed in pure 'bloc votes'; that is, exclusively with votes from the government's own 'bloc' to the left by a government led by the Social Democrats, or to the right by a Liberal-led government. The level varied between 6.5 and 12.2 per cent for the three governments under study.

6. The logic for the two topics may not be completely similar. The environment is a topic that unites left wing parties in parliament, and the centre-right government may have struggled to find a compromise with parties other than the DPP. Nevertheless, immigration was clearly the policy area that the DPP was most concerned about.

BIBLIOGRAPHY

Akkerman, Tjitske. 2012. Comparing radical right parties in government: Immigration and integration policies in nine countries (1996–2010). *West European Politics* 35, no. 2: 511–529.

Bale, Tim. 2003. Cinderella and her ugly sisters: The mainstream and extreme right in Europe's bipolarising party systems. *West European Politics* 26, no. 3: 67–90.

Bale, Tim, and Torbjörn Bergman. 2006. Captives no longer, but servants still? Contract parliamentarism and the new minority governance in Sweden and New Zealand. *Government and Opposition* 41, no. 3: 422–449.

Bale, Tim, Christoffer Green-Pedersen, André Krouwel, Kurt Richard Luther, and Nick Sitter. 2010. If you can't beat them, join them? Explaining social democratic responses to the challenge from the populist radical right in Western Europe. *Political Studies* 58, no. 3: 410–426.

Bille, Lars. 2001. *Fra valgkamp til valgkamp. Dansk partipolitik 1998–2001.* Copenhagen: Jurist- og Økonomforbundets Forlag.

Bille, Lars. 2006. *Det nye flertal. Dansk partipolitik 2001–2005.* Copenhagen: Jurist- og Økonomforbundets Forlag.

Bjerregaard, Mikkel. 2017. *En blåstempling der giver indflydelse. Et studie af regeringsdeltagelse og borgerlige partiers accept som forklaringer på radikale højrepartiers øgede indflydelse på lovgivning.* Unpublished MA thesis. Aarhus: Department of Political Science.

Carter, Elizabeth. 2005. *The Extreme Right in Western Europe.* Manchester: Manchester University Press.

Christiansen, Flemming Juul. 2016. The Danish People's Party: Combining cooperation and radical positions. In *Radical Right-Wing Populist Parties in Western Europe: Into the Mainstream?* edited by Tjitske Akkerman, Sarah L. de Lange, and Matthijs Rooduijn, 94–112. New York: Routledge.

Christiansen, Flemming Juul. 2017. Conflict and co-operation among the Danish Mainstream as a condition for adaption to the populist radical right. In *The European Mainstream and the Populist Radical Right*, edited by Pontus Odmalm, and Eve Hepburn, 49–70. Abingdon: Routledge.

Christiansen, Flemming Juul, and Erik Damgaard. 2008. Parliamentary Opposition under minority parliamentarism: Scandinavia. *Journal of Legislative Studies* 14, no 1/2: 46–76.

Christiansen, Flemming Juul, and Helene Helboe Pedersen. 2014. Minority coalition governance in Denmark. *Party Politics* 20, no. 6: 940–949.

Christiansen, Flemming Juul, and Rasmus Brun Pedersen. 2012. The Impact of EU on the coalition formation in a minority system: The case of Denmark. *Scandinavian Political Studies* 35, no. 3: 179–197.

Cole, Alexandra. 2005. Old right or new right? The ideological positioning of parties of the far right. *European Journal of Political Research* 44, no. 2: 203–30.

Dahl, Robert A. 1961. *Who Governs? Democracy and Power in an American City.* New Haven, CT: Yale University Press.

Damgaard, Erik, and Palle Svensson. 1989. Who governs? Parties and policies in Denmark. *European Journal of Political Research* 17, no. 6: 731–745.

De Lange, Sarah L. 2012. New alliances: Why mainstream parties govern with radical right-wing populist parties. *Political Studies* 60, no. 4: 899–918.

Ellemann-Jensen, Uffe. 2007. *Vejen, jeg valgte: ti mands minde-foredrag på Vartov.* Copenhagen: Gyldendal.

Green-Pedersen, Christoffer, and Jesper Krogstrup. 2008. Immigration as a political issue in Denmark and Sweden. *European Journal of Political Research* 47, no. 5: 610–634.

Green-Pedersen, Christoffer, and Pontus Odmalm. 2008. Going different ways? Right-wing parties and the immigrant issue in Denmark and Sweden. *Journal of European Public Policy* 15, no. 3: 367–381.

Ignazi, Piero. 2003. *Extreme Right Parties in Western Europe*. Oxford: Oxford University Press.

Jensen, Carsten, and Jens Peter Frølund Thomsen. 2013. Can party competition amplify mass ideological polarization over public policy? The case of ethnic exclusionism in Denmark and Sweden. *Party Politics* 19, no. 5: 821–840.

Kitschelt, Herbert. 1997. *The Radical Right in Western Europe*. Michigan, MI: The University of Michigan Press.

Kurrild-Klitgaard, Peter. 2011. Kontraktpolitik, kulturkamp og ideologi 2001–2011. *Økonomi og Politik* 84, no. 3: 47–62.

Meret, Susi, and Birte Siim. 2013. Multiculturalism, right-wing populism and the crisis of social democracy. In *Crisis of Social Democracy in Europe*, edited by Michael Keating, and David McCrone, 125–139. Edinburgh: Edinburgh University Press.

Mortensen, Hans. 2008. *Tid til forvandling: Venstres vej til magten*. Copenhagen: Gyldendal.

Norris, Pippa. 2005. *Radical Right. Voters and Parties in the Electoral Market*. Cambridge: Cambridge University Press.

Ringsmose, Jens. 2003. *Kedeligt har det i hvert fald ikke været.: Fremskridtspartiet 1989–1995*. Odense: Syddansk Universitetsforlag.

Rydgren, Jens. 2004. Explaining the emergence of radical right-wing populist parties: The case of Denmark. *West European Politics* 27, no. 3: 474–502.

Statsministeriet. 1999. Statsminister Poul Nyrup Rasmussens replik ved åbningsdebatten i Folketinget den 7. oktober 1999. Accessed 8 October 2018. http://www.stm.dk/_p_7628.html

Thomsen, Jens Peter Frølund. 2006. *Konflikten om de nye danskere*. Copenhagen: Akademisk Forlag.

Thomsen, Jens Peter Frølund. 2017. Indvandring som skillelinje blandt 'os'. In *Oprør fra udkanten*, edited by Kasper Møller Hansen, and Rune Stubager, 265–279. Copenhagen: Jurist- og Økonomforbundets Forlag.

Volkens, Andrea, Pola Lehmann, Theres Matthieß, Nicolas Merz, Sven Regel, and Annika Werner. 2015. The manifesto data collection. Manifesto project (MRG/CMP/MARPOR). Version 2015a. Berlin: Wissenschaftszentrum Berlin fur Sozialforschung/WZB.

Chapter 6

The Northern League (1991–2018)

Thriving Without Delivering? Or Harming Southern Italy for Decades by Its Very Existence?

Christophe Bouillaud

On the eve of the electoral contest for 4 March 2018 Italian general election, Matteo Salvini, leader of the Northern League (Lega Nord, LN) since 2013, decided to get rid of 'northern' in the name of his party. So he contested the run-off under the shortened name of *League* (Lega). Under the long-serving electoral symbol of northern regionalists (the sketched profile of Alberto da Giussano, a medieval warrior in helmet with a sword aiming at the sky, in use since the creation of the LN in 1991 through the merging of a few northern 'regional leagues' under the stewardship of Umberto Bossi's 'Lombard League' (LL), created in 1982, using it as symbol since then) and the word *Lega*, he put his campaign slogan, 'Salvini for Premiership' (Salvini Premier) echoing in Italian its campaign slogan, 'Italians First' (*Prima gli Italiani*). This personalized slogan, which asks for Matteo Salvini to be nominated President of the Council of Ministers, referred at the time both to the competition inside the rightist alliance and the overall electoral competition, and remains till today (April 2019) in use[1]. This U-turn to Italy-wide nationalism, after well-documented decades of Northern regionalism and Southern bashing (Mannheimer, 1991, Diamanti, 1993, 1996, 2003, 2009, Biorcio, 1997, 2010, Passalacqua, 2009, Dematteo, 2011, Zaslove, 2011), was by then a long awaited turn. Since he took office to chair a party in deep disarray in 2013, he intended to move it from a vocal spokesperson for the 'angry North' against Rome and the Italian 'South' to an even more vocal spokesperson for all 'angry Italians' against every kind of foreigner, be it unwelcomed immigrants on Italian soil or inefficient bureaucrats in Brussels (Albertazzi, Giovannini and Seddone, 2018). To signal his new nationalist strategy, Matteo Salvini has officially joined forces with the European mainstream of radical right populist parties (RRPP). Accordingly, LN's delegation elected in 2014 in the European Parliament was in June 2015 among the founding members of the new parliamentary group Europe of Nations and Freedom (ENL) alongside the National Front (Front National, FN), the Freedom Party of Austria (Freiheitliche Partei Österreichs, FPÖ), the Flemish Interest (Vlaams Belang, VB) the Party for Freedom (Partij voor de Vrijheid, PVV) and some other minor parties. Matteo Salvini's LN also helped to create a new party at the European level, the Movement for a Europe of Nations and Freedom (MENL) with the same allies (with the exception of the PVV). The ENL group organized on the 28 and 29 January 2016 its first convention in Milan with Marine Le Pen and Geert Wilders as guest stars to celebrate Matteo Salvini-led LN's adhesion to the European nationalist right.

From 2014 onwards, Matteo Salvini's strategy was aiming to win votes in every part of Italy, capitalizing on the long-standing LN's image of xenophobia and Euroscepticism among the general Italian public. But, with this nationalizing move, he contradicted one central basis of LN's political identity: fighting to deprive Italian southerners of any influence on Italian public policies and of any financial transfers from the rich northern regions through the Italian centralized tax system, and more specifically fighting to obtain some sort of autonomy, 'fiscal' or 'constitutional', for the Northern regions. In fact, at the very same time, Matteo Salvini decided to go full rightist or nationalist – even searching in 2015–2016 to join forces with House Pound Italia (Casa Pound Italia, CPI), a neo-fascist party created in 2009, following the illegal occupation since 2003 of a house in central Rome by neo-fascist grassroots militants, pretending to create 'the fascism of XXIth century', when some of LN's more traditionalist leaders decided to save the older agenda from oblivion. Two regions of northern Italy were ruled in the 2010s by rightwing majorities under the presidency of LN's long-time front-running politicians: the 'governors', Roberto Maroni in Lombardy and Luca Zaia in Veneto. Using a possibility given by the Italian Constitution (article 116 comma 3) and by the statutes of their respective regions, LN's 'governors', sustained by more regional councillors than their rightist majorities, called consultative referenda on the 22 October 2017. They (rhetorically) questioned their (affluent) constituencies if Lombardy or Veneto should ask 'Rome' for more (legal and fiscal) autonomy for all public policies where the Italian constitution opens the possibility to implement it. The legal technicalities and quorum requirements were different: in Lombardy, where no quorum was required to give validity to the vote, only 38 per cent of registered voters participated, but among them, 95 per cent asked (unsurprisingly) for more autonomy; in Veneto, where a quorum of 50 per cent was deemed necessary, 57 per cent of registered voters participated, and 98 per cent asked (even more unsurprisingly) for it. In substance and in both regions, a popular majority of voters accepted this (obvious) call by regional authorities for more autonomy, and, at the regional level, no significant partisan opposition to Roberto Maroni's and Luca Zaia's strategy was to be noticed. At the national level, Paolo Gentiloni's government, dominated by the Democratic Party (Partito democratico, PD), was unambiguously opposed to Veneto's and Lombardy's referenda, but mostly voiced concern on fiscal difficulties. But, after the results, a discussion was opened by this same central government with the two regions, and with a third guest to the table, Emilia-Romagna, a PD's long-standing northern stronghold. These negotiations did not give way to any decisions before the Italian 4 March 2018 general election. The LN's long-standing battle for more autonomy or more voice of Northern regions in Italian affairs seems to have kept its electoral appeal and popular legitimacy, and it could even be described in the late 2010s as the common sense of these regions. This enduring appeal of the LN among Northerners was duly confirmed during the 4 March 2018 Italian general election, when Matteo Salvini's 'nationalized' League built its overall national success – 17 per cent of the national electorate – also in the 'deep North' where it was born in the 1980s.

In fact, when one wants to assert LN's level of influence (or lack of influence) on Italian public policies on the whole span of its existence (1991–2018), one thinks primarily to what could be called today as Matteo Salvini's discourse, similar to most RRPP's discourse elsewhere in Western Europe, on *immigration* and *law and order* policies on the one side and on *Euroscepticism* on the other side, and to underestimate or even to neglect completely Roberto Maroni's or Luca Zaia's discourse, the long-standing *asymmetrical regionalist demands of the North*, that is to say LN's influence (or lack of influence) on the Italian fiscal and economic equilibrium between the 'North' and the 'South'. The reflection on the first topic – immigration and law and order issues, and Euroscepticism – is coherent with many other researches on the influence of the RRPP on public policies in contemporary Europe, as the present edited volume shows, the reflection on the second topic tends to be forgotten today since Matteo Salvini's League seems to be unable to stand for LN's old 'raison d'être'. To redress this effect, and to give a more accurate view of LN's influence on Italian public policies on the whole span of its existence (1991–2018), this chapter will argue that the LN's influence and impact on Italian public policies has to be searched in both directions. By influence, we mean mostly, building on previous literature on the LN, change in Italian legislation (or budgets). It could be direct influence (participation in government or in political majorities) or indirect influence (mainly through competition). By impact, we try to evaluate, when possible, the effective change of public policies 'on the ground', on each topic which was a core issue for the LN.

A LEGAL AND SYMBOLIC INFLUENCE
ON 'IMMIGRATION' ISSUES, BUT
WITH LIMITED EFFECTIVE IMPACT

Contrary to any retrospective illusion which would underline a deep change in the political orientation of the LN since the early days of its creation, this regionalist party was always clearly against 'extra-communitarian'[2] immigration in Italy, a deep-seated nativism linked to a clear-cut sentiment of (endangered) economic and cultural superiority of northern Italians on southern Italians, ethnic minorities (e.g. Romas) and foreigners alike (Mannheimer, 1991, Diamanti, 1993, 1996, 2003, 2009, Biorcio, 1997, 2010, Passalacqua, 2009, Huysseune, 2010). From this point of view, the LN might be rightly classified as both a RRPP *and* an (ethno-) regionalist party (McDonnell, 2006, 2007, Zaslove, 2007). In Italian context, since the late 1980s, this rightist aspect was blurred by the fact that the LN was yet not another neo-fascist or monarchist party. In fact, Italy, due the economic upturns of the 1980s and 1990s, the early degradation of Italian demography since the middle 1960s and the rise of education levels and work aspirations of younger generations, became for the first time since the time of the decline and fall of the Western Roman Empire, a territory of mass immigration and not of mass emigration. Immigration was needed to 'provide the labour market with the workforce that is still required by many sectors and activities where manual labour is necessary, but where working conditions, social status and wages no longer attract Italian workers' (Ambrosini, 2013). It was mainly the case in the most dynamic part of Italy, the northern industrial 'heartland' of Lombardy and Veneto, and in the post-industrial metropoles (Milan, Torino, Rome). Adaptation to this new situation was at first very slow in the 1980s, but the very *first* party to underline with success the threats of this wave of immigration was the LN at the end of this decade, and not the neo-fascist Italian Social Movement (Movimento Sociale Italiano, MSI). At the time, the MSI had not given salience to this emergent immigration issue. Most neo-fascist leaders were more interested to defend the rights of Italian emigrants in the world – and even their rights to be duly represented in the Italian Parliament. Some neo-fascists militants or leaders had also sympathies to the Arab world by hatred for 'Jewish' Israel, and so had not classified Islam or Islamism as their natural enemy. Following a distinction logic from historical fascism while using an anti-immigration rhetoric, one of the very first manifestoes of the LL, one of the main ancestors of the LN, denied any similarity with the French National Front (Front national, FN)'s xenophobia. So, from the very beginning, the LN denied any racist or xenophobic attitudes when expressing its radical views on immigration. Other parties (like the old Republican Party of Giorgio La

Malfa), tried to emulate this ambiguous formula ('anti-immigration, yet not xenophobe') in the early 1990s, but with no electoral success.

As any party which wished to politicize this new issue, it quickly underlined the link between immigration and more general law and order issues in the 'North'. It was not any more original for the European context of the early 1990s when the LN underlined both the fact that these new immigrants were stealing jobs to northern Italians and using the public and social services (as public housing, *case popolare*), which should be prioritized to 'poor and deserving' northern Italians. In quite a famous placard, the LN also dared to compare northern Italians to American Indians who were destroyed and subdued on their own land by immigration (Richardson and Colombo, 2013). This ordinary kind of xenophobic discourse had one originality: since most of the possible voters of the LN were to be found at the time in the most Catholic part of northern Italy (Mannheimer, 1991, Diamanti, 1993), traditional stronghold of Italian Christian Democrats (Democrazia Cristiana, DC) since 1946–1948, the leader of the LN, Umberto Bossi, accused the Catholic Church of a plot to reinforce immigration from the Catholic 'Third World', so as to find both new churchgoers and priests to replace the older generation of Italian Catholics. This accusation of complacency from the Catholic Church for an 'invasion' was in fact coherent with the fact that it was mostly civil society's associations linked to the Catholic Church, as 'Caritas', which searched first to alleviate the fate of the immigrants. It must also be underlined that members of the Church really helped to create some migration chains towards Italia, as the famous 'Filipina's connection', which intended to provide Italian families with 'badante'.[3] This conflict with the Catholic Church on immigration issues remains to this day one of the founding part of LN.

From the mid-1990s, the denunciation of immigration was also more and more linked to the denunciation of an 'Islamic invasion', and all the more so after the '9/11'. Some secondary leaders of the LN, like Marco Borghezio, gained great media exposition in Italian and European media, through reiterated provocations against Islamic institutions in Italy. So it is no surprise that one of the main aspects that was to be surveyed by scholars when the LN gained a place in a coalition government in 2001 was its influence on immigration policy. In fact, a new law on immigration, the 'Bossi-Fini' law (legge 189/2002) was passed in July 2002. The law took the name of Umberto Bossi and Gianfranco Fini, who were both ministers in Silvio Berlusconi's government at the time. Umberto Bossi was in charge of an ad hoc Ministry for Institutional Reforms and Devolution (2001–2003), and Gianfranco Fini was Vice Prime Minister (2001–2006). Gianfranco Fini was at the time the all-powerful leader and founding father of National Alliance (Alleanza Nazionale, AN), the post-neo-fascist party created in 1995 by the majority of the

MSI. At the time (2002), AN wanted to appear as strongly 'against immigration' as the LN. By the end of the 1990s and even more so after '9/11' events,
all neo-fascists had now joined LN's line on immigration issues.

Although the LN fared quite badly during 2001 general election with only
3.9 per cent of the national valid votes and its deputies and senators were not
crucial for the formation of Silvio Berlusconi's new parliamentary majority,
all observers of Italian politics at the time noted the existence of a 'Northern
Axis' dominating the government. It was the consequence, not only of the
renewed personal relation between Silvio Berlusconi and Umberto Bossi, but
of the deep convergence of their partisan interests at the local and regional
level in the 'North' for winning together and the contiguity of the socio-
economic interests both parties were representing.

When the long-standing Italian political system (the so-called First
Republic) collapsed in 1992–1993, under the revelation of systemic corruption inside and around the old 'moderate' parties of government (Christian
Democrat, Socialist, Social-Democrat, Liberal, Republican), and under the
threat of a generalized economic crisis for Italy due to the fixed-change system adopted in Western Europe ('European monetary system') a few years
before, it seemed for a short span of time that 'moderate' voters would have
no other solutions in the northern part of the country, but to vote for the LN
or to let the post-Communist dominated left alliance win. In fact, an unknown
and uncharismatic LN's candidate, Marco Formentini, won mid-1993 the
two-turn election[4] for Milan's local administration against the well-known
sociologist, Nando della Chiesa, son of General Carlo Alberto Della Chiesa,
killed by the Sicilian mafia in 1982, a candidate of a large centre-left coalition built around the Democratic Party of the Left (Partito democratico della
Sinistra, PDS). It was the new identity chosen by the social-democrat majority of the former Italian Communist Party (Partito comunista italiano, PCI), a
party excluded since 1947 from Italian governmental affairs.

Silvio Berlusconi, at the time only a very well-known media tycoon, had
evidently given orders to the personnel of his three television channels (Italia
Uno, Rete Quattro and Canale Cinque) and its daily conservative newspaper
published in Milan (*Il Giornale*) to flank LN's electoral campaign to keep
Milan, the economic capital of Italy, to the 'moderate' camp by sponsoring
Marco Formentini's reputation. So Silvio Berlusconi helped the LN's 'Bar-
barians', as they were nicknamed by the Italian media and pundits, although
he was also a long-standing personal friend of Bettino Craxi. A former Prime
Minister (1983–1987) and local politician in Milan, this socialist leader was
under the scrutiny of Italian judges, and one of Umberto Bossi's main political target with DC's leaders. When Silvio Berlusconi decided to enter the
political field himself officially by the early days of 1994 on the eve of the
Italian general elections after months of secret preparations with his 'personal

party', Forza Italia (FI), he immediately forged an electoral alliance with the LN in the Northern part in the country in the very name of 'anticommunism'. According the new electoral law ('Mattarellum') adopted in 1993 for parliamentary elections,[5] it was now essential for each political camp to stay as united as possible to win.

As many observers noted at the time, LN and the brand-new party of Silvio Berlusconi, Forza Italia, were complementary from the point of view of their electoral targets, geography and means. The LN was a labour-intensive party with a strong militancy on the ground, speaking mainly to working class and petty entrepreneurs of the 'Deep North', the small towns and villages where industrial districts had boomed since the 1960s. At the time, like later on, the LN was also the party of all thinkable provocations to get some media access. At the very beginning, FI had no militants, no organization on the ground, but it had the best marketing teams in Italian economic capital, Milan, and three commercial TV channels, also based in Milan. Officially, Silvio Berlusconi wanted to offer, for the first time since Italian Unity, the moderate (mainly Northern) bourgeoisie a party similar to the British Conservatives, and so he intended, with some success, to represent mostly owners and managers of Italian and foreign big enterprises (mostly) present in the North (especially in Milan and Torino). But FI was duly successful to win many votes among TV fans of Silvio Berlusconi's three TV channels all over Italy (especially among low-educated housewives in the South).

This political alliance LN/FI overwhelmingly won the 1994 general election in the 'North' and Silvio Berlusconi was able to access to power thereafter as Prime Minister. But this first LN/FI alliance dissolved after only eight months in December 1994. It appeared that Umberto Bossi had accepted the alliance with Bettino Craxi's old friend only tactically to survive Silvio Berlusconi's TV channels' firepower. To keep the LN as different as possible from the 'moderate' right alliance dominated by Silvio Berlusconi's party and sponsored by his three TV channels, he tried during the years 1995–1998 to lead the whole Northern part of Italy in the direction of the so-called Padania's independence. The rebranded Northern League for Padania's Independence, official name adopted in 1995, won 10,6 per cent of the vote during 1996 Italian general election. In fact LN's success appeared as a division of the 'moderate' camp in the 'North', the most populated part of Italy, and led to the defeat of both LN's and FI's rightist coalition to the very advantage of the leftist coalition. The Padania's independence proves itself a minority project among 'Northerners' during the year 1997–1998.

Considering this stalemate, which implied more victories for the former Communists, Umberto Bossi and Silvio Berlusconi renewed their alliance, first at the local and regional level, then at the national level since the 2001 Italian general election. It was rapidly called the 'Northern Axis' since it represented two simple facts: first, in contemporary Italy, all economic forces are concentrated in the 'North', both big businesses and small enterprises; second, the lesson of experience that the 'moderate' camp, corresponding in fact to the former voters of the government parties of the 'First Republic' (1946–1992), might win only *united* at local, regional and national elections. Since then, this 'Northern Axis' remained central for the definition of the goals of the rightist coalition. Till its electoral victory in 2018, the LN was always a junior partner, but with an outmost strategic importance for Silvio Berlusconi's alliance since its core voters corresponded geographically to the most export-oriented industrial districts of Northern Italy, whereas the rest of the rightist coalition was more important in the big 'post-industrial' cities or in the never-industrialized south. Since the LN was always a junior partner, its leaders, as Umberto Bossi, never departed from their 'populist style' and their provocative overtones, so the LN could play the 'bad guy' of the coalition, while Silvio Berlusconi could play the 'good guy'. This strategy, 'party of mobilization and of government' (partito di lotta e di governo), always played by a news-breaking 'charismatic' leadership, was one of the mean ingredients of LN's enduring successes (Albertazzi and McDonnell, 2005, Albertazzi, McDonnell and Newell, 2011, Bobba and McDonnell, 2016).

It must be remarked that this 'Northern Axis' corresponds to the long-standing official alliance of a RRPP's party and a so-called mainstream party. But it must also be remarked that Silvio Berlusconi's party, Forza Italia, is far less 'mainstream' than elsewhere in Western Europe, at the same moment. Created in 1994, to replace the former 'moderate' parties, like the Christian Democrats, the Liberals or the Socialists, it was admitted in the PPE only in 1998. It remained always a 'personal party', dominated by and identified with Silvio Berlusconi himself. Its militants and politicians were always some kind of vassals or employees of its all-powerful creator and main asset on the Italian political market. So LN's capacity to influence policies must take into account the peculiarity of the mainstream party of the right, FI, itself a new party without any solid foundations in a traditional mainstream ideology (liberalism, socialism or social-Christianism) or in any kind of long-standing grass-root mobilization. As far as we can figure it out, this case was unique in Western Europe at the time: in Italy, the main RRPP had a not-so mainstream rightist party to his own left. This explained why FI, a 'personal party' by many standards, was prone to accept whatever restriction to immigration and law and order measurers as long as 'no (Italian) capitalist nor (Italian) producer or (Italian) consumer was hurt'. This lack of moral or ideological resistance to LN's proposals was also explained by the fact that another party of FI-led coalition was competing with the LN to be the other 'bad guy' on immigration issues.

In fact, at the time, the post-neo-fascist party, National Alliance (Alleanza nazionale, AN), under the direction of Gianfranco Fini, decided to contest the issue of immigration to the LN. This explained why the revision of immigration regulations in 2002 happened to be known thereafter as the 'Bossi-Fini'. S. Berlusconi, whose own personality was not considered at all ordinary for a European national leader at the time, had so decided to delegate this public policy to his two more rightist allies. In fact, inside Silvio Berlusconi's large parliamentary majority, only one small party, the Union of Centre (Unione di Centro, UDC), tried to mitigate the new regulation, but with some success (Zaslove 2004, Albertazzi and McDonnell, 2005, Geddes 2008, Carvalho 2016). The UDC was the party created by some right-wingers of the old Christian Democratic Party (Democrazia Cristiana, DC) (1943–1994), allied with Silvio Berlusconi since 1994. In 2002, it decided to oppose the hardening of immigration regulations in the name of the 'colf' and 'badante' as a family's home-made substitute to non-existent welfare state provisions, and more generally of immediate needs of Italian small and medium-sized firms. The Catholic Church and business associations were also using the UDC to channel their discontent on the new regulation (Geddes, 2008). Although acting as a junior partner in Silvio Berlusconi's coalition, with only 3.2 per cent of the vote cast in 2001, the UDC could claim to have substantially modified the law, not operating on the symbolic and more general aspects of 'Bossi-Fini' law, but on many details changing the consequences of the law for immigrants. LN's leadership accepted these modifications, not only because they lacked the numbers to endanger Silvio Berlusconi's majority in both Houses, but also, since in its own main constituencies, a law really radical on the matter, with too great an impact, would have complicated the daily life of its own voters, be it families or entrepreneurs. The LN could also shift the blame for the real-world inefficiency of 'Bossi-Fini' law on its coalition partners (and on any other opponents: Church, associations, medias, intellectuals, etc.), so retaining its own radicalism in front of its core electorate (Zaslove, 2012). This method of blame shifting, experienced on the immigration issue, would be used on all over topics thereafter.

In fact, although this law was presented to the Italian public as a law intended to strongly regulate and limit immigration by linking the right to stay legally in Italy to the fact of having a legally declared job, and at the time was duly denounced by any party, institution or association intended to defend the humanitarian image of Italy (Geddes, 2008), the impact, that is to say the practical results of this new regulation, was a boom in the overall number of legal immigrants in Italy. It was the biggest 'sanatoria' (regularization) ever with no less than 600,000 persons regularized (Albertazzi and McDonnell, 2005). This boom was clearly linked to the needs of an Italian economy, searching for persons accepting very low levels of pay and bad working conditions, be it in agriculture (mostly in the South, for harvesting tomatoes, for example), industry (mostly in Lombardy and Veneto regions where the LN and FI were electorally stronger) or services (like the 'badante' taking care of old persons, children or handicapped persons) (Ambrosini, 2013). It was only the downturn of Italian economy after 2007/08, which reversed this epochal trend.

From the point of view of the impact, on this point, which was central to LN's ideology, the influence on Italian public policies by the LN was only 'symbolic'. A long-standing and extreme discourse against immigration was duly translated in laws and regulations, but with no measurable impacts on immigration as a social and economic phenomena. In the Northern part of Italy where the LN or more generally the rightist coalition of Silvio Berlusconi was in charge of most local authorities (regions, provinces or municipalities), grassroots public policies were even oriented towards integration of these migrants in local communities in the very name of economic realism. The need of a new workforce in the North, especially in Lombardy and Veneto, proved itself far greater in practical terms for local administrators, even from the LN, than the outspoken hatred of immigrants shown by their parties. In fact, some linked this benign attitude towards immigration from the right to the remaining strength of the Catholic Church in these northern regions and to their link with the business unions asking for 'manodopera' (workforce). Nevertheless, in the 2006 political election, the LN fared a little better than in 2001, with 4.5 per cent of the vote – but UDC was by then at 6.8 per cent. One could see LN's (limited) success as a consequence of this double line of action, speaking loudly against immigration, legislating and then accepting the good part of it for its own constituency.

In opposition after 2006, the LN continued its battle against uncontrolled immigration, for law and order, and gave even more proofs of its hatred of what it called 'islamization' (Bobba and McDonnell, 2016). It was rewarded by a good result at the 2008 Italian general election with 8.3 per cent of valid votes, acquired in the context of a smaller S. Berlusconi's rightist coalition (since the UDC was now outside it, and won 5.6 per cent of the valid votes). In consequence, during the years 2008–2011, the LN was again a junior partner in Silvio Berlusconi's government, but in a stronger position than in 2001–2006. Roberto Maroni, one of LN's historical leaders, was nominated Interior Minister by Silvio Berlusconi, and remained through the whole period 2008–2011 in this very important ministerial function. During the two years of opposition (2006–2008), the LN had hardened, if possible, its discourse on immigration and law and order. Since FI and AN had merged during the years 2007/2009 in the 'single party of the right' under the leadership of Silvio Berlusconi, Liberty's People (il Popolo della Libertà, PDL), the LN became the only party occupying the right wing of the coalition. Contrary to 2001–2006, LN's 2008 good electoral results ensured that no rightist parliamentary majority could exist without it.

Logically, in such a strong situation, Roberto Maroni promoted a 'security package' in 2008 and 2009 (Ambrosini, 2013) on law and order and immigration, this time without any rebuttal from other components of the coalition (Albertazzi and MacDonnell, 2010, Albertazzi and Mueller, 2013). Some aspects of this 'security package' were judged thereafter unconstitutional, by the Italian constitutional court or by the European Court of Justice. Apart from these legal aspects, as an Interior Minister, Roberto Maroni searched to prove by many actions, at the very limit of legality or clearly outside it, that he was tough on immigration and crime. But, as in 2002–2004, the new regulations on immigration seemed at first sight very restrictive, but were not effective at all in reducing the flow of immigrants. A new period of 'sanatoria' was even open, but with far smaller number of effective regularization than the first one (still around 300,000 demands were made before September 2009). It must be recalled that this immigration issue appeared far less important in 2008–2011, because the economic downturn of 2007–08 has ended the great immigration wave of the pre-crisis years, and, because the 'Arab Spring' of 2011, did not have at the time their consequences in terms of an overall 'migration crisis' for Italy and Europe in general as it did after 2015.

In conclusion, the LN did have influence on immigration and law and order public policies when it was in office, for three main reasons: importance of the LN in the competition potential of Silvio Berlusconi's alliance in the north ('Northern Axis'); very limited ideological opposition to this movement to the right on this topic from the coalition's partners, and so delegation of the topic to the LN by the other member of the coalition; choice of tough regulations in theory with soft aspects in practice, corresponding to the need of Italian society and economy, so escaping any hard conflict with coalition partners and 'civil society' (families and firms). Logically, Anna Cento Bull (2009, 2010) could so underline that the results were 'a politics of simulation that addresses the contradictory emotional and pragmatic needs of its electorate' – the fear of immigration as a challenge to its culture and the need for immigration to give northern industrial districts a cheap and abundant workforce, if possible with workers without any civic rights enabling them to complain. One could even underlined that 'the centre-right Italian governments are the biggest regularizers of undocumented migrants in Europe' (Ambrosini, 2013), with approximately 630,000 regularizations in 2002 and a little less than 300,000 in 2009.

It must be underlined with Anna Cento Bull (2010) that this strategy was electorally winning. After 2008, the LN confirmed its good electoral results in 2009 European elections and 2010 regional elections. It even began to make electoral inroads in the northern part of the centre regions (Emilia-Romagna and Toscana), normally under the domination of centre-left parties. After the direction crisis of the years 2012–2013, the LN, under the leadership of Matteo Salvini, has the opportunity to go back to this always-in-fashion LN's basics of 'immigration bashing' and 'law and order mantras'. On the medium term, its electorate was not troubled by the apparent inefficiency of 2002 'Bossi-Fini' law and 2009 'security package' and it asked for more and more restriction on any kind of immigration and law and order measures. So Matteo Salvini could win 2018 general election on this issues, with an Italian public opinion taking for granted that, as a LN's home-breed politician, he would be tough on immigration and crime.

A COMPLETE LACK OF INFLUENCE ON ITALY'S POSITION ABOUT EUROPEAN INTEGRATION

The role of the LN in the definition of Italian priorities about European integration is generally not even treated by existing literature (for an exception, see Verbeek and Zaslove, 2014), since it is too evident that this junior partner of Silvio Berlusconi's governments (1994, 2001–2006, 2008–2011) had no influence at all on Italy's stance on European integration, but from the point of view of an overall assessment of RRPP's influence on public policies, this European integration aspect should not be forgotten.

As late as 1998, the LN was a regionalist and xenophobe party fighting only 'Rome' centralism. At the very same time the LN was abandoning its splendid political isolation linked to its Padania's independence heralded since 1995 after its defeat in 1999 European election and so joined forces again with the rightist coalition under the direction of Silvio Berlusconi as a means to win first the regional elections of 2000 and then the general elections of 2001, it fully embraced a radical Eurosceptic discourse, already visible since Romano Prodi's centre-left government secured the entry of Italy inside the 'Eurozone' (Albertazzi and McDonnell, 2005). Umberto Bossi, LN's leader, made quite alone this decision to fight 'Brussels' centralism, but he was followed without much open difficulties by most rank-and-file militants and secondary leaders. To underline this U-turn from previous sympathies for European integration, Umberto Bossi multiplied offensive expressions against 'Brussels'. He took clear-cut positions against the 'Nice Treaty' and the 'Charter of Fundamental Rights of the European Union', which were both adopted during Nice European Summit in February 2001. LN's deputies and senators voted against both texts. The LN did not rejoice when the physical Euro was introduced in Italy, quite the contrary. The LN declared no sympathy of any kind for the 'Constitutional Treaty' of 2004 and voted against it, but, inside Silvio Berlusconi's majority (2001–2006),

LN's position on this European matter had no echo whatsoever. In fact, no ministerial posts (Prime Ministers, Foreign Affairs) was given to a member of the LN, which could have influence on the 'high politics' of European integration. These were under the strict control of Silvio Berlusconi himself, of members of his own party (FI) or of members of AN (party which at the time under the direction of Gianfranco Fini was willing to show its pro-European credentials to distance itself from its neo-fascist legacy). In contrast to the influence on immigration regulations, the LN was clearly in a minority inside Silvio Berlusconi's majority and government, and it did not have the force nor the will to break the rightist alliance on this topic. The 'Northern Axis' between Silvio Berlusconi and Umberto Bossi, so important on immigration issues, had only an internal validity, and its impact remained limited to the early resignation in 2002 of Renato Ruggiero, a 'technical' Minister for Foreign Affairs, deemed too integrationist for LN's taste.

When the LN returned to government, in 2008–2011, although it was stronger in numbers inside both chambers and could have endangered Silvio Berlusconi's rightist majority, the LN did not choose to break the majority on this topic. The LN even accepted to ratify in the immediate aftermath of 2008 political election the Lisbon Treaty of 2007 in the name of government solidarity – so assuring that inside both chambers of Italian Parliament the final votes of July 2008 were unanimously in favour of the Lisbon Treaty's ratification, but so neglecting, while strongly criticizing its content during the parliamentary debate, the obvious fact that the legal content of the new treaty was 99 per cent the same as the 'Constitutional Treaty' of 2004 (Cavatorto, 2012). So it is only after Silvio Berlusconi's resignation as Prime Minister in November 2011 that the LN decided to be coherent with its then own long-standing Eurosceptic discourses: the LN refused to vote for Mario Monti's government, this time in clear divergence with its long-standing allies. And, without any influence on Italy's final choice, LN's parliamentary groups voted against the ratification of the European 'fiscal compact' in 2012.

In the case of European integration 'high politics', we observe the opposite elements to the immigration issue, which explain LN's lack of influence: an opposition on European integration would have broken the 'Northern axis' (FI/LN) and endangered its electoral competitiveness in the Northern regions damaging both sides; the ideological distance with other allies on European integration was large (corresponding to different alliances in the European Parliament); the possible impact of LN's Eurosceptic demands on its own electorate would have been too detrimental to be neglected (since most LN's electoral Northern strongholds are export-oriented regions).

On this European topic, as in the former one, LN's traditional voters seemed not to remark, or not to take into account, when casting their vote in 2013 and 2018 for Italian general elections this long discrepancy between radical discourse, government participation and total lack of influence or impact. It is the clearest cut example of LN's verbal-only radicalism.

AN ENDURING INFLUENCE ON ITALIAN REGIONAL INSTITUTIONS AND 'NORTH–SOUTH' FISCAL EQUILIBRIUM

A more telling point of the influence of the LN on Italian public policies is its mostly indirect influence on Italian regional institutions, through the competition around this regionalism/decentralization/federalism issue heightened between Italian parties through its challenger status (for a complete account, see Massetti and Toubeau, 2013). In fact, since the LN in the early 1990s underlined that the territorial organization of the Italian state was deeply flawed, since it gave undue advantages to the 'lazy and corrupt South', this controversy did not remain without answers from other political forces. At first view, most of these answers were only instrumental and a counter-fire to LN's appeal to Italy's federalization in the name of Northern Italy's best interests, but, for most parties (Christian Democrats, Socialists, Republicans and even Communists), it was also an occasion to rediscover their own regionalist or federalist tradition. In fact, only the heirs of fascism, clearly centralist, and mostly electorally strong at the time in the 'South', resisted any temptation of such counter-move. If fascism did not show a disdain to praise the 'Italy of hundred towns' and the diversity of local and regional traditions, fascism as a regime (1922–1943) was statist and centralist. Due to the 'southernization' and 'romanization' of bureaucratic careers inside the Italian state apparatus during the fascist regime (1922–1943), and to the geography of Nazi and fascist war crimes during the Resistance years (1943–1945), the MSI (1946–1994) and then AN (1995–2008) did have their electoral stronghold in Rome and the South, and they were the natural opponents to any kind of federalization taking public money away from it. Still most Italian political ideologies did have in their near or remote past a federalist moment. It must be recalled that, from the very early days of Italian Unity (1861), it was always common knowledge to everybody that Italy as a country was deeply diverse and that some kind of practical or symbolic solutions had to be found to this diversity.

In the 1970s, under the compulsion of the Italian Communist Party, wanting to gain at regional level participation in public affairs it should not have at national government level for geopolitical reasons, the regional territorial organization of the Italian Republic, which was already in the Italian Republican Constitution of 1948, was finally implemented. The 'ordinary regions' were so created in 1970,[6] and the first regional elections for the 'ordinary regions' were organized in 1975. The Communist and socialist Left were so able to govern their regions in central Italy and used their 'buon governo' (good government) at this level as a tool to delegitimize the parties dominating 'Rome'. So it was no surprise if, at some points in the early 1990s, they were some points of convergence between the LN and the new left-of-the-centre party created by the majority of the PCI, the Democratic Party of the Left (Partito democratico della sinistra, PDS). The 'Emilian model' was in fact one of the main asset of the new PDS.

In 1995–1996, while isolated from the rightist alliance of Silvio Berlusconi but unable to discuss with the PDS, LN radicalized its own position from Italy's federalization, which was its program since its creation in 1991, to 'Padania's independence', 'Padania' – a nineteenth-century coined geographical name for the region around the Po between the Alps and the Apennines, not known in ordinary Italian language till the 1990s – should have been, according to the LN, a new independent, democratic and federal country, regrouping the Italian North (and member of the European Union). As we have already said, the LN renamed itself officially: Northern League for the Independence of Padania (Lega Nord per l'Independenza della Padania). With this new radicalized discourse, which promised to the northern voters to get rid of Rome and the South, and showing equidistance between the centre-right alliance headed by Silvio Berlusconi's party and the centre-left alliance organized around the PDS, the LN was able to win 10.6 per cent of the vote at the national level in the 1996 general election, meaning in fact more than 30 per cent in its strongholds, Lombardy and Veneto. Due to this division of the right and to the majoritarian part of the election system, the centre-left won the election under the leadership of Romano Prodi and felt obliged to do something to answer the Northern protest, which in 1997–1998 tended to get out of control of the LN's direction itself. A fringe group of Veneto's independentism militants, the 'Serenissimi', even gained international fame by occupying 'Piazza San Marco' with a fake armoured tank.

To answer what was accepted as a deep-rooted protest of the North and accordingly to its own evolution towards a more decentralized form of partisanship, the centre-left first used all the possibilities of ordinary legislation to reform the territorial asset of Italian state ('Bassanini Laws'), in a more general drive towards an overall state's reform in an overtly neoliberal spirit. After having failed to concord a consensual constitutional reform with the centre-right alliance and the LN, the centre-left parliamentary majority voted at the end of 1996–2001 legislature two important constitutional reforms. The first one, quite consensual between centre-left and centre-right, established the direct elections of regional presidents. From this time, these were nicknamed by the Italian press 'Governors' (using the English word), since this reform had an American taste. More important and far less consensual was the reform of the 'Title V' of the Italian constitution, the so-called federal reform. The LN was not satisfied, criticizing a 'fake federalism'. Since it was only voted less than a two-third parliamentary majority, Italian voters accordingly to Italian Constitution were called on 7 October 2001 to approve or disapprove it. In fact, against the wishes of the LN, and also against the views of more centralist parties as AN or hard-line communists, it was approved by 64.2 per cent of Italian voters, but with only an overall low turnout of 34 per cent. At the time, Italian government had returned in the hand of the rightist alliance of Silvio Berlusconi, who had won without difficulties in the spring of 2001 the general election, due to reintegration of the LN in his alliance. The rightist alliance, which was divided on the issue, having won a general election in the spring of 2001, had no other possibility but to take into account this modification of Italian Constitution.

Due to its return to the rightist alliance from 1999 on, linked to the fact that 'Padania's independentism' was unable to mobilize a majority of Italian Northerners, even more so after Italy as joined the 'Eurozone' under the leadership of Romano Prodi, the LN did not call anymore for Padania's immediate independence, but asked for a 'devolution' (in English) of state's competences to Northern regions on the model of what was happening since 1997 in the United Kingdom under the leadership of Tony Blair. The rightist alliance, although quite reluctantly formed the part of AN and of UDC, accepted this LN's demand (Albertazzi and McDonnell, 2005), and yet another constitutional reform was to be proposed. Umberto Bossi, LN's leader, was duly appointed Minister for Institutional Reforms and Devolution in Silvio Berlusconi's new government. After his stroke in 2004, another LN's leader, Roberto Calderoli, was in charge of this ad hoc ministry till the end of 2001–2006 legislature. Giving to the ordinary regions the exclusive legislative competence on matters of public health, local policing and education, changing the nature of the Italian Senate (on the model of the German 'Bundesrat') and reinforcing the role of the premiership, it was voted only in 2005 by Silvio Berlusconi's parliamentary majority. It designed an Italian republic at the same time more decentralized, to please the LN, and with a stronger national executive, to please FI and AN. Since it was only approved by less than a two-thirds parliamentary majority, the rightist constitutional reform, was like the previous leftist reform of 2001, submitted to a referendum on 25/26 June 2006 for public approval. But, this time, just a few months after the defeat of the centre-right during the general elections, it was disapproved by the Italian electorate, with 62 per cent of valid votes expressing a 'No', among the 53 per cent of Italian registered voters having chosen to participate. Only two regions expressed a popular majority (55 per cent) for the 'federal reform': Lombardy and Veneto. All the regions of southern Italy were overwhelmingly against this move.

Nevertheless, neglecting the evident divide inside the rightist alliance between northern and southern interests, quite the same idea was again at the centre of the common electoral program of Silvio Berlusconi's alliance for 2008. It was not anymore a full constitutional reform on Italian state's territorial organization, but only a 'fiscal federalism' reform intended to change Italian state's territorial budgetary asset (Albertazzi and McDonnell, 2010). The overall idea, as publicized by the LN, was to give less money to the Southern regions and more to the Northern regions, without hurting too much the quality of public services in the South. Of course, southerners never bought the argument. A law authorizing the government to reform many aspects of local finance and territorial overall organization – not only regional, but also communal – was voted in 2009[7] and a period of implementation was open for two years till November 2011. The discussion, mostly inside Silvio Berlusconi's majority between the 'Northern Axis' and the other member of the majority, had rapidly become very technical, and it was strongly impacted by the consequences of 2008 economic crisis on Italian public finance, constraining the rightist government to ask all local, northern and southern, authorities to spend as far less as (im)possible (Zanardi, 2011).

More generally, be it in 2001–2006 or 2008–2011, they were always an acute internal debate inside the rightist coalition on the use of public finance as viewed through the prism of territorial 'equity', because the LN intended to keep most of the taxes levied in the North itself. This 'fiscal autonomy' was always contentious with the other parties of the rightist coalition, since it means more difficulties to finance the Southern regions and/or difficulties of the Italian state to finance itself on the international markets.

While there were many discussions and controversies since the failure of 2006 constitutional reform, the constitutional situation of the regions remained without any change till 2013–2016. At this point, the regional institutions had totally changed for the worst their public image. In the 1970s, 'regions' and 'regional autonomy' meant public efficiency and honesty in public affairs, in the 1990s, one could underline the difference in efficiency between northern and southern regions (as the world-famous book of Robert Putnam did), in the 2010s, 'regions', as any Italian public institution, meant in Italian public sphere more or less shameless public robbery, even in the 'red regions' (Emilia-Romagna, Toscana, Umbria) dominated by Communists or their political heirs and allies since the 1970s. So one of the many aspects of the overall constitutional reform voted by Matteo Renzi's centre-left majority in 2014–2016 intended to drastically limit regional autonomy in the name of fiscal 'responsibility'. This counter-revolution, from the point of view of regional autonomy, which intended to re-centralize all relevant economic powers in Rome in the hand of a future all-powerful Prime Minister designed by Matteo Renzi's constitutional reform (Baldi, 2018), was clearly rejected on 4 of December 2016 during a much-disputed referendum (contrary to 2001 and 2006 referenda), with 68.5 per cent of Italian electors choosing to vote, and 59 per cent of valid votes were counted against the reform. Matteo Renzi, totally defeated, has no choice as to leave thereafter the Premiership to one of his ministers and closest political ally, Paolo Gentiloni. Of course, the LN mobilized in the north, with all the rightist alliance, against Renzi's constitutional reform, but also against Renzi himself and his more general political stance (e.g. immigration, law and order, European affairs). The electorate of the 'deep North', which rejected Matteo Renzi's re-centralized Constitution, may be proving itself more attached to the regional institutions than what had appeared formerly in media and opinion pools. And, at the same time, the Southern electorate protested against the dire economic situation of the South and also voted 'no', even more massively. In fact, 2016 vote was more a referendum on Matteo Renzi's government than a choice on federalism.

Anyhow, this encouraging results in the north and the enduring internal fight inside the LN since 2013 after the dismissal of Umberto Bossi and the choice by the new leader Matteo Salvini of a nationalist (Italian) line paved the way, as we have said in the introduction, for to the two regional referendums at the end of 2017 asking inhabitants of Lombardy and Veneto if their regions should obtain more fiscal autonomy. In both cases, regional presidents, long-standing politicians of the LN, Roberto Maroni in Lombardy and Luca Zaia in Veneto – deeply dissatisfied by Matteo Salvini's line – were followed by their regional rightist majorities, and so took advantage of a possibility given by 2001 constitutional reform to organize such consultative referenda. Their legal character, due to their consultative nature and their conformity to regional statutes, was admitted by Italian Constitutional Court. As commentators noted, these were obvious questions for northern electorates, so why one should bother to participate? In both cases, it was in fact a clear 'yes' with a relevant level of participation – maybe helped by the Italian media's coverage of the Catalonia crisis happening at the very same moment. In particular, Veneto's vote and level of participation confirmed the long-standing dissatisfaction of voters with Italian state organization and the fact that it was by far broader than LN's own electoral audience. Presidents of both regions, dominated by the LN and its rightist allies, asked for an immediate answer on fiscal matters from the central government, dominated by the centre-left. Due to the natural end of 2013–2018 legislature and the impending general elections, Paolo Gentiloni's government did not take any relevant decision on the matter, giving one more reason for Northerners to vote for LN in the 2018 general elections.

So, to summarize, even if the LN was always a small- or medium-sized party in the Italian political landscape, and quite unable to mobilize for its utopian (dystopian?) project of 'Northern independence', it was able to channelize the Italian constitutional debate and overall territorial organization in a more regionalist direction than prior to its existence (for an adverse view, see Basile, 2015). And judging by results of the referenda in 2016 (national) and 2017 (regional), no U-turn on this matter is now possible. Of course, this trend towards more decentralization of public policies is general in the Western world and depends on more profound factors than the existence of a specific party, but, without the very existence of the LN, this trend would have been far weaker in Italy or could have taken different forms. Another possibility was to channel the demand of grassroot government in direction of municipal autonomy, and in the 1990s, there were major demands of Italian mayors to re-think Italy on the basis of municipalities.

VETOING ANY OTHER SOUTHERN POLICY FOR ITALY OTHER THAN CRUDE 'NEOLIBERALISM'

Since most recent presentations and overall views of the LN tends to assimilate this party to the Italian version of a RRPP, all the more so since the takeover of the party by Matteo Salvini in 2013, one tends to forget the more enduring influence of the very existence of the LN on Italian public policies: creating a veto point in Italian political arena on *thinking* or even *discussing* any other solutions than crude 'neoliberalism' or illusory 'endogenous development' to the woes of Southern Italy (Davis, 2015). By crude neoliberalism or endogenous development, we mean here that Italian state intervention should limit itself to ensure law and order against all kinds of mafia organizations, and let the 'endogenous' market forces, liberated from the mafia's debilitating consequences, ensure in due consequence Southern development. Money transfer, public investment or long-term territorial planning were deemed ineffective; only the *rule of law* was necessary, and the *free market* will save the South. This aspect is, of course, intertwined with the question previously treated of territorial institutions, but it is far more diffuse and difficult to assign to a single specific provision.

At first, the LN was created in 1989–1991, under the leadership of the 'lumbard' Umberto Bossi, by a confederation of regional leagues (Lega Lombarda, Liga Veneta, etc.) of the North to protest against the fact that 'Rome' was stealing Northern taxpayer money to give it to the Southern clienteles of the then governing parties. '*Roma ladrona*' (Thieving Rome) was the well-known motto to symbolize this 'anti-meridionalist' line. More profoundly, the emergence of the northern regional leagues at the beginning of the 1980s in the heartland of the conservative North, dominated till then by the Italian Christian Democrats and their allies, was an unintended consequence that, during the 1970s and early 1980s, for the first time in its post-war history, all great leaders of the Christian Democrats (Ciriaco De Mita, Giulio Andreotti, Andrea Forlani) were clearly southerners and clearly channelling Italian public money in direction of the 'lazy and corrupt South' in the very name of economic development, but without few positive effects and many defects (as corruption around the European 'structural funds').

As a matter of fact, during the 1970s and 1980s, the fringe northern 'regional leagues' were not at all the only Italian political actors to describe the 'Meridional policy' in place since the 1950s as fruitless in terms of sound economic development and costly to the Italian budget, and to denounce the high level of political corruption and the enduring linkage between the diverse territorial mafias and the ruling parties. It was even a discourse common to the greatest part of the economics profession, be it in Italy or abroad, to underline that this 'Meridional policy' was too much state-oriented and not enough market-oriented. Many underlined that transferring public money to the Southern regions to create jobs in public administration, helping to create there public infrastructure or giving 'pensione d'invalidità' (disability subsidies) to unemployed persons as a substitute to a lack of minimal income scheme, were not a realistic path to Southern economic development. Many also underlined that this huge pouring of state money was controlled by corrupt politicians, 'brokers', intended to develop their electoral clienteles, or even directly by members of Southern criminal organizations (*mafia*, *camorra*, etc.). So, even before that the LN became an important electoral challenger in the Northern part of the country, it was already deemed self-evident that the 'Meridional policy' was a complete failure on all its relevant aspects (Davis, 2015). So it must be clear that the LN was *not* the only political actor to underline this failure – the 'Radicals' of Marco Pannella or all the neoliberal factions of the great traditional parties for example were on the same line. In fact, all the actors believing in the neoliberal stream of solutions to public policies problems were prone to giving a quick and clear end to any kind of statist 'Meridional policy'.

So, from the beginning of the 1990s, meridional development's problem was only thinkable in terms of a neoliberal agenda, underlining that only 'endogenous development' or 'neoliberalism' could save the South from its long-standing woes, and LN's discourses on this topic were in Italian context more mainstream than extreme (Huysseune, 2008). Very few southerner politicians dare to criticize this new 'neoliberal' common sense and praise the old 'Meridionalist policy' and they had no influence, even on their own party. This does not mean that public transfer of wealth through the Italian state was totally stopped since the early 1990s – in fact, in Italy as elsewhere in the world, rich regions of a state 'subsidize' through fiscal transfers poor regions. Quite the contrary, in fact, these interregional transfers remained on all the period an enduring aspect of Italy's political economy. From time to time, some academics or research institutions tried to quantify with new methods the exact amounts of these interregional transfers. In fact, when in charge of Italian government (1994, 2001–2006 and 2008–2011), LN's ministers had no choice but to admit this reality. Of course, on many occasions, they tried to negotiate, or reform the fiscal mechanism, as we have already seen in 2008–2011, inside the rightist majority they were part of, less money for the South under diverse guise – but they duly failed to stop this enduring transfer of public money. Without these interregional transfers, Italian statehood would dissolve itself immediately since the southern part of the country could not function only on local fiscal resources.

So it was not really in a day-to-day basis that the influence of the LN on the 'South' has to be considered as the most important – even if southerners tend to denounce it – but, on a more reflexive way. As historians of the Italian economy and current observations by statisticians (Davis, 2015, Iuzzolino, Pellegrini, Viesti, 2013) showed without any reasonable doubt that the 'South' is now in a dire situation, the choice of a neoliberal way of development for the 'South' can now be viewed as an economic disaster in the long run – or, in a more benign view, a non-solution. The long-standing difference in the level of economic development between 'North' and 'South', which was reducing itself at the time of the 'Meridional policy' between the 1950s and the 1980s, has grown again and returned to its 'historical level' of post-Unification years (1861 onwards). The great recession beginning in 2007–2008 has accentuated this medium-term phenomena, being far more acute in the 'South' than in the 'North'. This negative trend was already visible before 2007–2008, especially as young highly educated Southerners ('laureati') did go north again (like in the 1950s and 1960s) to find work in the trendier metropoles of the north (Milano especially), and the southern component of the rightist majority – mostly AN – had already duly complained at the end of the 2001–2006 legislature about the lack of a comprehensive new strategy for the 'South'. The same scenario was played again in 2008–2011: the southern components of the rightist alliance complained, the LN refused to discuss any real innovation other than more fiscal responsibility for the regions, and the status quo finally prevailed and no new innovative strategy emerged. The left-of-centre alliances and parties of the 1990s and 2000s (Progressisti in 1994, Ulivo in 1996 and 2001, then Partito democratico in 2008 onwards) were not any better at taking into account the failure of the 'neoliberal' view of Southern problems, since the main leaders of these alliances or parties were in fact the most convinced followers of 'neoliberalism' in matter of public policies in the very name of European integration.

So one could argue that, in the last quarter of century, the enduring presence of the LN in the Italian political arena, even when the LN tried in 2008 an alliance with a southern regional party[8] (Movimento per l'Autonomia [MpA]), stopped any kind of discussion on the future of the South not based on the very idea that *the South should not receive more transfers of public money*. One so came back always to the idea of 'endogenous development'. For the LN's politicians, most of the time, it meant 'tourism' and 'agriculture' for the South. This ancillary view of the South, as a group of sunny regions not prone to industry or advanced services, was a long-term peculiarity of LN's leaders, militants and voters, but no other political party dared to advance a more strategic view of the future of the South. On this topic, one could argue that the LN had both an enduring direct and indirect influence, stopping any large-scale legal or budgetary initiative to alleviate the woes of the South, and a strong impact on the public policies regarding this part of Italy.

Ironically, this enduring crisis of the 'South' led during the 1990s, 2000s and 2010s to a continuous flow of young, mostly educated, Southerners to the North. 'Ethnically', the North became then an even more a mixed region from the point of view of internal Italian migration. Like in the 1950s and 1960s, the 'South' went to the 'North'. Even more ironically, a part of the remaining Southerners in the 'South' decided to vote in March 2018 for Matteo Salvini's 'national' League, deciding to endorse his xenophobic message and to forget that he had no real proposition to renew the vision of Southern development. With Matteo Salvini as Interior Minister and Vice-President of Giovanni Conte's government since June 2018, regional elections held in Southern regions (Sardinia, Abruzzo, Basilicata) till today (April 2019) could be described as a triumph for the League and the rightist alliance: southern electoral majorities were even prone to endorse Italy's new strongmen as the only person able to convey state's resources to them. The irony of League's destiny was complete.

CONCLUSION

When trying to estimate the impact of the LN on Italian public policies as a RRPP, one tends generally to underline that the presence of the LN at the executive level of Italy as a junior partner in Silvio Berlusconi's governments (1994, 2001–2006 and 2008–2011) had some influence on immigration laws, but less impact on the objective reality of immigration trends – and more generally no influence nor impact on overall public policies, since the LN was always pinpointing in its own propaganda and political action few issues (immigration/law and order, 'Northern Question' and Euroscepticism). But one so forgets that, from the beginning, the LN had many declared enemies. One of these enemies was clearly the Southern population of Italy (in Italian northern slang, 'terroni'), which were not from their point of view real Italians, that is to say Europeans (or 'Celts'), but some kind of Africans

Table 6.1. Synthesis of LN's influence and impact on Italian public policies (1994-2011)

Public policy	LN's Influence (measured by legislation or budget)	LN's Impact (as measure by on the ground public policies)	Factor 'Northern Axis' (FI + LN = majority in the most populated part of Italy)	Ideological unity inside S. Berlusconi's coalition	Ex-ante negative consequences of PP for 'Northern Axis' electorate	Ex-ante negative consequences of PP for 'rightist' Southerners	Opposition of the centre-left
Restriction of immigration/ Law and order	Medium	Feeble	Yes	Yes (only a small minority [UDC] against, and less important in 2009 than in 2002)	Yes (businesses, pro-migrant associations, own electorate)	Neutral or not relevant	Yes (mild)
Refusal of further European integration	Null	Null	Yes	No (LN Eurosceptic from 1999/FI [1998 EPP] and AN [under G. Fini] pro-integration)	Yes (free access to European markets, value of Italian savings as labelled in Euros)	Yes (European structural funds)	Yes (strong)
Italy's asymmetric federalization	Feeble	Medium	Yes	No (LN and 'northern' FI for, UDC, AN and 'southern' FI against)	No (implicit model of the 'regions with special statutes like Trentino-Alto Adige'	Yes (diminution of state's transfer to local authorities)	Yes (mild)
North – South divide, solved by market forces (statu quo)	Strong	Strong	Yes	Yes (incapacity or unwillingness of rightist 'Southerners' to formulate an alternative)	Yes (if they were to finance a new 'meridional policy')	No (statu quo)	No (in favour of neoliberalism)

Source: Own elaboration on literature quoted in the present chapter.

('marrochini' as was said in the 'North' on the southern immigrants as late as the 1960s).

In the early 1990s, LN's discourse was duly described as a special kind of xenophobia, where the limit between the 'in-group' and the 'out-group' was built between Italian nationals. By chance, the LN was unable to give all the advantages of the Italian statehood only to Northerners – as with its failed project of Padania's secession, which could be summarized as the will to create 'an Italy without the burden of the South and the Southerners'. Nevertheless, the enduring presence of the LN as a challenger in the Italian political system stopped any revision of 'neoliberal' public policy towards the 'South', which was, as can be said now without reasonable doubts, impoverishing it. Any revision, which would have implicated more public money for the 'South' or a more state-oriented public policy, was deemed impossible, because it would have arisen the wrath of Northerners taxpayers.

Without this consideration, it should have been long evident that the 'neoliberal' approach to southern Italy's development adopted in the 1990s was deeply flawed. Of course, it must be underlined that, in the present state of the world, this kind of consciousness of the failure of a 'neoliberal' policy in any domain of public action is very difficult to appropriate by any kind of mainstream politicians (left, right or centre), since no fully legitimate economic alternatives exist to 'neoliberalism' in the Western world. But, in Italy, one could argue that the very presence of the LN stopped any reflexion in this direction. It may even be argued that the surprising success of the Five Star Movement (Movimento Cinque Stelle, M5S)[9] in the Southern regions in the 2013 general election, the very negative results of 2016 referendum and then the triumph of the M5S on 4 March 2018 general elections in the same regions are in fact indirect results of this absence of reflection. At the end, the neoliberal approach to Southern development and the impoverishment of the 'South' it implied give rise to a deep and general protest from southerners, a movement of protest that the League, not more Northern, of Matteo Salvini also wanted to integrate in its own nationalist and xenophobe party, a development which is not the lesser paradox of this whole story. The electoral success of the Salvini's League in the Southern regions is mostly due to the personal capacity of Matteo Salvini to attract voters here on the theme of immigration and law and order. After the formation of a government between the M5S and the League, the same old prejudice against the southerners remained in public discussion: the idea of creating a minimum income for the poorest Italians was immediately viewed by most LN's leaders and grassroot militants as a way to help once again 'lazy' ('by nature' or 'by choice') southerners. When the M5S/League government was formed in early June 2018, most observers noted that, in fact, it would be difficult to satisfy the northern electorate of the LN and the southern electorate of the M5S.

In fact, this North/South aspects were not discussed in the early months of M5S/League government (apart from doubts around a minimal income encouraging 'laziness'), and Matteo Salvini, as Interior Minister (like Roberto Maroni in 2008–2011), runs the show, at the Italian and European levels, with an all-out attack on 'illegal immigration', leading his party to score more than 30 per cent of intended votes in all opinion polls after a few weeks in power. One of the very first law voted by this new majority during the second part of 2018 was once again a 'Security Decree' (*Decreto Sicurrezza*), intended to reinforce the fight against illegal immigration and mafia activities. Matteo Salvini was so seen by everybody as the 'strong man' of the M5S/League government: a junior partner, with less deputies and senators than the M5S, but far stronger by its agency than its bigger partner, the M5S. '*Bis repetita placent*', as one could say in ancient Rome. The M5S/League government also made the show with the European Commission with its Italian State's 2019 budget, but, at the very last minute, in December 2018, the leaders of the LN/M5S 'government of change' decided to bow to European fiscal rules. 'Much noise for nothing', as one could say using Shakespeare's words. And the 'Southern question' was not, one more time, on Italian public agenda, although the electoral success of the M5S in the 'South' in 2018 was a clear cry of despair from this part of Italy and although all objective proofs were here to show that it was still here. 'Nothing new under the sun', a philosopher could say.

So, from a more general standpoint, the example of the indirect influence of the LN on the sorrow fate of Southern Italy should be replaced by a more general reflection on the impact of regional-oriented RRPP on the distribution of state resources. The Belgian example (with the concurrence on the right of the Flemish side, between VB and the N-VA) has many similarities with the Italian case. In fact, one should not forget that exclusion of others from the benefits of a state could be targeted *at the same time* both against foreigners *and* nationals without any contradiction, quite the contrary.

NOTES

1. The Facebook page of Matteo Salvini is titled *'legasalvinipremier'* in one word (https://www.facebook.com/legasalvinipremier).

2. That is to say coming from outside the European Community (EC).

3. This term means 'person taking care of'. It served to name any legal, or mostly illegal, employee of an Italian family taking care of an old person, a child or a handicapped person. Most 'badante' were women from Filipina and Eastern Europe (Romania, Ukraine, and countries of former Yugoslavia).

4. According to the new electoral law for municipalities with more than 15,000 inhabitants (Legge 25 marzo 1993, n. 81), which was to prove thereafter a strong factor of bipolarization.

5. The new electoral law was adopted in 1993 to mark the shift from the 'First Republic' to the 'Second Republic'. Sergio Mattarella, a Christian-Democrat deputy, engineered it, so it was named 'Mattarellum'. To simplify, it was a mix of 75 per cent uninominal First Past the Post (FPTP) and of 25 per cent proportional representation based on blocked list. A similar electoral system was in place, as before, for both chambers.

6. One speaks of 'ordinary regions' to contrast them to the 'special statute regions' (e.g. Sicilia, Valle d'Aosta, Trentino Alto-Adige), which were created, mostly in 1944–1948, to control separatist movements or solve geopolitical disputes with Italy's neighbours (France, Austria and Yugoslavia). All these regions were dominated by conservative majorities.

7. Law n. 42/2009 of 5 May 2009, *Delega al Governo in materia di federalismo fiscale, in attuazione dell'articolo 119 della Costituzione.*

8. The MpA was created in the 2000s by a Sicilian politician (Riccardo Lombardi) as a liberal-conservative party asking for more fiscal autonomy for the South. It was mostly present in Sicily and finally completely failed when its links with the local criminal organizations were revealed by the judiciary.

9. As a protest movement against all traditional parties created in 2009 by a northerner, the comedian Beppe Grillo from Genova (Liguria), and winning its first vote in the Northern regions during 2010 regional elections, one should have predicted difficulties for the M5S in southern Italy.

BIBLIOGRAPHY

Albertazzi, Daniele, Arianna Giovannini and Antonella Seddone. 2018. 'No regionalism please, we are Leghisti!' The transformation of the Italian Lega Nord under the leadership of Matteo Salvini. *Regional and Federal Studies*, 28 (5): 645–671.

Albertazzi, Daniele and Duncan McDonnell. 2005. The Lega Nord in the second Berlusconi government: In a league of its own. *West European Politics*, 28 (5): 952–972.

Albertazzi, Daniele and Duncan McDonnell. 2010. The Lega Nord back in government. *West European Politics*, 33 (6): 1318–1340.

Albertazzi, Daniele, Duncan McDonnell and James L. Newell. 2011. Di lotta e di governo: The Lega Nord and Rifondazione Comunista in office. *Party Politics*, 17 (4): 471–487.

Albertazzi, Daniele and Sean Mueller. 2013. Populism and liberal democracy: Populists in government In Austria, Italy, Poland and Switzerland. *Government and Opposition*, 18 (3): 343–371.

Ambrosini, Maurizio. 2013. Immigration in Italy: Between economic acceptance and political rejection. *Int. Migration Integration*, 14: 175–194.

Baldi, Brunetta. 2018. Second chamber reform in Italy: Federalism left behind. *South European Society and Politics*, 23 (3): 387–403.

Basile, Linda. 2015. A dwarf among giants? Party competition between ethnoregionalist and state-wide parties on the territorial dimension: The case of Italy (1963–2013). *Party Politics*, 21 (6): 887–899.

Biorcio, Roberto. 1997. *La Padania promessa*. Milan: Il Saggiatore.

Biorcio, Roberto. 2010. *La rivincita del Nord: la Lega della contestazione al governo*. Bari: Laterza.

Bobba, Giuliano and Duncan McDonnell. 2016. *South European Society and Politics*, 21 (3): 281–299.

Carvalho, João. 2016. The impact of extreme-right parties on immigration policy in Italy and France in the early 2000s. *Comparative European Politics*, 14 (5): 663–685.

Cavatorto, Sabrina. 2012. Il trattato di Lisbona nel Parlamento italiano, oltre il permissive consensus. In *Gli italiani e l'Europa. Opinione pubblica, élite politiche e media*, edited by Paolo Bellucci and Nicolo Conti. Rome: Carroci editore.

Cento Bull, Anna. 2009. Lega Nord: A case of simulative politics? *South European Society and Politics*, 14 (2): 129–146.

Cento Bull, Anna. 2010. Addressing contradictory needs: The Lega Nord and Italian immigration policy. *Patterns of Prejudice*, 44 (5): 411–431.

Davis, John A. 2015. A tale of two Italy? The 'Southern Question' past and present. In *The Oxford Handbook of Italian Politics*, edited by Erik Jones E. and Gianfranco Pasquino, DOI: 10.1093/oxfordhb/9780199669745.013.5. Oxford: Oxford University Press.

Dematteo, Lynda. 2011. *L'idiota in politica: anthropologia della Lega Nord*. Milan: Feltrinelli.

Diamanti, Ilvo. 1993. *La Lega. Geographia, storia e sociologia di un nuovo soggetto politico*. Roma: Donzelli.

Diamanti, Ilvo. 1996. *Il male del Nord: Lega, localismo, secessione*. Rome: Donzelli.

Diamanti, Ilvo. 2003. *Bianco, Rosso, Verde . . . e Azzurro: Mappe e Colori dell'Italia politica*. Bologna: Il Mulino.

Diamanti, Ilvo. 2009. *Mappe dall'Italia politica. Bianco, rosso, verde, azzurro . . . e tricolore*. Bologne: Il Mulino.

Geddes, Andrew. 2008. Il rombo dei cannoni: Immigration and the centre-right in Italy. *Journal of European Public Policy*, 15 (3): 349–366.

Huysseune, Michel. 2008. Come interpretare l'Altro. Il Mezzogiorno nel discorso della Lega Nord. *Meridiana*, 63: 173–192.

Huysseune, Michel. 2010. Defending national identity and interests: The Lega Nord's asymmetric model of globalization. *Studies in Ethnicity and Nationalism*, 10 (2): 221–233.

Iuzzolono, Giovanni, Guido Pellegrini and Gianfranco Viesti. 2013. Chapter 20. Regional convergence. In *The Oxford Handbook of The Italian Economy since Unification*, edited by Gianni Toniolo: 571–598. Oxford: Oxford University Press.

Mannheimer, Renato, ed. 1991. *La Lega Lombarda*. Milan: Feltrinelli.

Massetti, Emanuele and Simon Toubeau. 2013. Sailing with northern winds: Party politics and federal reform in Italy. *West European Politics*, 36 (2): 359–381.

McDonnell, Duncan. 2006. A weekend in Padania: Regionalist populism and the Lega Nord. *Politics*, 26 (2): 126–132.

McDonnell, Duncan. 2007. 'Beyond the radical right straitjacket: A reply to Andrej Zaslove's critique of 'regionalist populism and the Lega Nord'. *Politics*, 27 (2): 123–126.

Passalacqua, Guido. 2009. *Il vento della Padania: storie della Lega Nord 1984–2009*. Milan: Mondadori.

Richardson, John E. and Monica Colombo. 2013. Continuity and change in anti-immigrant discourses in Italy: An analysis of the visual propaganda of the Lega Nord. *Journal of Language and Politics*, 12 (2): 180–202.

Verbeek, Bertjan and Andrej Zaslove. 2014. The impact of populist radical right parties on foreign policy: The Northern League as a junior coalition partner in the Berlusconi Governments. *European Political Science Review*, 7 (4): 525–546.

Zanardi, Alberto. 2011. Federalismo fiscale: prove di attuazione. In *La finanza pubblica italiana. Rapporto 2011*, edited by Maria Cecilia Guerra and Alberto Zanardi A: 225–256. Bologna: Il Mulino.

Zaslove, Andrej. 2004. Closing the door? The ideology and impact of radical right populism on immigration policy in Austria and Italy. *Journal of Political Ideologies*, 9 (1): 99–118.

Zaslove, Andrej. 2007. Alpine populism, Padania and beyond: A response to Duncan McDonnell. *Politics*, 27 (1): 64–68.

Zaslove, Andrej. 2011. *The Re-invention of the European Radical Right: Populism, Regionalism and the Italian Lega Nord*. Montreal: McGill-Queens University Press.

Zaslove, Andrej. 2012. The populist radical right in government: The structure and agency of success and failure. *Comparative European Politics*, 10 (4): 421–448.

Chapter 7

The Populist Performance of Urban Crisis

The Policy Influence of Radical Right Populist Parties in Leadership of Local Government in Austria and Italy

Fred Paxton

Local governments led by radical right populist parties (hereafter RRPP) have received increasing media attention in recent years.[1] Many such cases have been framed as significant for understanding the contemporary populist phenomenon more broadly; their actions in local government claimed to provide an insight into the parties' ideological priorities and their likely forms of influence if in national government. Sub-national government can indeed function as a 'laboratory' in which parties test policy (Egner, et al., 2018, 329; Hendriks, et al., 2010). Yet the particular influence of RRPP in such contexts remains an under-researched area, with only a few examples that focus on them at the sub-national rather than national level (for example: Bolin et al., 2014; van Ostaijen and Scholten, 2014). Research into the policy-making influence of RRPP in local government thus offers a fitting and fresh perspective on the new structuring conflicts of European society produced, and represented, by the contemporary populist challenge (Kriesi, 2014).

Recent research on the participation of RRPP in national government has refuted earlier accounts of them being 'doomed to fail' in power (Canovan, 1999; Heinisch, 2003; Luther 2011; McGann and Kitschelt, 2005; Mény and Surel, 2002). Rather than an inevitable ideological taming and premature collapse, recent examples have shown greater policy efficacy and longevity in such positions (Albertazzi and McDonnell, 2015; Zaslove, 2012). This chapter transfers the focus to the local level of government and asks the following research question: to what extent and how do RRPP influence policy in leadership of local government in different institutional settings? Furthermore, it tests the conception of populism as a performative style that creates, rather than merely responds to, a sense of crisis and insecurity, and the contribution made by such a performance of crisis towards their policy influence (Lacey, 2018; Moffitt, 2015).

The empirical part of the chapter uses a qualitative content analysis of policy documents and government newsletters to analyse two cases of local government leadership by RRPP: Wels in Austria (led by the FPÖ Mayor Andreas Rabl since October 2015) and Padua in Italy (led by the Lega Nord Mayor Massimo Bitonci between June 2014 and November 2016[2]). In line with theoretical expectations, I first establish that the RRPP attempt to create a sense of crisis through their actions, rather than simply respond to pre-existing crisis conditions. Second, regarding the form of the crisis, I find that their policies focus upon a threat to public order caused by an ethnicised out-group and promote a new ethnocentrically defined cultural order. Third, I show the differences in the performances of crisis and policy outputs can be explained with reference to the degree of policy-making autonomy afforded to Austrian and Italian local governments. The two governments have given different relative prominence to either the nativist or populist elements of party ideology. The government of Padua utilized its autonomy to introduce measures that exclude migrants from urban space and society, while in Wels, lacking many such competences, the government has given higher priority to rhetorical attacks against (national) government elites.

The chapter begins with its theoretical framing: the role of crisis and (in)security in the ideology and actions of RRPP, as well as the moderating force of local government autonomy upon ideologically distinctive action from governing parties. The methodological approach is then outlined, after which the empirical results are explored. Finally, I conclude with clarification of the contribution of the research and discussion of future research directions.

POPULISM AS A PERFORMANCE OF CRISIS

Explanations for rising support for RRPP have long pointed to objective, systemic crisis conditions producing new grievances to which non-mainstream political actors are able to respond (e.g. Bell, 1964; Laclau, 2005; Lipset, 1960; Ramet, 1999). Different scholars have stressed the political, economic and cultural sides of the crisis: whether a crisis of political representation, of economic deprivation or of cultural backlash. For Taggart (2000), a sense of crisis is the critical factor in producing conditions to which the usual politics is perceived as unable to respond, providing a distinct opportunity for novel political actors. A constructionist argument proposes that crises are diffuse phenomena that only gain political salience through the mediation of political action, or in crisper terms: crises are in fact only perceived as such due to their performance by political actors (Hay, 1995, 1999; Moffitt, 2015). Rather than being a reaction to a pre-existing crisis, populist political actors (of left or right) create a sense of crisis through a number of performed stages, such as (Moffitt, 2015, 198):

(1) Identify failure.
(2) Elevate to the level of crisis by linking into a wider framework and adding a temporal dimension.
(3) Frame 'the people' vs. those responsible for the crisis.
(4) Use media to propagate performance.
(5) Present simple solutions and strong leadership.
(6) Continue to propagate crisis.

This study examines this conception of populism at the local level of government through an investigation of whether and how the policies of local governments led by RRPP demonstrate the creation of a sense of crisis.

Different varieties of populism – itself a 'thin-centred' ideology – can be distinguished based on its combination with other concepts and ideological traditions. As a result, both an inclusionary left populism and an exclusionary populism of the radical right can be distinguished (Mudde and Kaltwasser, 2013). The latter hold an ethnocentric definition of 'the people' and fundamental nativist antagonism towards out-groups representative of multicultural society (March, 2017, 298; Rydgren, 2005). Investigations of RRPP in (national) executive power have tended to focus on the ethnically exclusionary effects of their influence on government policy (Akkerman and de Lange, 2012; Albertazzi and McDonnell, 2015; Albertazzi and Mueller, 2013). Rather than being 'tamed' by power, these parties have influenced public policies, party systems and, more fundamentally, democratic functioning, through measures that initiate a transformation of democracy into ethnocracy (Minkenberg, 2001, 19).

However, whether the theorized centrality of crisis performance to populism parties is also evident in their government practice lacks empirical support. The local level of government is an environment particularly well suited to such an investigation. The salience of the issue of urban security, and the idea of 'urban crisis', has increased in recent years, in academic literature as well as public debates (Barbehön and Münch, 2017; Jabareen et al., 2017; Weaver, 2017). Security is a policy area in which local authorities possess significant responsibility, which increases its importance in local political debates for all parties (Castelli Gattinara, 2016, 35). Furthermore, it is a 'golden issue' of RRPP, located at the nexus of their key ideological tenets of authoritarianism, populism and nativism (Lacey, 2018; Mudde, 2007, 2010). Like security, migration is another policy area over which sub-national governments have significant responsibility and one of ideological centrality to RRPP (Alexander, 2003; Penninx et al., 2004; Rogers and Tillie, 2001). Analyses of Italian local governments have revealed the compatibility of these policy areas in this country at least, and the resulting security-oriented migration policy, or migration-oriented security policy (Bonnet, 2009; Caponio and Graziano, 2011; Gilbert, 2009). Despite these existing research avenues, the particular exploitation of the two issues of migration and security by PRR actors in local government has so far been neglected (an exception: van Ostaijen and Scholten, 2014). Based on this theoretical framing, I expect the policies of local governments led by RRPP to be focused on the threat to security posed by an ethnicised out-group.

LOCAL GOVERNMENT AUTONOMY MODERATING IDEOLOGICAL ACTION

There is considerable academic scepticism regarding the possibility of distinctive partisan influence over local politics due to particular legal, political and economic constraints at this level (Gerber and Hopkins, 2011, 327). According to some urban scholars (Harvey, 1989; Jouve, 2005; Swyngedouw, 2010), the move towards more entrepreneurial, investment-oriented urban governance methods from the 1970s onwards has resulted in a consensual 'post-political' approach to governing alongside private sector actors and the preclusion of space for policy disagreements. Much of the empirical literature on local government policy-making is distinctly functionalist, without sufficient attention given to the levels of autonomy that enable distinctive partisan choices (Lascoumes and Le Gales, 2007). Attempts to measure and compare government autonomy cross-nationally cover a number of measures such as policy scope and effective political discretion, but have one consistent absence: partisanship (Goldsmith and Page, 2010; Ladner et al., 2016; Pierre, 2000; Sellers and Lidström, 2007).

Mayoral partisanship has been shown to have little influence over American local government policy, being only somewhat evident in specific policy areas in which autonomy is relatively high (Gerber and Hopkins, 2011).[3] The weakness of the connection between local government partisanship and policy is attributed to the constraints of the American context, both in legal and political-cultural terms (Einstein and Glick, 2018). The influence of party actions might be expected to be greater in Western European contexts where a culture of partisanship is stronger, particularly where greater autonomy is afforded to local governments (DiGaetano and Strom, 2003, 364). RRPP are expected to seek to implement their 'full' ideological commitments in local government – that is, the nativist and authoritarian elements characteristic of the radical right as well as the 'thin' populism – but be constrained by the level of policy-making capacity provided to local government.

METHODOLOGICAL APPROACH

This study follows a comparative case study approach and focuses on the actions of two European RRPP when in leadership of local government. Austria and Italy are selected as the locations of the case studies, being examples of varying degrees of local policy-making autonomy. Although both Austrian and Italian local government have a similarly high level of overall autonomy according to some measures (for example: Ladner et al., 2016[4]), there are crucial differences in government capacity regarding security policy. Most importantly, the introduction of mayor-issued emergency ordinances to Italian local government in 2008 enables policy responses to their own defined threats to security, which Austrian local governments lack.

The specific cases within Austria and Italy are selected based on current local government control by RRPP, including the position of mayor. Cities with a larger population are favoured in order to maximize the potential powers of decision-making, resource distribution, and therefore politically distinctive action. The two cities selected for research are Wels in Austria (led by the FPÖ Mayor Andreas Rabl since October 2015) and Padua in Italy (led by the Lega Nord Mayor Massimo Bitonci between June 2014 and November 2016). In both cases, the RRPP hold the position of mayor and are the senior partner of the governing coalition. In Wels, the FPÖ formed a coalition with the ÖVP after the election, having contested the election separately. As a result they secured an absolute majority in the proportionately allocated council and executive, in a partnership in which the FPÖ were dominant.[5] In Padua, the Lega Nord had contested the election as part of the same list as Forza Italia, and the two parties continued to work together in a governing coalition. Although the Lega Nord mayor was dominant, and able to select the members of the executive, the seats held by Forza Italia were crucial to attaining a majority within the council.[6]

The empirical focus is on the policies proposed and implemented by RRPP local government actors on the themes of crisis, migration and security, due to the theoretical framing of populism as a political style performing crisis, and the RRPP ideology as one that draws from the increased political salience of security and aims for ethnic homogeneity. The timeframe of the analysis begins after the election of the RRPP into local government. For Padua, the end date is the collapse of the governing coalition in November 2016; for Wels, the analysis continues until March 2017. The policy-making instruments held by local governments in each case context determine the data gathered for the policy analysis: for Padua, the mayor issued emergency ordinances were analysed, and for Wels, the resolutions made within the monthly council meetings. Council newsletters are analysed for the surrounding rhetoric in both cases. Semi-structured interviews are also conducted with nine experts and seven high-level political actors to corroborate the findings. In an effort to further triangulate the findings, additional data sources are used: local and national press reports and statistical measures of population development and crime rates.

I make use of a qualitative content analysis of the material, with two cycles of coding. In the first cycle, descriptive codes are inductively created with grounding in the study's theoretical framing. In the second cycle, pattern codes are created to draw together the data into meaningful groups based on three core themes of analysis. First, the codes are based on the six steps outlined in the populist performance of crisis theory of Moffitt (2015), to evaluate the presence and form of each one. Second, the role of party ideology in local government policies – both the 'thin' populism and the radical right elements with which it combines, in particular ethnocentrism and (in)security. Third, the influence of varying levels of local government policy-making autonomy over their actions.

The process by which RRPP create a sense of crisis through their performance in local government, and the extent of influence thereby exerted on policy-making, is analysed here in three parts. First, via policies related to a negatively defined public disorder of migrant threat; second, those related to an ethnocentric public order constructed in opposition; and third, with reference to the moderating force of local government autonomy, the differences in evident policy influence between the two cases are explored.

EMPIRICAL FINDINGS

The Performance of a Local Migration-Security Crisis

The idea that populism is not simply a reaction to a pre-existing crisis, but a political practice in which the creation of a sense of crisis is central (Moffitt, 2015), is corroborated by both cases of RRPP in leadership of local government. A fundamental stage in the process is the identification of failure. RRPP government actors in Wels and Padua have accused political elites of the facilitation of local socio-economic and demographic changes that have produced threats to public order. The national level of government has been blamed by both local administrations for the rise of immigration in particular. Figure 7.1 shows the number of foreign residents who have risen rapidly in

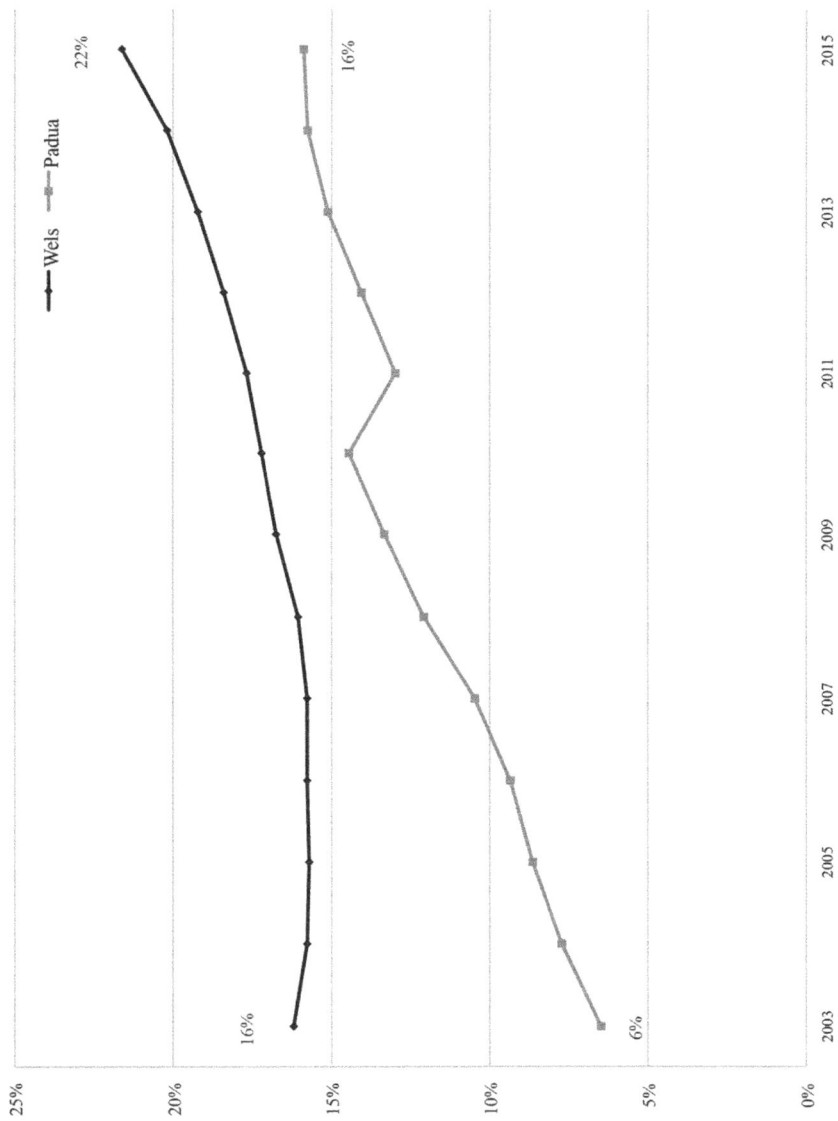

Figure 7.1. Increasing share of foreign nationals in Wels and Padua, 2003–2015.

Wels and Padua over the past decade, while the population of national citizen residents declined.[7] The mayor of Padua used the council newsletter to blame the Italian government for an overly generous and wasteful immigration policy, against the wishes of taxpayers 'who pay taxes for security and justice, not illegals [sic] in their home' (PiC January 2016). Furthermore, he depicted the preceding centre-left local government as neglectful in matters of crime and responsible for a rise in levels of reported crime (PiC Apr. 2015). The deputy mayor of Padua responsible for security stressed that 'the role of the mayor, in issues relating to security, is not a mere spectator as [the preceding centre-left mayors] have been, but can and should legitimately intervene to ensure the safety of citizens' (PiC September 2015).

The prime source of threats to the security of 'the people' communicated by both governments is the figure of the migrant. In the policies of Padua, a connection with immigrants is explicitly stated in four of the eleven security policy ordinances issued by Mayor Bitonci, and justified using a web of threatening concepts, such as safety, civility and hygiene. An example of such a rhetorical combination is shown in a policy that bans street prostitution (Ord. 5 February 2015). The policy also blames the national immigration system, given that a substantial percentage of offenders are migrants and therefore less amenable to (local) control. Furthermore, the metaphorical framing in emotionally evocative terms – the 'social alarm and discomfort' felt by the 'local people' – portrays a shared sense of vulnerability for those within the victimized group.

The FPÖ-led government in Wels has followed a similar exclusionary approach, but has defined the group responsible for the crisis conditions to include the wider non-Austrian resident population. Their opposition to federally proposed placement of migrants within the city has repeatedly been justified by the strain already caused in attempts to integrate the existing 32 per cent of the population without Austrian citizenship (WG January 2016; WG February 2016; WI February 2016; WI May 2016). The Wels local government does not have the legal powers to practically resist the placement, however they have fixated on the subject in four of the seven security related council resolutions.[8] Mayor Rabl has repeatedly asserted his opposition as follows: 'the goal must continue to be closed as a city and to be united against the federal and regional governments in order to achieve the best possible result for Wels' (WI February 2016; WI May 2016).

The escalation to the level of crisis has been attempted through the linkage of a number of incidents of threatened public order with a broader framework in order to make them symptomatic of a wider criminal-migrant threat. In the connection of topics as wide-reaching as immigration, crime and the incompetence of preceding governments in dealing with them, RRPP actors consistently draw upon the common conceptual framework provided by wider contemporary trends, specifically of an ongoing European migrant crisis and a heightened security threat from radical Islamic terrorism. In Wels, reference to the migrant crisis, and crimes committed by migrants as part of this movement, has been a repeatedly used rhetorical tool of the Wels government. From September 2015, the month before the election of the FPÖ in Wels, 40,000 refugees passed through Wels to Germany, 24,000 of whom were temporarily accommodated, during which time no criminal incidents were recorded (WI December 2015). Yet in order to justify an increase in police numbers the following month, the FPÖ councillor blamed the strain caused by transit refugees (WG February 2016). A similar threat is presented in justification of heightened security measures in Padua: to justify health checks on migrants in the city, the policy blamed the 125,000 arrivals to Europe due to the Mediterranean refugee rescue operation Mare Nostrum (Ord. 42 November 2014). Another salient contemporary issue to which migration and crime is linked is terrorism. Following the terror attacks in Paris in November 2015, Mayor Bitonci related the threat of similar attacks on Padua, as an important Christian site (PiC November 2015). Such a sense of danger is used to reinforce a sense of the local culture and heritage as being under threat.

The framing of crisis produces a layer of seeming 'objectivity' and the attainment of a wider consensus in their execution of their ethnocentric and nativist ideology in power than would be possible otherwise (Moffitt 2015, 202). The implications of the specific nature of the crisis being evoked in Wels and Padua – a growing insecurity in the city amidst a context of uncontrolled migration and terrorism – clearly frame the nature of the threat to urban security; that is, the non-native group represented by, and thus responsible for, the threat. The following survey of the policies proposed and implemented by both RRPP local governments reveals a concentration on the issues of migration and security, and their analysis reveals a simplistic quality, as well as an exclusionary logic.

The governments in Wels and Padua have justified new security policies with reference to the threat to safety and quality of life in public space posed by migrants, conceived as a homogenous group. This conception of an ethnically specific and collectively pre-determined threat distinguishes these policies from more typical exclusionary strategies to protect urban standards (Smith, 1996). The policies that have pursued public order through the exclusion of the threatening migrants can be grouped along a sliding scale of severity: from obstruction, to displacement and, most severely, removal. Obstructive measures have made life more difficult for individuals within the defined out-group by, for instance, restricting cultural expression through a proposed ban on the Islamic headscarf in Wels (Herzog, 2017), or limiting commercial operations around Padua train station, where the concentration of migrants is particularly high (Comune di Padova, 2012)[9]. The stated aim of the latter policy was to 'prevent and combat urban decay, and protect urban security and public safety' (Ord. 12 2015). Further examples include a blanket curfew imposed on an asylum centre housing young men in Wels following an isolated incident of sexual assault (WI September 2016), or the implementation of hygiene checks on municipal housing in Padua (Ord. 17 2015), publicized with reference to the specific foreign nationalities identified in the process (PiC September 2016).

Other policies have sought to displace the threatening physical presence in particular urban areas. The first major project of the Wels government was an expansion of CCTV surveillance within the city centre, passed within the first month of the government despite its prior rejection by an independent consultation. The scale of the crisis described by government actors of RRPP is used to demand an increased speed of response. Against the protests of other councillors for its excessive cost and ineffectiveness (WG November 2016), the surveillance was justified as 'urgently necessary' (WI November 2015). The Padua government similarly used the external event of the terror attacks in Paris of November 2015 to demand urgent security changes locally in response (PiC November 2015). Other measures in Padua have sought to limit certain commercial operations and the consumption of alcohol, and focused on displacing the activities from areas notable for being both central and therefore sites of investment and symbolic importance, while also gathering points for migrants (Cancellieri and Ostanel, 2015). The idea of the security measures only managing to displace, rather than solve outright, criminal activity is one acknowledged by Wels Mayor Rabl, and serves as a justification for further security changes to combat its new manifestations (WelsInt4 2017).

To sustain the relevance of the issues conjoined into the created crisis requires continued active RRPP support, as much as for its initiation. The sense of crisis, and the proposed counter-measures, have been publicized through simple and often direct communication with citizens such as the newsletters analysed in this study. Following the first year of the RRPP leadership of the local governments, there were reports of declining crime in both cities.[10] Figure 7.2 shows the existing trend of gradually declining crime prior to the election of the RRPP governments. In both cases, RRPP actors responded to these reports with the reiteration of the continuing threat, rather than, for instance, simply claiming credit for the decline in crime levels (PiC November 2015; Stadt Wels 2017). This perpetuation of the sense of crisis for political gain, and indeed its necessity for their political survival, is one factor which distinguishes the 'populist performance of crisis' from typical 'crisis politics' (Moffitt, 2015, 209). The so-called crisis politics – the formation of political strategy defined in its response to particular crises – is common for political actors of all party backgrounds. In the urban setting,

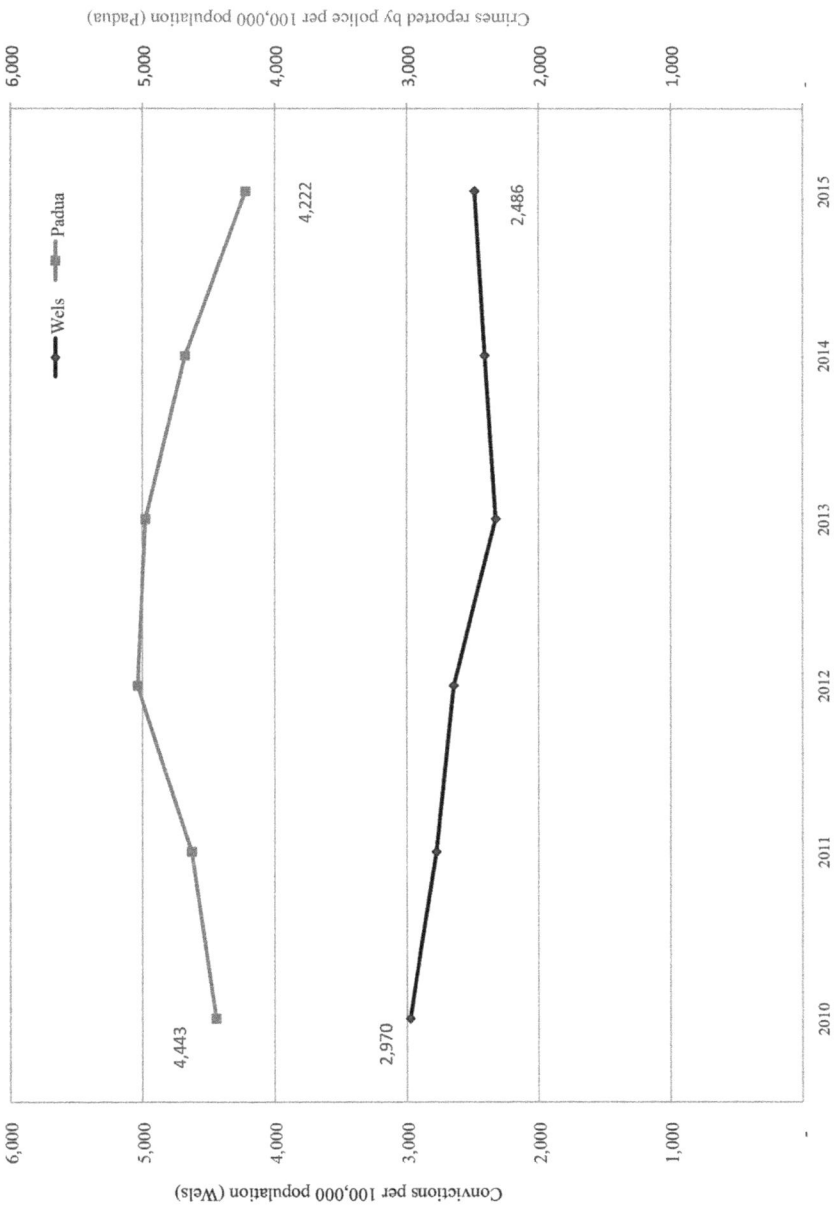

Figure 7.2. Stability of crime rate in Wels and Padua, 2010–2015.

measures heightening the perception of insecurity are evident in widespread programmes of 'revanchist urbanism' (Uitermark and Duyvendak, 2006) and 'military urbanism' (Graham, 2011). However, such examples of 'crisis politics' do not necessitate the perpetuation of crisis; in fact, political actors seek to accrue political benefits through perceived responsibility for resolution of a crisis. To the extent that the continued success of populist parties is dependent on the maintenance of a sense of crisis, this performance can be seen as a central component of populism.

THE CONSTRUCTION OF A NEWLY ETHNOCENTRIC FORM OF PUBLIC ORDER

Implicit in the discursive construction of a crisis is an absent or departed condition of normality; the crisis is thus a decision point from which a different direction can be taken towards a new or restored state of normality. RRPP local government actors in Wels and Padua have sought to create a different model of urban order through new policy measures. The sense of crisis is used by these RRPP to frame underlying local societal threats and enable their connection into a programme of action. In Wels, the refugee crisis was raised by the incoming mayor as a catalyst for discussions of integration, culture and values, claimed as necessary due to long-term problematic developments (WI February 2016). The threatening combination of crime and migration, by drawing upon a wider framework of the dual crises of migration and terrorism, is used to politicize other societal issues, as well as local culture and identity.

Cultural policy is a particularly important route for urban governments to form collective identities for their cities, and attract investment and tourism. These RRPP-led governments have pursued an ethnocentrically defined culture, with the escalation of security concerns as an integral part of the process. In Wels, the mayor has raised the profile of the annual cultural festival Volksfest and emphasized its traditional elements (WI February 2017). The failure of a prominent previous attempt of cultural change, the Welios Science Centre, to evoke the so-called Bilbao effect of cultural regeneration also contributed to a wider reorientation towards a more nostalgic vision of the city (Schmidt-Lauber and Wolfmayr, 2016, 201). Such a recourse to nostalgia and rationalization has been characterized as a 'post-modern response to fear' (Ellin, 2001), as opposed to the rational efforts towards progression characteristic of earlier modernism. The first Wels Volksfest under the FPÖ government in 2016 was held with highly publicized added security, following an incident of alleged assault by a migrant, showing the use of culture to support the image of a threatened urban order (WI September 2016; WG November 2016). A threatened urban heritage – to be restored after the neglect of preceding governments – was presented by the mayor of Padua in populist terms through homogenizing a threatened citizenry (PiC May 2015). The combination of ethnocentric nostalgia and fear is exemplified in the agenda of the cultural festival introduced by the mayor – Babel – that offered discussions on both the historic Venetian dialect and, 'following [the January 2016 terror attacks in] Nice, the most difficult issues of fundamentalism, of war, of fear [. . . and] the big question of Muslim women and basic civil rights' (PiC February 2016, October 2016).

A heightened focus upon public order enables local government actors to represent themselves as 'guardians of safety, dignity and social order', defending the people from the 'others' considered to be dangerous and invading urban space (Ambrosini, 2013, 143). Furthermore, in opposition to the 'others' – the criminal outsiders and the neglectful, even malevolent, elites – an identity of 'the people' can be more clearly constructed, who in contrast are presented as vulnerable, victimized but an ultimately virtuous group. The rhetorical centrality given to the antagonistic relationship between 'the people' and their enemy is another crucial feature that distinguishes the populist performance of crisis from 'crisis politics' more generally (Moffitt, 2015, 208). Government actors from RRPP in Wels and Padua have aimed to present themselves as distinctively capable of expressing the 'will of the people', through an emphasis on their leadership qualities and straightforward solutions to the crisis. The adoption of a performative populist style is not only unusual amidst a long-term trend for professionalization of local government and an expansion of the civil service (Berg and Rao, 2005, 7), it is also made difficult by the professional and partisan background of both mayors. Such a performance requires a process of personal adaptation and requires a delicate balancing act to simultaneously establish an image of competence and professionalism in government. The mayor of Wels has sought to present an image of competence and expertise in public appearances, and his 'utmost diligence, excellent expertise and tireless perseverance' has been praised in the mainstream German press (Gürgen, 2016). This performance of competence in governing is presented alongside the more typically populist stylistic features, such as spectacles and symbolic usage of bottom-up governing methods like referendums, thereby exhibiting a kind of 'technocratic populism' (De la Torre, 2013, 42).

The overall process by which a new urban order is formed through the populist performance of crisis demonstrated in both cases combines a closely linked process of the depiction of disorder and the potential for (re-)construction of order. The nature of this new form of urban order not only, of course, contrasts with the disorder, and functions to exclude those social groups held responsible, but actually depends upon a continued sense of disorder in its discursive formulation. The new cultural festivals of Padua and Wels are not only traditional, they are also threatened. The following section will explore how the mechanism followed by the RRPP-led local governments to create this new sense of urban order – defining the threat, excluding the threat and emphasizing a new, and threatened, order – has significant variations in the two contexts.

LOCAL GOVERNMENT AUTONOMY AS A FACTOR MODERATING POLICY INFLUENCE

A comparison of the varying amount of autonomy held by local governments in Wels and Padua helps to explain the extent and manner of policy influence in the two cases. The concept of autonomy provides contextual variables that shape the mechanism that links their performance of crisis to the discursive creation of a new urban order, in moderating how these performances are converted and formalized into policy changes.

Italian local governments have a higher degree of autonomy over security policy due to the introduction of mayor-issued emergency ordinances in 2008, which enable policy responses to their own defined threats to security. The most severe form of exclusionary remedy to the crisis of public order is the complete removal of the out-group from the city boundaries. The measures implemented in Padua are distinctively forceful compared to Wels in this respect. Austrian local governments lack the legal competences to place such localized restrictions on migrant entries as the measures in Padua to ban the anti-Roma measure banning the arrival of tents and caravans (Ord. 30 2015) and prohibit residence of migrants without a medical certificate (Ord. 42 2014). The efforts to prevent further settlement of migrants within the city, as documented in four of the eleven security-related resolutions from the Wels Council here examined during the period October 2015 to January 2017, show a similar desire to (pre-emptively) remove a security threat to the city, defined by the status of migrant. Yet, lacking the legal capacity to carry out such a level of exclusion, the Wels government has had to rely on the tactics of obstruction and displacement described above (for example: Ord. 42 2014; Ord. 17 2015).

The exclusionary measures are combined with actively ethnocentric policies, which again demonstrate differences due to national variations in autonomy. For example, a measure obstructing public housing for non-Italians was labelled as the 'Paduans First' policy, and resulted in 92 per cent of public housing allocated to Italian citizens between March and September 2016, in comparison to 67 per cent between 2010 and 2012 (PiC September 2016). On the other hand, the intention of Wels mayor Rabl to restrict welfare benefits to Austrian nationals, has never been implemented, due to Austrian local government lacking the necessary autonomy (Rohrhofer, 2015).

Furthermore, the Wels executive has to a greater degree resorted to resolutions with symbolic purpose, directed upwards towards the national and regional governments. As stated by a Wels councillor from the governing coalition: 'I and our group are aware that we do not decide this in the town council. But it is a crucial signal when this body clearly expresses its freedom' (WG February 2016). Regarding their opposition to plan migrant settlements in Wels, the rhetorical stress by the RRPP has been placed on the inability of a local government response, due to the power being held by central government. Such denigration of existing political institutions and processes, particularly those of institutional checks and balances, is a typical anti-elite populist strategy.

Thanks to the higher degree of legal autonomy held by Italian local government, the security actions of the RRPP-led local government in Padua have more specifically targeted the social group held as directly responsible, with greater scope for exclusion. Diverging from the case of Padua, the activation of a crisis of urban security in Wels has produced, to a greater degree, rhetorical performances and symbolic actions focused upon political opponents and elites rather than the population group depicted as the security threat themselves. A relationship is therefore suggested between the level of local government policy-making autonomy and the relative prominence given to either the populist anti-elitism or the nativist anti-migrant elements of the ideology of RRPP.

CONCLUSION

This analysis has demonstrated the relevance of the theory of a populist performance of crisis to the exercise of executive power by RRPP at the sub-national level. Their policies are shown to create the sense of a security crisis related to the presence of migrants, rather than to simply react to crisis conditions already existing. The crisis is one of public disorder, caused by an ethnicized out-group and facilitated by the neglect and incompetence of political elites. Significantly, their policies also promote a new ethnocentrically defined, and locally specific, cultural order in its place.

The degree of policy-making autonomy held by local governments within the particular context shapes the relative focus upon either the ethnicized out-groups or political elites. With greater autonomy, the nativist ideology of the RRPP is more evident in the policies and rhetoric of the Lega Nord government in Padua, through the exclusion of migrants depicted as responsible for the security crisis. However, with less autonomy, the FPÖ government in Wels has put greater rhetorical emphasis upon political elites and their claimed antagonistic relationship with (native-born) residents. This study therefore supports the interpretation of populism as a 'thin' ideology that is combined with other 'thicker' ideological components such as nativism.

Furthermore, the substitution of populism for nativism in contexts of relatively high autonomy indicates the 'thin' populism may act as a vehicle for the implementation of the 'thicker' nativism by governing RRPP when the institutional context allows.

The findings suggest new research directions at this level in order to systematically test the influence of local government autonomy over partisan influence over policy, as well as the extent to which populism is of rather instrumental value for the execution of nativist policy by local governments led by RRPP in different institutional settings. A sub-national government perspective provides new avenues through which to contribute to debates on the policy-making influence of RRPP. Future research with a similar focus should look beyond policies directly related to security to investigate the role played by populism and nativism in governance more broadly. Further consideration of the particularities of this local level of government would be worthwhile, for instance how the principles and instruments of supposedly apolitical, consensual new public management and other forms of urban governance interact with the decidedly ideological and contentious aims of RRPP. Questions remain about the extent to which the approach of RRPP actors in these contexts is distinctive, in the form and intensity of the crisis performed at a time in which 'crisis politics' is common. Future comparative studies that include further cases of local governments that involve parties of other ideological families, populist and otherwise, should examine the extent to which populist forms of crisis performance and security concerns are used by local government party actors to exclude migrants from urban space and society, beyond the confines of RRPP.

NOTES

1. Examples include *The Guardian*'s 'Fear of migrants and loathing of elites drive a small Austrian town to far right' (Oltermann, 2016), Die Zeit's 'The Blue (FPÖ) model city' (Kapeller, 2016) and *Time* magazine's 'European politics are swinging to the right' (Shuster, 2016). Beziérs, the French city governed by the independent but Front National-aligned Robert Menard, has been similarly framed in many international press features, for example: *The Atlantic*'s 'Inside Béziers, France's far-right laboratory' (Masih, 2017), *The Guardian*'s 'Talk of the town: French mayor's "laboratory of the far right"' (Chrisafis, 2015) and the *Financial Times*'s 'The French town that shows how Marine Le Pen could win' (Chassany, 2017).

2. In November 2016, the governing coalition led by the Lega Nord collapsed. The subsequent election in June 2017 was won by a centre-left coalition.

3. As Minister of the Interior in 2008 (now President of the Veneto region), Lega Nord representative Roberto Maroni introduced the mayor issued emergency ordinances in the 2008 Security Decree No. 92 (converted into law No. 125). The

opportunity was enthusiastically taken up by municipalities in northern Italy, with 788 such ordinances issued between 2008–09 (Ambrosini, 2013).

4. As of 2014, Austria and Italy are placed closely together on the LAI, with scores of 25.17 and 25.5 respectively, and ranked thirteenth and eleventh of the thirty-nine European countries measured (Ladner, et al., 2016). Their similarity is a new phenomenon, achieved after a dramatic increase in Italian local government autonomy between 1990 and 2014, due above all to increases in institutional depth, financial self-reliance and freedom from administrative supervision. The most significant change was the reform introducing directly elected mayors in 1993, bringing Italy in line with Austria in having a 'strong mayor' form of local government, according to the typology of Mouritzen and Svara (2002, 55).

5. The FPÖ gained sixteen seats in the council of thirty-six seats. With the additional six seats of the ÖVP, the governing coalition holds an absolute majority. In the eight-member executive, the FPÖ gained four seats. The coalition with the ÖVP enabled the addition of their one executive member to hold an absolute majority in that body too.

6. The electoral list of the Lega Nord mayoral candidate, Massimo Bitonci, gained a total of seventeen seats in the council of thirty-two seats in total. Within these seventeen, ten were of the personal list of Bitonci, three of the Lega Nord and four of Forza Italia.

7. In Wels, 24.11 per cent of residents were foreign citizens in 2017, the largest of any Austrian city besides Vienna; and between 2002 and 2015, migration from abroad amounted to 4,258 while internal migration in the same period was –2,346 (Stadt Wels 2016). In Padua, the foreign population has more than doubled between 2002 and 2015, in both absolute and proportionate terms, from 13,545 (6.48 per cent) to 33,395 (15.87 per cent) (Comune di Padova, 2016).

8. According to the *Durchgriffsrecht des Bundes* ('Intervention Right of the State'), the Austrian federal government has the right to place refugees within federal property in any location when a region (i.e. Upper Austria) does not meet its 1.5 per cent quota, without reference to the population of individual cities (WG January 2016). More on the significance of local government autonomy in section 5.2.

9. Immigrants comprise 27.1 per cent of the population in this area, territorial unit numbers 5.2 ('Stazione') and 25.1 ('Arcella').

10. One per cent in Padua between November 2014 and October 2015 compared to the previous year (PiC Nov. 2015) and 4.5 per cent in Wels over 2016 (Stadt Wels 2017).

BIBLIOGRAPHY

Akkerman, Tjitske, and Sarah L de Lange. 2012. Radical right parties in office: Incumbency records and the electoral cost of governing. *Government and Opposition* 47, no. 4: 574–96.

Albertazzi, Daniele, and Duncan McDonnell. 2015. *Populists in Power*. Abingdon: Routledge.

Albertazzi, Daniele, and Sean Mueller. 2013. Populism and liberal democracy: Populists in government in Austria, Italy, Poland and Switzerland. *Government and Opposition* 48, no. 3: 343–71.

Alexander, Michael. 2003. Local policies toward migrants as an expression of Host-Stranger relations: A proposed typology. *Journal of Ethnic and Migration Studies* 29, no. 3: 411–30.

Ambrosini, Maurizio. 2013. 'We are against a multi-ethnic society': Policies of exclusion at the urban level in Italy. *Ethnic and Racial Studies* 36, no. 1: 136–55.

Barbehön, Marlon, and Sybille Münch. 2017. Interrogating the city: Comparing locally distinct crisis discourses. *Urban Studies* 54, no. 9: 2072–86.

Bell, Daniel. 1964. The dispossessed. In *The Radical Right*, edited by Daniel Bell, 1–45. Garden, NY: Anchor.

Berg, Rikke, and Nirmala Rao. 2005. *Transforming Political Leadership in Local Government*. London: Palgrave Macmillan.

Bolin, Niklas, Gustav Lidén, and Jon Nyhlén. 2014. Do anti-immigration parties matter? The case of the Sweden Democrats and Local Refugee Policy. *Scandinavian Political Studies* 37, no. 3: 323–43.

Bonnet, François. 2009. Managing marginality in railway stations: Beyond the welfare and social control debate. *International Journal of Urban and Regional Research* 33, no. 4: 1029–44.

Cancellieri, Adriano, and Elena Ostanel. 2015. The struggle for public space: The hypervisibility of migrants in the Italian urban landscape. *City* 19, no. 4: 499–509.

Canovan, Margaret. 1999. Trust the people! Populism and the two faces of democracy. *Political Studies* 47, no. 1: 2–16.

Caponio, Tiziana, and Paolo Graziano. 2011. Towards a security-oriented migration policy model? Evidence from the Italian case. In *Migration and Welfare in the new Europe: Social Protection and the Challenges of Integration*, edited by Emma Carmel, Alfio Cerami, and Theodoros Papadopoulos, 105–20. Bristol: The Policy Press.

Castelli Gattinara, Pietro. 2016. *The Politics of Migration in Italy: Perspectives on Local Debates and Party Competition*. Abingdon: Routledge.

Chassany, Anne-Sylvaine. 2017. The French town that shows how Marine Le Pen could win. *Financial Times*, 10 April 2017. https://www.ft.com/content/309292d4-1a28-11e7-a266-12672483791a.

Chirisafis, Angelique. 2015. Talk of the town: French mayor's 'laboratory' of the far right. *The Guardian*, 29 August 2015. https://www.theguardian.com/world/2015/aug/29/french-mayor-beziers-accused-of-laboratory-of-the-far-right.

Comune di Padova. 2012. *Municipal Statistical Yearbook (Annuario Statistico Comune di Padova)*. Accessed 12 August 2017. http://www.padovanet.it/dettaglio.jsp?id=9840#.VXq7yPntlBd.

Comune di Padova. 2016. Relazione sulla Performance 2015. Accessed 1 April 2017. http://www.padovanet.it/informazione/piano-e-relazione-sulle-performance.

De la Torre, Carlos. 2013. In the name of the people: Democratization, popular organizations, and populism in Venezuela, Bolivia, and Ecuador. *European Review of Latin American and Caribbean Studies* 95: 27–48.

DiGaetano, Alan, and Elizabeth Strom. 2003. Comparative urban governance: An integrated approach. *Urban Affairs Review* 38, no. 3: 356–95.

Egner, Björn, Adam Gendźwiłł, Pawel Swianiewicz, and Werner Pleschberger. 2018. Mayors and political parties. In *Political Leaders and Changing Local Democracy*, edited by Hubert Heinelt, Annick Magnier, Marcello Cabria and Herwig Reynaert, 327–58. Cham: Springer International Publishing.

Einstein, Katherine Levine, and David M Glick. 2018. Mayors, partisanship, and redistribution: Evidence directly from U.S. mayors. *Urban Affairs Review* 54, no. 1: 74–106.

Ellin, Nan. 2001. Thresholds of fear: Embracing the urban shadow. *Urban Studies* 38, no. 5–6: 869–883.

Gerber, Elisabeth R, and Daniel J Hopkins. 2011. When mayors matter: Estimating the impact of mayoral partisanship on city policy. *American Journal of Political Science* 55, no. 2: 326–39.

Gilbert, Liette. 2009. Immigration as local politics: Re-bordering immigration and multiculturalism through deterrence and incapacitation. *International Journal of Urban and Regional Research* 33, no. 1: 26–42.

Goldsmith, Michael, and Edward Page. 2010. *Changing Government Relations in Europe: From Localism to Intergovernmentalism.* Abingdon: Routledge.

Graham, Stephen. 2014. *Cities under Siege: The New Military Urbanism.* London: Verso.

Gürgen, Malene. 2016. AfD einfach entzaubern reicht nicht. *TAZ*, 24 September 2016. http://www.taz.de/Wochenend-Wahlbilanz-2/!5339951.

Harvey, David. 1989. From managerialism to entrepreneurialism: The transformation in urban governance in late capitalism. *Geografiska Annaler. Series B, Human Geography* 71, no. 1: 3–17.

Hay, Colin. 1995. Rethinking crisis: Narratives of the new right and constructions of crisis. *Rethinking Marxism* 8, no. 2: 60–76.

Hay, Colin. 1999. Crisis and the structural transformation of the state: Interrogating the process of change. *The British Journal of Politics and International Relations* 1, no. 3: 317–44.

Heinisch, Reinhard. 2003. Success in opposition – failure in government: Explaining the performance of right-wing populist parties in public office. *West European Politics* 26, no. 3: 91–130.

Hendriks, Frank, Anders Lidström, John Loughlin, Frank Hendriks, John Loughlin, and Anders Lidström. 2010. European subnational democracy: Comparative reflections and conclusions. In *The Oxford Handbook of Local and Regional Democracy in Europe*, edited by John Loughlin, Frank Hendriks, and Anders Lidström, 715–743. Oxford: Oxford University Press.

Herzog, Philip. 2017. Integrationsreferent Kroiß will Kopftücher vom Magistrat verbannen. *Bezirks Rundschau Wels*, 19 January 2017. https://www.meinbezirk .at/wels/politik/integrationsreferent-kroiss-will-kopftuecher-vom-magistrat-verban nen-d1996863.html.

Istat. 2017. Istituto Nazionale di Statistica. Accessed 12 August 2017. http://www .istat.it.

Jabareen, Yosef, Efrat Eizenberg, and Omri Zilberman. 2017. Conceptualizing urban ontological security: 'Being-in-the-city' and its social and spatial dimensions. *Cities* 68: 1–7.

Jouve, Bernard. 2005. From government to urban governance in Western Europe: A critical analysis. *Public Administration and Development* 25, no. 4: 285–94.

Kapeller, Lukas. 2016. Die Blaue Musterstadt. *Die Zeit*, 12 September 2016. http://www.zeit.de/2016/38/fpoe-wels-buergermeister-andreas-rabl.

Kriesi, Hanspeter. 2014. The populist challenge. *West European Politics* 37, no. 2: 361–78.

Lacey, Joseph. 2018. Populist nationalism and ontological security: The construction of moral antagonisms in the United Kingdom, Switzerland and Belgium. In *Trumping the Mainstream: The Conquest of Democratic Politics by the Populist Radical Right*, edited by Lise Esther Herman and James Muldoon, 109–125. Abingdon: Routledge.

Laclau, Ernesto. 2005. *On Populist Reason*. London: Verso.

Ladner, Andreas, Nicolas Keuffer, and Harald Baldersheim. 2016. Measuring local autonomy in 39 countries (1990–2014). *Regional and Federal Studies* 26, no. 3: 321–57.

Lascoumes, Pierre, and Patrick Le Gales. 2007. Introduction: Understanding public policy through its instruments – from the nature of instruments to the sociology of public policy instrumentation. *Governance* 20, no. 1: 1–21.

Lipset, Seymour Martin. 1960. *Political Man: The Social Bases of Politics*. Garden City, NY: Doubleday.

Luther, Kurt Richard. 2011. Of goals and own goals: A case study of right-wing populist party strategy for and during incumbency. *Party Politics* 17, no. 4: 453–70.

March, Luke. 2017. Left and right populism compared: The British case. *The British Journal of Politics and International Relations* 19, no. 2: 282–303.

Masih, Niha. 2017. Inside Béziers, France's far-right laboratory. *The Atlantic*, 3 May 2017. https://www.theatlantic.com/international/archive/2017/05/beziers-france-menard-le-pen/524931.

McGann, Anthony J., and Herbert Kitschelt. 2005. The radical right in the Alps: Evolution of support for the Swiss SVP and Austrian FPÖ. *Party Politics* 11, no. 2: 147–171.

Mény, Yves, and Yves Surel. 2002. The constitutive ambiguity of populism. In *Democracies and the Populist Challenge*, edited by Yves Mény and Yves Surel, 1–21. London: Palgrave Macmillan.

Minkenberg, Michael. 2001. The radical right in public office: Agenda-setting and policy effects. *West European Politics* 24, no. 4: 1–21.

Moffitt, Benjamin. 2015. How to perform crisis: A model for understanding the key role of crisis in contemporary populism. *Government and Opposition* 50, no. 2: 189–217.

Mouritzen, Poul Erik, and James H Svara. 2002. *Leadership at the Apex: Politicians and Administrators in Western Local Governments*. Pittsburgh, PA: University of Pittsburgh Press.

Mudde, Cas, and Cristóbal Rovira Kaltwasser. 2013. Exclusionary vs. inclusionary populism: Comparing contemporary Europe and Latin America. *Government and Opposition* 48, no. 2: 147–74.

Oltermann, Philip. 2016. Fear of migrants and loathing of elites drive a small Austrian town to far right. *The Guardian*, 22 May 2016. https://www.theguardian.com/world/2016/may/21/fear-of-migrants-austria-wels-norbert-hofer.

van Ostaijen, Mark, and Peter Scholten. 2014. Policy populism? Political populism and migrant integration policies in Rotterdam and Amsterdam. *Comparative European Politics* 12, no. 6: 680–699.

Pierre, Jon. 2000. *Debating Governance: Authority, Steering, and Democracy*. Oxford: Oxford University Press.

Ramet, Sabrina P. 2010. *Radical Right in Central and Eastern Europe since 1989*. University Park: Penn State University Press.

Rohrhofer, Markus. 2015. Welser Bürgermeister will Sozialleistungen für Nicht-EU-Bürger streichen. *Der Standard*, 17 October 2015. http://derstandard.at/2000024000669/Welser-Buergermeister-will-Sozialleistungen-fuer-Nicht-EU-Buerger-streichen.

Rydgren, Jens. 2005. Is extreme right-wing populism contagious? Explaining the emergence of a new party family. *European Journal of Political Research* 44, no. 3: 413–37.

Sellers, Jefferey M, and Anders Lidström. 2007. Decentralization, local government, and the welfare state. *Governance* 20, no. 4: 609–32.

Shuster, Simon. 2016. European politics are Swinging to the right. *Time*, 22 September 2016. http://time.com/4504010/europe-politics-swing-right.

Smith, Neil. 2005. *The New Urban Frontier: Gentrification and the Revanchist City*. London: Routledge.

Stadt Wels. 2016. Statistisches Jahrbuch der Stadt Wels 2015. Accessed 1 April 2017. http://www.wels.gv.at/Politik-Service-Verwaltung/Pressecorner/Presseaussendungen-Archiv/20160728-Neues-Statistisches-Jahrbuch-der-Stadt-Wels.html?:hp=3.

Stadt Wels. 2017. Kriminalitätsstatistik 2016: Licht und Schatten in Wels. Accessed 1 April 2017. http://www.wels.gv.at/Politik-Service-Verwaltung/Pressecorner/Presseaussendungen/20170308-Kriminalitaetsstatistik-2016-Licht-und-Schatten-in-Wels.html?:hp=3.

Statistik Austria. 2017. Bundesanstalt Statistik Österreich. Accessed 12 August 2017. http://www.statistik.at.

Swyngedouw, Erik. 2007. The post-political city. In *Urban Politics Now: Re-Imagining Democracy in the Neoliberal City*, edited by BAVO, 58–76. Rotterdam: NAi Publishers.

Taggart, Paul A. 2000. *Populism*. Buckingham: Open University Press.

Uitermark, Justus, and Jan Willem Duyvendak. 2008. Civilising the city: Populism and revanchist urbanism in Rotterdam. *Urban Studies* 45, no. 7: 1485–1503.

Weaver, Timothy. 2017. Urban crisis: The genealogy of a concept. *Urban Studies* 54, no. 9: 2039–55.

Wolfmayr, Georg, and Brigitta Schmidt-Lauber. 2016. Doing city. Andere Urbanität und die Aushandlung von Stadt in alltäglichen Praktiken. *Zeitschrift für Volkskunde* 112: 187–208.

Zaslove, Andrej. 2012. The populist radical right in government: The structure and agency of success and failure. *Comparative European Politics* 10, no. 4: 421–448.

Other Sources

Resolutions from Wels Council meetings (WG), October 2015 – January 2017.
Wels council newsletters 'Wels Informiert' (WI), October 2015 – March 2017.
Emergency Ordinances issued by the mayor of Padua (Ord.), June 2014 to November 2016.
Padua council newsletters 'Padova in Comune' (PiC), March 2015 to October. 2016.
Elite and expert interviews in Wels (WelsInt).
Elite and expert interviews in Padua (PaduaInt).

Chapter 8

The Political Influence of the Austrian Freedom Party

Farid Hafez and Reinhard Heinisch

In this chapter we ask about the policy impact of one of the most successful and long-lasting radical right populist parties (RRPP), the Austrian Freedom Party (FPÖ). Specifically we wonder how decisive it has been in influencing policy-making and which policy areas were most affected. At the national level, the FPÖ has been in national government twice (2000–2006 and 2017 to present) since its conversion to RRPP. At the state level, it has of late entered two regional governments as full coalition partner. Otherwise the Freedom Party has largely remained frozen out of power for most of the time since the mid-1980s. The FPÖ is thus an important case not only because it has a long track record of policy proposals and changes in programmatic direction but also because its involvement in regional and national government has put it in a position to affect policy changes and implement its policy agenda at different levels.

Thus, our objective is to explain under which circumstances the Austrian Freedom Party (FPÖ) exercises its influence on politics. Since we know that opposition parties as well as parties without parliamentary representation can also be influential actors in the policy-making process (Williams, 2006), the FPÖ is an apt case to examine such a party's policy impact in and out of power. In particular, we will discuss the question of influence by analysing the impact of the FPÖ on agenda-setting, policy implementation, and political discourse. Examining the history of the FPÖ's policy impact and its behaviour in public office adds to a growing literature on convergent trends between conservative mainstream and far right parties (cf. van Spanje and Graaf, 2017; van Spanje and van der Brug, 2007; Spies and Franzmann, 2011; Loxbo, 2014; Treib, 2014; van Spanje and Graaf, 2017).

In this chapter we will first give a brief history of the FPÖ (section 2) and show how, and to what extent the FPÖ managed to shape Austrian politics

145

by influencing policymaking directly and indirectly (section 3). We examine the FPÖ's impact in the current government position (section 4). We argue that particularly with respect to questions of identity, culture, religion and immigration the influence of the FPÖ has been substantial, even when it was out of power.

THE FPÖ IN THE AUSTRIAN POLITICAL SYSTEM

Founded in 1956, the Austrian Freedom Party was initially dominated by Nazi sympathizers, German nationalists and libertarians, which branded the FPÖ a political pariah for no other party wanted to cooperate with it. Luther calls this phase in the FPÖ's development 'political-ghetto-period' (cf. Luther, 1995, 138). Over time the party's liberal wing grew stronger and, thus, the FPÖ became more acceptable to other political parties in the late 1960s and early 1970s. Thus, it was considered a potential partner for Austrian Social Democratic Party (SPÖ) and the Christian Conservatives (ÖVP), both of which dominated Austria's consociationalist political system in the decades after the war. Throughout that period, the FPÖ was polling mostly between 5 and 6 per cent of the votes in national elections.

Finally, in 1983 the FPÖ joined the Social Democrats after their three successive terms of absolute majorities in parliament had come to an end. The FPÖ's inexperience in government and its role as junior coalition partner of a major party used to controlling all levers of power and a loyal civil service threw the Freedom Party into turmoil. Particularly, it intensified a long simmering conflict within between the far-right nationalists and the more moderate liberals. The situation came to a head when the young and charismatic leader of a regional party faction, Jörg Haider, deposed the liberal party leader Norbert Steger in 1986. When the Social Democrats terminated the coalition, Haider transformed the FPÖ from a libertarian-nationalist formation into a rightwing populist protest party (Hauser and Heinisch, 2015, 4). As a result, the party shifted its electoral focus and support base from both libertarians and anti-Catholic German nationalists, who were typically small town and rural small business owners, professionals and civil servants, to urban and blue collar voters (McGann and Kitschelt, 2005).

As a consequence, the FPÖ increased its electoral share, as table 8.1 shows, from 4.8 per cent in 1986 to 26.9 per cent in 1999.

Already by the mid-1990s, the FPÖ had become a major force in regional politics, emerging as the second biggest party in five (including the capital city of Vienna) of Austria's nine provinces. Haider even served as governor of the state of Carinthia from 1989 to 1991 and then again from 1999 until his death in 2008. Hence, the FPÖ's opportunities to set the agenda and

Table 8.1. Elections to the National Parliament (Lower House)

		Political Parties[a]					
Year of election[b]	Greens	Social Democrats (SPÖ)	People's Party (ÖVP)	Freedom Party (FPÖ)	Alliance (BZÖ)	Team Stro-nach	Liberals/ NEOS
1983		47.7	43.2	5.0	–	–	–
1986	4.8	43.1	41.3	9.7	–	–	–
1990	4.8	42.8	32.1	16.1	–	–	–
1994	7.3	34.9	27.7	22.5	–	–	6.0
1995	4.8	38.1	28.3	21.9	–	–	5.5
1999	7.4	33.2	26.9	26.9	–	–	–
2002	9.5	36.5	42.3	10.0[c]	–	–	–
2006	11.1	35.3	34.3	11.0	4.1	–	–
2008	10.4	29.3	26.0	17.5	10.7		–
2013	12.4	26.8	24.0	20.5	–	5.7	5.0
2017	3.8	26.8	31.4	25.9	–	–	5.3

Source: Federal Ministry of the Interior. https://www.bmi.gv.at/412/Nationalratswahlen/.

a The parties are ordered along the left-right dimension. Grey cells indicate the parties forming the government after the respective elections.
b Legislative and government periods do not always correspond exactly. Most new governments take office at the beginning of the following year (e.g. in 1987, 1996, 2000, 2003 and 2007).
c The second ÖVP–FPÖ cabinet lasted only until April 2005, when the BZÖ formally replaced the FPÖ as the ÖVP's coalition partner, without new elections being called.

Source: Own elaboration on literature quoted in the present chapter.

shape public policy grew significantly. On the regional level, the other parties' acceptance of the Freedom Party as a partner and their willingness to cooperate with it also increased. Due to the so-called *Proporz* rule practiced in several Austrian provinces, which mandates that every party with a certain number of seats in the state legislature can automatically take part in state government in proportion to the party's strength, the FPÖ ended up in executive government in six Austrian states (Hauser and Heinisch, 2015, 5).

The growing political influence of the FPÖ culminated in the 1999 parliamentary elections, when the party came in second, besting the Christian Democratic People's party (ÖVP). Remarkably, FPÖ was for the first time also able to attract more blue-collar workers than the Social Democrats. The ascent of the Freedom Party permanently changed the duopoly of the Austrian party system into one marked by three roughly equal political parties, two of which needed to form a coalition to be able to form a government. From 2000 to 2005 the ÖVP was in a coalition with the FPÖ whereas the SPÖ went into opposition. The subsequent decade was marked by a coalition between the SPÖ and the ÖVP. Then, following the 2017 national elections the ÖVP once again entered into a coalition with the FPÖ.

In order to achieve their impressive electoral gains, the FPÖ tailored its message to the expectations of the voters most discontented with the direction of Austrian politics. However, the motives of protest voters changed over time and thus the Freedom Party followed suit. As Hauser and Heinisch note there 'is no Austrian party that has changed its political direction more frequently than the Freedom Party' (cf. Hauser and Heinisch, 2014, 4). Thus, by the latter part of 1990s, the FPÖ had embraced an economically rather neoliberal but culturally more Catholic conservative orientation to minimize the political gap with positions held by the Christian Democratic ÖVP. This was clearly an effort to become a more suitable partner for the aforementioned intended coalition with the ÖVP, which commenced in 2000. Yet once again, unpreparedness for government and clashing views over the party's direction between the leadership and radical-populist rank-and-file caused a near permanent crisis in the FPÖ, which eventually brought down not only the party's leadership but also the government. In the subsequent elections in 2002, electoral support for the party plummeted by nearly two-thirds, rendering the FPÖ (10 per cent) a substantially weakened partner for an ÖVP that had achieved its best result (42.3 per cent) in twenty years (cf. table 8.1) (Luther, 2003, 139–141). In the new coalition, the FPÖ controlled only three ministries instead of the previous six from a total of twelve portfolios. As a policy consequence, the FPÖ moved further to the left on social policy, casting itself as the defender of the 'man in the street' (Hauser and Heinisch, 2014, 11). As such however, it was more a spoiler of political initiatives from the ÖVP than an agenda-setter and partner.

Due to the permanent tensions within the FPÖ, its former leader Haider, who was pushing a policy-seeking strategy and supporting the party moderates, formed a new political party in 2005 named Alliance Future Austria (BZÖ). De facto, nearly all the senior members of the FPÖ in government and parliament transferred to the new party. In essence, the 'old' FPÖ split into a radical right-wing populist formation dominated by the grassroots membership, focused on protest politics and a more moderate right-wing group around the old leadership pursuing public office. Whereas the former represented hard Eurosceptical, nativist, xenophobic and blue-collar protectionist positions, the latter aimed their comparatively more moderate and decidedly more economically liberal message at middle-class voters looking for an alternative to the Christian conservative ÖVP. As a result, the ÖVP served out the government's term with the BZÖ as their new coalition partner until 2007, which consisted for the most part the same individuals who had made up the old and familiar FPÖ leadership.

The 'rump FPÖ' reverted to its radical populist roots under the leadership of Heinz-Christian Strache. Its campaigns embraced the familiar radical populist repertoire emphasizing identity, immigration, crime and opposition to European integration. While the BZÖ achieved moderate success by gaining 10 per cent of votes in the 2007 elections, the FPÖ's returned to political strength by achieving 17.5 per cent (cf. table 8.1). With the sudden death of Haider in 2008 who had been the acknowledged leadership figure of Austrian far right, the BZÖ was subsequently unable to galvanize voters and faded politically. Those for whom the FPÖ was too radical and economically illiberal divided their support among three smaller new populist protest formations, which gained some support in different state, national and European elections between 2009 and 2014. Of these, the Team Stronach (TS), a more centrist populist protest formation and personal party of the Austro-Canadian business tycoon Frank Stronach, was the most successful. Yet, all these parties proved unable to sustain, or even build on their initial successes as a result of which the Freedom Party remains today the only radical right populist party in Austria of political significance and continues to be in a position to shape policy-making. As Hauser and Heinisch conclude, the FPÖ 'must be qualified as major party because it attracts a share of the electorate roughly equal to that of the traditional government parties' (cf. Hauser and Heinisch, 2015, 18).

This conclusion is even more true after the 2017 national elections when FPÖ reentered government alongside the ÖVP and is thus in the best position yet to affect policy-making. In order to avoid repeating the mistakes made during its stint in government from 2000 to 2005, which were largely the result of being ill-prepared and having poorly skilled, if not to say incompetent people, in public office (Heinisch, 2003), the FPÖ turned to networks of hard right-wing academic fraternities that had been sidelined in the FPÖ when Haider was party leader. These German nationalist groups recruited from academic circles have a long tradition in Austrian and German universities, dating back the early days of pan-German nationalism in the mid-nineteenth century. Whereas these groups typically possess the professional expertise the FPÖ needs when filling important ministerial, judicial or board positions, their affinity to anti-Semitic, extremist right-wing, neo-fascist thinking serves as a frequent public embarrassment at a time when the party wants to signal respectability. For the FPÖ to return to public office, it had to shed its toxic political image regarding its 'governing fitness' (Fallend and Heinisch, 2017, 48) and began a process of relative moderation after 2008 (cf. Fallend, 2009, 890).

Currently, the FPÖ in power represents a mix of professional message control and political deftness on one hand and repeated political blunders due to lapses in judgement on the other. As a result, the FPÖ has become more dependent on the ÖVP for support to help cover over a string of embarrassing episodes. This situation is undoubtedly caused to some extent by the fact that a radical opposition and protest party like the FPÖ will find governing invariably difficult, especially in a coalition with a typical mainstream party. Yet, these problems are also due to the need for the FPÖ to maintain its distinct profile in the eyes of voters. Thus, occasional radical messages and policy proposals can also be seen a clear signal to the base that even in government the Freedom Party remains true to itself.

THE FPÖ'S LONG-STANDING AND INDIRECT POLICY IMPACT

Before moving on to the FPÖ's impact on policies, it should be noted that the Freedom Party has always been an important agenda-setter with a significant impact on political discourse and public rhetoric since 1986 when Haider took the reins of the party. Even while the party was ostracized politically by the other parties, the rhetoric and positions of the FPÖ tended to seep into the agenda of other parties. Yet, as already mentioned, the Freedom Party changed direction several times, which also affected its agenda-setting capacity and subsequently its policy influence. Hauser and Heinisch (2014, 4) distinguish three distinct periods of the FPÖ under Haider's leadership: The 'protest phase' (1986–1991) during which the FPÖ focused especially on the political establishment, the civil service and labour market organizations, charging them with public corruption. By styling itself a middle-class protest party, the FPÖ managed to attract more voters from the Conservatives (Heinisch, 2002, 113–121). The 'social populist phase' (1991–1996) was marked by the FPÖ's emphasis on 'going after welfare cheats' protecting the country from economic and social 'dangers posed by immigrants', attracting more the blue-collar electorate (Heinisch, 2002, 121–215). The 'identitarian phase' (1996–2000) meant that the FPÖ shifted its emphasis more towards socio-cultural issues (Heinisch, 2002, 125–131). Overall, the Freedom Party adopted positions on immigration and foreign cultural influences (Hauser and Heinisch, 2014; Kryzanowski and Wodak, 2009) as well as Islam (Hafez, 2010; Hafez, 2017; Hafez and Heinisch, 2018) and on supporting Euro-scepticism (Heinisch et al., 2018) that subsequently affected the other parties notably the Conservatives. As we will show below, this did not only affect the political discourse in that the FPÖ's rhetoric entered the communication of other parties but also their policy positions. By contrast, on issues of social and economic policy changes, the Freedom Party was less effective because it was divided on this question and contending with a political competitor, the ÖVP, which itself became more economically liberal over time. Thus, on the questions of culture and identity, the Christian Conservatives were especially susceptible to the FPÖ's message and their claims and related policy positions have found their way into ÖVP manifestos and policies. This confirms the literature suggesting that the center-right in Western Europe is moving closer to positions of the radical right (Pytlas, 2015; Mondon, 2016). We can argue that, by being a RRPP, the FPÖ is highly effective in launching provocative messages that shift the discursive frame especially in policy dimensions where mainstream competitors have ambivalent programmatic preferences or 'blur' their position (Rovny, 2012).

The most important area of RRPP impact is that of public policy-makers because it is the most consequential. According to a study of how election manifestos from 1945 to 2008 were drafted, the FPÖ was found among Austria's party to be the one that devoted least time to developing its programme (Dolezal et al., 2012, 875). In contrast to the SPÖ and ÖVP, the Freedom Party's drafting process is highly centralized with the party secretary general being the main actor (ibid., 879). Insider interviews confirm that this process is often governed by an assessment of how likely the FPÖ is to join a future government (ibid., 889).

When the FPÖ launched its 'Austria First' initiative in 1992, it had successfully positioned itself as an anti-immigrant social populist party. The initiative had proposed a constitutional amendment, declaring that Austria was not a country of immigration. In addition, the initiative advocated a list of measures to be undertaken to dissuade foreigners from making Austria their home such as limiting access to education benefits, healthcare, public welfare and public housing. The programmatic claims linked foreigners with crime and created a pressure for the Social Democrats and the Christian Democrats to counteract these claims (Fallend and Heinisch, 2017, 41). The government composed in the 1990s of the SPÖ and ÖVP responded by adopting ever more restrictive immigration and asylum policies (Bauböck and Perchinig, 2006, 732–735). In short, the FPÖ was exercising influence on legislative behaviour and policy outcomes by its ability to frame the issue a certain way. This confirms trends we see also in other European countries (Mudde, 2013, 10).

As a result, nowhere was the impact of the FPÖ more obvious than in immigration policy. During its term in office from 2000 to 2005, the FPÖ implemented one of the internationally most restrictive regimes on family reunions for foreigners despite calls from the industry for some 165,000 additional workers by 2005 (Hauser and Heinisch, 2014, 10). The same discussion and set of policy measures returned when another ÖVP–FPÖ coalition was formed in 2017.

The other and closely related area of indirect policy influence was, as already reported, the government's policy towards Islam. The SPÖ was internally divided but left this issue to their ÖVP coalition partner (Hafez and Heinisch, 2018). In the People's Party, the relative hardliners led by Sebastian Kurz – who was at the time foreign minister and also responsible for the integration portfolio but not religion per se – took control of the issue. In 2011, he introduced a new policy process that radically broke with the traditional government approach to dealing with organized religion when it comes to Islam. Previously, Austria had been known for its tolerance towards the Islamic community, granting Islam full religious equality since the country adopted rather progressive legislation already early in the twentieth century, the Islam Act of 1912. It provided the Islamic community with a measure of autonomy to regulate its own affairs and religious training. The new Islam Act of 2015 introduced discriminatory policy measures that seemed to go against the Austrian constitution by treating people differently based on their religion (Dautovic and Hafez, 2018). Thus, the resulting legislation was a departure from granting autonomy to recognized religious communities by instituting a regime of government supervision and involving the government in matters (including teacher training) that previously were handled independently by the Islamic community (for details see Dautovic and Hafez, 2017; Hafez and Heinisch, 2018).

The policy history of the FPÖ also shows that it could moderate and change direction when that was expedient. After the FPÖ presented a new party programme in 1997, which was more measured in tone, it laid the groundwork for an alliance with the ÖVP (Müller and Fallend, 2004). The FPÖ then adopted positions in the fields of family policy, national administrative and deregulatory reforms, expanding the privatization of state enterprises and national security (i.e. NATO membership) that brought the party closer to the Christian Conservatives. In return, the FPÖ's tougher stance on immigration and asylum was shared by many conservatives. As Müller and Jenny (2000, 143–51) suggest in their analysis of national MPs in 1997–98, many members of the ÖVP parliamentary faction were in reality closer to FPÖ than to their Social Democratic coalition partner both on socio-economic and socio-cultural matters. Hence, it is not surprising that once in government, FPÖ and the ÖVP jointly favoured deregulatory policies and aimed at reducing the central role of the Social Democrats and unions in matters of economic governance and social policy (Hauser and Heinisch, 2014, 9).

Ennser-Jedenastik showed in his analysis of the social policies presented in the Freedom Party election manifestos between 1983 and 2013 that the primary elements of the FPÖ's ideology – nativism, authoritarianism and populism – structure the FPÖ's social policy domain. Thus, the FPÖ moved from welfare populism and some retrenchment proposals under Haider to strong welfare chauvinism after the leadership change in 2005. The analysis specifically reveals that the FPÖ demands nativist policies in the following areas: (1) child care benefits; (2) family allowances (both universal); and (3) social housing (means-tested). Furthermore, the FPÖ proposed the introduction of a special guest worker category in the existing social insurance schemes

(Ennser-Jedenastik, 2016, 419). Thus, while the FPÖ wants to strengthen the insurance principle for non-natives, it grants citizens the benefit of tax-funded (i.e. non-insurance-based) compensation payments to maintain benefit levels (Ennser-Jedenastik, 2018, 308).

We may conclude that the FPÖ's long-standing and indirect policy impact has been most pronounced in the areas of identity politics and socio-cultural policy. This pertains first and foremost to issue areas such as European integration, immigration, asylum and Islam. Related to these issues, we also notice important policy influences in other areas such as education, security and crime, as well as social and economic policy where socio-cultural and identity-related aspects play a role. It is here that the FPÖ is able to frame the discourse in its favour and that other political actors concede credibility to the Freedom Party.

THE FPÖ'S DIRECT POLICY IMPACT IN THE CURRENT GOVERNMENT

When the FPÖ reentered government in 2017 it was arguably in the best position in its history to shape national policy-making. Compared to 2000, the party was now far better prepared, its leadership is much broader and the party is significantly more cohesive. The 2017 election results provided the FPÖ with a comfortable and close third-place finish, which allowed it to claim half of the ministerial portfolios and also corresponding programmatic influence. Importantly, the election victory by ÖVP leader Kurz was based on appropriating large parts of the FPÖ's socio-cultural agenda and as such the Freedom Party can justly claim to have a mandate to move public policy in the direction of their agenda. The FPÖ was also very successful in claiming for itself all the high-profile portfolios that matter especially to Freedom Party supporters such as Ministry of the Interior, the Ministry of Social Affairs, the Ministry of Defense and the Foreign Ministry. We may therefore expect the FPÖ to have a significant direct policy impact despite the fact that formally all policies are subject to the coalition agreement between ÖVP and FPÖ and require unanimity in the Council of Ministers (the cabinet).

If we group the policy claims made in FPÖ election manifesto by policy dimension, we notice in table 8.2 that by far the dominant area was immigration with 24 per cent all claims (defined as quasi-sentences stating a policy preference). Other policy areas that received significant attention were the environment, public safety and not surprisingly sovereignty.

While it appears that, apart from immigration, the election manifesto of Freedom Party is conceptually broad in its policy priorities, table 8.3 reveals that populist, sovereignist and socio-cultural demands in fact permeate also

Table 8.2.   FPÖ claims by policy area in the 2017 election manifesto

FPÖ claims and policy area by frequency	
Immigration	24%
Environment (incl. water/opposition to nuclear power)	14.6%
Social Policy/Welfare State	12.1%
Public Safety (incl. policing/law enforcement)	12.1%
Sovereignty (reclaiming authority)	12.1%
Euro-Zone/Economy	9.7%
Education	9.7%

Source: 2017 FPÖ election manifesto. Claims are individual quasi sentences coded as expressing or referring to a policy preference.

Source: Own elaboration on literature quoted in the present chapter.

the other policy areas. For example, environmental policy includes claims against 'selling out' Austrian water resources, thus reflecting a nativist and identitarian understanding of collective resources. Also the area of welfare policy includes measures having to do with curtailing work-related social benefits to labourers (including from the EU) from countries with lower levels of income if their families stay behind in the home country. Although the government fully expects this and other policy question[1] to be found in violation of EU law by the European Court of Justice, the government seems to welcome this opportunity to show that it is standing up for nativist interests.

Table 8.3 provides a detailed overview of the policy claims that both FPÖ and ÖVP made in their manifestos and summarizes the respective policy actions taken by the ÖVP–FPÖ government since it took office in December 2017. Essentially, we may divide the policy role of the FPÖ into three parts. First, it plays the role of a *policy enabler* and willing supporter such as in areas of social insurance reform, labour flexibilization and business deregulation. As these policies were vehemently opposed by organized labour, they would have been opposed by the SPÖ in any previous governments. While the initiative for these reforms was largely taken by the ÖVP, and here especially the business wing of the party, the FPÖ's support was critical and quite consistent with the role the Freedom Party played in this regard when it was in government from 2000 to 2005.

Second, the FPÖ acts as a *policy intensifier*. This concerns areas like immigration and border security, which were shared concerns of FPÖ and ÖVP. However, it can be argued that FPÖ help push policies further to the extreme. This either happened outright or Conservative hardliners were able to overcome internal resistance by moderates by pointing to the pressure from Freedom Party. An example is the government's decision to make asylum seekers waiting for their cases to be decided suddenly ineligible for apprenticeships despite the fact that they often wait for years and that are sever labour

Table 8.3. ÖVP and FPÖ claims by policy area in the 2017 election manifesto

Policy Field	ÖVP	FPÖ	Policy action taken 2017–2018
Immigration	• Severely curtail immigration, selectivity, more national autonomy, differential treatment, safety first	• Stop immigration, counteract illegal activities, replace European HR convention with 'Austrian HR convention'	• New restrictions of asylum laws (tightening quotas, quicker deportation, cuts in benefits, relaxation of protective custody rules) • Austria opted not to sign UN immigration pact at the behest of FPÖ
Sovereignty/euro	• Protect cash in circulation, force ECB to raise interest rates, expand national say in currency matters	• Protect cash in circulation • Need for higher interest rates, pull out of mutual bailout mechanism	No action taken
Culture/tradition/values	• Protect and revive Austrian culture, opposes 'false' tolerance vis-a-vis religion • Zero-tolerance against political Islam • Prevent parallel societies from emerging	• Strengthen identity through promoting local customs and traditions.	• Banning headscarves in kindergarten and schools for pupils up to ten years of age. • FPÖ proposal on whether teachers should be restricted from wearing headscarf
Direct democracy	• Strengthen voluntarism, more direct democracy, more citizen initiatives/referenda • Expand preferential voting	• Direct democracy following the Swiss model • Enable blocking referenda against legislations	• FPÖ demanded that 640,000 signatures on a ballot initiative trigger an automatic plebiscite; the compromise reached with ÖVP as it obtained 900,000 signatures
Public safety/order	• More effective policing, more competences/means, stricter punishment, more effective European border security	• Increase police corps, stricter border controls against illegal immigrants and 'crime tourism' • Increase defense expenditures	• Extension and expansion of border control through FPÖ-led Ministry of Interior • Exercises by security forces simulating border crisis. New protective custody rules for asylum seekers

(Continued)

Table 8.3. (Continued)

Policy Field	ÖVP	FPÖ	Policy action taken 2017–2018
Youth/ schooling	• Extra year of kindergarten for students with insufficient German language skills • Special German class for kids with inadequate German	• Restrictive admission of foreigners to school classes to protect Austrian students, good German skills are required for Austrian school attendance	• Move immigrant children with poor German language skills into special classes • Proposal to mandate German in schoolyards during breaks
Labour/ Social policies	• For foreigners, access to work-related social benefits after five years of work • Remittances of family benefits for foreign workers (including from the EU) to be proportional to cost of living in receiving country	• Sector-wide closures of labour market to foreigners • Access to labour-related benefits only after five years	• Ending practices of making vocational training available to asylum seekers awaiting a ruling about their stay • Reducing child benefits for EU labour where children reside abroad
Environment	• Focus more strongly on energy independence and renewables	• No sell-out of Austrian water resources, reliance on Austrian energy sources	No action taken
Economy		• No more competences to be transferred to the EU, CETA, TTIP never to be enacted contrary to national sovereignty.	• Regular calls for ending (EU) economic sanctions with Russia • Reducing NGO and third party access to speed up infrastructure projects
European Union	• New subsidiarity agreement with Europe • directly election of European Commission President • Oppose Turkish accession	• Greater sovereignty, secure external borders, stop uncontrolled immigration, exit ESM-EFSF-vehicles • Oppose Turkish accession and any payments going to Turkey	• Supports expanding external border control. Closing down migration routes. Repatriation agreements with Africans states. Holding facilities for asylum seekers in North Africa • Opposition to Turkish accession

Source: Own elaboration on literature quoted in the present chapter.

shortages. This policy decision was criticized by businesses groups affiliated with the ÖVP and numerous Christian Conservative politicians outside the government.[2]

Third, the FPÖ acts as *a policy instigator* on issues where the ÖVP would probably not have moved at all. This concerns, for example, the decision by the Austrian government not to sign the UN immigration pact,[3] or the proposal to award Austrian citizenship to German-speaking minority living in the Italian province of South Tirol.[4]

As was to be expected, the government acted most noticeably in the area of immigration and identity politics. The FPÖ argued for a general closure of Islamic kindergartens and to further amendment of the Islam Act. In response, the ÖVP presented its own list of measures that can only be described as anti-Islamic (Hafez and Heinisch, 2018). The goal is clearly to regulate Muslim life even further (Hafez, 2017c). This includes new legislation declaring the hijab in kindergartens (Hafez, 2018b) and elementary schools (for girls up to 10 years of age) illegal as well as banning symbols of what the government terms 'political Islam', which much more threatens Muslim civil society (Hafez, 2018c; Hafez, 2018d). This was not the case from 2000 to 2005 when the FPÖ seemed to have been constrained by the ÖVP because the latter attempted to highlight its good relations with Austria's Muslims. This was intended to position the party as non-racist at a time when it was under an international microscope after fourteen EU governments had decided to boycott the Conservative-Freedom Party government in Vienna (Hafez, 2010b).

In social and economic terms, scholars see a general trend towards neoliberalism in the FPÖ's programme and policy proposal despite the party's rhetoric to protect Austria from foreign economic interests and the EU's pro-market policies. Empirical longitudinal studies of Austrian party manifestos show neoliberal positions to be especially pronounced in ÖVP and FPÖ programs (Grimm, 2018, 144–149). However, as the Freedom Party often lacked the know-how and qualified policy experts in social and economic policy matters, its influence was traditionally limited (Heinisch, 2003; Hecking and Marchart, 2016). Learning from past mistakes, the FPÖ prepared before 2017 a 150-page economic program defining twenty-four economic goals. Its programme included proposals that would provide the basis for collaboration with either the SPÖ or the ÖVP. However, on balance, it was clear that a coalition with the People's Party would be the better match. For example, cutting the top income tax rate to 40 per cent, abolishing automatic income tax progression and eliminating taxes on inheritance, property and machinery would clearly be favoured by the ÖVP but opposed by the SPÖ (Lampl, 2017). Since being in power, it seems that the FPÖ and ÖVP have implemented a business-friendly agenda including tax cuts and introducing a measure that allows employees to work voluntarily for up to twelve instead of eight hours per day. This measure was rather controversial and met with resistance by organized labour, which was excluded from the drafting process of the legislation. Other measures resulted in a reduction in the guaranteed minimum income and eliminating a national programme assisting unemployed people older than fifty years.

With respect to European integration, the government's direction is not fully clear yet. The portfolio was taken away from the FPÖ-run Ministry of Foreign Affairs and attached to the ÖVP controlled chancellery. Despite remarks rather critical of the EU by Kurz and Strache during the campaign, the rhetoric has been rather muted thus far. In part this is clearly owed to the fact that Austria has the EU presidency in the second semester of 2018. Thus, it has to play special role and is dependent on the goodwill of other countries and the European Commission if it does not want its presidency to be a visible failure. Moreover, being in the presidency also provides the Austrian government with the opportunity to push for immigration restrictions and an external border security regime that is dear to many ÖVP and FPÖ voters. Moreover, several of the areas where Austria, as mentioned earlier, is possibly in violation of EU law are likely to be decided only in the intermediate future. Should the government wish to recast itself as a defender of Austrian national interest against overbearing European institution, then that would present a far better opportunity for a more euro-sceptical direction than the current situation. Lastly, the current and possibly future EU is likely to include countries dominated by RRPP parties that could serve as allies on the European level. For now, the government has made it quite clear that in immigration and identity it prefers the policies of Central European Visegrad states and Italy to that of Merkel's Germany. Both ÖVP Chancellor Kurz and especially the FPÖ have been pushing for closer relations with Russia. In fact, Austria has been steady critic of the West's sanctions regime against Moscow for its annexation of the Crimea.

We may conclude that the policies in which the FPÖ had the biggest impact all relate to immigration, national sovereignty and identity. This concerns these issues themselves but extends to other policy dimensions such as education, religion and social policy. In the area of economic policy, the FPÖ threw its support behind the pro-business reforms of the ÖVP and in doing so moved further to the right economically. In terms of foreign policy, the FPÖ has taken a back seat to Chancellor Kurz but has several party political allies in other European countries to ensure a significant measure of influence. Its arguably biggest coup was to prevent the government from signing the UN Migration Pact, which, in turn, induced other European countries to follow suit and prompted a debate even in Germany where the local far right is pointing to the Freedom Party as an example. Overall, the FPÖ is politically better prepared than in 2000 and the government is more cohesive and better at controlling the message. Despite this, there have been a series of gaffs and embarrassing scandals that frequently required the coalition partner to come to the rescue.

CONCLUSION

We started out by looking at the policy impact of the RRPP Freedom Party. We can confirm research conducted by Bale that showed that center-right parties and the far right converge on policy in the areas of immigration and culture (Bale, 2003). These issues have been the FPÖ's most consistent policy input dating back to the early days of Haider. The cultural 'other' is the central problem to be regulated, banned, or reeducated. Whereas the cultural others used to be an autochthonous Slavic minority such as the Slovenes in the Southern province of Carinthia, or Turkish and former Yugoslav guest workers in the 1990s or, more recently, asylum seekers, Muslims and workers from neighbouring EU countries, the agenda remains the same by claiming to preserve the nativist vision of culture, order and lifestyle. Ancillary are the issues of security and sovereignty. The research has also shown that the FPÖ has impacted policy-making long before it entered government at the regional and national level by acting as an agenda-setter and shaping the public discourse through provocative framing. Over time, mainstream parties are taking up both the policy positions and in part the rhetoric, thereby legitimating claims that had previously be denounced as too radical.

Our research has also shown that in a structured relationship between a RRPP party and a Conservative mainstream party, the former impact policy-making be acting as enablers, intensifiers and instigators. As such the influence of a party like the Freedom Party exceeds the nativist agenda in distinct core areas and permeates a wide range of policies. Lastly, we also need to bear in mind that the impact of the Freedom Party on policy formation extends beyond its specific policy proposals and capacity to shape legislation. Since the 1990s the FPÖ has been a potent force in state and regional politics by being part of coalition governments or in one case even occupying the governorship for over a decade. These regionals settings serve as a venue for launching policy initiatives and test the public acceptance of policy measures, which are then proposed nationally. Moreover, the Freedom Party has also functioned as an important agenda-setter and framer of political debate. In doing so, it has moved the public position significantly to the right and thus affected the policy positions of other parties that felt a need to make their own stance more restrictive. This was especially the case on immigration, the universal eligibility of social benefits, Islam, public safety and to some extent European integration. Within the constraints of this publication, we could not explore these other aspects and they need to await further research. One is forced to conclude nonetheless on the evidence presented that the policy impact of the Freedom Party has not only been profound and sustained but clearly extends beyond the time the FPÖ was in public office.

NOTES

1. In the policy area of cutting family allowances, see: Der Standard. 2018. Familienbeihilfe: Warnungen vor EU-rechtswidriger Kürzung. *Der Standard*, 16 February 2018. https://derstandard.at/2000074401786/Familienbeihilfe-Warnungen-vor-EU-rechtswidriger-Kuerzung. In the area of restricting basic support payments for asylum seekers below minimal levels granted to Austrians, see: Der Standard. 2018. Mindestsicherung: Rotes Licht der EU zu Kürzung erwartet. *Der Standard*, 27 June 2018. https://derstandard.at/2000082374880/EU-soll-Mindestsicherung splaene-der-Regierung-skeptisch-sehen.

2. Kleine Zeitung. 2018. Viele greifen sich an den Kopf. *Kleine Zeitung*, 16 August 2018. https://www.kleinezeitung.at/politik/innenpolitik/5486218/Aus-fuer-Lehre-fuer-Asylwerber_Viele-greifen-sich-an-den-Kopf.

3. Der Standard. 2018. UN-Migrationspakt wäre laut Strache 'Bruch der Regierungsvereinbarung'. *Der Standard*, 31 October 2018. https://derstandard.at/2000090424127/UNO-Migrationspakt-waere-laut-Strache-Bruch-der-Regierungsvereinbarung.

4. Kurier. 2018. Thema Doppelpässe: Das schwierige Südtirol-Engagement der FPÖ. *Kurier*, 16 October 2018. https://kurier.at/politik/inland/thema-doppelpaesse-das-schwierige-suedtirol-engagement-der-fpoe/400147046.

BIBLIOGRAPHY

Bauböck, Rainer, and Bernhard Perchinig. 2006. Migrations – und Integrationspolitik. In *Politik in Österreich: Das Handbuch*, edited by Herbert Dachs et al., 726–742. Vienna: Manz.

Dautovic, Rijad, and Farid Hafez. 2018. Institutionalising Islam in contemporary Austria: A comparative analysis of the Austrian Islam Act of 2015 and Austrian religion acts with special emphasis on the Israelite Act of 2012. *Oxford Journal of Law and Religion* 2018(0): 1–23.

Dolezal, Martin, et al. 2012. The life cycle of party manifestos: The Austrian case. *West European Politics* 35(4): 869–895.

Deutsche Welle. 2018. Austria to withdraw from UN migration treaty. *Deutsche Welle*, 31 October 2018. https://www.dw.com/en/austria-to-withdraw-from-un-migration-treaty/a-46097012.

Die Presse. 2016. OÖ-Landtag stimmt über Kürzung der Mindestsicherung ab. *Die Presse*, 16 June 2016.

Die Presse. 2017. Neue FPÖ-Plakate: 'Vordenker' Strache gegen 'Spätzünder'. *Die Presse*, 25 September 2017. https://diepresse.com/home/innenpolitik/national ratswahl/5291629/Neue-FPOePlakate_Vordenker-Strache-gegen-Spaetzuender-Kurz

Ennser-Jedenastik, Laurenz. 2016. A welfare state for whom? A group-based account of the Austrian Freedom Party's policy profile. *Swiss Political Science Review* 22(3): 409–27.

Ennser-Jedenastik, Laurenz. 2018. Welfare chauvinism in populist radical right platforms: The role of redistributive justice principles. *Social Policy and Administration* 52(1): 293–314.

Fallend, Franz. 2009. Austria. *European Journal of Political Research Political Data Yearbook* 48: 884–902.

Fallend, Franz, and Reinhard Heinisch. 2017. The impact of radical right parties on the austrian political system. In *Absorbing the Blow: Populist Parties and Their Impact on Parties and Party Systems*, edited by Zaslove, Andreij, and Steven Wolinetz, 27–54. Lanham: Rowman & Littlefield International.

FPÖ. 2015. *Landeswahlprogramm 2015* (Manifesto).

Frankfurter Allgemeine Zeitung. 2016. Weniger Geld für Flüchtlinge in Österreich. *Frankfurter Allgemeine Zeitung*, 6 June 2016.

Geden, Oliver. 2005. Identitätsdiskurs und politische Macht: Die rechtspopulistische Mobilisierung von Ethnozentrismus im Spannungsfeld von Opposition und Regierung am Beispiel von FPÖ und SVP. In *Populistenan der Macht. Populistische Regierungsparteien in West- und Osteuropa*, edited by Frölich-Steffen, Susanne, and Lars Rensmann, 69–83. Vienna: Braumüller Verlag.

Grimm, Christian. 2018. Wirtschaftspolitische Positionen österreichischer Parteien im historischen Verlauf. Die Ausgestaltung österreichischer Parteiprogrammatiken hinsichtlich neoliberalen Gedankenguts. *Momentum Quarterly – Zeitschrift für Sozialen Fortschritt* 7(3): 136–154.

Gruber, Oliver, and Astrid Mattes. 2015. 'Integration durch Leistung'. Zur kritischen Verortung eines neuen Narratives österreichischer Integrationspolitik. In *Minderheiten im Dilemma zwischen Selbstbestimmung, Integration und Segregation*, edited by Karin Schnebel: 89–116. Wiesbaden: Springer.

Hafez, Farid. 2010a. *Islamophober Populismus: Moschee-und Minarettbauverbote österreichischer Parlamentsparteien*. Wiesbaden: Springer VS.

Hafez, Farid. 2010b. Österreich und der Islam – eine Wende durch FPÖVP? Anmerkungen zur Rolle von Islamophobie im politischen Diskurs seit der Wende. In *Die beschämte Republik: Zehn Jahre nach Schwarz-Blau in Österreich*, edited by Baker, Frederick and Petra Herczeg, 130–141. Vienna: Czernin Verlag.

Hafez, Farid. 2014. Shifting borders: Islamophobia as the cornerstone for building pan-European right-wing unity. *Patterns of Prejudice* 48(5): 479–499.

Hafez, Farid. 2017a. Debating the 2015 Islam law in Austrian parliament: Between legal recognition and islamophobic populism. *Discourse and Society* 28(4): 392–412.

Hafez, Farid. 2017b. Islamophobia in Austria. National Report 2017. In *European Islamophobia Report 2017*, edited by Bayraklı, Enes, and Farid Hafez, 49–83. Ankara: SETA.

Hafez, Farid. 2017c. Austria's new programme for government. En route to a restrictive policy on Islam? *Quantara*, 21 December 2017. https://en.qantara.de/content/austrias-new-programme-for-government-en-route-to-a-restrictive-policy-on-islam.

Hafez, Farid. 2018a. Alte neue Islampolitik in Österreich? Eine postkoloniale Analyse der österreichischen Islampolitik. *ZfP – Zeitschrift für Politik* 65(1): 22–44.

Hafez, Farid. 2018b. Austrian McCarthyism: Banning symbols. *Anadolu Agency*, 18 October 2018. https://www.aa.com.tr/en/analysis-news/analysis-austrian-mccarthyism-banning-symbols/1285083.

Hafez, Farid. 2018c. Banning symbols of extremism in Austria: Targeting extremism or civil society? *SETA Perspective* 49 (December 2018). https://setav.org/en/assets/uploads/2018/12/49_Perspective.pdf.

Hafez, Farid. 2018d. Muslim civil society under attack: The European Foundation for Democracy's role in defaming and delegitimizing Muslim civil society. In *Islamophobia and Radicalization: Breeding Intolerance and Violence*, edited by Derya, Iner, and John Esposito, 117–137. Basingstoke: Palgrave.

Hafez, Farid, and Reinhard Heinisch. 2018. Breaking with Austrian consociationalism: How the rise of rightwing populism and party competition have changed Austria's Islam politics. *Politics and Religion* 11(3): 649–678.

Heinisch, Reinhard. 2003. Success in opposition – failure in government: Explaining the performance of right-wing populist parties in public office. *West European Politics* 26(3): 91–130.

Heinisch, Reinhard. 2002. *Populism, Proporz and Pariah – Austria Turns Right: Austrian Political Change, Its Causes and Repercussion.* New York: Nova Science Publishing.

Heinisch, Reinhard, Duncan McDonnell, and Annika Werner. 2017. Equivocal euroscepticism: How some radical right parties play between 'reform' and 'rejection' lines. Paper prepared for the European Union Studies Association Conference, Miami, USA, 4–6 May 2017.

Heinisch, Reinhard, Annika Werner, and Fabian Habersack. 2019. Reclaiming national sovereignty: the case of the conservatives and the far right in Austria, European Politics and Society, first online: 24 Jun 2019 – DOI: 10.1080/23745118.2019.1632577

Hecking, Claus, and Jan Michael Marchart. 2016. Dagegen sein ist alles. *Die Zeit*, 19 May 2016. https://www.zeit.de/2016/22/fpoe-oesterreich-norbert-hofer-wirtschaft/komplettansicht.

Hellmuth, Thomas. 2002. 'Patchwork' der Identitäten. Ideologische Grundlagen und politische Praxis des Populismus in Frankreich und Österreich. In *Populismus: Ideologie und Praxis in Frankreich und Österreich, Studien zur Gesellschafts- und Kulturgeschichte*, Vol. 12, edited by Gabriella Hauch, Thomas Hellmuth, and Peter Gutschner, 9–43. Vienna/Innsbruck: Studien Verlag.

Krzyzanowski, Michal, and Ruth Wodak. 2009. *The Politics of Exclusion. Debating Migration in Austria. Transaction Publishers.* New Brunswick, NJ: Transaction Publishers.

Lampl, Andreas. 2017. Wirtschaft durch die blaue Brille – das FPÖ-Programm. *TREND*, 19 May 2017. https://www.trend.at/politik/fpoe-wirtschaftsprogramm-neuwahlen-8152689.

Loxbo, Karl. 2014. Voters' perceptions of policy convergence and the short-term opportunities of anti-immigrant parties: Examples from Sweden. *Scandinavian Political Studies* 37(3): 239–262.

Luther, Kurt Richard. 1995. Zwischen unkritischer Selbstdarstellung und bedingungsloser externer Verurteilung: Nazivergangenheit, Anti-Semitismus und Holocaust im Schrifttum der Freiheitlichen Partei Österreichs. In *Schwieriges Erbe. Der Umgang mit Nationalsozialismus und Antisemitismus in Österreich, der DDR und der Bundesrepublik Deutschland*, edited by Werner Bergmann, Rainer Erb, and Albert Lichtblau, 138–167. Frankfurt: Campus Verlag.

Luther, Kurt Richard. 2003. The self-destruction of a right-wing populist party? The Austrian parliamentary election of 2002. *West European Politics*, 26(2): 107–121.

McGann, Anthony, and Herbert Kitschelt. 2005. The radical right in the Alps: Evolution of support for the Swiss SVP and Austrian FPÖ. *Party Politics* 11: 147–71.

Mudde, Cas. 2013. Three decades of populist radical right parties in Western Europe: So what? *European Journal of Political Research* 52(1): 1–19.

Müller, Wolfgang, and Franz Fallend. 2004. Changing patterns of party competition in Austria: From multipolar to bipolar system. *West European Politics* 27(5): 801–835.

Mondon, Aurélien. 2016. *The Mainstreaming of the Extreme Right in France and Australia: A Populist Hegemony?* London: Routledge.

Pytlas, Bartek. 2015. *Radical Right Parties in Central and Eastern Europe: Mainstream Party Competition and Electoral Fortune. Extremism and Democracy.* London: Routledge.

Rosenberger, Sieglinde. 2013. Das Staatssekretariat für Integration. Von der 'Integration durch Leistung' zur ‚Vorintegration'. In *Gaismair-Jahrbuch 2014*, edited by Elisabeth Hussl, Lisa Gensluckner, Martin Haselwanter, Monika Jarosch, and Horst Schreiber, 59–66. Bozen, Innsbruck, Vienna: Studienverlag.

Rovny, Jan. 2012. Who emphasizes and who blurs? Party strategies in multidimensional competition. *European Union Politics* 13(2): 269–292.

Schultheis, Emily. 2017. A new right-wing movement rises in Austria. *The Atlantic*, 16 October 2017. https://www.theatlantic.com/international/archive/2017/10/austria-immigration-sebastian-kurz/542964/

Sedlak, Maria. 2000. You really do make an unrespectable foreign policy . . . Discourse on ethnic issues in the Austrian parliament. In *Racism at the Top: Parliamentary Discourses on Ethnic Issues in six European States*, edited by Ruth Wodak and Teun Van Dijk: 107–168. Klagenfurt: Drava-Verlag.

SORA/ISA. (2015a). Wahlanalyse Landtagswahl Oberösterreich.

SORA/ISA. (2015b). Wahlanalyse Landtagswahl Burgenland.

Spies, Dennis, and Simon Franzmann. 2011. A two-dimensional approach to the political opportunity structure of extreme right parties in Western Europe. *West European Politics* 34(5): 1044–1069.

Treib, Oliver. 2014. The voter says no, but nobody listens: Causes and consequences of the Eurosceptic vote in the 2014 European elections. *Journal of European Public Policy* 21(10): 1541–1554.

Van Spanje, Joost, and Nan Dirk de Graaf. 2017. How established parties reduce other parties' electoral support: The strategy of parroting the pariah. *West European Politics* 41(1): 1–27.

Van Spanje, Joost, and Wouter Van Der Brug. 2007. The party as pariah: The exclusion of anti-immigration parties and its effect on their ideological positions. *West European Politics* 30(5): 1022–1040.

Williams, Michelle Hale. 2006. *The Impact of Radical Right-Wing Parties in West European Democracies*. New York: Palgrave MacMillan.

Wodak, Ruth, and Anton Pelinka. 2003. *Dreck am Stecken – Politik der Ausgrenzung*. Vienna: Czernin Verlag.

Wodak, Ruth, and Teun van Dijk. 2000. *Racism at the Top: Parliamentary Discourses on Ethnic Issues in Six European States*. Klagenfurt: Drava-Verlag.

Chapter 9

Populism and Democracy

The Best Foes? A Comparison of the Policy Influence of Radical Right Populist Parties in Switzerland, France and Belgium

Benjamin Biard

Radical right populist parties (RRPPs) are on the rise in many countries in Western Europe. Defined as political parties that cultivate a populist communication style (Jagers and Walgrave, 2007) and an ideology based on nativism and authoritarianism (Mudde, 2007), these parties are often considered as a threat to the quality of democracy, mainly regarding their rejection of the liberal principles of democracy (Albertazzi and Mueller, 2013; Urbinati, 2014). As a reaction, mainstream parties have traditionally adopted measures aiming at ostracizing RRPPs, for instance by adopting a *cordon sanitaire* or by demonizing them (Capoccia, 2001; Heinze, 2018).

Despite the adoption of such measures, RRPPs are often considered as political actors that theoretically influence policy-making, mainly regarding immigration and law and order issues (e.g. Mudde, 2007). Better understanding the policy influence of RRPPs allows for better apprehension of the role of RRPPs in democracy and the real threat they might represent. This thus raises the following research question: what influence do RRPPs exercise on policy-making and how? By answering that question, this chapter aims at contributing to the literature on populism but also to the 'do parties matter' literature.

Using the process-tracing method, this study provides an analysis of RRPPs' policy influence by closely looking at the policy-making processes in Switzerland, France and Belgium on the issue of 'foreigners' criminality'. These cases are analysed and compared since they have different relationships with power. It thus allows for assessing the influence of RRPPs in different settings. The issue of 'foreigners' criminality' is particularly relevant since both criminality and nativism are RRPP cornerstones (Mudde, 2007), and because parties mostly try to influence their 'own' issues (Walgrave et al., 2012). In addition, foreigners' criminality has been highly debated in many countries during the last decade, notably in a context characterized by terrorism. Focusing on that issue thus makes sense both from a scientific and a societal point of view.

The chapter proceeds as follows: First, it sets the theoretical and analytical frameworks by reviewing the literature on RRPP policy influence, and by defining and characterizing the notion of influence. Using the process-tracing method, the data – collected through 104 interviews, archival research and direct observations – and the cases are discussed in the second section. The three following sections present the empirical analysis for each case. The causal mechanisms representing the translation of each RRPP's pledge into a decision are summarized in a table at the end of each section. This provides an easier way to map and understand where and how RRPPs exercise their influence. Eventually, the three cases are compared and discussed, and several concluding lessons are drawn.

RADICAL RIGHT POPULIST PARTIES
AND INFLUENCE: THEORETICAL
AND ANALYTICAL FRAMEWORKS

Theoretical Framework

The 'do parties matter' literature has extensively analysed the policy influence exercised by mainstream political parties based on three different approaches: the study of the evolution of electoral pledges, the study of the correspondence between the issues defended by RRPPs and policy agendas, and the study of the effects of a government change (Guinaudeau and Persico, 2018). Studies mobilizing one of these approaches mostly indicate that political parties matter and can influence policy-making, even if their influence may vary in intensity. For instance, Pétry (2012) analyses the implementation of parties' electoral pledges and conclude that they matter since the majority of their pledges are implemented.

Yet, despite this attention paid to the policy influence of mainstream parties and despite the great attention paid to various aspects of RRPPs in the literature (Rovira Kaltwasser et al., 2017), the policy influence of RRPPs on policy-making has barely been investigated. The first studies dealing with the policy influence of RRPPs were conducted in the early 2000s and specifically focused on RRPPs in power. Minkenberg (2001) and Zaslove (2004), as well as others after them (e.g. Albertazzi and McDonnell, 2015), have indeed compared RRPPs in power and found that the legislation regarding immigration and asylum issues evolves and becomes more restrictive when RRPPs are in government. According to them, RRPPs are not only able to shape coalition agreements but also the content of reforms.

Research has also pointed out that the policy influence of RRPPs, even when it is verified, can be severely limited (Minkenberg, 2001; Williams, 2006; Carvalho, 2014; Afonso and Papadopoulos, 2015). For instance, Akkerman and de Lange (2012) have shown that even when legislation becomes more restrictive while RRPPs are in power, the changes are initiated by mainstream parties and not by RRPPs. Other scholars have gone further, suggesting that the policy influence of RRPPs is so limited that these parties cannot be called influential, may they be in power or not (e.g. Howard, 2010; Akkerman and de Lange, 2012).

In order to better understand this disagreement between scholars, the notion of influence should be unpacked. Two types of influence can indeed be distinguished: direct and indirect influence (Schain, 2006). Direct influence occurs when they directly contribute to shaping public policies; indirect when, even if not in power, RRPPs exercise influence by exerting pressure on other parties. The process-tracing method allows for detecting which kind of influence is exercised since it rebuilds causal mechanisms.

Analytical Framework

The notion of influence is widely discussed in political science, but many different definitions and ways to operationalize it have been proposed. The definition proposed by Arts and Verschuren (1999, 413) – and according to which 'the achievement of (a part of) an actor's goal in political decision-making, which is either caused by one's own intervention or by the decision-makers' anticipation' – has been widely used by researchers interested in the policy influence of interest groups (e.g. Arts, 2000; Betsill and Corell, 2001; Coolsaet and Pitseys, 2015). This definition is used in this research since it offers the advantage of going beyond the interactionist approach, focusing on the influence of RRPPs on the policy-making process rather than on the behaviour of other actors intervening in the process.

Because the notion of influence is complex, assessing influence is also particularly difficult. One single study cannot pretend to assess each dimension of influence and several approaches may be used to assess one's influence (*cf. supra*). In this chapter, RRPPs' influence is assessed based on their electoral pledges, by tracing the trajectories of those pledges and finding critical sequences in the policy-making process where RRPPs intervened with the effect of translating them into decisions. Studying this specific dimension of RRPPs' influence is original but also relevant in several respects: First, political parties aim to translate their electoral pledges into decisions through policy-making (Thomson et al., 2017). Translating their electoral pledges may be a goal per se, but it is also a way to gain votes or offices (Strom, 1990). Second, political parties own some issues. This means they grant more attention to particular issues. Immigration and law and order are two issues owned by RRPPs. Therefore, the electoral pledges they make regarding these issues are first and foremost defended by RRPPs (Mansergh and Thomson, 2007). Operationalizing the notion of influence via the translation of electoral pledges into decisions is thus also relevant in that regard. Third, some studies have focused on the extent to which decisions are coloured 'radical right' (e.g. Bouillaud, 2007). These tend to observe if penal or immigration policy become more restrictive when RRPPs are in power. If these studies bring interesting insights to the literature, it is by assessing the influence of radical right ideology more than the influence of RRPPs themselves. Because several RRPPs can coexist in the same country (as in Switzerland, for instance), the approach of examining electoral pledges allows us to better distinguish which party exercises such influence. Finally, focusing on electoral pledges is a good way to study the whole policy-making process.

Therefore, for the purposes of this study, the notion of influence is operationalized as follows: influence can be detected when RRPPs intervene through an action (any kind of action) during a sequence in the policy-making process, and provoke a new sequence, in order to translate a pledge into decision. For instance, that action may be writing a law proposal, and the consequence may be obtaining the support from other parties. Both intervention during a sequence and the fact it provokes a new sequence in the process towards the adoption of the pledge are thus necessary conditions for recognizing whether a RRPP exercises influence during the policy-making process.

The distinction made in the literature between direct and indirect forms of influence (Schain, 2006) is taken into account in this research in order to increase the accuracy of the analysis. This distinction helps us to better understand to what extent other actors contribute to RRPPs' influence, and to what extent RRPPs are autonomous in the exercise of their influence. Empirically, a direct influence is found when RRPPs provoke a new sequence without an intermediary; an indirect influence is found when RRPPs provoke a new sequence in the process through other actors – for instance by putting pressure on mainstream parties.

CASES AND METHOD

This chapter focuses on the influence exercised by the Swiss Schweizerische Volkspartei (SVP),[1] the French Front national (FN)[2] and the Belgian Vlaams Belang (VB)[3] on policy-making in their respective countries. This selection comes with the different relationships that these parties have to power. The three cases are characterized by important differences: the Belgian VB has faced a strong *cordon sanitaire* since 1989 and has never exercised power, the Swiss SVP is fully integrated into the political landscape and exercised executive power since its foundation, and the French FN does not suffer from a formal *cordon sanitaire* but is rejected from executive power at the national level by way of an informal *cordon sanitaire* in combination with a majoritarian electoral system (Carter, 2005).

The process-tracing method is one of the most accurate tools for apprehending political actors' influence since it helps to go beyond a mere correlation by identifying causal mechanisms. Figure 9.1 theoretically illustrates such mechanisms.

Causal mechanisms are 'ultimately unobservable physical, social, or psychological processes through which agents with causal capacities operate, but only in specific contexts or conditions, to transfer energy, information, or matter to other entities. In so doing, the causal agent changes the affected entities' characteristics, capacities, or propensities in ways that persist until subsequent causal mechanisms act upon it'. (George and Bennet, 2005, 137)

Three data collection methods are used to triangulate the data, and to gather strong evidence about the sequences of the causal mechanisms: 104 interviews were conducted in French, Dutch and English in Switzerland, France and Belgium (with actors participating in the policy-making process, first based on a selection of policy-makers and party leaders, then based on the snowball method),[4] direct observations were realized (of events organized by RRPPs in each of the three countries) and archival research was done (manifestos, law proposals, minutes in the parliament, roll-cast votes, etc.). Each of these data collection methods are necessary for rebuilding causal mechanisms. For instance, while the minutes in the parliament provide information about the process in the parliament, interviews also provide information about the pressure MPs might have experienced. Direct observations also contribute to rebuild causal mechanisms, for instance by providing information about the atmosphere of an event that can be considered as a sequence of the process. The process-tracing method is designed to rebuild causal mechanisms in order to understand to what extent and how pledges made by RRPPs

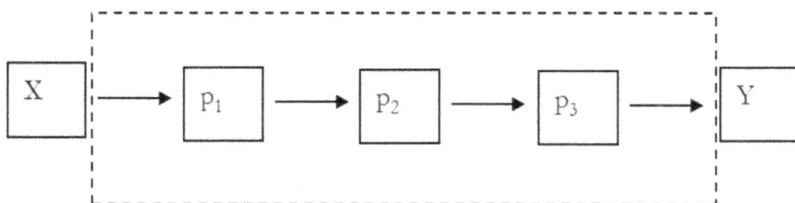

Figure 9.1.   Causal mechanism.
(adapted from Beach & Pedersen, 2013)

are developed in the policy-making process. Therefore, it becomes possible to precisely know if, when, how and to what extent RRPPs intervene in the process and, thus, exercise influence on the policy-making process.

The evidence can be considered as empirical fingerprints of the influence of RRPPs in the policy-making process. Of course, some evidence has a stronger inferential weight than others, and these differences are taken into account in the analysis, notably by distinguishing direct from indirect forms of influence. This results from the fact it can be more difficult to shed light on some sequences of a causal mechanism than others.

Assessing one's influence through this method leads to reconsidering the notion of influence. Indeed, an actor is not 'influential or not', but can exercise various forms of influence at various points of a policy-making process. It is thus important to cut these processes into a set of necessary sequences. In figure 9.1, for instance, a RRPP could be considered as an influential actor if it intervenes in P2 (i.e. the second part – or sequence – of the causal mechanism) by developing a specific action and, therefore, provoking P3 (i.e. the third part – or sequence – of the causal mechanism). Some RRPPs could also act on the next sequences or not. This results from the fact that a wide variety of actors intervene in every policy-making process (Birkland, 2005). In addition, influence is not exclusive. Even if the focus of this chapter is to grasp the influence exercised by RRPPs, other actors may also influence the same sequence of a process.

Three steps are necessary for the analysis: First, one should find 'where are the pledges'. This means the development of pledges should be traced in order to know if pledges on 'foreigners' criminality' were cultivated and, if so, to what extent. Second, if pledges have been developed (even if they are not decisions *per se*), the black boxes of the policy-making processes should be opened in order to precisely know if, where, when, and how RRPPs intervene in the process. Specific attention is given to other actors (other parties and civil society actors, but also institutional actors, such as the Department of Justice), the social context and institutional specificities. Yet, the aim of this research is to better apprehend the influence exercised by RRPPs and not other actors. Therefore, the figures illustrating the processes will mostly focus on sequences where RRPPs intervene. In order to be recognized as exercising an influence on the policy-making process, they should intervene at some point by provoking – alone or not – a new sequence in the process. This means their action should be followed by another action made by themselves or by another actor. Finally, the obstacles RRPPs face in their effort to be influential should be summarized in order to provide a typology of obstacles, and to get a fine-grained understanding of RRPPs' influence.

The pledges under scrutiny (cf. bellow), as units of analysis, are selected in the same time frame, that is, between 2010 and 2018. The pledges are thus recent enough in order to tackle such a current phenomenon, but also old enough in order to offer enough hindsight for the analysis. They are collected based on two criteria suggested by Royed (1996): their testability and their clarity. These pledges are thus clearly defined party commitments – that is, clear statements of policy positions whose fulfilment can be assessed, not general statements. Based on these criteria, eight pledges are analysed in this study. The SVP pledges come from its 2011 manifesto, the FN pledges come from its 2012 manifesto and the VB pledges come from its 2010 manifesto. In 2011, the SVP held 54 out of 200 MPs; in 2012 the FN held 2 out of 577 MPs; in 2010, the VB held 12 out of 150 MPs.

SVP pledges:

The SVP wants to revoke Swiss nationality from persons having dual nationality who have committed a serious crime. (2011 manifesto, p. 58)
The SVP wants to arrange a trial period for naturalization in order to have the possibility of revoking Swiss citizenship from any naturalized citizen who became an offender. (2011 manifesto, p. 58)
The SVP pledges to expel criminal foreigners. (2011 manifesto, p. 45)

FN pledges:

The FN promises to expel criminal foreigners to their country of origin. They should also serve their prison sentence in their country of origin. (2012 manifesto, p. 12, p. 16)
Racism against the French as a motivation for crime or offence will be considered as a particularly aggravating circumstance. The sentence will be tougher. (2012 manifesto, p. 12)
Deprivation of nationality should be pronounced [for those who have been naturalized for less than 10 years] in the case of a crime or offence leading to a sentence of more than 6 months imprisonment. (2012 manifesto, p. 6)

VB pledges:

We require statistics about criminality according to nationality of origin. (2010 manifesto, p. 11)
The VB wants to expel criminal foreigners and, when possible, to make them serve their prison sentence in their country of origin. (2010 manifesto, p. 16)

THE SWISS SVP AND FOREIGNERS' CRIMINALITY

The Swiss SVP only acted in the parliament on one of the three identified pledges, despite the fact that the Swiss SVP recognizes criminality among foreigners as a key party issue: 'One of our most important themes is foreigners' criminality. It is clear' (SVP MP, 2016a). When it comes to deprivation of nationality or a trial period for naturalization, no pledges have been developed around these themes since 2011. The SVP itself has been quite passive. The party only intervened once in the parliament in 2006, in order to propose the deprivation of nationality (parliamentary initiative n° 06.486), and once in 2010 in order to propose a trial period for naturalization (interpellation n° 10.3965), but both these proposals were quickly rejected by the other parties without parliamentary debate. If some party leaders recognized these pledges should be translated into decisions (SVP party official, 2016), some SVP members of the parliament do not remember these two pledges (SVP MP, 2016a; SVP MP, 2016b). No empirical fingerprint shows that the SVP exercised influence regarding these pledges.

The analysis is different regarding the pledge dealing with the expulsion of criminal foreigners. As a matter of fact, the SVP intervened many times in the parliament in order to translate this pledge into a decision. If these interventions sometimes provoked debates, other parties systematically rejected them. This rejection is justified on the basis that the proposal is 'radical' or 'extreme' (e.g. PDC[5] MP, 2015). Because the SVP could not manage to influence policy-making in the institutional arenas, it decided to launch a popular initiative in order to influence policy differently:

> The Federal Council and the majority of the parliament did not want [a law about the expulsion of criminal foreigners] and the SVP has used the popular initiative in order to force the decision. (SVP party official, 2016)

In Switzerland, popular initiatives are direct democracy tools that can be used to modify the federal constitution if the majority of the people and the majority of the cantons vote for an initiative. It is also a way of forcing other parties to take a stance. The majority of the parliament can indeed propose a counter-initiative to citizens. Even if the SVP was the only party to support its initiative, it was accepted on 28 November 2010. This has resulted in an amendment to the federal constitution (Article 121, § 2), stating that 'foreign nationals may be expelled from Switzerland if they pose a risk to the security of the country'.

This quick narrative is helpful in order to detect how a pledge becomes a decision or, in other words, who furnishes causal energy and at which stage of the policy-making process. The SVP managed to put the issue on the agenda via its parliamentary activity but for a very short period. In addition, its parliamentary interventions practically never provoked any debate or new sequence in the policy-making process. Therefore, the party tried to develop a different type of causal energy by addressing the question directly to the Swiss people. By mobilizing a direct, harsh and provocative communication style, the SVP managed to convince the people. This way, the SVP thus directly influenced the policy-making process as a whole.

Table 9.1. Causal mechanism explaining the translation of the SVP pledge relating to the expulsion of criminal foreigners

SVP electoral pledge	
SVP parliamentary interventions	
No effect	Effect
–	Short-term debate in the parliament
–	The texts are rejected in the parliament
Popular initiative by the SVP	
Other parties fight against the initiative and propose a counter-initiative	
The SVP uses an 'atypical' communication style in its campaign for the initiative	
The people adopt the initiative	
The pledge becomes a constitutional article	

> Sometimes it is useful to set the cat among the pigeons. It provokes a debate and you can discuss solutions. (SVP MP, 2015a)
> We are able to use simple words to talk about real problems that people face day-to-day. (SVP MP, 2016b)

Table 9.1 synthesizes how the SVP manages to translate its pledge into decision, by indicating which are the observed empirical fingerprints of its influence. Some of the causal energies do not directly lead to any new sequence. It is the case of some parliamentary interventions. Yet, others are crucial and can be observed based on the collected evidence.

THE FRENCH FN AND FOREIGNERS' CRIMINALITY

Three pledges are found in the 2012 FN manifesto regarding the issue of criminality among foreigners. According to FN party officials (e.g. FN party official, 2016), this has been a central issue for the party since its foundation.

As the SVP, the French FN also first tries to develop its electoral pledges through the parliamentary arena. Nevertheless, its weak representation in the parliament[6] makes it difficult for the FN to incite debate around one of its interventions. In addition, the popular initiative is a nonexistent tool in France. Therefore the FN has to act differently in order to develop its electoral pledges.

The FN considers the expulsion of criminal foreigners a priority (FN party official, 2016), and it is the only party to defend the issue over several decades. Moreover, this is verified through an analysis of the parties' manifestos. Yet, no empirical fingerprint can attest to the FN having any influence on the policy-making process. It has not even proposed a text in the parliament to defend it. The only evolution on the topic occurred before 2012, when Nicolas Sarkozy suppressed the 'double penalty', that is, the possibility to expel criminal foreigners from France. In that regard, the FN did not manage to avoid this decision in spite of its pledge.

The FN has also not deployed any causal energy to develop its pledge to increase sentences in the case of racism against the French. Again, no empirical fingerprint was detected during the analysis, neither from the FN nor from any other political actor. In addition, even if they agree with it in principle, several FN party officials and elected officials do not remember the pledge:

To Be Honest I Do Not Know That Proposal (FN parliamentary assistant, 2017)

While no causal energy was found for the two first pledges, this is not the case for the last one, which deals with deprivation of nationality. One law proposal was written by an FN Member of Parliament in 2016 (law proposal n° 4011), but it was not even put on the agenda of the National Assembly. Therefore the proposal did not provoke any new sequence in the policy-making process. Yet, the FN promoted the law proposal on social media in order to show that it addresses the issue, and to exert pressure on other political parties. Here, there is thus a trace of influence in spite of the weak inferential weight of the evidence. This is helpful for grasping the FN's influence since it means its influence was, at most, indirect in that moment.

The issue appeared at the forefront of the agenda in 2015, directly after the terrorist attacks in Paris on 13 November 2015. This context is crucial for understanding why the issue gained in saliency during that period. President Hollande recognized it himself:

It is not really in the substance of the text. You can or not agree with the deprivation of nationality. I am myself against that principle. But I did it because of the context and because it could have been an opportunity to bring people together. (François Hollande, in Davet and Lhomme, 2017, 433)

Quickly after the attacks, François Hollande met representatives from other parties at Versailles in order to find consensual solutions against terrorism. Deprivation of nationality was proposed during these meetings by the FN but also, and mostly, by the LR.[7] Nicolas Sarkozy – representative from the LR – made an agreement with François Hollande according to which the LR would support the President and his set of measures against terrorism if he agreed to include several specific measures, among which was deprivation of nationality (as explained by: LR MP, 2017; PS representative, 2016; PS MP, 2017). The FN also proposed this measure to the president (as explained by an FN party official, 2017), but its lack of representation in the parliament meant François Hollande's proposal to constitutionalize the deprivation of nationality could not be concluded. While empirical traces are found that support the conclusion that the LR exerted influence upstream of the policy-making process in that period, no empirical traces support the idea that the

FN had any influence. François Hollande himself identified the influential party as the LR:

> It was the only possibility to obtain the support from the right in order to modify the Constitution. It was tactic. If I had withdrawn the extension of the deprivation of nationality, it is clear the right would have never voted for the text. (François Hollande, in Davet and Lhomme, 2017, 722)

Soon after the President proposed to constitutionalize deprivation of nationality, the PS was divided. Many PS members of the National Assembly, but also PS members of the government declared that they were against the measure. In the parliament, and mostly in the Senate, the text was seriously amended both by the right and by the left. As a consequence, the president withdrew his text on 30 March 2016. No empirical fingerprint supports the idea that the FN intervened during the parliamentary process in order to amend the text or to support it.

The only empirical fingerprints explaining the role of the FN during the policy-making process are those showing its 'permanent pressure' on other parties – such as underlined above – but, first and foremost, on public opinion through the (new) media. The influence exercised by the FN is thus severely limited, that is, the inferential weight of the evidence is quite weak. Indeed, its influence is exercised upstream of the policy-making process and only indirectly. The FN has never intervened in the process alone to provoke a decisive sequence. It has only intervened in order 'to prepare the ground' for the right context.

The FN thus only exercised an influence towards one out of the three pledges. Table 9.2 synthesizes how the FN tries to translate that pledge into decision, by indicating that several empirical fingerprints of its influence

Table 9.2. Causal mechanism explaining the translation of the FN pledge relating to deprivation of nationality (cf. comment regarding table 9.1)

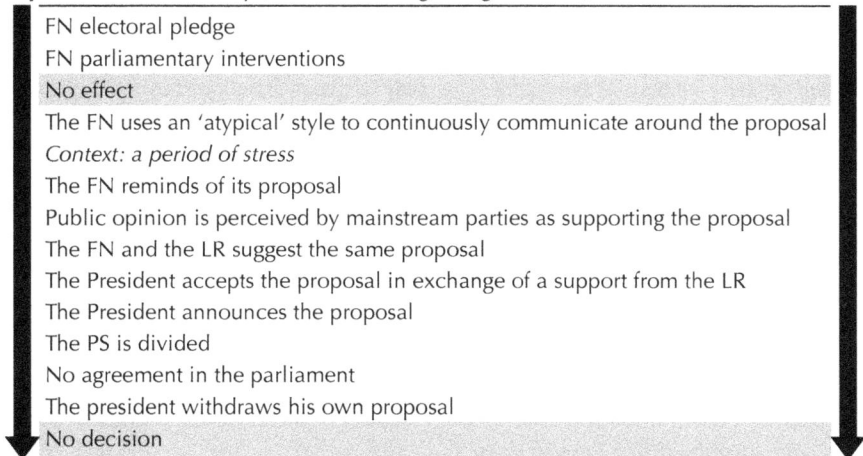

FN electoral pledge
FN parliamentary interventions
No effect
The FN uses an 'atypical' style to continuously communicate around the proposal
Context: a period of stress
The FN reminds of its proposal
Public opinion is perceived by mainstream parties as supporting the proposal
The FN and the LR suggest the same proposal
The President accepts the proposal in exchange of a support from the LR
The President announces the proposal
The PS is divided
No agreement in the parliament
The president withdraws his own proposal
No decision

are observed but also that their effects are limited: only few causal energies directly lead to a new sequence. In addition, the table shows that the role of the context is crucial.

THE BELGIAN VB AND FOREIGNERS' CRIMINALITY

As stated by several VB representatives and leaders (e.g. VB party official, 2017a), foreigners' criminality is a key issue for the VB. Yet only two proposals were made by the Belgian VB in its 2010 manifesto regarding the issue of 'foreigners' criminality'.

The first one – dealing with the will to keep statistics about criminality according to the nationality of origin – has never been debated and no empirical fingerprint from the VB was detected during the empirical analysis. A VB representative himself (2017b) recognized the party had not influenced policy-making at all on that specific question. The VB never intervened on the question in the parliament, and no empirical data shows the party addressed the question outside the institutions.

If the first pledge remains a simple electoral pledge, the second one – dealing with the expulsion of criminal foreigners – was partially developed in Belgium. First and foremost, the VB tried to translate this pledge into decision through the parliamentary arena. Yet its interventions never provoked any reaction from other parties, and there has thus never been any opportunity to put the issue on the agenda.

The government put forward two law proposals to the parliament on 9 February 2017 in order to facilitate the expulsion of criminal foreigners. The empirical analysis shows that the motivations of the government and the parliament to pass such a law are mostly linked to the context, that is, to terrorist attacks in France and Belgium. This results from analysis of the minutes of the parliament but was corroborated in the interviews:

> The terrorist context. Very clearly. The party has been influenced by the context in the society. For sure. (CD&V[8] MP, 2017)
>
> The pressure outside and inside was so strong on that topic. Yes, we were influenced by the terrorist context. (PS[9] MP, 2017)
>
> Pressure from public opinion to talk more about it? Yes, of course. It is often a theme [. . .] Yes, yes. Public opinion is very [. . .] It is easy. Everybody says 'I do not like foreigners'. (Ex-cdH[10] federal minister, 2017)

After the terrorist attacks, more and more demands to be more severe were formulated (Ex-CD&V federal minister, 2017).

No empirical fingerprint from the VB can be found in the process beyond its communication role through leaflets, parliamentary interventions (e.g. question by Filip Dewinter to the Minister of Justice, on 7 April 2017, in order to learn the number of criminal foreigners expelled from Belgium) and social networks. Communication around the issue is permanent, and aims at garnering public opinion in order to put pressure on mainstream parties. The party defended the proposal this way for several decades. By 1992, the VB had already defended the expulsion of criminal foreigners through a leaflet published by the VB president (Dillen, 1992, 30–32), for instance. This measure is also systematically present in its manifestos. In order to make the proposal salient, the VB uses an atypical communication style, using provocation and radicalism but also non-technical words:

> We have provoked. It is true. But our goal was to implement our manifesto. (VB party official, 2017c)
> We have formulated the problem in a harsh way, in an extreme way in order to attract attention. (VB party official and MP, 2017)
> We need to convince people. And you do not convince people with technical and nuanced discourses. You should be clear in your communication. (Ex-VB party official and MP, 2017)

By these means, the VB has exercised indirect influence on policy-making, acting in order to contribute (the empirical analysis cannot attest that it is the only political actor to do so) to shaping public opinion and, consequently, to shaping mainstream parties' preferences and the decisions they contribute to adopting. Yet, this influence is only exerted during the first stages of the process. Beyond that limited role – because the inferential weight of the evidence, such as for the French case, is weak – context and perceived pressure from public opinion are the main factors explaining the adoption of two laws expanding the possibilities for expulsion of criminal foreigners.

The VB thus exercised an influence regarding one out of two pledges. Table 9.3 shows the empirical evidence that are found in order to understand how the VB has tried to translate that pledge into decision.

Table 9.3. Causal mechanism explaining the translation of the VB pledge relating to the expulsion of criminal foreigners

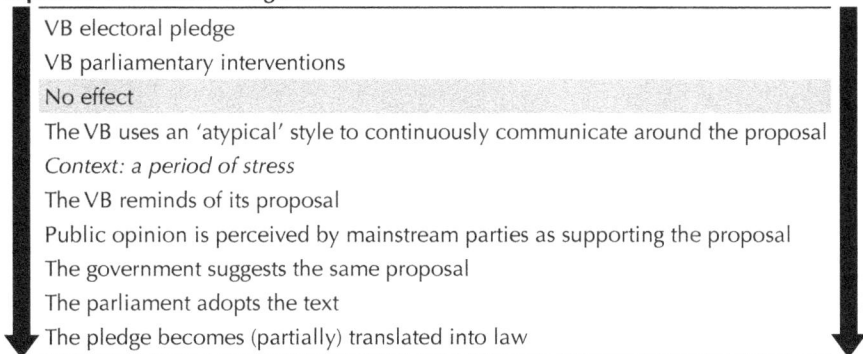

VB electoral pledge
VB parliamentary interventions
No effect
The VB uses an 'atypical' style to continuously communicate around the proposal
Context: a period of stress
The VB reminds of its proposal
Public opinion is perceived by mainstream parties as supporting the proposal
The government suggests the same proposal
The parliament adopts the text
The pledge becomes (partially) translated into law

COMPARISON AND DISCUSSION

The in-depth comparison of the three cases suggests interesting results on the policy influence exercised by RRPPs. Several patterns can indeed be detected in terms of the influence exercised by RRPPs on policy-making, the stages during which influence is exercised, the type of influence (direct or indirect), the way RRPPs proceed to exercise such an influence and the obstacles they face.

First, none of them can fulfil all the pledges they formulate regarding foreigners' criminality despite the fact that they all consider it an essential issue for them. In each case, they only exercised influence over one pledge. For the other pledges, no empirical fingerprint of their influence can be detected at any stage of the policy-making process. At most, they submit a text to the parliament that provokes no reaction (any new sequence, in the terms used in this chapter) from the other parties. This results from the fact that mainstream parties consider these parties undemocratic or too radical for their proposals to be taken seriously. Sometimes, RRPPs' party officials do not even remember their party manifesto contains such pledges.

Yet, the three RRPPs remain influential political actors. This corroborates the findings of several authors (Minkeberg, 2001; Zaslove, 2004; Afonso and Papadopoulos, 2015; Albertazzi and McDonnell, 2015) but also expands them since these new results also suggest that being in opposition also carries the potential to influence policy-making. In cases where these parties exercise policy influence, several regularities can be highlighted. Firstly, they all try to translate their electoral pledges foremost through the parliamentary arena. This is the cheapest way to proceed since they have seats in the parliament, and since their interventions can be disseminated through the (new) media. The result of such interventions varies: it may provoke debate (and thus a new sequence in the process) or not. Switzerland is the only country in this study where RRPPs have the potential to provoke a debate following a law proposal. This is because of its high share of votes (it is the first party at the National Council in terms of seats). In the other cases, parliamentary interventions never provoked any reaction or debate. Even the debates provoked in the Swiss parliament, though, are always short term and do not lead to any agreement or decision. An issue can thus be set on the agenda, but for a very short period of time. That lack of influence in the parliament corroborates the suggestion made by Minkenberg (2001), according to whom a mere parliamentary presence is not sufficient for a RRPP to exercise policy influence.

Because the parliamentary arena does not help RRPPs to develop their electoral pledges, they try to do so differently. In Switzerland, the availability of direct democracy tools is a very important factor to take into account since the SVP can use popular initiatives in order to directly appeal to the people to vote for its pledge. In the case of the expulsion of criminal foreigners, this resulted in a decision, despite strong opposition to the pledge. The SVP thus exercised influence at each stage of the process, and directly. Differently, the French FN and the Belgian VB cannot resort to direct democracy tools to be influential. Therefore, and as suggested by the literature (Schain, 2006), they can only indirectly influence policy-making, that is by making other parties adopt their own electoral pledges. This is explained by the fact that mainstream parties systematically reject any agreement with the FN or the VB because they are perceived as undemocratic:

> We never co-sign any text with the Front national. This is a matter of principle. (LR MP, 2016)
> We systematically vote against. When the Vlaams Belang proposes a text, regardless of the content, we are against. This is a matter of principle. (cdH MP, 2017)

In order to indirectly influence policy-making, RRPPs develop an atypical communication style: they tend to be provocative, harsh and direct. Interviewees from these parties all recognize that communication style. According to them, they do so in order to be heard by the public. They also think it is easier to spread their message through society via the media. Because of the weak inferential weight of the evidence, the indirect influence exercised by RRPPs is thus weaker than more direct influence. It is an influence *a maxima*.

The pledges made by RRPPs are not new and have been made for several decades, as shown in the manifesto analysis at the beginning of each case study. Because they repeat the same proposals over a long period, and because they use an atypical communication style when they do so, the effect of their actions is permanent pressure on public opinion and, *in fine*, on mainstream parties. When a specific context – or a 'period of stress' (Almond and Verba, 1963, 140) – happens (terrorist attacks), mainstream parties believe that public opinion supports RRPPs' pledges as a consequence of the action by RRPPs and, therefore, develop the same pledge – albeit not to the same extent. In other cases, other parties that initially wanted to develop that kind of pledge – but they did not do so because they were afraid to be assimilated into RRPPs – to take advantage of such a window of opportunity to develop the pledge. In both these cases, RRPPs intervene in order to 'prepare the ground'. Yet their intervention is never direct. This means the empirical fingerprints show that their interventions facilitate the adoption of measures translating their electoral pledge, but does not show they are provoking a new sequence in the policy-making process. The findings thus support the idea that two crucial factors have to be taken into account in order to understand how RRPPs' pledges become decisions: context and perceived public opinion

(Howard, 2010). This also means that RRPPs' policy influence is mostly exercised upstream of the policy-making process.

Finally, the study shows that the three RRPPs face the same difficulties in trying to exercise influence on the issue of foreigners' criminality. The more direct and full (i.e. exercised at several stages of policy-making) influence exercised by the Swiss SVP is explained by the Swiss political system, which allows the SVP to submit a popular initiative to the people in order to translate its electoral pledges regardless of the support of other political parties. Generally, the influence exercised by RRPPs is thus 'indirect' (Schain, 2006), mostly in the first stages of the policy-making process, and aims to make other parties 'co-opt' their own electoral pledges (as suggested by Carvalho, 2014). Their influence is thus nuanced. Their communication style – characterized as 'populist' (Jagers and Walgrave, 2007; Jamin, 2009) – is crucial for them to exercise that permanent pressure.

CONCLUSION

This chapter has contributed to a better apprehension of the influence exercised by RRPPs on policy-making regarding the most salient issue for them, i.e. foreigners' criminality. The findings suggest RRPPs matter, even when they face difficulties to attain power (because of a formal *cordon sanitaire* in Belgium, for instance). This chapter thus enriches the 'do parties matter' literature by showing that not only mainstream parties but also anti-system and anti-democratic parties such as RRPPs influence policy-making and thus matter. Yet, if RRPP are influent, they also face great challenges when trying to influence policy-making. Because these challenges are specific to RRPPs, their influence is less intense and different from the influence exercised by mainstream parties. The influence is indeed mostly exercised upstream of policy-making and indirectly.

While Switzerland is often studied as a country where the SVP does not suffer from measures excluding RRPPs from power, the chapter shows that such measures indeed exist in Switzerland. It takes the form of a denial of the legitimacy of RRPPs and/or their proposals. This means other parties avoid debating or making agreements with the SVP on the issue of foreigners' criminality (the SVP core pledges). Yet, that strategy is issue-specific and less visible in Switzerland than in France or Belgium. Mainstream parties have never adopted any (formal or informal) *cordon sanitaire* towards the SVP and they can collaborate on other issues, as Afonso and Papadopoulos (2015) remind us. In Belgium and France, a *cordon sanitaire* (formal in Belgium, informal in France) does exist. Of the three cases examined here, the direct influence of RRPPs is thus severely limited (even if not completely stopped). Strategies adopted by mainstream parties towards RRPPs thus have an impact on the policy influence of RRPPs. RRPPs indeed have to develop other strategies for exerting influence on policy-making, and they manage to do so only over the long term, directly via a popular initiative (when available) or indirectly via public opinion.

Finally, the results of this chapter contribute to the debate over the way direct democracy tools can help improve the quality of democracy. While studies have already mentioned that direct democracy tools do not necessarily lead to a real democratization of the political game (Mottier, 1993; Cherix, 2016), this study also suggests that these tools can increase the policy influence of political parties considered to be threatening liberal democracy (Urbinati, 2014). Populism and democracy are thus intrinsically linked. While mainstream parties adopt disengagement strategies towards RRPPs because they are a threat to the quality of democracy, populist parties use direct democracy tools in order to increase their capacity of influence. There is thus a paradox. RRPPs and democracy are thus the best foes but also the best friends.

If this research focuses on a key issue for RRPPs, other studies could enrich the contribution of the analysis by systematically analysing the influence of RRPPs on a broader range of issues. This paves an avenue for further research.

NOTES

1. In the parliament, the SVP has held 68/200 seats in the Lower House (National Council) and 6/46 seats in the Upper House (Council of States) since 2015. Between 2011 and 2015, the SVP held 57/200 seats in the Lower House and 6/46 seats in the Upper House. The SVP was the most important party during these periods in terms of seats in the Lower House. The party was also a member of the federal government (coalition) during these periods.

2. In the parliament, the FN has held 8/577 seats in the Lower House (National Assembly) since 2017. Between 2012 and 2017, the party held 2/577 seats in the Lower House. The FN also has held 2/348 seats in the Upper House (Senate) since 2014. The party has never participated to the national executive.

3. In the parliament, the VB has held 3/150 seats in the Lower House (House of Representatives) and 2/60 seats in the Upper House (Senate) since 2014. Between 2010 and 2014, the VB held 12/150 seats in the Lower House and 5/71 in the Upper House. The party has never participated in the national executive.

4. 104 interviews (65.23 minutes per interview in average) were realized in all.

5. Christian Democratic People's Party.

6. The FN held two seats in the National Assembly between 2012 and 2017, and has held eight since 2017. The FN also held two seats in the Senate in 2014. The FN thus cannot form a parliamentary group (15 MPs are necessary to form a parliamentary group).

7. The Republicans.
8. Christian Democratic and Flemish.
9. Socialist Party.
10. Humanist Democratic Centre.

REFERENCES

Afonso, Alexandre and Yannis Papadopoulos. 2015. How the populist radical right transformed Swiss welfare politics: From compromises to polarization. *Swiss Political Science Review* 21, no. 4: 617–635.

Akkerman, Tjitske and Sarah L. de Lange. 2012. Radical right parties in office: Incumbency records and the electoral cost of governing. *Government and Opposition* 47, no. 4: 574–596.

Albertazzi, Daniele and Duncan McDonnell. 2015. *Populists in Power*. New York: Routledge.

Albertazzi, Daniele and Sean Mueller. 2013. Populism and liberal democracy: Populists in government in Austria, Italy, Poland and Switzerland. *Government and Opposition* 48: 343–371.

Almond, Gabriel and Sidney Verba. 1963. *The Civic Culture. Political Attitudes and Democracy in Five Nations*. Princeton, PA: Princeton University Press.

Arts, Bas and Piet Verschuren. 1999. Assessing political influence in complex decision-making: An instrument based on triangulation. *International Political Science Review* 20, no. 4: 411–424.

Arts, Bas. 2000. Political influence of NGO's on international environmental issues. In *Power in Contemporary Politics: Theories, Practices, Globalizations*, edited by Henri Goverde, Philip Cerny, Mark Haugaard and Howard Lentler. London: Sage.

Beach, Derek and Rasmus Pedersen. 2013. *Process-tracing: Foundations and Guidelines*. Ann Arbor, MI: University of Michigan Press.

Betsill, Michele and Elisabeth Corell. 2001. NGO influence in international environmental negotiations: A framework for analysis. *Global environmental politics* 1, no. 4: 65–85.

Birkland, Thomas. 2005. *Policy Process: Theories, Concepts and Models of Public Policy Making*, 2nd ed. New York: ME Sharpe Inc.

Bouillaud, Christophe. 2007. La législation italienne des années 2001–2005 porte-t-elle la marque des nouvelles droites? In *Extrême droite et pouvoir en Europe*, edited by Pascal Delwit and Philippe Poirier, 265–290. Brussels: Université libre de Bruxelles.

Canu, Isabelle. 1997. *Der Schutz der Demokratie in Deutschland und Frankreich. Ein Vergleich des Umgangs mit politischem Extremismus vor dem Hintergrund der europäischen Integration*. Opladen: Leske and Budrich.

Capoccia, Giovanni. 2001. Defending democracy: Reactions to political extremism in interwar Europe. *European Journal of Political Research* 39, no. 4: 431–460.

Carter, Elisabeth. 2005. *The Extreme Right in Western Europe: Success or Failure?* Manchester: Manchester University Press.

Carvalho, Joao. 2014. *Impact of Extreme Right Parties on Immigration Policy. Comparing Britain, France and Italy*. New York: Routledge.

Cherix, François. 2016. *Qui sauvera la Suisse du populisme?* Genève: Slatkine.

Coolsaet, Brendan and John Pitseys. 2015. Fair and equitable negotiations? African influence and the international access and benefit-sharing regime. *Global Environmental Politics* 15, no. 2: OnlineFirst.

Davet, Gérard and Fabrice Lhomme. 2016. *Un Président ne devrait pas dire ça. Les secrets d'un quinquennat*. Paris: Stock.

Dillen, Karel. 1992. *Vlaams Blok: partij van en voor de toekomst*. Brussels: Uitgeverij Vlaams Blok.

George, Alexander and Andrew Bennett. 2005. *Case Studies and Theory Development in the Social Sciences*. Cambridge, MA: The MIT Press.

Guinaudeau, Isabelle and Simon Persico. 2018. Tenir promesse. Les conditions de réalisation des programmes électoraux. *Revue française de science politique* 68, no. 2: 215–237.

Heinze, Anna-Sophie. 2018. Strategies of mainstream parties towards their right-wing populist challengers: Denmark, Norway, Sweden and Finland in comparison. *West European Politics* 41, no. 2: 287–309.

Howard, Marc. 2010. The impact of the far right on citizenship policy in Europe: Explaining continuity and change. *Journal of Ethnic and Migration Studies* 36, no. 5: 735–751.

Invernizzi Accetti, Carlo and Ian Zuckerman. 2017. What's wrong with militant democracy? *Political Studies* 65, no. 15: 182–199.

Jagers, Jan and Stefaan Walgrave. 2007. Populism as political communication style. *European Journal of Political Research* 46, no. 3: 319–345.

Jamin, Jérôme. 2009. *L'imaginaire du complot: discours d'extrême droite en France et aux États-Unis*. Amsterdam: Amsterdam University Press.

Mansergh, Lucy and Robert Thomson. 2007. Election pledges, party competition, and policymaking. *Comparative Politics* 39, no. 3: 311–329.

Minkenberg, Michael. 2001. The radical right in public office: Agenda-setting and policy effects. *West European Politics* 24, no. 4: 1–21.

Mottier, Véronique. 1993. La structuration sociale de la participation aux votations fédérales. In *Citoyenneté et démocratie directe*, edited by Hanspeter Kriesi, 123–144. Zurich: Seismo.

Mudde, Cas. 2007. *Populist Radical Right Parties in Europe*. Cambridge: Cambridge University Press.

Pétry, François. 2012. Les partis tiennent-ils leurs promesses? In *Les partis politiques québécois dans la tourmente. Mieux comprendre et évaluer leur rôle*, edited by Réjean Pelletier, 95–225. Québec: Presses de l'Université Laval.

Rovira Kaltwasser, Cristobal, Paul Taggart, Paulina Ochoa Espejo and Pierre Ostiguy (eds.). 2017. *The Oxford Handbook of Populism*. Oxford: Oxford University Press.

Royed, Terry. 1996. Testing the mandate model in Britain and the United-States. *British Journal of Political Science* 26, no. 1: 45–80.

Schain, Martin. 2006. The extreme-right and immigration policy-making: Measuring direct and indirect effects. *West European Politics* 29, no. 2: 270–289.

Strom, Kaare. 1990. A behavioral theory of competitive political parties. *American Journal of Political Science* 34, no. 2: 565–598.

Thomson, Robert, Terry Royed, Elin Naurin, Joaquin Artes, Rory Costello, Laurenz Ennser-Jedenastik, Mark Ferguson, Petia Kostadinova, Catherine Moury, Francois Petry and Katrin Praprotnik. 2017. The fulfillment of parties' election pledges: A comparative study of the impact of power sharing. *American Journal of Political Science*. Online First.

Urbinati, Nadia. 2014. *Democracy Disfigured: Opinion, Truth, and the People*. Cambridge, MA: Harvard University Press.

Walgrave, Stefaan, Jonas Lefevere and Anke Tresch. 2012. The associative dimension of issue ownership. *Public Opinion Quarterly* 76: 771–782.

Williams, Michelle. 2006. *The Impact of Radical Right-wing Parties in West European Democracies*. New York: Palgrave Macmillan.

Zaslove, Andrei. 2004. Closing the door? The ideology and impact of radical right populism on immigration policy in Austria and Italy. *Journal of Political Ideologies* 9, no. 1: 99–118.

Chapter 10

Who's to Blame

Radical Right Populist Party and Mainstream Parties' Roles in Adoption of Welfare Chauvinist Policies

Juliana Chueri

Although welfare chauvinism – the notion that the welfare state should only benefit the citizens (Andersen and Bjørklund, 1990) – appears as an important component of RRPP (radical right populist party) anti-immigrant appeal (Rydgren, 2004; de Koster, et al., 2013; Afonso and Rennwald, 2018; Ennser-Jedenastik, 2018), the academic literature has barely explored the relationship between the success of RRPPs and the adoption of restrictive legislation towards immigrants' social rights (Bolin et al., 2014; Mudde, 2013). The few existing studies that focus on the influence of RRPPs on policy outcomes take a broad approach by addressing, often indistinctly, immigration and integration policies (Minkenberg, 2001; Williams, 2006; Schain, 2006; Akkerman, 2012). Exceptions are Howard (2010), who focuses on the effect of RRPPs on immigrants' access to citizenship, and Koning (2013), who analyses the influence of RRPPs on immigrants' access to the welfare state. Also, these works address one or few cases, with the valuable exception of Akkerman (2012), who analyses nine Western European countries.

The general conclusion is that the increasing presence of RRPPs in politics is associated with the adoption of restrictive policies. Nevertheless, rather than considering this outcome a result of parliamentary or ministerial activity of RRPPs' personnel, these studies mainly highlight those parties' constrains to adapt to public office (Minkenberg, 2001; Akkerman, 2012). Therefore, the state of the art indicates that RRPPs' influence on immigrants' rights occurs mainly through indirect channels, and their interaction with mainstream parties (Akkerman, 2012; Williams, 2006; Schain, 2006; Howard, 2010; Koning, 2013). Indeed, studies that focus on party manifesto data show that the success of RRPPs has a contagious effect on mainstream parties

(Norris, 2005; van Spanje, 2010; Bale et al., 2010; Alonso and da Fonseca, 2012; Schumacher and van Kersbergen, 2016). However, the nature of this interaction is yet to be clarified. First, studies are not clear about the different policy responses of mainstream left- and right-wing parties in light of the increasing presence of RRPPs in politics. Second, the differences in RRPPs' levels of bargaining power have so far been ignored.

Therefore, this study aims to shed light on the influence of RRPP policy outcomes, by responding to two research questions. The first one is if RRPPs had an influence on the adoption of welfare chauvinist polices and, the second one is by which mechanism those parties influence immigrants' entitlement to social rights. This chapter tests three main hypotheses. The first is that RRPPs are able to restrict immigrants' access to social policies by participating in the government, a mechanism called *direct influence*. The second one is that even when RRPPs are not part of the government coalition, the increase of RRPPs participation in parliament influences the adoption of welfare chauvinist policies, the *indirect influence*. The third hypothesis is that welfare chauvinist policies are adopted independently of RRPPs participation in governments or parliaments.

Clarifying the influence of RRPPs in the adoption of welfare chauvinist policies is fundamental for, at least, three reasons. First, considering the governmental challenge of ensuring inclusion of new immigrants in society, policy changes that reduce immigrant eligibility to social rights enhance immigrants' vulnerability to poverty and social exclusion. Second, the deprivation of basic rights could not only harm the integration of newcomers in the society, but also affect the integration of future generations. Finally, integration policies are linked to solidarity towards immigration, while restrictive integration reinforces public perception that immigrants are a threat (Crepaz, 2008).

Compared to previous studies, the scope of this study is wider. It performs a large-N analysis with data from seventeen Western European countries between 1990 and 2014. The analysis relies on the Determinants of International Migration Policy data (DEMIG POLICY). Additionally, data from Support and Opposition to Migration (SOM) and Migrant Integration Policy Index (MIPEX) are considered for cross-validation. The remainder of this chapter is structured as follows. First, I discuss the populist right-wing ideology and the role of welfare chauvinism in their agenda. Second, I present the hypotheses of the study. Third, I outline the data and discuss the analyses. And lastly, I present the conclusions.

CONTEMPORARY RADICAL RIGHT POPULISM

The emergence of new parties on the right was one of the most important political occurrences in contemporary advanced European democracies. In conjunction with the Green parties, these new RRPPs ended the stability of Western European party systems, increased polarization and party competition (Kriesi et al., 2006). In addition, such parties have been relatively successful in recent years, enlarging their electoral pool, winning seats in national parliaments and participating in governments.

This work adopts Cas Mudde's definition of populism: a 'thin-centered ideology that considers society to be ultimately separated into two homogeneous and antagonistic groups, "the pure people" and "the corrupt elite", and which argues that politics should be an expression of the *volonté general* (general will) of the people' (2004, 543). Therefore, as defined by Laclau (1977), the central feature of the populism is a discourse that pits 'the people' against the elite, or institutions. Also, by considering population as a homogeneous group and denying intermediations between peoples' will and policies, populism is the opposition of elitism and multiculturalism. Therefore, populist parties are essentially anti-liberal, as they believe that the majority should rule without limits, denying the existence of minority rights, and defending a positive discrimination in favour of the 'silent majority' (Copsey, 2007). Because populism is a thin ideology, it is usually combined with other ideologies, such as nationalism, socialism and liberalism.

I restrict my analysis to parties located on the right side of the political spectrum, excluding the populist left-wing parties, such as the Greek SYRIZA. Finally, like many scholars, I adopt the term 'radical', 'in addition to 'populist right' in order to designate parties that, besides populism, have (at least) nativism and authoritarianism in their ideologies (Mudde, 2007). These parties claim that there is homogeneous native group in opposition to an alien minority that represents a cultural or economic threat to the nation. In addition, they argue that crimes should be punished severely and they defend strict law and order policies. Finally, those parties associate foreigners with crime, advocate for stricter punishment and defend extradition of immigrants involved in crimes.

RRPPs AND WELFARE CHAUVINISM

Welfare chauvinism is the notion that welfare benefits should be exclusive to citizens (Andersen and Bjørklund, 1990). However, empirical evidence shows that strict welfare chauvinism, that is, the belief that immigrants' access to social services should be banned, is rare. More commonly, people believe immigrants should receive benefits after meeting some preconditions or making some contribution (Kolbe and Capaz, 2016). This moderate version of welfare chauvinism is also present in RRPPs' agenda. They openly argue that immigrants' access to the welfare state should not be equal to citizens' access, and that restrictions to aliens' social rights are necessary to meet fairness criteria, avoid abuse and ensure the sustainability of social protections. Although it was not explored during the emergence of RRPPs, welfare chauvinism has become an important component of RRPP rhetoric since 1990 (Andersen and Bjørklund, 1990; Rydgren, 2004; Ivarsflaten, 2008; de Koster et al., 2013; Afonso and Rennwald, 2018; Ennser-Jedenastik, 2018).

The emergence of welfare chauvinism as a central political platform coincides with the shift in those parties' positions regarding distributive issues, from a liberal to a more pro-welfare state rhetoric (Betz, 1994; Afonso and Rennwald, 2018). By the early 1990s, many RRPPs discovered the electoral appeal of an anti-immigrant agenda, and gradually adopted anti-immigration as a primary issue. Moreover, to expand the number of voters who were likely to be dependent on the welfare state, those parties abandoned their strong defence of neoliberalism and embraced instead a welfare state defence (Betz, 1994; Kriesi et al., 2006).

However, this pro-welfare state platform is significantly different from the traditional left. The strong anti-immigrant position of RRPPs prevents true egalitarianism; thus, they defend distribution only for those who deserve it, that is, the nationals who contribute to the society's wealth and have the right to fully enjoy social benefits. This welfare chauvinism is supported by the view that immigrants abuse the welfare state, or simply that natives should have preference in receiving benefits (de Koster et al., 2013). Empirical studies have confirmed that welfare chauvinism has become a crucial component of anti-immigrant agendas and it is an important variable for right-wing populist voting (Rydgren, 2004; Ivarsflaten, 2008; de Koster et al., 2013). Therefore, the hypotheses of this study hold the premise that, once in power, RRPPs will be responsible to their voters and will have the restriction of immigrants' entitlements to social rights as their primary policy goals.

HYPOTHESES

Many scholars have argued that political parties have a decisive influence on policy outcomes. Focusing generally on left-to-right positioning, studies have shown a significant relationship between right-wing parties and welfare state retrenchment (Castles, 1982; Hicks, Swank and Ambuhl, 1989; Allan and Scruggs, 2004). From the perspective that parties affect policy designs, this study argues that the recent electoral success of RRPPs in Europe is the central explanatory element for the extent of the gap between citizens' and immigrants' entitlements to social rights.

This chapter tests three main hypotheses. The first is that RRPPs are a central element in understanding the restrictions on immigrants' entitlements, and that RRPP participation in national governments is the main channel by which they influence other parties to adopt welfare chauvinist policies. This perspective is based on the notion that governmental participation, as a formal member of the government or as a stable supporter party of the governing coalition, leads to the legitimization of RRPP political platforms and constitutes a channel of communication whereby RRPPs can persuade ally parties to adopt welfare chauvinist policies.

This interpretation is supported by Akkerman and de Lange's study (2012), which shows that the entrance of RRPPs does not lead to moderation in issues that are central to RRPPs. Also, this study relies on the claim that, though junior members of the coalition, RRPPs can sway policy outcomes because the requirement to build majorities gives them bargaining power or allows them to blackmail the other parties of the coalition to assert their policy preferences, which is supported by empirical results (Strom, 1990; Downs, 1957). Therefore, as welfare chauvinism has become one important component of RRPP political platforms and voting (de Koster et al., 2013; Ivarsflaten, 2008), it is reasonable to expect that, once in power, RRPPs will aim to reduce immigrants' entitlement to rights.

H1: The participation of a RRPP in the governing coalition increases the likelihood of a reduction in immigrants' social rights.

Due to their share of seats in a parliament, RRPPs are most frequently junior members in the government coalition. However, in some cases, RRPPs have equitable power with other coalition partners, for example, in Austria from 2000 to 2002, and Switzerland from 2003. Therefore, in order to access the importance of RRPPs power resource inside the coalition on the adoption of welfare chauvinist policies, a slightly different model that has RRPP participation's share in coalition as dependent variable will also be tested.

Finally, literature generally treats indistinctly the RRPP status of support party, that is, the stable legislative support of a RRPP to the winning coalition without receiving a portfolio, an informal participation, and its formal participation in the government (Akkerman, 2012; Akkerman and de Lange, 2012; Afonso, 2015). I draw attention to the particularities of the RRPPs' status of legislative supporter party. First, this outsider position might put RRPPs in a better position to influence policy outcomes, as it allows those parties to peruse a vote-seeking strategy, without risking a crack in the cabinet (Christiansen and Pedersen, 2014; Akkerman, de Lange and Rooduijn, 2016; Thesen, 2016). Second, it overcame the lack of qualified personnel to occupy executive positions, as negotiations occur at the leadership level. Therefore, this chapter investigates if informal governmental participation of a RRPP increases the likelihood of a reduction in immigrants' social rights versus formal participation.

The second hypothesis is that RRPPs influence policy outcomes indirectly. Literature has called significant attention to the contagious effect of RRPPs in mainstream parties (Norris, 2005; Schain, 2006; Bale et al., 2010; van Spanje, 2010; Alonso and da Fonseca, 2012). The electoral success of RRPPs signifies to other parties, especially right-wing parties, that immigration and integration issues have gained significant political visibility. This may nudge mainstream right-wing parties towards policy convergence to prevent RRPPs from gaining ownership of those issues, that is, being considered by the electorate as the most competent party to deal with those issues (Budge, Farlie and Laver, 1983; Meguid, 2005). Therefore, the growing presence of a RRPP in politics is perceived by mainstream as right-wing parties as an electoral threat, which leads those parties to adopt RRPP's policies regarding immigration and integration (Norris, 2005; van Spanje, 2010, Meguid, 2005; Bale et al., 2010, Schumacher and van Kersbergen, 2016).

H2a: The presence of RRPPs in a parliament increases the likelihood that right-wing governments adopt restrictions to immigrants' entitlement to rights.

The mainstream left has a much more complicated choice. On one hand, mainstream left parties attract highly educated voters and those with liberal social-cultural values, which favour social egalitarianism policies and a broader concept of solidarity. On the other hand, those parties cast votes from the working class, a group that has become a supporter of RRPPs in recent years. Those voters feel particularly threatened by immigration and wronged by the social welfare state (de Koster et al., 2010). Therefore, they are generally inclined to approve restrictions towards immigrants' access to rights.

Nevertheless, left parties are less likely to change their political positions in response to changes in other parties' positions in the political spectrum. Studies attribute this behaviour to left-wing parties' decentralized structure of decision, which gives substantial power of influence to party activists (Kitschelt, 1994; Adams et al., 2009). Therefore, left-wing parties are less likely to abandon their ideological commitments to tolerance on immigration and integration.

Empirical studies present inconclusive results. Alonso and da Fonseca (2012) show that the mainstream left tend to increase the salience of the immigration issue, and adopt a tough discourse on immigration in response to the threat of RRPP. On the other hand, Bale and his colleagues (2010) found that the Social Democratic response to the rise of the populist radical right, and to the rise of immigration and integration issues' salience, is not uniform. However, it rarely involves adoption of RRPP's positions. Therefore, in contrast to the mainstream right, I expect that if RRPPs gain ground in national politics, the mainstream left will not restrict immigrants' access to rights.

H2b: Left-wing governments are not likely to restrict immigrants' entitlement to social rights in response to increased RRPP parliament participation.

The third hypothesis posits that RRPP is not a necessary element for a restriction of immigrant social rights. This perspective assumes that mainstream parties can access citizen sentiments regardless the electoral success of those parties. Thus, if anti-immigrant sentiments become a salient issue in society, mainstream parties will adapt their policies in order to maximize their electoral results. This last hypothesis is in line with Mudde's perspective (2007) that the influence of RRPPs has been exaggerated by scholars, and the fact that restrictive policies have been enacted by mainstream governments and by governments that have faced no significant populist right competitor (Bale, 2008).

H3: Independently of RRPPs electoral success or government participation, right-wing governments are more likely to adopt a restriction on immigrants' entitlements to social rights compared to left-wing governments.

DATA AND RESEARCH DESIGN

Data will be collected from the following seventeen countries: Austria, Belgium, Denmark, Finland, France, Germany, Greece, Ireland, Italy, Luxembourg, the Netherlands, Norway, Portugal, Spain, Sweden, Switzerland and the United Kingdom. The data has a longitudinal structure and covers the period from 1990 to 2014. This starting year correspond to RRPPs' adoption of a welfare chauvinist rhetoric in most of the countries studied. Following Inglehart and Norris' study (2017), parties that scored more than 80 points on the standardized 100-point Chapel Hill expert survey's cultural scale, and scored more than 50 in the left–right dimension were considered in this study. Nevertheless, only parties that had parliament representation during the period of this study were included. The complete list of right-wing populist parties considered in this study is found in table 10.1. The empirical analysis involves a statistics study based on a random logistic regression, with an ordinal dependent variable.[1,2]

Dependent Variable

The dependent variable of the model is the degree of the change (increase, maintenance or decrease) of immigrants' rights, produced by a legislation (or the absence of legislation). It assumes the value zero if no change in entitlement occurred in the year, positive ordinal values if inclusive legislation was adopted, and negative ordinal values if restrictive legislation was adopted. Note that I consider citizens' entitlement as the baseline, so an increase in immigrants' entitlement is a change that equates or approximates immigrants' rights to citizens' rights. Similarly, a decrease in immigrants' social rights represents a change that increases the gap between immigrants' and citizens' entitlement to social rights. Therefore, changes in legislation that target both immigrants' and citizens' rights are not considered.

Data on immigrants' entitlement to rights comes from three databases. First, I use the DEMIG POLICY data from Oxford University (DEMIG, 2015), a

Table 10.1.   Populist right-wing parties with parliament representation from 1980 to 2014

Country	Party Name	Acronym
Austria	Freedom Party of Austria	FPÖ
	Alliance for Austria's Future	BZÖ
Belgium	National Front Belgium	FN(b)
	Flemish Interest/Flemish Block	VB
Denmark	Danish People's Party	DF
	Progress Party	FRP(d)
Finland	Finns Party/True Finns	Ps
France	National Front	FN
Greece	Popular Orthodoxy Rally	LAOS
	Independent Greeks	AE
	Popular Association – Golden Dawn	LS-CA
Italy	Italian Social Movement/National Alliance	MSI/AN
	Northern League	LN
Luxembourg	Action Committee Pensions/Alternative Democratic Reform Party	AR-ADR
Netherlands	Centre Party/Centre Democrats	CP/CD
	Pim Fortuyn List	LPF
	Party for Freedom	PVV
Norway	Progress Party (Norway)	FRP(n)
Sweden	New Democracy	ND
	Sweden Democrats	SD
Switzerland	Swiss People's Party/Democratic Union of the Centre	SVP/UDC
	Swiss Automobile Party/Freedom Party of Switzerland	FPS
	Ticino League	LdT
	Geneva Citizens' Movement	MCG
	Vigilance	V
	Swiss Democrats (SD/DS)	SD/DS
UK	United Kingdom Independence Party	UKIP

qualitative database that provides information about legislation changes that affect immigrants' entitlement to social rights. Then, the explanation tables of MIPEX and SOM databases were also consulted to cross-check information and include missing data. In this last step, four new legislation changes were incorporated in the study (see appendix 1 for the entire list of legislation).

The choice of prioritizing the DEMIG POLICY database rather than other databases (Niessen et al., 2007; Economist Intelligence Unit, 2008; Oxford Analytica, 2008; Klugman and Pereira, 2009; Ruhs, 2011) is four-fold. First, DEMIG covers the countries and years examined in the current study. Second, it appropriately differentiates the diverse policy areas of immigration (immigration, integration and citizenship policies) and their subcategories. Third, the DEMIG POLICY database makes a clear distinction between outputs and outcomes, and it catalogues only legislation changes, that is, policy outputs. Some databases mix information about policy outputs, legislation and norms with outcomes.[3] Finally, it provides information about policies that restrict and expand immigrants' entitlement to social rights. This feature allows the present study to make inferences about both movements.

Figure 10.1 shows that, instead of a constant restriction of immigrants' entitlement to rights, most of the countries combine inclusive and restrictive changes in legislation. In total, thirty-three restrictive and twenty-three inclusive legislations were passed.[4] The United Kingdom and Belgium are the notable exceptions; those were the most restrictive nations and approved six and five bills that reduced immigrants' entitlement to rights, respectively. Denmark approved five restrictive legislations, but also two expansions over the twenty-five-year period. On the other hand, Portugal was the most inclusive country, adopting four bills to increase immigrants' entitlement to welfare state.

However, the number of measures adopted does not provide a complete information about changes in immigrants' entitlement, as scope of the legislation varies. A granular study that has as unity of analysis the immigrant group and counts the number of restrictions or expansions by social policy targeted revealed seventy-nine restrictive and fifty-six inclusive measures. This shows that those legislations are far-reaching in terms of immigrant group and polices affected. Therefore, in order to better access the content of the bills, the numerical dependent variable of this study was obtained by a codification of the qualitative information of DEMIG POLICY database.

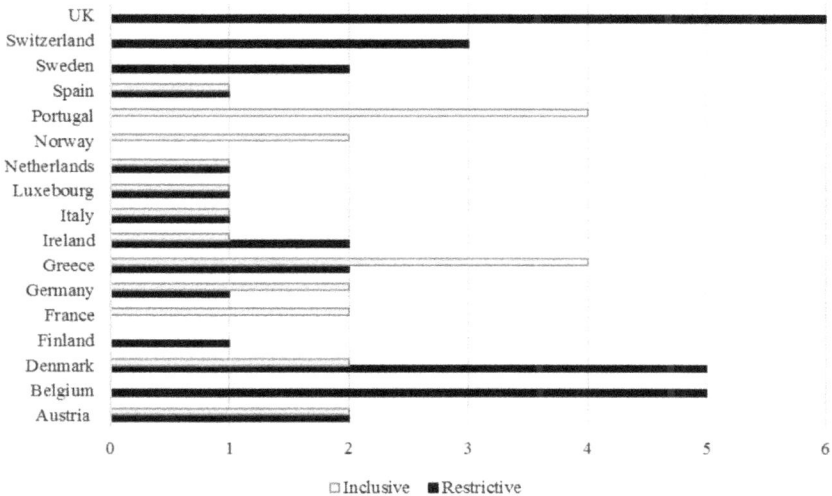

Figure 10.1. Number of approved legislations that changed immigrants' entitlement to social rights from 1990 to 2014.

This final variable takes into account the change in coverage engendered by the law, the number of immigrant groups targeted and the number of polices affected by the legislation (see appendix 2 for a detailed information of the coding process).

Independent Variables

This study uses ten explanatory variables. The first independent variable is the share of seats occupied by RRPPs in parliament,[5] which was taken from the Parliaments and Governments Database (ParlGov).[6] The second variable of interest is RRPP government participation. This variable is a dummy that assumes a value of 1 if RRPP participates at government (formally or informally), and assumes the value of 0 otherwise. A slightly different version of the second variable is the RRPP government participation type that considers the following three situations: RRPP's formal participation in the government, RRPP's informal support of the winning coalition and no RRPP government participation. Table 10.2 shows the years of formal and informal participation of RRPPs in governments for the countries and period considered in this study.

Table 10.2 shows twelve examples of RRPPs participating in governments, three of which were informal. The Netherlands and, recently, Norway had combined experiences of formal and informal participation.

The third explanatory variable is government orientation. This variable is equal to the sum of each party's position in the left–right scale, weighted by party's participation share in the cabinet:

$$\text{Government orientation} = \sum_{party=1}^{n} \text{party's position}_i \text{ X party's government participation}_i$$

Table 10.2.   RRPP's formal and informal participation in governments from 1980 to 2014

Country	Formal	Informal
Austria	2000–2006	
Denmark		2002–2011
Greece	2011	
Italy	1994	
	2001–2005	
	2008–2011	
Netherlands	2002–2003	2010–2011
Norway	2014-	2002–2005
Switzerland	1990–2007	
	2009–2014	

In the case of minority governments, this study takes two approaches. The first approach is to look for stable supporter parties. If the minority government had one or more supporter parties that were not formal members of the coalition, such parties are considered in the calculation as they were members of the coalition. If the minority government had no stable legislative supporter party and looked for ad hoc allies to pass bills, the calculation of this variable considers the entire parliament position in left–right scale multiplied by its participation in the coalition, which is the additional share necessary to build a simple majority of 50 per cent.[7]

I also considered the following four other rival explanations: welfare state type, unemployment rate, elderly dependence rate, public debt and immigrant influx. Budget deficits and unemployment increase the likelihood of welfare state retrenchment and might disproportionately impact immigrants' entitlement (Pontusson, 1995). Some studies have concluded that ethnic homogeneity is essential to building trust, which is critical to supporting collective action (Putnam, 2007; Soroka et al., 2006). Therefore, immigrant influx can have a negative impact on welfare state solidarity. Finally, demographic factors can also play a role, as a high elderly dependence rate may negatively affect welfare state sustainability and lead to the adoption of restrictive measures.

STATISTICAL ANALYSIS

As shown in table 10.3, four models were tested. Model 1 assessed the influence of RRPP government participation on the adoption of restrictive or expansive policies towards immigrants' access to rights, controlled by RRPP parliament participation, RRPP government participation, government orientation, welfare state type, immigrant influx, unemployment rate, elderly dependence rate, and public debt. Model 2 tests the influence of RRPP share of participation in coalition. Model 3 includes two dummy variables for RRPP government participation, informal and formal. Model 4 considers the interaction between RRPP parliament participation and government orientation.

As the coefficients of the ordinal logistic regression model represent the log odds, their interpretation are not straightforward. Therefore, table 10.3 shows the odds ratio, that is, the exponential transformation of the models' coefficients. The odd ratio represents the probability of obtaining greater values of the dependent variable for a unit of change in the predictable variable. If the odds ratio is smaller than one, a marginal increase in the dependent variable will increase the odds of obtaining lower values of the dependent

Table 10.3. Model result in odds ratio and standard errors in parenthesis (N = 425, 1990–2014, 17 countries)

	Model 1	*Model 2*	*Model 3*	*Model 4*
RRPP parliament participation	1.00 (0.02)	1.00 (0.02)	1.00 (0.02)	1.06 (0.07)
RRPP government participation	0.32** (0.18)			0.42 (0.28)
RRPP coalition participation		0.97** (0.02)		
RRPP government participation type (baseline non-participation)				
Informal participation			0.23* (0.18)	
Formal participation			0.38* (0.25)	
Government orientation	0.73** (0.09)	0.74** (0.09)	0.74** (0.09)	0.78* (0.12)
Interaction between RRPP parliament participation and government orientation				0.99 (0.01)
Welfare state type (baseline continental)				
Liberal	0.43* (0.19)	0.36** (0.16)	0.41* (0.19)	0.37** (0.18)
Social Democrat	0.59 (0.27)	0.54 (0.25)	0.64 (0.30)	0.58 (0.26)
South European	2.89** (1.39)	2.63** (1.24)	2.87** (1.39)	2.76** (1.34)
Public debt	0.99** (0.01)	0.99* (0.01)	0.99* (0.01)	0.99* (0.01)
Elderly dependence rate	1.02 (0.05)	1.01 (0.05)	1.01 (0.05)	1.01 (0.05)
Immigrant influx	0.97 (0.03)	0.97 (0.03)	0.97 (0.03)	0.97 (0.03)
Unemployment	0.97 (0.04)	0.97 (0.04)	0.97 (0.04)	0.97 (0.04)
Probability > chi-square	0.00	0.00	0.00	0.00

(*) Significant at the 0.1 level, (**) significant at the 0.05 level and (***) significant at the 0.01 level.

variable. However, if the odds ratio is greater than one, a marginal increase in the dependent variable will increase the odds of obtaining higher values of the dependent variable.

Model 1 supports the first hypothesis, which states that RRPPs' government participation has a negative influence on immigrants' entitlement to rights. The model shows that RRPP government participation increases the odds of getting lower values of the dependent variable (reduction in immigrants' entitlement to rights) by 3.13 times.[8]

The second model considers the variable 'RRPP coalition participation'. This coefficient shows that a marginal increase in RRPPs' participation share in the coalition increases the odds of a decrease in immigrants' entitlement to rights by 1.03 times, confirming the slightly different version of the first hypothesis.

Model 3 tests different types of government participation. Both types of participation, formal and informal, have significant coefficients and negative impacts on immigrants' entitlement to social rights. However, informal participation has a greater negative influence. Holding all variables constant, the informal participation of RRPPs in the government increases the chance of obtaining lower values in the dependent variable (reduction of immigrants' entitlement to rights) by 3.57 times, in comparison to non-participation. On the other hand, formal participation increases this chance by 2.63 times. This result suggests that informal participation involves an exchange: RRPP forgo holding offices in order to obtain policy space in issues that are relevant to their voters.

The last model includes the interaction between the participation of RRPPs in parliament and government orientation, which slightly changes the interpretation of the coefficients. The coefficient 'government orientation' corresponds to the influence of the variable when RRPP's parliament participation is zero. This coefficient shows that a marginal increase in government orientation increases the odds of a decrease in immigrants' entitlement to rights by 1.28 times when RRPP parliament participation is zero. The variable 'RRPP parliament participation' is not significant in this model.

The interaction variable represents the influence of RRPPs parliament participation mediated by the government's position on the left–right scale. The interpretation of an interaction between two constant variables is not straightforward, since its coefficient may have different signs for different values of covariates. Therefore, figure 10.2 shows the linear marginal influence of an increase in RRPPs participation in parliament on the dependent variable, for different fixed values of government orientation.

As displayed in the below figure, the influence of RRPP's parliament participation in immigrants' entitlement to social rights is dependent on government orientation. The marginal influence is positive for governments that score 5 and below in the left–right party position dimension and negative for governments that score above 5. Therefore, a marginal increase in RRPP participation in parliament enhances the chance of a restriction on immigrants' social rights when a right-wing government is in power. On the other hand, this enhances the chance of an expansion of immigrants' social rights when a left-wing coalition is in power. However, those results are not significant, with a confidence level of 90 per cent. Therefore, I cannot accept hypothesis 2a, which states that the presence of RRPPs in a parliament increases the likelihood that right-wing governments adopt restrictions to immigrants' entitlement to rights. Similarly, I cannot accept hypothesis 2b, which states that left-wing governments are not likely to restrict immigrants' entitlement

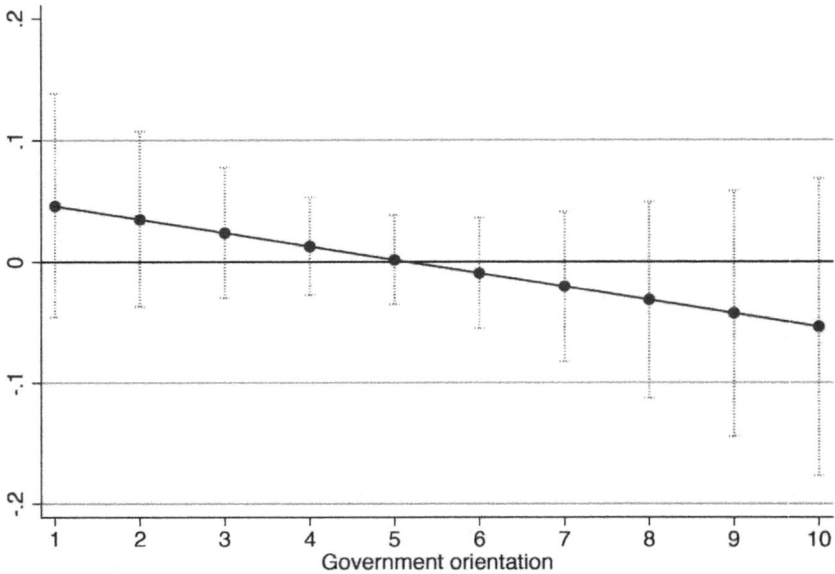

Figure 10.2. Linear marginal influence of the participation of RRPPs in parliament on the dependent variable for different levels of government orientation, when RRPPs do not participate in government, with 90% confidence interval.

to social rights in response to increased RRPP parliament participation. Additionally, models 1, 2 and 3 show that controlling for RRPP government and parliament participations, a marginal increase of government orientation (towards the right) increases the chance of obtaining lower values in the dependent variable (reduction of immigrants' entitlement to rights) by 1.37, 1.35 and 1.35 times, respectively, confirming hypothesis 3.

Finally, in all models, the variables 'elderly dependence rate', 'unemployment' and 'immigrant influx' are not statistically different from zero. Nevertheless, the variable 'public debt' is significant. The study shows that a marginal increase in this variable leads to a 1 per cent higher change of a restriction in immigrants' social rights. Additionally, models have significant coefficients for South European and Liberal welfare states dummies. Controlled by other independent variables, the presence of this South European welfare state increases the chance of an expansion in immigrants' access to rights compared to the Continental welfare state. Conversely, compared to Continental welfare states, the presence of a Liberal welfare state increases the chances of a decrease in immigrants' entitlement to rights. Finally, the last line of table 10.3 shows the result of the chi-squared test, which has as null hypothesis that all predictors are simultaneously equal to zero. The small p-values (smaller than 0.01) lead to the conclusion that at least one coefficient of the model is different from zero.

CONCLUSION

This chapter sought to clarify RRPPs' influence on immigrants' entitlement to social rights and the influence of the interaction between RRPPs and mainstream parties on the adoption of welfare chauvinist policies. Therefore, this study tested three main hypotheses. The first is that RRPPs are able to restrict immigrants' access to social policies by participating in the government, mechanism called *direct influence*. The second one is that even when RRPPs are not part of the government coalition, the increase of RRPPs participation in parliament influences the adoption of welfare chauvinist policies, the *indirect influence*. The third hypothesis is that welfare chauvinist policies are adopted independently of RRPPs participation in governments or parliaments.

In line with previous studies, it confirmed the direct influence of RRPP on immigrants' entitlement to social rights. RRPPs participation in governments increases the odds of a reduction in immigrants' entitlement to welfare benefits. Also, a marginal increase of RRPP's participation share in the coalition increases the likelihood of changes in immigrants' entitlement to rights. This last point shows that their bargaining power explains the influence of those parties on the adoption of welfare chauvinist policies. Finally, the statistical study showed that the influence of formal and informal RRPP government participation on immigrants' entitlement to social rights differs in terms of magnitude, with the negative influence being greater when a RRPP informally participates in a coalition. A possible explanation for this result is that RRPPs trade offices for policy outcomes. One important limitation of this outcome, though, is that it is mainly the result of the Danish case; therefore, it cannot be generalized for other parties. Nevertheless, a case study is needed to identify and clarify how this trade mechanism works to verify that hypothesis.

Additionally, the study did not confirm the indirect influence hypothesis. Another finding is that mainstream parties affect immigrants' entitlement to social rights. All variables held constant, a marginal shift in government orientation towards the right increases the odds of restrictions to immigrants' rights. This result suggests that mainstream right-wing parties adopt welfare chauvinist measures regardless of the electoral success of RRPPs and level of RRPPs' government participation. This finding supports Mudde's observation

(2007) that governments that do not face competition with a RRPP or have a RRPP in their coalition still adopt restrictive policies towards immigrants.

It is important to note that the present research relies on a small database made up of seventeen cases studied over twenty-five years. It reduces the power of the statistical tests, which increases the probability of rejecting a true hypothesis (type II error). However, this feature does not alter the reliability of the significant results (type I error). Therefore, the associations found in the study are likely to be true. Additionally, due to the size of the dataset, the results are sensitive to changes in my database. In that scenario, the accuracy of the data is even more determinative to obtain reliable results.

Therefore, this study illustrates that the role of RRPPs in the adoption of welfare chauvinist polices cannot be ignored. The analysis supports the claim that the participation of a RRPP in the coalition is the predominant mechanism of RRPPs' influence on immigrants' rights. Additionally, unlike previous studies, which highlighted the technical incapacity of RRPPs to obtain policy results, this work suggests that RRPPs use their bargaining power inside coalitions to implement strategies to influence policies. Finally, traditional left and right dimensions also explain changes to immigrants' entitlement to rights. Controlled by the presence of RRPPs in politics, the higher a government scores on the left–right scale, the more likely they are to adopt welfare chauvinist policies.

NOTES

1. I chose to apply the random effects model because I have time-independent explanatory variables. The estimator is the method of maximum likelihood.

2. In order to ensure results' reliability, I also ran survival models. The results support the conclusions presented in this chapter and are available upon request.

3. Refer to Helbling (2013) for a full discussion about the topic.

4. To maintain coherence with the hypotheses developed previously, I excluded changes in legislation that address economic rights (access to the labour market), target exclusively the rights of immigrants from the diaspora and legislation adopted due to judicial decision.

5. If there is more than one RRPP in the parliament, this variable represents the share of the sum of all seats occupied by RRPPs.

6. For electoral years, I considered preponderant data, that is, information that lasts more than six months.

7. For example, if the government has 35 per cent of the parliament seats and its position is 3.5, the position of the entire parliament, excluding the government parties, is 6.0. This variable will assume the value of 4.25: $(((0.35)(0.50)) * 3.5) + (((0.15)(0.50)) * 6.0)$.

8. The calculation 1/odd gives the odds of obtaining lower values of the dependent variable given a marginal rise in the independent variable.

9. Policy coverage corresponds to rules regarding who can receive social rights and under what conditions. Policy reforms may or may not introduce fundamental changes in the criterion of social policy distribution. Introduction or removal of bureaucratic requirements to receive benefits is considered a minor change in coverage. On the other hand, exclusion or inclusion of an immigrant group from receiving the benefits and the introduction or removal of long waiting periods are considered major changes. The increase or decrease of waiting periods up to one year and exclusion or inclusion of only part of an immigrant group are considered mid-level changes.

10. In proportional odds models, it is common practice to collapse adjacent categories. For a detailed discussion about the pros and cons of this method, refer to Murad, Fleischman, Sadetzki, Geyer and Freedman (2003).

BIBLIOGRAPHY

Adams, James, Andrea B. Haupt and Heather Stoll. 2009. What moves parties? The role of public opinion and global economic conditions in Western Europe. *Comparative Political Studies*, 42(5): 611–639.

Afonso, Alexandre. 2015. Choosing whom to betray: Populist right-wing parties, welfare state reforms and the trade-off between office and votes. *European Political Science Review*, 7(2): 271–292.

Afonso, Alexandre and Line Rennwald. 2018. The changing welfare state agenda of populist radical right parties in Europe. *Welfare Democracies and Party Politics: Explaining Electoral Dynamics in Times of Changing Welfare Capitalism*, edited by Philip Manow, Bruno Palier and Hanna Schwander, 171–196. New York: Oxford University Press.

Akkerman, Tjitske. 2012. Comparing radical right parties in government: Immigration and integration policies in nine countries (1996–2010). *West European Politics*, 35(3): 511–529.

Akkerman, Tjitske and Sarah L. de Lange. 2012. Radical right parties in office: Incumbency records and the electoral cost of governing. *Government and Opposition*, 47(4): 574–596.

Akkerman, Tjitske, Sarah L. de Lange and Matthijs Rooduijn. 2016. Inclusion and mainstreaming? In *Radical Right-Wing Populist Parties in Western Europe: Into the Mainstream?* edited by Tjitske Akkerman, Sarah de Lange and Matthijs Rooduij, 1–28. New York: Routledge.

Allan, James P. and Lyle Scruggs. 2004. Political partisanship and welfare state reform in advanced industrial societies. *American Journal of Political Science*, 48(3): 496–512.

Alonso, Sonia and Sara Claro da Fonseca. 2012. Immigration, left and right. *Party Politics*, 18(6): 865–884.

Andersen, Jørgen Goul and Tor Bjørklund. 1990. Structural change and new cleavages: The progress parties in Denmark and Norway. *Acta Sociologica*, 33(3): 195–217.

Bale, Tim. 2008. Turning round the telescope. Centre-right parties and immigration and integration policy in Europe. *Journal of European Public Policy*, 15(3): 315–330.

Bale, Tim, Christoffer Green-Pedersen, André A. Krouwel, Kurt Richard Luther and Nick Sitter. 2010. If you can't beat them, join them? Explaining social democratic responses to the challenge from the populist radical right in Western Europe. *Political Studies*, 58(3): 410–426.

Betz, Hans-Georg. 1994. *Radical Right-wing Populism in Western Europe*. Hampshire: Macmillan.

Boeri, Tito. 2010. Immigration to the land of redistribution. *Economica*, 77(308): 651–287.

Bolin, Niklas, Gustav Lidén and Jon Nyhlén. 2014. Do anti-immigration parties matter? The case of the Sweden Democrats and local refugee policy. *Scandinavian Political Studies*, 37(3): 323–343.

Budge, Ian, Dennis Farlie and Michael Laver. 1983. Shifts of meaning within explanations of voting and party competition. *Electoral Studies*, 2(1): 23–38.

Castles, Francis Geoffrey, ed. 1982. *The Influence of Parties: Politics and Policies in Democratic Capitalist States*. London: Sage Publications.

Christiansen, Flemming Juul and Helene Helboe Pedersen. 2014. Minority coalition governance in Denmark. *Party Politics*, 20(6): 940–949.

Copsey, Nigel. 2007. Changing course or changing clothes? Reflections on the ideological evolution of the British National Party 1999–2006. *Patterns of Prejudice*, 41(1): 61–82.

Crepaz, Marcus M. L. 2008. *Trust beyond Borders: Immigration, the Welfare State, and Identity in Modern Societies*. Ann Arbor, MI: University of Michigan Press.

De Koster, Willem, Peter Achterberg and Jeroen Van der Waal. 2013. The new right and the welfare state: The electoral relevance of welfare chauvinism and welfare populism in the Netherlands. *International Political Science Review*, 34(1): 3–20.

DEMIG. 2015. DEMIG POLICY, version 1.3, Online Edition. Oxford: International Migration Institute, University of Oxford. www.migrationdeterminants.eu.

Downs, Anthony. 1957. *An Economic Theory of Democracy*. New York: Harper-Collins Publishers.

Economist Intelligence Unit. 2008. Global Migration Barometer. Methodology, Results and Findings. London: WesternUnion, The Economist.

Ennser-Jedenastik, Laurenz. 2018. Welfare chauvinism in populist radical right platforms: The role of redistributive justice principles. *Social Policy and Administration*, 52(1): 293–314.

Esping-Andersen, Gosta. 1990. *The Three Words of Welfare Capitalism*. Cambridge: Polity Press.

Helbling, Marc. 2013. Validating integration and citizenship policy indices. *Comparative European Politics*, 11(5): 555–576.

Hicks, Alexander, Duane H. Swank and Martin Ambuhl. 1989. Welfare expansion revisited: Policy routines and their mediation by party, class and crisis, 1957–1982. *European Journal of Political Research*, 17: 401–430.

Howard, Marc Morjé. 2010. The influence of the far right on citizenship policy in Europe: Explaining continuity and change. *Journal of Ethnic and Migration Studies*, 36(5): 735–751.

Inglehart, Ronald and Pippa Norris. 2017. Trump and the populist authoritarian parties: The silent revolution in reverse. *Perspectives on Politics*, 15(2): 443–454.

Ivarsflaten, Elisabeth. 2008. What unites right-wing populists in Western Europe? Re-examining grievance mobilization models in seven successful cases. *Comparative Political Studies*, 41(1): 3–13.

Kitschelt, Herbert. 1994. *The Transformation of European Social Democracy*. New York: Cambridge University Press.

Klugman, Jeni and Isabel Medalho Pereira. 2009. Assessment of national migration policies: An emerging picture on admissions, treatment and enforcement in developing and developed countries. *Human Development Research Paper*, no. 48.

Kolbe, Melanie and Markus M. L. Crepaz. The power of citizenship: How immigrant incorporation affects attitudes towards social benefits. *Comparative Politics*.

Koning, Edward. 2013. Selective solidarity: The Politics of immigrants' social rights in Western welfare states. PhD thesis, Queen's University.

Kriesi, Hanspeter, Edgar Grande, Romain Lachat, Martin Dolezal, Simon Bornschier, and Timotheos Frey. 2006. Globalization and the transformation of the national political space: Six European countries compared. *European Journal of Political Research*, 45: 921–956.

Laclau, Ernesto. 1977. *Politics and Ideology in Marxist Theory: Capitalism, Fascism, Populism*. London: Verso.

Meguid, Bonnie M. 2005. Competition between unequals: The role of mainstream party strategy in niche party success. *American Political Science Review*, 99(3): 347–359.

Minkenberg, Michael. 2001. The radical right in public office: Agenda-setting and policy influences. *West European Politics*, 24(4): 1–21.

Mudde, Cas. 2004. The populist Zeitgeist. *Government and Opposition*, 39(4): 541–563.

Mudde, Cas. 2007. *Populist Radical Right Parties in Europe*. Cambridge: Cambridge University Press.

Mudde, Cas. 2013. Three decades of populist radical right parties in Western Europe: So what? *European Journal of Political Research*, 52(1): 1–19.

Murad, Havi, Anat Fleischman, Siegal Sadetzki, Orna Geyer and Laurence S. Freedman. 2003. Small samples and ordered logistic regression: Does it help to collapse categories of outcome? *The American Statistician*, 57(3): 155–160.

Niessen, Jan, et al. 2007. *Migrant Integration Policy Index (MIPEX)*. Brussels: British Council and Migration Policy Group.

Norris, Pippa. 2005. *Radical Right: Voters and Parties in Electoral Market*. Cambridge: Cambridge University Press.

Oxford Analytica. 2008. *Labour Migration Policy Index Phase II*. IOM, October 01, 2008. Peters, M.

Pontusson, Jonas. 1995. Explaining the decline of European social democracy: The role of structural economic change. *World Politics*, 47(4): 495–533.

Putnam, Robert D. 2007. E pluribus unum: diversity and community in the twenty-first century: The Johan Skytte Prize Lecture. *Scandinavian Political Studies*, 30(2): 134–167.

Ruhs, Martin. 2011. Openness, Skills and Rights: An Empirical Analysis of Labor Immigration Programs in 46 High- and Middle-Income Countries. *COMPAS Working Paper. 88*. Centre on Migration, Policy and Society. Oxford.

Rydgren, Jens. 2004. Explaining the emergence of radical right-wing populist parties: The case of Denmark. *West European Politics*, 27(3): 474–502.

Schain, Martin A. 2006. The extreme-right and immigration policy-making: Measuring direct and indirect influences. *West European Politics*, 29(2): 270–289.

Schumacher, Gijs and Kees Van Kersbergen. 2016. Do mainstream parties adapt to the welfare chauvinism of populist parties? *Party Politics*, 22(3): 300–312.

Soroka, Stuart, Keith Banting and Richard Johnston. 2006. Immigration and redistribution in a global era, in: S. Bowles, P. Bardhan, and M. Wallerstein (eds.). *Globalization and Egalitarian Redistribution*. Princeton, PA: Princeton University Press and Russell Sage Foundation, 261–288.

Strom, Kaare. 1990. *Minority Government and Majority Rule*. Cambridge University Press.

van Spanje, Joost. 2010. Anti-immigration parties and their influence on other parties' immigration stances in contemporary Western Europe. *Party Politics*, 16(5): 563–586.

Thesen, Gunnar. 2016. Win some, lose none? support parties at the polls and in political agenda-setting. *Political Studies*, 64(4): 979–999.

Williams, Michelle. 2006. *The Influence of Radical Right-Wing Parties in West European Democracies*. Basingstoke: Palgrave Macmillan.

Appendix 1

Country	Year	Resume	Policies(s) affected	Immigrant group(s)	Change in coverage	Ordinal variable
Austria	1991	1991 Law on Federal Care for Asylum Seekers ('Bundesbetreuung') was established – stipulating that the federal government is responsible for health, nutritional and accommodation of asylum seekers. However, there is no legal entitlement to these benefits.	Health, minimum income and housing	Asylum seekers	Mid-level change	3
Austria	1997	Revision of the Law on Unemployment Assurance – made all third country nationals eligible for emergency benefits (after unemployment benefits) but enshrined the priority of people born in Austria. This amendment is a reaction to a judgement of the ECHR, which considered the exclusion of third country nationals from emergency benefits do not conform with human rights. Before, only refugees and those with permanent residence permit were eligible.	Minimal income	Temporary immigrants	Mid-level change	1
Austria	2002	Internal order of the Ministry of Interior – restricted access to state benefits to asylum seekers from certain countries which were likely to be rejected (a list of safe third countries was created)	Minimal income	Asylum seekers	Mid-level change	–1
Austria	2004	Seasonal workers are no longer eligible for unemployment benefits.	Minimal income	Temporary immigrants	Mid-level change	–1
Belgium	2000	Two measures have been introduced in 2000 in the field of asylum – replacing the granting of financial assistance to asylum seekers by a material assistance distributed in open reception centres created for this purpose	Minimal income	Asylum seekers	Mid-level change	–1

Belgium	2007	Reception Law introduced material support during the entire asylum procedure (replacing, as was the case in the past, the situation where asylum seekers could apply for financial support from social welfare centres)	Minimal income	Asylum seekers	Minor change	−1
Belgium	2010	Amendment of the 2007 Reception Law – changed in reaction to the reception crisis the right of reception and/or material aid for certain categories of asylum seekers and other foreigners. (1) Fedasil may exclude asylum seekers, who applied for asylum the third or further times (2) the end terms of material aid for asylum seekers and certain other categories of foreigners is specified: if an asylum claim is henceforth concluded with a negative decision of the appeal instance or the Court of Cassation, the material aid is ending after a term of five days after the issue date of the decision. (3) in exceptional circumstances, it is allowed to assign asylum seekers to a local Public Centre for Social Welfare (OCMW/CPAS) for inscription.	Minimal income	Asylum seekers	Minor change	−1
Belgium	2011	Bill of 27 October 2011 – stipulated that asylum seekers introducing a subsequent asylum application can no longer benefit form material assistance, unless their asylum claim is deemed admissible by the Immigration office.	Minimal income	Asylum seekers	Minor change	−1

(Continued)

(Continued)

Country	Year	Resume	Policies(s) affected	Immigrant group(s)	Change in coverage	Ordinal variable
Belgium	2012	The Belgian Public Centre for Social Welfare (CPAS/OCMW) has restricted its support to EU citizens and their family members since 27 February 2012. In detail, this means that – All EU citizens and their family members are excluded from entitlement to CPAS/OCMW social services, (urgent) medical assistance and employment provisions during the first three months of their stay in Belgium. – After the first three months, EU citizens and their family members are entitled to CPAS/OCMW social services, medical assistance and employment provisions, provided that they are not job seekers. Irregularly staying individuals are only entitled to urgent medical assistance. – Once they obtain an E or F card, all EU citizens and their family members qualify for social integration (income support and employment provisions) if they meet the conditions regarding the Right to Social Integration provided by Belgian Law.	Minimal income and health assistance	EU citizens	Minor change	–1
Denmark	1999	On 26 June 1998 the Danish Parliament passed its first Integration Act, which entered into effect on 1 January 1999 – created the Start Help, a very low level of social benefits for newly arrived refugees, so that their benefits were much lower than the benefits for Danish citizens.	Minimal income	Refugees and asylum seeker	Mid-level change	–2

Country	Year	Description	Benefit type	Target group	Change type	Score
		> This was a drawback from the general entitlement to social benefits enacted in 1976. The official argument was that the level of benefits should function as a positive incentive to integrate refugees into the labour market.				
Denmark	2000	The start help for newly arrived refugees was abolished in January 2000 only thirteen months after its introduction. > The official argument was that it was not possible to demonstrate that the lower rates had given work to more refugees and that the rules might be contravening the 1951 refugee convention.	Minimal income	Refuges and asylum seeker	Mid-level change	1
Denmark	2002	Amendment to the Integration Act in 2002 Reduces the amount of assistance granted to newly arrived immigrants in order to encourage them to look for a job more rapidly.	Minimal income and housing	Temporary immigrant, asylum seeker and refugees	Mid-level change	–3
Denmark	2003	In July 2003, a new law regarding asylum seekers and refugees came into effect – creating a contract that needs to be fulfilled by an applicant in order to receive basic cash allowances from the state.	Minimal income	Asylum seekers and refugees	Minor change	–1
Denmark	2009	Act No. 982 of 2 October 2009 Section 2: old age pension requires 10 years of legal residence in Denmark OR (convention or quota refugees), cf. The size of the pension depends of the length of stay. Full pension is possible after forty years of legal residence.	Unemployment assistance	EU citizens, permanent immigrant, temporary, refugees and asylum seeker	Mid-level change	–3

(Continued)

(Continued)

Country	Year	Resume	Policies(s) affected	Immigrant group(s)	Change in coverage	Ordinal variable
Denmark	2010	Law no.1609 (L79): adopted: December 12 2010 and January 1 2011: Introduced an earnings principle, which was used to discriminate in the payment of child – and youth benefits to families in Denmark, effectively barring newly arrived immigrant families from receiving child – and youth benefits equivalent to that of ethnically Danish families until they had held residence in Denmark for two years. Newly arrived families thereby only had the right to 25 per cent of the benefits after six months, 50 per cent of the benefits after twelve months, 75 per cent of benefits after eighteen months and 100 per cent after two years. Law 1382 (L31)	Family Assistance	EU citizens, temporary immigrants	Mid-level change	−2
Denmark	2012	From January 2012, cash allowances for newly arrived refugees and immigrants, as well as the starter allowances for persons having resided in Denmark for less than seven of the preceding eight years will be eliminated – instead, new immigrants will be entitled to social assistance from the moment they arrive in Denmark.	Minimal income	Temporary immigrant, asylum seeker and refugees	Mid-level change	3
Finland	2010	Amended Decree entered into force on 2 February 2010 on living allowance paid in cash to asylum seekers – reducing the cash portion of basic living allowance paid to an asylum seeker by 30 per cent compared to other residents of Finland.	Minimal income	Asylum seekers	Mid-level change	−1

Country	Year	Description	Policy area	Target group	Magnitude	Score
France	1998	Law 98-349 of 11 May 1998 relative to the conditions of entry and stay of foreigners (Loi Chevènement) – extends social benefits to irregular migrants. > For instance, living allowance for an adult asylum seeker living alone will be €292.22 per month (compared to €375.11 previously).	Housing and family assistance	Non-documented immigrants	Major change	3
France	2010	Law Arrete du 15 mars 2010	Housing	Permanent immigrants, temporary, asylum seekers and refugees	Mid-level change	3
Germany	1993	1993 law on financial support of asylum seekers (Asylbewerberleistungsgesetz) – creates a specific allowance for asylum seekers, which is lower than the mainstream social benefits	Minimal income	Asylum seekers	Minor change	−1
Germany	1993	1993 law on financial support of asylum seekers (Asylbewerberleistungsgesetz) – grants illegally resident migrants entitlement to medical care. > In particular, medical services are granted in cases of acute sickness and pain, pregnancy and childbirth.	Health assistance	Non documented immigrants	Mid-level change	1
Germany	2014	In November 2014, over two years after the Constitutional Court ruling, both houses of the German Parliament finally passed revisions to the Asylum Seekers' Benefits Act. According to the amendment, from March 2015 onwards allowances for asylum seekers will be similar to the ones provided under the transitional arrangement.	Minimal income	Asylum seekers	Mid-level change	1

(Continued)

Country	Year	Resume	Policies(s) affected	Immigrant group(s)	Change in coverage	Ordinal variable
Greece	1991	Act No 1975/1991 regulating the admission of aliens (replaced by Act 2910/2001) – stipulates that all public services and legal persons under public law, the local self-administration authorities, public utilities ventures and social security fund organizations are obliged to refrain from offering their services to irregular immigrants. This obligation is also extended to hospitals, sanatoriums and clinics, unless there is an emergency or children need medical care.	Health assistance and family benefits	Undocumented immigrants	Major change	–3
Greece	1996	Law 2452/1996 – defined the requirements and the procedure for granting assistance, both to recognized refugees and to those who have submitted a request for refugee status.	Minimal income	Asylum seekers and refugees	Major change	3
Greece	1999	Presidential Decree 266/1999 – covered issues like social protection of the recognized refugees and asylum seekers.	Minimal income	Asylum seekers	Major change	3
Greece	2001	Act 2910/2001 on the entry, residence and naturalization of immigrants in Greece (entered into force on 2 June 2001; amended by Act 3013/2002) – guarantees equal access to the courts, social services and health care to legal migrants, as well as access to education for undocumented children. > Since 2001, immigrants who work and pay taxes in Greece have the same rights as Greek workers. For example, they can benefit from the housing	Housing and basic education	Undocumented immigrants, temporary immigrants, permanent immigrants	Major change	3

Country	Year	Description	Benefit	Target group	Change	Score
		program of the Organisation of Labour Housing (OEK) as long as they fulfil certain requirements that also apply to Greek workers. This housing program is supervised by the Ministry of Employment and Social Protection and it gives immigrants the opportunity to either receive a monthly rent subsidy or reside in public (labor) housing.				
Greece	2005	In February 2005, the Minister of Health issued a ministerial circular to state hospitals stating that free routine health care to immigrants who are not legal residents is against the law.	Health assistance	Undocumented immigrants	Major change	−2
Greece	2006	Act 3386/2005 on the entry, residence and integration of immigrants (voted in May 2005 and to be implemented in 2006) – made legally resident immigrants eligible for social security insurance and benefiting of the same social, labor and security rights as Greek workers.	Family Assistance and social pension	Temporary and permanent immigrants	Minor change	2
Ireland	2004	The Social Welfare (Miscellaneous Provisions) Act 2004 – restricts access to social assistance and Child Benefit payments by introducing a 'Habitual Residence Condition'. Migrants have to demonstrate two years of 'habitual' residency in Ireland and the intention to stay in the country in order to be eligible for benefits. > As in the UK, Accession State nationals face restrictions on access to Ireland's social welfare system. Ireland proposed the restrictions in February 2004 after the UK had done so. The test applies to all persons but was introduced to protect the Irish welfare system.	Minimal income, housing allowances, child benefits, pension assistance	EU citizens, temporary, asylum seeker	Major change	−3

(Continued)

(Continued)

Country	Year	Resume	Policies(s) affected	Immigrant group(s)	Change in coverage	Ordinal variable
Ireland	2006	2006 Amendments to the Habitual Residence Condition – eased the requirement of the habitual residence condition to access social benefits nearly completely for EEA and to a certain extent for non-EEA residents. The amendment granted all EEA workers who have work history in the state access to the Supplementary Welfare Allowance (includes a basic allowance, rent allowance, emergency payments and medical cards).	Minimal income, housing allowances, child benefits and social pension	EU citizens	Major change	3
Ireland	2009	Since December 2009, asylum seekers no longer have access to the Irish welfare system.	Minimal income, housing allowances, child benefits and social pension	Asylum seekers	Major change	−3
Italy	1999	'Turco-Napolitano' law (Act 40) granted access to education and the national health system for all immigrants regardless of their legal status, including irregular migrants, but in this case limited to urgent and/or essential treatment.	Health care and education	Undocumented immigrants	Mid-level change	2
Italy	2002	(Law no. 189 called Bossi-Fini). TCNs need a two-year temporary permit for an equal access to housing. The claim of a permit at least two years was introduced in 2002.	Housing	Temporary immigrants and EU citizens	Major change	−3

Country	Year	Description		Change	
Luxembourg	2002	Grand Ducal Regulation of 4 July 2002 – defines the modalities and conditions of social aid for asylum seekers	Housing and minimal income	Asylum seekers	Major change	3
Luxembourg	2012	Grand Ducal Regulation of 8 June 2012 on social aid for international protection applicants, significantly reduced the financial allocation received.	Housing and minimal income	Asylum seekers	Mid-level change	−1
Netherlands	1996	Linking Act. Law passed in November 1996 and went into effect on 1 July 1998. Since then, undocumented migrants are barred from all social benefits and provisions with the exception of education for under-aged children, legal counselling and emergency medical care.	Non-compulsory education, health care, housing and minimal income	Undocumented immigrants	Major change	−3
Netherlands	2001	Aliens Act of April 2001 introduced the same social benefits for all asylum seekers. In its place, only one asylum status is possible, granting the same temporary ('fixed-term') residence permit and entitlements to all refugees: to be eligible for student financing and subsidized accommodation.	Non-compulsory education and housing	Asylum seeker	Mid-level change	2
Norway	1997	1997 policy on refugees – granted those under collective protection the same rights as those granted refugee status, including the right to receive education and social security payments.	Housing, family allowances, minimal income and non-compulsory education	Asylum seeker	Major change	3

(Continued)

(Continued)

Country	Year	Resume	Policies(s) affected	Immigrant group(s)	Change in coverage	Ordinal variable
Norway	2008	New Immigration Act of 15 May 2008 entered into force on 1 January 2010 – grants all asylum applicants who are entitled to protection refugee status. Pursuant to the Act, persons who were previously granted asylum in accordance with the Geneva Convention and persons who are protected from deportation (*refoulement*) according to other conventions will be given the same status as refugees, entitling the former to the same rights as the latter.	Housing, family allowances, minimal income and non-compulsory education	Asylum seeker	Minor change	2
Portugal	2001	Law establishing a framework on health stipulates that any foreign citizen living legally in Portugal has access to health care and services of the National Health Service (NHS), like all nationals. Those staying irregularly may have access to NHS by presenting a residence certificate (that can be obtained in the local councils) at the health service located in their area of residence, proving that they had been in Portugal for at least 90 days.	Health assistance	Non-documented immigrants	Minor change	1
Portugal	2006	Decree Law 41/2006 of 21 February – extended the attribution of family social allowance to foreign children and youngsters who hold a legal title of permanence, to refugees, and to holders of temporary protection titles. Thereby, the mentioned Decree Law puts on the same level resident foreigners, the holders of	Family assistance	Permanent immigrants, temporary and refugees	Major change	3

Portugal	2009	permanence permit, the refugees and the holders of temporary protection title for attribution of family social allowance to children and youngsters. Such social benefits were formerly only granted to foreigners holding residence permits.

Decree Law 204/2009 of 31 August – allows foreign students who hold a permanent residence permit or benefit from the status of long-term resident to access social action benefits in the field of higher education. | Non-compulsory education | Permanent immigrants | Mid-level change | 1 |
| Portugal | 2010 | Circular 11258/2010 of 7 June approved the Regulations for Advanced Training and the Qualification of Human Resources 2010 – facilitating the conditions for the applications of foreign students to Portuguese education resources | Non-compulsory education | Temporary immigrants | Minor change | 1 |
| Spain | 2000 | Law 4/2000 on the Rights and Freedoms of Foreigners in Spain and Their Integration widened most socio-economic rights to aliens in an irregular situation, such as the right to education in the same conditions as Spanish people; the right of all aliens, whatever their legal situation might be, to emergency public health care, and the right to public health care for all aliens who are minors and for pregnant women before and after the birth; the right to assistance as regards housing for aliens registered in the municipal census; and the right to basic social services and facilities (although such basic facilities were not clarified). | Health care, housing, compulsory education | Undocumented immigrants | Major change | 3 |

(Continued)

(Continued)

Country	Year	Resume	Policies(s) affected	Immigrant group(s)	Change in coverage	Ordinal variable
Spain	2001	Law 8/2000 amending Law 4/2000 makes the Immigration Law more restrictive by removing nearly all socio-economic rights that had been granted to irregular migrants under the January 2000 Law, except the right to health care and access to education for minors. The most important exception is the right to public health care, which remains unaltered by the modification.	Housing and non-emergency health care	Undocumented immigrants	Major change	−3
Sweden	2003	Bill 'Measures to clarify the identity of asylum seekers, etc' entered into force on 1 July 2004 – allowed to partially reduce or entirely remove the daily allowance and housing allowance of an alien over the age of 18 under the Act on the Reception of Asylum Seekers and Others Act (1994) if she or he hinders the investigation of a case concerning a residence permit by not assisting in clarifying his or her identity.	Housing and minimal income	Asylum seeker	Mid-level change	−3
Sweden	2009	In late 2009, the government in Stockholm announced that students from abroad will have to pay for university studies in Sweden from the winter semester 2011 onwards.	Non-compulsory education	Temporary and permanent immigrants	Mid-level change	−2
Switzerland	2004	Asylum seekers with a decision to dismiss an application without entering into the substance of the case (DAWES) have been excluded from social assistance since 2004,	Health care, minimum income and housing	Asylum seeker	Mid-level change	−3

Country	Year	Description	Policy area	Target group	Change	Score
Switzerland	2007	New Asylum Act approved in a referendum in September 2006 (phased in between 2007 and 2008) – excludes individuals with a legally binding rejected decision on asylum from social assistance. They are only eligible for emergency assistance (Nothilfe) and have limited access to health care > They are only eligible to emergency assistance and in some cantons they only get access to the public health system in case of emergency.	Health care and minimum income	Asylum seekers	Minor change	–1
Switzerland	2010	In February 2010, the Federal Council approved a number of measures aimed at limiting potential abuses in the framework of the freedom of movement – including restrictions of access to the welfare system of persons from the EU/EEA.	Family allowances and minimal income	EU citizens	Minor change	–1
UK	1993	Asylum and Immigration Appeals Act 1993 – reduced the benefit entitlements of persons who claim asylum in the UK, as well as their dependents.	Minimal income	Asylum seekers	Minor change	–1
UK	1996	Asylum and Immigration Act 1996 – withdraw eligibility to non-contributory benefits from asylum seekers who did not lodge their application at the port of entry or who are appealing on a negative decision on their claim. > This resulted in a High Court judgement in October 1996, which established that local authorities have a duty under the National Assistance Act to provide services to asylum seekers with no other means of support.	Minimal income	Asylum seekers	Mid-level change	–1

(Continued)

(Continued)

Country	Year	Resume	Policies(s) affected	Immigrant group(s)	Change in coverage	Ordinal variable
UK	1999	Immigration and Asylum Act 1999 – introduces the National Asylum Support Service (NASS) to co-ordinate the arrangements for supporting asylum seekers and dispersing them to different areas of the UK. The act replaces welfare benefits for asylum seekers with vouchers worth £35 a week for an adult and provides accommodation on a no-choice basis around the UK.	Housing and minimum income	Asylum seekers	Minor change	–1
UK	2004	2004 EU enlargement – workers from the new EU countries only become eligible for benefits such as Jobseeker's Allowance and income support after working continuously in the UK for at least a year.	Minimal income	EU citizens	Minor change	–1
UK	2004	Asylum and Immigration Act 2004 – Limits eligibility for refugee support. > Failed asylum seekers with children can be refused support if they are not 'cooperating with the removals process'.	Minimal income	Asylum seekers	Minor change	–1
UK	2009	Borders, Citizenship and Immigration Act 2009 – restricts the access to public services and benefits during Probationary Citizenship	Housing, old age assistance, minimum income and family allowances	EU citizens and temporary immigrants	Mid-level change	–3

Source: DEMIG (2015) and author.

Appendix 2

As discussed, the number of legislations adopted does not provide a complete information about countries' change in exclusion (or inclusion) of immigrants in the welfare state as scope of the legislation varies. Therefore, in order to have a clear understanding about the scope of those measures, I coded the qualitative information present in DEMIG POLICY database in a numerical variable that considers not only the number or legislation adopted, but also its reach. To this end, the following dimensions were considered:

1. The change in policy coverage, which corresponds to a comparison between the initial degree of coverage and the policy coverage after the legislation change. Three levels of change are considered: minor change, mid-level change and major change. Those categories are respectively coded as 1, 2 and 3 if the change corresponds to an extension of coverage, or −1, −2 and −3 if the change corresponds to a restriction of coverage.[9]
2. The number of immigrant groups affected. The entitlements of six categories of immigrants are considered: EU citizens, permanent residents, temporary residents, asylum seekers, refugees and non-documented immigrants.
3. The number of policies affected (compulsory education, non-compulsory education, family allowances and childcare benefits, old age assistance, minimal income and long-term unemployment, social housing and public health or subsidies for insurance fees).

For each country, the following eight social policies will be considered: minimum income, social pension, guaranteed income for the elderly, children's allowances, housing allowances, healthcare aid, compulsory education and non-compulsory education. These are all non-contributory policies, which means they are generally financed by taxes and that the benefits received do not depend on previous contributions.

The choice of non-contributory policies stems from three factors. First, they represent a greater fiscal burden to the state because they are not linked to contributions. Second, immigrants have a higher exposure to social risks, such as poverty and unemployment, so they are relatively more dependent on these types of benefits than the general population (Boeri, 2010). Therefore, such policies are likely targets of restrictions. Finally, the literature reports that, generally, immigrant access to contributory policies has no restrictions (Fix and Laglagaron, 2002).

The dependent variable applied in this study is calculated in a two-step process. First, I multiply the values of criterion 1, 2 and 3 aforementioned. For example, if the change corresponds to a mid-level restriction of rights, two immigrants' groups are affected, and the bill affects one social policy, this legislation change receives the value −4. As a result, I have an ordinal variable with values form from −36 to 36. Second, I collapse the outcome of the first step into an ordinal scale from −3 to 3.[10] Legislations that score less (more) than −5 (5) were considered major restrictions (expansions) and received the code −3 (3). Legislation changes scored between −3 and −4 (3 and 4) were considered mid-level restrictions (expansions) and were coded −2 (2). Legislation changes scored between −1 and −2 (1 and 2) were considered minor restrictions (expansions) and were therefore scored −1 (1).

Negative values correspond to decreases in entitlement, positive values correspond to increases in entitlement and zeroes correspond to the absence of change. Absolute values of 3 correspond to major changes in terms of polices and immigrants' groups affected, as well as the degree of the adoption of a restrictive legislation. Likewise, absolute values of 2 correspond to mid-level changes, and absolute values of 1 correspond to minor modifications.

For example, in 2002, Denmark approved an amendment of the integration act of 2002. The legislation reduced the amount of assistance granted to newly arrived immigrants in order to encourage their integration into labour market. The legislation targeted one social policy (minimal assistance) and three immigrant groups (refugees, asylum seekers and temporary immigrant). As the change in legislation reduced the level of benefit for a period, it is considered a mid-level change. The multiplicative formula leads to −6, which in the framework of this study is considered a major restriction and receive the ordinal number of −3.

Chapter 11

Law and Order Populism?

Assessing the Influence of Right-wing Populist Parties on Law and Order Policies in Europe

Georg Wenzelburger and Pascal D. König

Does the electoral success of radical right populist parties (RRPP) bear on mainstream parties' law and order policies? Although hardly studied in this context (cf. chapter 1 of this volume), RRPP seem a likely candidate for helping to explain mainstream or government party policy shifts in the area of law and order. A solid body of research has shown how RRPP affect immigration policies and how they drive mainstream parties to adopt more restrictive positions with regard to immigration. In fact, while the analyses by Akkerman (2015) and Green-Pedersen and Krogstrup (2008) question a direct effect on mainstream parties' immigration policy positions a number of contributions offers clear evidence that radical right populists do pull mainstream parties to a more restrictive position regarding immigration (Abou-Chadi, 2016; Alonso and da Fonseca, 2011; Dalton, 2009; Pettigrew, 1998; Schain, 1987, 2006; van Spanje, 2010). In a similar vein, the findings by Han (2015) indicate that the rise of radical right-wing parties induces mainstream parties to take more restrictive positions regarding multiculturalism.

Following the line of this research, we argue that a similar pattern is likely to also hold for law and order policies. There are several reasons why it makes sense to look at radical right populists as a possible cause for changes in law and order policy, reasons that do not stretch far from the cited research on immigration policy. First, RRPP seem to emphasize law and order, especially in association with their core issue of immigration (Betz, 1993; Mudde, 1996; Akkermann, 2015). Second, voters for whom the issue of immigration is important also are concerned with law and order (see e.g. Shields, 2007). Thus, RRPP have the potential to heighten the competitive pressure on mainstream parties specifically with regard to the law and order issue. Mainstream parties have to fear RRPP occupying this issue and attracting votes based on it. In other words, there are solid reasons to expect that mainstream parties in general and center-right parties in particular respond to the presence of a radical right populist challenger with a stronger emphasis on law and order in their programmes and adopt harsher policies when in government.

Investigating this role of RRPP can shed light on processes of party competition and policy-making. It is, however, also relevant from a criminological perspective and gains particular importance in light of research which has shown that, beginning in the early 1990s, law and order policies have become increasingly tough in several Western industrialized countries – a tendency that has been labelled 'punitive turn' (Downes, 2011; Tonry, 2007). Several explanations for this increasing harshness as well as for persisting cross-national differences have been put forward in the literature (for an overview, see Wenzelburger, 2015). Among others, there are explanations related to developments in crime (Garland 2001; Miller 2016), to broad trends such as globalization and neoliberalism (Wacquant, 2010), to attitudes of the citizens (Roberts et al., 2003; Enns, 2016), the type of the political economy (Cavadino and Dignan, 2006; Lacey, 2008) or the media (Cere et al., 2014). Only recently, the ideology of governing political parties has been identified as a further important cause of harsher law and order policies, not only in case studies (e.g. on the UK, Morgan, 2006; Newburn, 2007) but also in large-N quantitative analyses (Wenzelburger, 2015, 2016). Furthermore, the case study of the Swiss radical right populist SVP by Biard (2018) suggests a marked influence by that party on law and order policy, primarily during the agenda-setting stage.

Overall however, the reasons for policy shifts by mainstream and government parties are, to date, not well understood. More precisely, we lack an understanding of *why* parties harden their tone and policy action with regard to law and order policy and what role party competition plays in this connection (but: Miller, 2016). While RRPP are a plausible driver behind such policy shifts there is a lack of systematic evidence on the influence of their electoral successes on law and order policy, and on how mainstream parties might differ in their policy reactions to a rise of RRPP. To address this void in the literature, this paper investigates whether the strength of radical right populist parties is a relevant force that makes (1) mainstream parties shift their attention to law and order as an issue and eventually (2) adopt harsher policies when in government.

We thus investigate the influence of RRPPs looking at two dependent variables: (1) the emphasis of law and order issues by mainstream parties in their manifestos and (2) law and order policy outputs measured by public spending on public order and safety. The analysis assesses the influence of the strength of RRPP on these two variables by means of a quantitative large-N-analysis of European countries. The theoretical foundation is rooted in an issue competition framework, which departs from a purely positional model (mostly used for the studies on immigration) and takes into account the valence component involved the law and order politics (see also: Miller, 2016).

Our research adds to the state of the art in several respects. First, we contribute to the literature on the influence of RRPP by moving beyond the policy of immigration and by examining their influence not only on the salience of an issue but also on actual policies. And second, we advance the mostly criminological research on the 'punitive turn', by examining the role of RRPP pressuring mainstream parties to adopt a tougher stance.

The remainder of the chapter is structured as follows. The next section describes the theoretical framework for our analysis and presents the hypotheses that guide our empirical analysis. After having discussed the research design and data in the third section, the fourth section presents the findings of a series of regression analyses focusing on law and order issue salience as well as on policy outputs as dependent variables. The fifth section provides a brief discussion and closes with a conclusion.

THEORETICAL FRAMEWORK AND HYPOTHESES

Analyses of party policy change and party reactions to competitors are usually placed within the spatial model of party competition (e.g. Adams et al., 2005; Downs, 1957; Laver and Sergenti, 2012; Laver and Hunt, 1992; Meyer, 2010). Such models locate parties via positions they take on one or more dimensions and explain party electoral success based on the distance between voter preferences and party positions. Hence, the distribution of voter preferences and party positions determine a party's electoral success (Downs, 1957). The issue of law and order, however, does not easily fit into the spatial model because it involves both a valence component and a positional aspect.

The importance of a valence component (Stokes, 1963; Clarke et al., 2009) is based on the incontestable adherence of people to policy goals like high levels of security and successful crime fighting – issues on which parties agree as a desirable state or goal (Bélanger and Meguid, 2008, 483; see also Ansolabehere and Iyengar, 1994; Egan, 2013, 5). As political actors are therefore hardly inclined to openly state that they want less law and order, issue ownership, that is, to be perceived as the party that is best able to deal with the issue (Petrocik, 1996), is a crucial advantage in electoral competition. Acknowledging this valence component means that the issue of law and order requires a view on party competition that goes beyond the spatial conception of positionality and policy distances.

At the same time, however, law and order involves a positional element, too. It is linked to the preferred means of how to achieve high levels of security and low crime rates, and political parties diverge in their views, positioning themselves as more liberal or more repressive in party competition. Liberal parties advocate a less restrictive stance while emphasizing the importance of civil rights whereas more repressive parties propose tougher sanctions or more surveillance (Morgan, 2006; Newburn, 2007; Wenzelburger, 2015).

Moreover, this positional aspect is not unrelated to the question of how to achieve or defend issue ownership. Parties at least have to signal that they are committed to tackling the issue, which involves stating how exactly they aim to promote security and law and order, for instance by advocating to step up their efforts and thus to take a tougher stance on crime.[3] Consequently, issue ownership regarding law and order inherently contains a positional aspect, a consideration that is underscored by studies arguing that political actors cannot afford to present themselves as soft on crime (Roberts et al., 2003, 161).

The law and order issue is usually owned by those parties that take a tough stance on crime, and it is center-right parties that usually emphasize law and order comparatively more than other mainstream parties and are also more likely to own these issues (Heywood, 2017, 67–78). What makes their issue ownership status, at least in part, hard to challenge is that other parties would not be seen as credible if they were to take a harsh stance to deal with the law and order issue. In other words, they are unable to achieve the same valence.

Based on these assumptions, emphasizing law and order can generally be expected to go hand in hand with advocating a stronger effort and tougher stance in that area.[4] One would furthermore expect that those parties place a greater emphasis on this issue, which have issue ownership and can expect to attract more votes in this way (Bischoff, 2005; Green, 2007; Green and Hobolt, 2008; Green-Pedersen, 2007; Green-Pedersen and Mortensen 2010; Petrocik, 1996). This also means that the existence and popularity of a RRPP is primarily a threat to these issue-owner-parties because both most directly compete for voters.[5] RRPP have repeatedly been shown to emphasize law and order (Betz, 1993; Heinisch, 2003; Mudde, 2013), including as a way to underscore their anti-immigration stance (Akkerman, 2015; Smith, 2010).

Even if radical right populist parties do not own the law and order issue as such, they may still have strong incentives to emphasize and politicize the issue. When conceiving issue ownership as a question of degree (Geys, 2012) center-right parties may profit from a greater emphasis on law and order, specifically in comparison to its leftist competitors, but RRPP may well profit even more. Due to the relative strength in valence of these parties they have much more to win than to lose by emphasizing it. Moreover, they can scandalize cases of crime and violations of national security, for instance, and connect them to their core issue of immigration to boost their reputation on that issue. Therefore, RRPP may politicize law and order either because they expect to be competitive with that issue or because it helps them to increase their issue ownership with respect to immigration. In any case, they constitute a threat primarily to those parties that traditionally own the law and order issue, leading to the following expectation.

Hypothesis 1a: The party that traditionally owns the law and order issue in a country will react strongly to the increasing strength of a radical right populist party challenging its issue ownership by emphasizing the issue more strongly itself.

There are, however, reasons for expecting that RRPP do not only affect parties with issue ownership but mainstream parties in general. As Seeberg (2013) has argued, opposition parties can influence mainstream party and especially government party policies through politicizing an issue and setting it on the public and political agenda. This expectation is based on the idea that law and order forms a potentially problematic issue for governing parties as it can appear that the government is not doing enough and thus becomes susceptible to blame (Seeberg, 2013, 92). The government then has an incentive to respond and avoid this risk.

Developing this argument further, opposition parties can be presumed to strive for being and staying competitive on the issue or use the opportunity of a politicized law and order issue to attack the government. Hence, they also have an incentive to emphasize this issue as a reaction to a radical right populist challenge that is accompanied by a greater salience of law and order. Moreover, if this issue salience is accompanied by an increase in voter support of RRPP this forms a strong signal that the populist agenda is attractive to voters. Mainstream parties in general, then, have an incentive to respond to the law and order issue emphasis by stressing this issue themselves as they have to fear that they are perceived as giving too little attention to this sensitive issue. This relationship is expressed in the following hypothesis.

Hypothesis 1b: The more vote shares a radical right populist party wins while emphasizing law and order, the more mainstream parties emphasize the law and order issue.

Advertising a policy is, however, not the same as actual policy action, and RRPP might pressure mainstream parties to place a greater emphasis on the law and order issue but ultimately fail to influence policies. In fact, for policies, differences between issue owner parties and the remaining mainstream parties should be more pronounced. Following a 'bifurcation' argument (Frase, 2001, 263), several criminologists have found that some governments only pay lip service to the calls for harsher law and order policies without implementing harsher laws (Aharonson, 2013, 167; Kunz, 2013, 38)[6] whereas others also toughen the policy stance. Relating this argument to the literature on issue ownership leads us to expect that this difference is due to the importance of the law and order issues to the respective parties in governments. Whereas government parties that own the issue are very likely to defend (and enhance) their issue ownership in the light of a radical right populist threat by adopting tougher law and order policies, such policy change is riskier for other mainstream parties as a stark policy turn involves a much higher risk of alienating core voters than merely emphasizing the issue more strongly. Consequently, whereas it is likely that center-right parties indeed react with tougher policies to an attack on their issue ownership by RRPP, we would expect that other mainstream parties may change their position on paper, but not in actual policies (see also Albrecht, 2004). In sum, we only expect an influence on policy for governments in which issue-owner parties are present:

Hypothesis 2: The more vote shares a radical right populist party wins while emphasizing law and order, the more likely are government parties that traditionally own the law and order issue in a country to adopt tougher law and order policies.

DATA AND METHOD

Data and Measurement

In order to test the theoretical expectations developed above, we have constructed an original dataset, which includes sixteen European countries and covers, depending on data availability in the respective country, the years from the mid-1980s to 2014. The panel dataset is structured based on 'election periods in countries', that is, a single election period in a certain country counts as one observation.[7] Opting for this approach instead of the more common country-year-structure not only has methodological advantages (Schmitt, 2016), but it is also adequate for conceptual reasons because one of our main variables of interest, the salience of the law and order issue, is measured via party programs as coded in the Manifesto Project Dataset (Volkens et al., 2013).

Our analysis comprises three different *dependent variables*. To test the first hypothesis (H1a), we have calculated the average importance of law and order issues for the parties that own the issue of law and order. We identified a party as owning the issue of law and order by looking at the supply side of the party system. Two sources have been used: First, we looked at qualitative literature on the party systems of the respective countries (Christensen et al., 2015; Green and Jennings, 2017; Seeberg, 2016); and second, we calculated the long-term averages of the issue salience of all parties in the respective party system. In most cases, the major parties of the right emerged as issue owners and were coded as such (e.g. the Austrian ÖVP, the French Gaullists [UMP, LR], the German CDU or the Swedish Moderaterna, for the complete list, see Appendix). The law and order issue importance (LOI) of these parties has been assessed via the salience of law and order (number of quasi-sentences related to law and order relative to the length of the manifesto) for issue owner parties according to the Manifesto Project Dataset (Volkens et al., 2013) (MARPOR-variable per605). In order to test hypothesis 1b, namely the overall ideological stance of all mainstream parties, we have calculated the salience of law and order for all relevant mainstream-parties (excluding RRPP) in the respective party system and weighted the salience by the strengths of the parties in terms of seats. Hence, bigger parties affect the overall value of the measure more strongly than smaller ones. For both measures, we would therefore expect the LOI to increase if the pressure of RRPP grows.

Figure 11.1 depicts how the average LOI for the mainstream parties has developed over time in the countries under review. The graphs do not indicate a uniform trend in all countries, but, instead, point to remarkable differences between the countries with some nations exhibiting a point in time, in which law and order issues gained considerable importance (France, Belgium, Denmark and others with a more continuous development, Switzerland and Ireland).

Hypothesis 2 moves the analysis beyond the question of issue importance, postulating that the strength of a RRPP also affects actual policies. In order to approximate the law and order policy stance, we use public spending on 'public order and safety' according to the international Cofog classification (see Wenzelburger, 2015).[8] Again, due to poor data availability (valid time series are only available in the beginning of the 1990s, see figure 11.2), we lose some observations in the regression analyses – but spending is one of the rare indicators, which is reliably available for many countries and over a number of years. If we plot the development of spending data over time, there is a clear upward tendency in several countries (Belgium, Netherlands, Greece) pointing to what is often called a 'punitive turn' by criminologists. However, it is also visible that the development is more incremental in nature compared to the LOI where we see pronounced spikes in attention to the issue.

Our main *independent variable* of interest relates to the strength of RRPP and the question whether the RRPP create competitive pressure through emphasizing law and order issues. Hence, conceptually, our independent variable covers two dimensions: The electoral strength of RRPP and the issue emphasis of RRPP on law and order. For our hypothesis to hold, both conditions have to be fulfilled: A RRPP has to be strong and emphasize law and

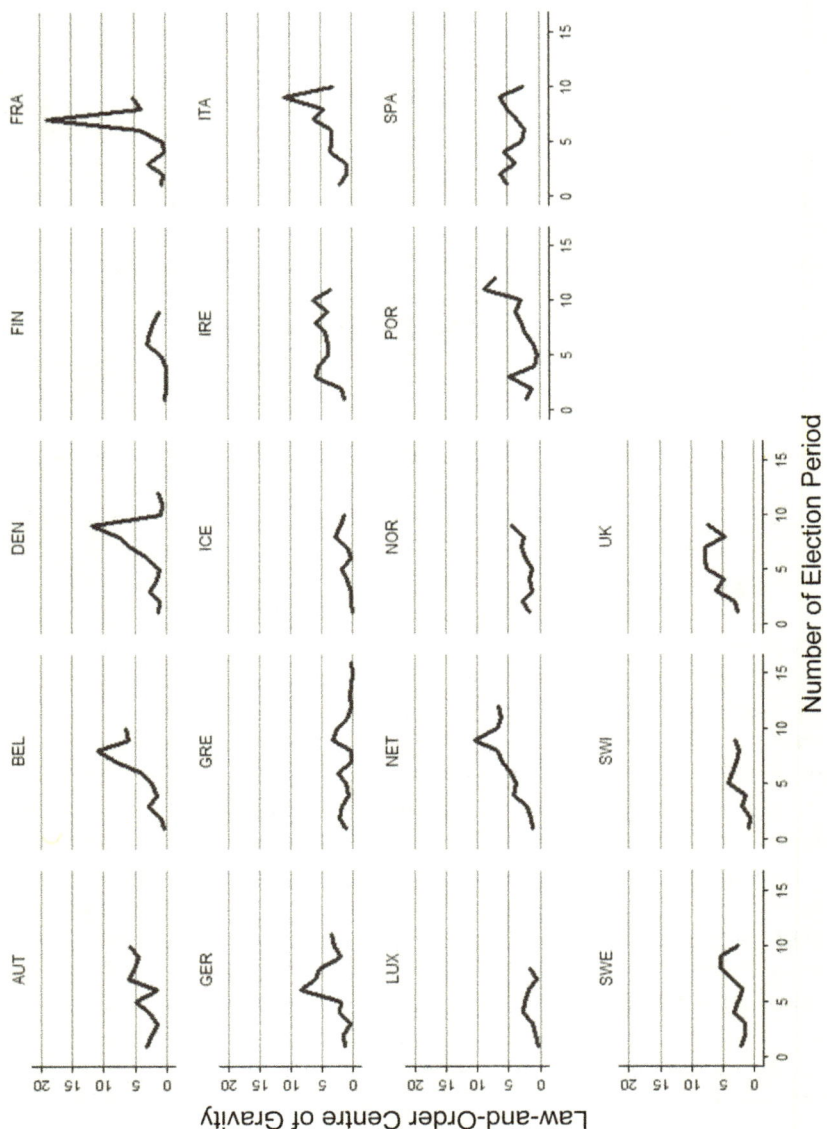

Figure 11.1. Importance of law and order issues (LOI).

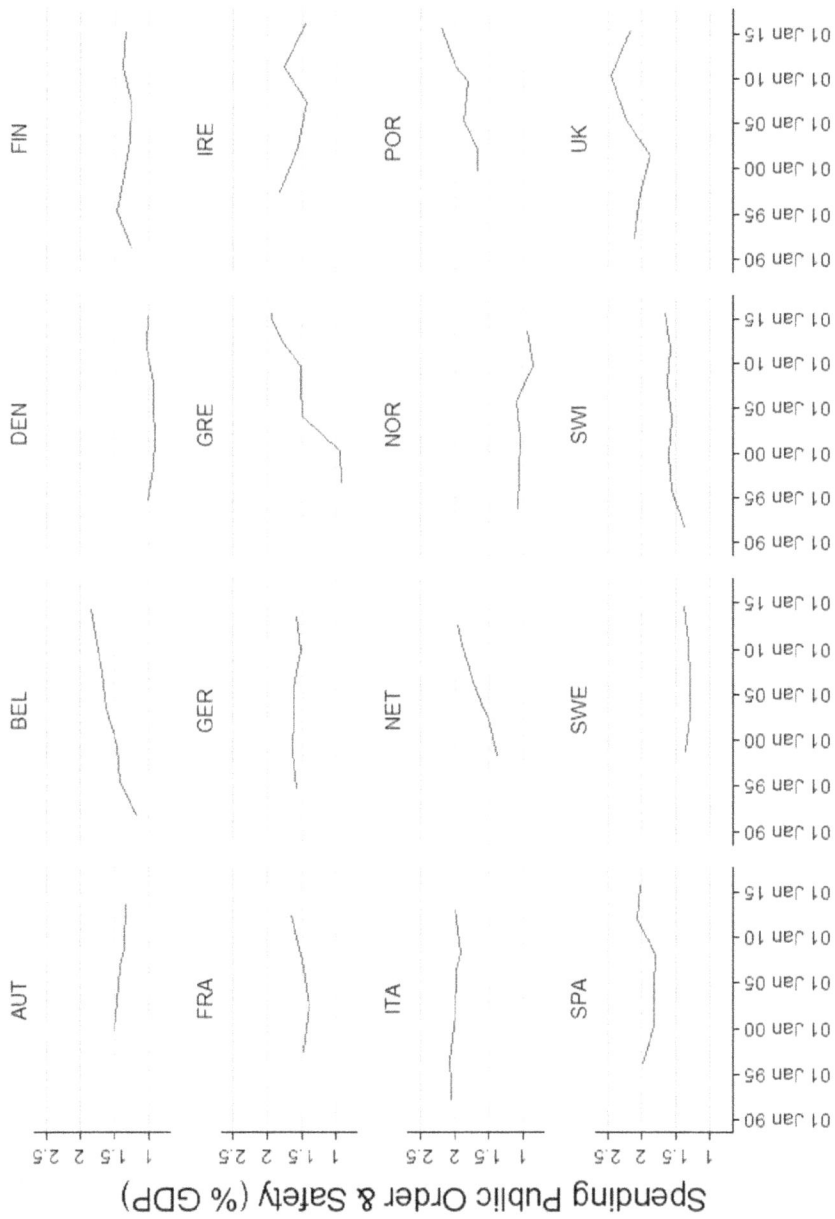

Figure 11.2. Public spending on law and order.

order in competition with the mainstream parties in order to exert pressure on its competitors so that those also emphasize law and order more strongly. The combination of conditions comes down to a multiplicative relationship, which is why we construct an index of 'radical right populist law and order pressure' (RLOP) calculated as the product of the vote share of the respective RRPP[7] in the national election and its issue emphasis of law and order (again, based on MARPOR per605).[8]

Table 11.1 summarizes the mean and standard deviation (over time) of the RLOP variable as well as the two components for all countries of our sample. Looking at the average over the years, it is evident that the strongest pressure to act on law and order was exerted in Switzerland (by the Swiss Peoples Party) whereas other RRPP, for instance the Sweden Democrats, were not only electorally weaker but also emphasized law and order less strongly, resulting in a lower RLOP value. In the regression analyses below, we lag the variable by one election period in order to account for the fact that the pressure has to build up before parties react and in order to exclude any suspicion of reverse causality.

Evidently, our regression models also have to account for possible confounders – variables that affect both the pressure exerted by RRPP and our two main dependent variables. Three kinds of possible confounding variables can be distilled from the literature on party competition and law and order politics.

Table 11.1. Index: Radical right populist law and order pressure (RLOP)

	Vote share RPP		L&O Issue Emphasis RPP		RLOP	
	Mean	*sd*	*Mean*	*sd*	*Mean*	*sd*
Austria	16.60	*8.12*	3.16	*3.38*	**54.89**	*63.45*
Belgium	6.73	*5.11*	5.30	*5.10*	**30.80**	*45.89*
Denmark	6.14	*7.43*	4.15	*5.79*	**47.76**	*74.76*
Finland	4.35	*7.52*	1.94	*2.34*	**12.76**	*31.63*
France	8.56	*5.45*	6.16	*5.27*	**76.61**	*72.23*
Germany	0.00	*0.00*	0.00	*0.00*	**0.00**	*0.00*
Greece	2.61	*3.43*	2.35	*2.97*	**15.28**	*21.63*
Ireland	0.00	*0.00*	0.00	*0.00*	**0.00**	*0.00*
Italy	4.77	*3.93*	3.31	*3.35*	**20.49**	*22.40*
Netherlands	4.51	*6.41*	5.01	*7.15*	**49.06**	*74.69*
Norway	11.59	*7.89*	3.64	*1.93*	**46.81**	*51.46*
Portugal	0.00	*0.00*	0.00	*0.00*	**0.00**	*0.00*
Spain	0.00	*0.00*	0.00	*0.00*	**0.00**	*0.00*
Sweden	2.77	*4.46*	2.18	*3.56*	**9.22**	*18.81*
Switzerland	16.09	*12.48*	5.61	*4.83*	**115.71**	*123.42*
United Kingdom	1.40	*4.21*	0.54	*1.61*	**6.76**	*20.28*

Note: No RRPP in Germany, Ireland, Portugal and Spain; Please note that the mean values of the first two variables cannot simply be multiplied to obtain the value of RLOP because the variables vary over time.

First, actual crime rates may increase the strength of RRPP and affect LOI as well as spending or imprisonment. As criminologists have convincingly shown that total police recorded crime rates are problematic not least because of non-reporting (Matthews 2005), we follow the standard practice here and use the most reliable data on the mortality of assaults as reported by the World Health Organization (WHO). Second, the economy may influence our results in two possible ways. On the one hand, an economic crisis with high unemployment, low growth rates and soaring deficits may lead to both an increase in votes for populist parties as well as a shift to more repressive policies by mainstream parties because they can no longer compete in the field of social policies – a prominent explanation for the 'punitive turn' in the criminological literature. On the other hand, high economic growth can decrease party competition on the economic dimension, which is why parties move to other issues, such as law and order, to differentiate themselves from each other. In any case, it becomes clear that we need to include growth, unemployment and budget deficits as controls in our regression equations (we take this data from Armingeon et al., 2015). Moreover and third, migration is an issue that has to be taken into account in order to avoid spuriousness. High migration rates may lead to higher importance of law and order for mainstream parties as well as to higher support for populist parties and a tougher stance on law and order issues. We therefore include the net migration rate as registered by the UN in the regression equations. In order to avoid reverse causality, we calculate the averages of the three first years of the respective election period and use these values for the regression on the data for the following election (for a similar approach, see Schmitt 2016). Finally, we include a dummy to all regressions that indicates whether RRPP have been part of the government.

Method

In order to investigate the influence of RRPP on mainstream parties' law and order issue emphasis and resulting policies, we perform a panel regression analysis based on our data, which varies over space and time. When estimating regressions for such data it is important to take into account common peculiarities of that data, especially unit heterogeneity, temporal dependence and heteroscedasticity. We test for these potential problems and use econometric solutions, which we will briefly discuss in the following.

Unit heterogeneity is an issue for our dependent variables. As heterogeneity is not substantially reduced after including theoretically meaningful variables, we resort to the standard econometric solution and run FE-models (including country dummies). This comes down to de-meaning our dependent variables, that is, to investigate the deviations from the country-specific means of the LOI variable or the spending/imprisonment indicators in specific years. In other words: We investigate whether law and order was a more than average or less than average issue in a certain country at a given point in time. Even theoretically, this is a relevant question as we are more interested in the over-time variance than in the cross-country variance. In any case, an *F*-test on the necessity of fixed effects clearly suggests their inclusion.

Whereas *temporal dependence* is not a big issue for the LOI variable, public spending on law and order is highly correlated even though the periodization of the data by electoral periods should have reduced autocorrelation. Therefore, for statistical reasons, we either include a lagged dependent variable (spending one year before) into the regression equations or use the Prais-Winston-estimator (AR-1) (see: Plümper et al., 2005) in the models below. However, as one could also argue that the inclusion of a lagged dependent variable makes sense from a substantive point of view regarding the LOI variable – because it indicates that law and order issue importance in one manifesto is related to the issue importance in the next manifesto of the same party (or that spending is temporally dependent on the last election period) – we include the lagged values of the respective variables (i.e. the LOI of the last election manifesto) in some of the regression equations, too.

Finally, as *panel-heteroscedasticity* is present in all estimations, we estimate panel corrected standard errors (PCSE) (Beck and Katz, 1995). All regressions have been checked in terms of robustness by excluding one country at a time and estimating the regressions without this country. If results are not robust, this will be reported in a footnote.

EMPIRICAL FINDINGS

Importance of Law and Order Issues

Our first two hypotheses relate to the question whether the RLOP drives mainstream parties, and especially the parties that traditionally own the law and order issue, to emphasize this issue more in their manifestos. In order to see whether this proposition holds, we ran several panel regressions with the LOI of all mainstream parties (models 1–4) as well as the LOI of the issue owner party (models 5 and 6) as dependent variables. In model 4, we have estimated a more parsimonious model excluding two insignificant covariates, the assault death rate and the unemployment rate. The third model replaces the assault death rate by the homicide rate, which leads to loss of around one third of the observations but only minor changes to the substantive interpretations of the results.

Table 11.2 tentatively shows that the pressure exerted by RRPP that challenge mainstream parties on law and order issues does indeed seem to drive these parties, on average, to talk more about law and order in their election

Table 11.2. Regressions LOI

	(1)	(2)	(3)	(4)	(5)	(6)
	Average LOI	Average LOI	Average LOI	Average LOI	LOI issue ownership party	LOI issue ownership party
RLOP	0.014***	0.014**	0.011*	0.0086	0.033***	0.031***
	(4.04)	(2.30)	(1.85)	(1.64)	(6.28)	(4.02)
Assault death ratio	0.086	0.60			0.085	0.58
	(0.15)	(0.56)			(0.11)	(0.53)
Net migration rate	0.19***	0.17***	0.11	0.16***	0.32***	0.28***
	(3.27)	(3.27)	(1.01)	(3.58)	(3.23)	(3.12)
Econ growth	0.35***	0.39***	0.34***	0.29***	0.29*	0.26
	(3.07)	(2.83)	(4.40)	(3.62)	(1.80)	(1.59)
Unemployment rate	-0.11	-0.072	-0.23**		-0.12	-0.096
	(-0.80)	(-0.49)	(-2.31)		(-0.80)	(-0.59)
Debt ratio	0.030	0.025	0.058***	0.019**	0.020	0.018
	(1.41)	(1.07)	(3.39)	(2.01)	(0.79)	(0.71)
Inclusion of RRPP in government	2.48***	2.47***	1.19	2.57***	3.31***	3.83***
	(4.18)	(3.32)	(1.45)	(4.30)	(3.82)	(2.81)
LDV: LOI, t-1		0.26**		0.27*		0.15*
		(2.08)		(1.72)		(1.80)
Intent. homicide (subsample)			2.64***			
			(2.58)			
Constant	-5.88***	-6.86**	-3.91***	-4.20***	4.26*	5.33**
	(-3.17)	(-2.33)	(-5.17)	(-2.94)	(1.94)	(2.06)
R^2	0.408	0.455	0.543	0.439	0.421	0.444
N	132	132	84	155	125	123

Note: All estimations include country fixed effects and PCSE.

manifestos. Although the significance of the coefficients for the RLOP variable in the first four specifications, is not overwhelming and the coefficient loses significance in some models, the direction of the relationship is consistently positive: Hence, in line with H1b, a higher pressure by RRPP seems to drive mainstream parties to emphasize law and order in their manifestos more strongly, although the robustness of the results is somewhat questionable.

While the evidence for H1b is not entirely convincing, H1a is strongly supported by our data: As expected, the parties which own the law and order issue are affected particularly strongly by RRPP that challenge them on law and order. This is evident from the regression table where the coefficient of the RLOP variable is highly significant and substantially higher for models 5 and 6, that is, where the issue emphasis of law and order by the issue owner parties is used as dependent variable. This strong relationship is also evident, if we plot the marginal effects of RLOP on the importance of the law and order issue for the two dependent variables analysed here (figure 11.3, Appendix): The slope of the line indicating the relationship between the strength of radical right populist law and order pressure and the LOI is much steeper for the parties traditionally owning the issue (graph on the right) than for the average mainstream parties in a party system (graph on the left). In sum, the evidence strongly supports H1a, which expected exactly this relationship.

Finally, concerning the co-variates, the results show a significant effect of the migration rate on the LOI with high migration leading to a stronger emphasis of law and order. The different economic variables seem to be less relevant with the exception of the economic growth rate, which is positively correlated with an emphasis of law and order in the manifestos: It thus appears that when economic growth is high and therefore the economic dimension of party competition less contested, parties move to other issues such as law and order to gain electoral advantages. In contrast, the assault death ratio in a country, that is, a co-variate that is directly related to the issue of law and order, shows no influence on how strongly political parties emphasize law and order issues. Finally, the presence of RRPP at the government also increases the issue emphasis by both mainstream parties and the issue owners, which is easily explainable by the agenda-setting power that RRPP in government can be presumed to have.

Law and Order Policies

After having shown that mainstream parties and especially center-right parties (i.e. generally those owning the issue of law and order) indeed seem to react to the presence of RRPP challengers by emphasizing law and order issues in their programs, this section goes one step further and investigates whether the pressure exerted by RRPP also affects actual law and order policies. In the following, we present results of regression analyses that examine whether tougher law and order policies can be explained with RLOP (H2).

What emerges from table 11.3 is that, as expected, there is no direct influence of RLOP on the general repressiveness of law and order policies as implemented by all kinds of governments (models 1 and 2). The coefficient for RLOP is non-significant in all estimations and the statistical effect on law and order spending is rather weak. Instead, law and order spending emerges as highly path dependent, that is, highly influenced by the amount of money

Table 11.3. Regressions public spending on law and order

	(1)	*(2)*	*(3)*	*(4)*
RLOP	0.000031	−0.00022	0.00012	−0.00042
	(0.15)	(−0.97)	(0.50)	(−1.43)
LDV (spending, t-1)		0.46***	0.47***	
		(2.62)	(2.75)	
Assault death ratio	−0.10*			−0.12*
	(−1.72)			(−1.88)
Net migration rate	−0.018*	−0.0041	−0.0036	−0.017
	(−1.67)	(−0.47)	(−0.40)	(−1.50)
Economic growth	−0.033**	−0.030***	−0.030***	−0.036**
	(−2.20)	(−2.91)	(−2.94)	(−2.11)
Unemployment rate	0.014	0.0073	0.0064	0.016
	(1.02)	(0.69)	(0.60)	(1.07)
Public debt ratio	−0.0013	−0.00060	−0.00034	−0.0013
	(−0.67)	(−0.85)	(−0.51)	(−0.67)
Institutional constraints	0.0025	0.00013	0.0016	0.0015
	(1.11)	(0.04)	(0.51)	(0.61)
Government ideology	−0.010	−0.0017	0.0064	
(Schmidt-index)	(−1.12)	(−0.24)	(0.76)	
Inclusion of RRPP in	0.0020	−0.030	−0.029	−0.018
government	(0.13)	(−0.99)	(−1.11)	(−0.42)
Issue owner party leads				−0.036
government				(−0.56)
RLOP*			−0.00024**	
Government ideology			(−2.32)	
RLOP*Issue owner party				0.0011*
leads government				(1.93)
Constant	2.04***	1.04***	0.93***	1.93***
	(6.96)	(5.41)	(4.64)	(10.32)
R^2	0.877	0.948	0.950	0.880
N	93	82	82	93
Serial correlation	AR1	LDV	LDV	AR1

Note: All estimations include country fixed effects and PCSE. The assault rate was excluded in LDV estimations in order to keep enough observations to calculate PCSE. Results do not change substantially, if we include the assault rate and run an estimation with robust s.e. instead of PCSE.

spent during the last election, and very much as a function of economic growth (which is not surprising at all given that it is measured in % of GDP). All other variables, be it socio-structural indicators or political ones, are not significantly related to public spending on law and order.

However, the results suggest that this picture changes dramatically if we look at specific governments – and particularly if we consider the question whether an issue owner party leads the government. In line with H2, which posits that especially right-wing parties traditionally owning the law and order issue will react to RRPP challengers by toughening policies, we find such a conditional relationship (see the significant coefficients for the interactions in models 3 and 4): The more leftist a government is, the less it reacts to RLOP by toughening policies (see the marginal effects plot in the Appendix: figure 11.4, left); and if an issue-owner party leads the government, we find a significant positive relationship indicating that such governments indeed react to RLOP by increasing expenditure in this area (Appendix: figure 11.4, right). In both cases, the coefficient of the interaction effect is significant on conventional levels. Hence, H2, according to which policies change toward a more repressive pole if the issue owner is challenged by a RRPP on law and order issues, is supported by our data.

DISCUSSION AND CONCLUSION

In this contribution we have asked the basic question whether the pressure from RRPP that challenge mainstream parties on law and order issues makes mainstream parties move – in terms of party programs and in terms of policies. The answer from our empirical analysis of party manifestos and public spending on law and order is straightforward: It depends on the party. We find that those parties traditionally owning law and order issues (essentially center-right or conservative parties) do not only talk more about law and order in their electoral manifestos but also spend more on this policy when they govern if they are pressured by RRPP. In contrast, we do not find such a relationship for the average of all mainstream parties in a party system. If at all, our results indicate that other mainstream parties might emphasize the issue a bit more in their programs, but there is no sign whatsoever of a change in policies (as measured by public spending). Hence, while mainstream parties may chant in with radical right populist challengers, this change in tone, however, does not necessarily translate into actual tougher law and order policies. This evidence supports a nuanced view about the possible impact of RRPP even in policy areas that are strongly linked to the ideological core of these parties, such as law and order and crime issues.

Nevertheless, there are potential limitations of the findings that have to be addressed and will be discussed in the following. First, given the sample of countries in the analysis, the results, strictly speaking, can be taken as valid only for the Western European context. One might thus call into doubt the generalizability of the findings. However, our main argument concerns a very general mechanism in party competition dynamics, competitive incentives due to a party's issue ownership regarding law and order. Thus, one would expect the registered relationships to hold true in other contexts as well – as long as there are mainstream parties that traditionally own that issue within a country's party system. This should be kept in mind for further analyses that aim to change or widen the scope.

Second, the quantitative analysis in the preceding section uses a wide lens to look at the relationship between RRPP and mainstream parties and government reactions. It is therefore well-suited to finding systematic patterns in a large-N dataset. However, it cannot provide an in-depth view in the processes that have led parties to harden their tone on law and order and especially governments to introduce more restrictive policies. Future studies should build on these insights and focus on the causal mechanisms that are at work. There is a growing literature on law and order and penal policies in comparative criminology (Tonry, 2001; Lacey, 2008) as well as in political science (Gottschalk, 2008; Barker, 2009; Miller, 2016) that uses case studies for that purpose. However, the influence of RRPP on party competition is mostly overlooked (but see Biard, 2018). The present study, which pointed out some patterns on the aggregate level, can therefore provide a starting point for a deeper case study-based analysis of how exactly mainstream parties perceive the challenge from the right and in what way they react.

Beyond the specific research question and the literature on RRPP, the findings from our analysis also contribute to the wider discussion on party competition. In fact, the pattern we find is very much in accordance with assumptions of the issue competition framework, as issue ownership emerges as a crucial strategic factor that conditions parties' reactions to challengers: the rise of RRPP with their strong emphasis on law and order is followed by a stronger emphasis on this issue and tougher actual policy decisions largely by those mainstream parties that traditionally own that issue. Consequently, if we want to understand how party competition and policy outputs are interlinked in policy areas in which the issues are characterized by a strong valence component, it seems to be key to look more closely at the issue ownership of the party leading the government – and not, as the traditional parties matter approach does (Castles and McKinlay, 1979) – at the general ideological stance of the government.

NOTES

1. Of course, those voters who strongly disagree with the means a party advocates to deliver on the law and order issue will hardly be influenced by the party's ability and commitment in dealing with that issue (Bélanger and Meguid, 2008, 483).

2. An argument that points in a similar direction can be found in a study by Abou-Chadi (2016) on mainstream parties' reactions on radical right populist parties. He argues that position changes carry with them an increase in salience of the issue in question, as parties also have to advocate their changed positions – and thus politicize the issue in question, putting it higher on the agenda (Abou-Chadi, 2016, 419–420).

3. For a similar argument expressed using propositions of the spatial model see Akkerman (2015).

4. Another interpretation of the thesis suggests that governments only act out on very severe cases whereas they do not adopt a general increase in the toughness of law and order policies (Bottoms, 1995, 40–41).

5. That leaves us with a total of 199 observations from 1979 to 2014 of which around 130 are usually used in the regression analyses due to missing values for early years (see the regression tables below).

6. We acknowledge that this is an imperfect measure of law and order policies, but it is one of the few indicators that takes up law and order policies in a reliable manner and that is available over time for a bigger sample of countries. We have used general government data here, although this measure of overall spending may also be driven by political decisions on a sub-national level. Using central government spending data, instead, would underestimate the fact that decisions by central governments often also affect sub-national spending. Ultimately, the best measure would be one of legislative outputs, where partisan effects have already been found (but which has so far only been studied for individual countries [Staff, 2018; Wenzelburger and Staff, 2016]).

7. The classification of a party as RRPP follows the standard practice in the literature (Mudde, 2007). For a list, see Appendix.

8. We have not z-standardized the variables as the means are not too different for both variables and because we wanted to keep the substance of the raw values in terms of variance (e.g. particularly high vote shares or strong emphasis). A z-standardization would have artificially reduced this variance.

BIBLIOGRAPHY

Abou-Chadi, Tarik. 2016. Niche party success and mainstream party policy shifts: How green and radical right parties differ in their impact. *British Journal of Political Science* 46(2): 417–436.

Adams, James, Samuel Merrill, and Bernard Grofman. 2005. *A Unified Theory of Party Competition: A Cross-National Analysis Integrating Spatial and Behavioral Factors*. Cambridge: Cambridge University Press.

Aharonson, Ely. 2013. Determinate sentencing and American exceptionalism: The underpinnings and effects of cross-national differences in the regulation of sentencing discretion. *Law and Contemporary Problems* 76(1): 161–187.

Akkerman, Tjitske. 2015. Immigration policy and electoral competition in Western Europe: A fine-grained analysis of party positions over the past two decades. *Party Politics* 21(1): 54–67.

Albrecht, Hans-Jörg. 2004. Öffentliche Meinung, Kriminalpolitik und Kriminaljustiz. In *Alltagsvorstellungen von Kriminalität*, edited by Michael Walter, Harald Kania, and Hans-Jörg Albrecht, 491–520. Münster: Lit Verlag.

Alonso, Sonia, and Sara Claro de Fonseca. 2012. Immigration, left and right. *Party Politics* 18(6): 865–884.

Ansolabehere, Stephen, and Shanto Iyengar. 1994. Riding the wave and claiming ownership over issues: The joint effects of advertising and news coverage in campaigns. *Public Opinion Quarterly* 58(3): 335–357.

Armingeon, Klaus/Isler, Christian/Knöpfel, Laura/Weistanner, David/Engler, Sarah (2015): Comparative Political Dataset 1960–2013, in: Institute of Political Science, University of Bern (Hg.) Bern.

Barker, Vanessa. 2009. *The Politics of Imprisonment*. Oxford: Oxford University Press.

Beck, Nathaniel, and Jonathan Katz. 1995. What to do (and not to do) with time-series cross-section data. *American Political Science Review* 89(3): 634–647.

Bélanger, Éric, and Bonnie M. Meguid. 2008. Issue salience, issue ownership, and issue-based vote choice. *Electoral Studies* 27(3): 477–491.

Betz, Hans-George. 1993. The new politics of resentment: Radical right-wing populist parties in Western Europe. *Comparative Politics* 25(4): 413–427.

Biard, Benjamin. 2019. The influence of radical right populist parties on law and order policy-making. *Policy Studies*, 1: 40–57.

Bischoff, Ivo. 2005. Party competition in a heterogeneous electorate: The role of dominant-issue voters. *Public Choice* 122(1–2): 221–243.

Bottoms, Anthony. 1995. The philosophy and politics of punishment and sentencing. In *The Politics of Sentencing Reform*, edited by Chris Clarkson and Rod Morgan, 17–49. Oxford: Oxford University Press.

Castles, Frank, and Robert D. McKinlay. 1979. Does politics matter: An analysis of the public welfare commitment in advanced democratic states. *European Journal of Political Research* 7(2): 169–186.

Cavadino, Michael, and James Dignan. 2006. *Penal Systems: A Comparative Approach*. London: Sage.

Cere, Rinella, Yvonne Jewkes, and Thomas Ugelvik. 2014. Media and crime. In *The Routledge Handbook of European Criminology*, edited by Sophie Body-Gendrot, Mike Hough, Klára Kerezsi, René Lévy, and Sonja Snacken, 266–279. London/ New York: Routledge.

Christensen, Love, Stefan Dahlberg, and Johan Martinsson. 2015. Changes and fluctuations in issue ownership: The case of Sweden, 1979–2010. *Scandinavian Political Studies* 38(2): 137–157.

Clarke, Harold D, David Sanders, Marianne C. Stewart, and Paul F. Whiteley. 2009. *Performance Politics and the British Voter*. Cambridge: Cambridge University Press.

Dalton, Russell J. 2009. Economics, environmentalism and party alignments: A note on partisan change in advanced industrial democracies. *European Journal of Political Research* 48(2): 161–175.

Downes, David. 2011. Comparative criminology, globalization and the 'punitive turn'. In *Comparative Criminal Justice and Globalization*, edited by David Nelken, 27–47. Farnham: Ashgate.

Downs, Anthony. 1957. *An Economic Theory of Democracy*. New York: Harper.

Egan, Patrick J. 2013. *Partisan Priorities: How Issue Ownership Drives and Distorts American Politics*. New York: Cambridge University Press.

Enns, Peter. 2016. *Incarceration Nation: How the United States Became the Most Punitive Democracy in the World*. Cambridge: Cambridge University Press.

Frase, Richard S. 2001. Comparative perspectives on sentencing policy and research. In *Sentencing and Sanctions in Western Countries*, edited by Michael Tonry and Richard S. Frase, 259–292. Oxford: Oxford University Press.

Garland, David. 2001. *The Culture of Control: Crime and Social Order in Contemporary Society*. Oxford: Oxford University Press.

Geys, Benny. 2012. Success and failure in electoral competition: Selective issue emphasis under incomplete issue ownership. *Electoral Studies* 31(2): 406–412.

Gottschalk, Marie. 2008. Hiding in plain sight: American politics and the carceral state. *Annual Review of Political Science* 11 (June): 235–260.

Green, Jane. 2007. When voters and parties agree: Valence issues and party competition. *Political Studies* 55(3): 629–655.

Green, Jane, and Sara B. Hobolt. 2008. Owning the issue agenda: Party strategies and vote choices in British elections. *Electoral Studies* 27(3): 460–476.

Green, Jane, and Will Jennings. 2017. *The Politics of Competence: Parties, Public Opinion and Voters*. Cambridge: Cambridge University Press.

Green-Pedersen, Christoffer. 2007. The growing importance of issue competition: The changing nature of party competition in Western Europe. *Political Studies* 55(3): 607–628.

Green-Pedersen, Christoffer, and Jesper Krogstrup. 2008. Immigration as a political issue in Denmark and Sweden. *European Journal of Political Research* 47(5): 610–634.

Green-Pedersen, Christoffer, and Peter B. Mortensen. 2010. Who sets the agenda and who responds to it in the Danish parliament? A new model of issue competition and agenda-setting. *European Journal of Political Research* 49(2): 257–281.

Han, Kyung Joon. 2015. The impact of radical right-wing parties on the positions of mainstream parties regarding multiculturalism. *West European Politics* 38(3): 557–576.

Heinisch, Reinhard. 2003. Success in opposition – Failure in government: Explaining the performance of right-wing populist parties in public office. *West European Politics* 26(3): 91–130.

Heywood, Andrew. 2017. *Political Ideologies: An Introduction*. 6th ed. London: Macmillan Education, Palgrave.

Kunz, Karl-Ludwig. 2013. Die Unersättlichkeit des Strebens nach Sicherheit: Eine Bedrohung unserer Freiheit? In *Politische Ökonomie und Sicherheit*, edited by Daniela Klimke and Aldo Legnaro, 28–43. Weinheim/Basel: Beltz Juventa.

Lacey, Nicola. 2008. *The Prisoners' Dilemma*. Cambridge: Cambridge University Press.

Laver, Michael, and W. Ben Hunt. 1992. *Policy and Party Competition*. New York: Routledge.

Laver, Michael, and Ernest Sergenti. 2012. *Party Competition: An Agent-based Model*. Princeton, PA: Princeton University Press.

Matthews, Roger. 2005. The myth of punitiveness. *Theoretical Criminology* 9(2): 175–201.

Meyer, Thomas. 2010. *Party Competition over Time*. Mannheim: Universität Mannheim.

Miller, Lisa. 2016. *The Myth of Mob Rule. Violent Crime and Democratic Politics*. New York: Oxford University Press.

Morgan, Rod. 2006. With respect to order, the rules of the game have changed: New Labour's dominance of the 'law and order' agenda. In *The Politics of Crime Control: Essays in Honour of David Downes*, edited by Tim Newburn and Rod Morgan, 91–115. Oxford: Oxford University Press.

Mudde, Cas. 1996. The war of words defining the extreme right party family. *West European Politics* 19(2): 225–248.

Mudde, Cas. 2007. *Populist Radical Right Parties in Europe*. Cambridge: Cambridge University Press.

Mudde, Cas. 2013. Three Decades of populist radical right parties in Western Europe: So what? *European Journal of Political Research* 52(1): 1–19.

Newburn, Tim. 2007. 'Tough on crime': Penal policy in England and Wales. *Crime and Justice* 36(1): 425–470.

Petrocik, John R. 1996. Issue ownership in presidential elections, with a 1980 case study. *American Journal of Political Science* 40(3): 825–850.

Pettigrew, Thomas F. 1998. Reactions toward the new minorities of Western Europe. *Annual Review of Sociology* 24(1): 77–103.

Plümper, Thomas, Vera Troeger, and Philip Manow. 2005. Panel data analysis in comparative politics: Linking method to theory. *European Journal of Political Research* 44(2): 327–354.

Roberts, Julian V., Loretta J. Stalans, David Indermaur, and Mike Hough. 2003. *Penal Populism and Public Opinion*. Oxford: Oxford University Press.

Schain, Martin A. 1987. The National Front in France and the construction of political legitimacy. *West European Politics* 10(2): 229–252.

Schain, Martin A. 2006. The extreme-right and immigration policy-making: Measuring direct and indirect effects. *West European Politics* 29(2): 270–289.

Schmitt, Carina. 2016. Panel data analysis and partisan variables: How periodization does influence partisan effects. *Journal of European Public Policy* 23(10): 1442–1459.

Seeberg, Henrik Bech. 2013. The opposition's policy influence through issue politicization. *Journal of Public Policy* 33(1): 89–107.

Seeberg, Henrik Bech. 2016. How stable is political parties' issue ownership? A cross-time, cross-national analysis. *Political Studies* 65(2): 475–492.

Shields, James. 2007. *The Extreme Right in France: From Pétain to Le Pen*. London: Routledge.

Smith, Jason Matthew. 2010. Does crime pay? Issue ownership, political opportunity, and the populist right in Western Europe. *Comparative Political Studies* 43(11): 1471–1498.

van Spanje, Joost. 2010. Contagious parties: Anti-immigration parties and their impact on other parties' immigration stances in contemporary Western Europe. *Party Politics* 16(5): 563–586.

Staff, Helge. 2018. Partisan effects and policy entrepreneurs: New Labour's impact on British law and order policy. *Policy Studies* 39(1): 19–36.

Stokes, Donald E. 1963. Spatial models of party competition. *The American Political Science Review* 57(2): 368.

Tonry, Michael. 2001. Punishment policies and patterns in Western countries. In *Sentencing and Sanctions in Western Countries*, edited by Michael Tonry and Richard S. Frase, 3–28. Oxford: Oxford University Press.

Tonry, Michael. 2007. *Crime, Punishment, and Politics in Comparative Perspective.* Chicago, IL: University of Chicago Press.

Volkens, Andrea, Pola Lehmann, Nicolas Merz, Sven Regel, and Annika Werner. 2013. *The Manifesto Data Collection. Manifesto Project (MRG/CMP/MARPOR). Version 2013b*. Wissenschaftszentrum Berlin für Sozialforschung (WZB).

Wacquant, Loïc. 2010. Crafting the neoliberal state: Workfare, prisonfare, and social insecurity. *Sociological Forum* 25(2): 197–220.

Wenzelburger, Georg. 2015. Parties, institutions and the politics of law and order. *British Journal of Political Science* 45(3): 663–687.

Wenzelburger, Georg. 2016. A global trend toward law and order harshness? *European Political Science Review* 8(4): 589–613.

Wenzelburger, Georg, and Helge Staff. 2016. German exceptionalism? An empirical analysis of 20 years of law and order legislation. *Politics & Policy* 44(2): 319–350.

Appendix

SUPPLEMENTARY FIGURES

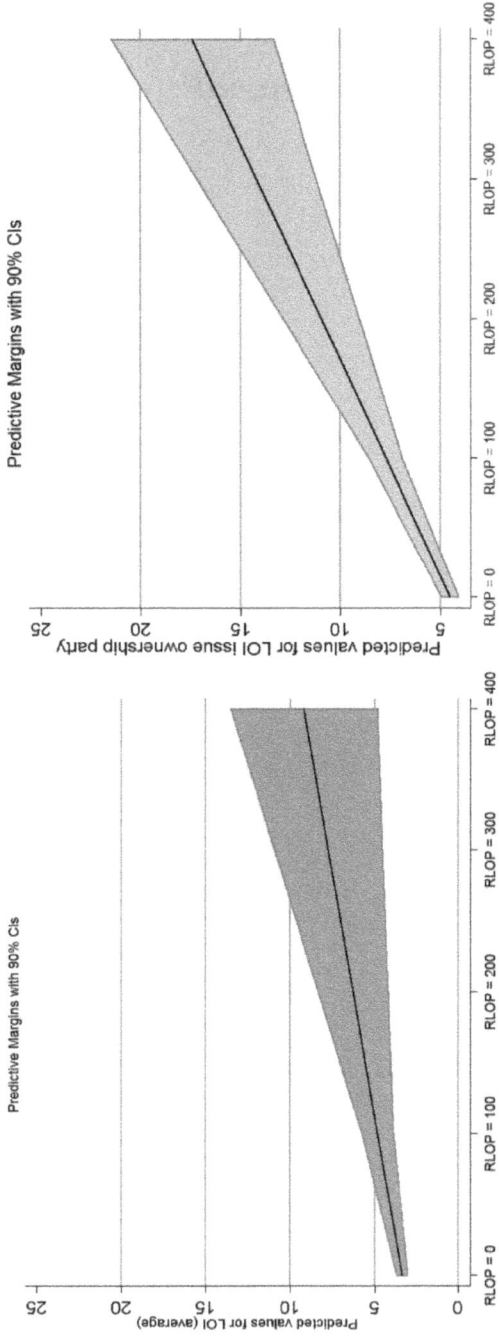

Figure 11.3. Predictive margins for RLOP. *Note:* Predictive margins of LOI (y-axis) for different levels of RLOP (x-axis). **Left graph: Average LOI all mainstream parties (H1b); Right graph: LOI issue owner (H1a).**

Marginal effect RLOP

Dependent Variable: L&O Spending

Marginal effect RLOP

Dependent variable: L&O Spending

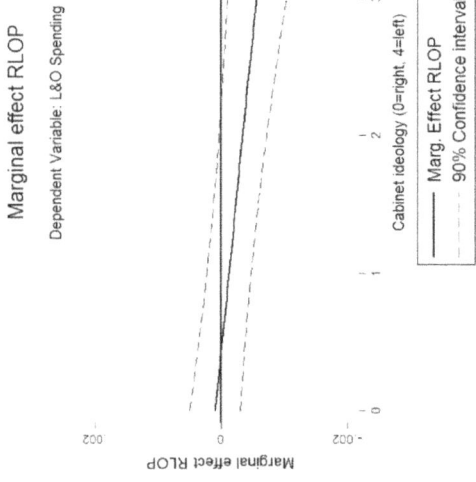

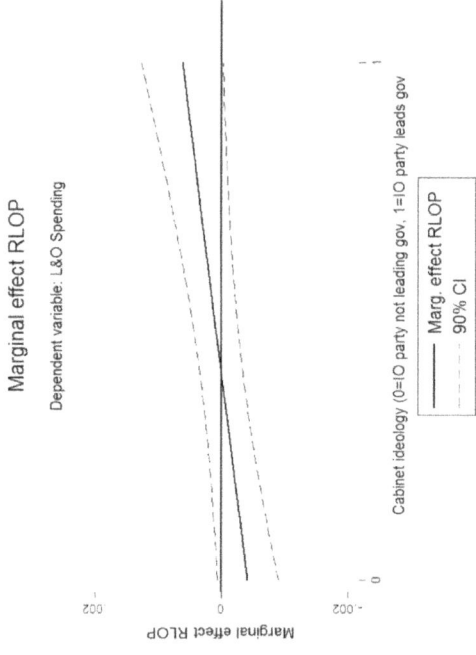

Figure 11.4. RLOP and right-wing government's policy stance. *Note*: Graph to the left: Based on model 4 in table 11.3; Graph to the right: Based on model 3 in table 11.3; Please note the coding of the conditional effect is different for the two graphs; Low values in the left graph indicate a more right-wing government (expected positive relationship) and a zero in the graph to the right indicates a more liberal government that does not own the issue of law and order.

CODING RULES

General coding rules	
General rule	Coding of vote share for populist parties if party is – member of Parliament or – an important player in the party system (according to national sources).
Law and order issue importance (LOI)	Arithmetic mean for per605 (salience law and order) of non-right-wing-populist parties in Parliament weighted by their respective seat shares (in % of seats for non-right-wing populist parties).
Issue importance for right- wing populist parties	Arithmetic mean for per605 (salience law and order) for right-wing-populist parties in Parliament weighted by their respective seat-shares (in % of total seat shares for right-wing populist parties).

Coding of right-wing populist parties in individual countries		
Country	*Party/Parties*	*Remarks*
Austria	FPÖ (since 1994) BZÖ since 2006	Salience of per605 of FPÖ in early elections 1995 is derived from 1994 program
Belgium	Vlaams Blok Front National	No manifesto data for Front National, position not included
Denmark	Dansk Folkeparti	
Finland	True Finns	
France	Front National (and in the 1970s also Parti Front National)	Election results from the first round of general legislative elections
Germany	–	
Greece	LAOS (Laïkós Orthódoxos Synagermós) Golden Dawn	
Ireland	–	
Italy	Movimento Sociale Italiano (until 1994) Lega Nord (since 1992)	Lega Veneta and Lega Lombarda (active since the 1980s are not included)
Luxemburg	–	
Netherlands	List Pim Fortuyn PVV	
Norway	Fremskrittspartiet (since 1981)	
Portugal	–	
Spain	–	
Sweden	Ny demokrati (1991–1994) Sverigedemokraterna	
Switzerland	SVP (since 1991)	
United Kingdom	UKIP	

CODING OF PARTIES OWNING THE ISSUE OF LAW AND ORDER IN INDIVIDUAL COUNTRIES

Issue ownership has been coded via the supply-side of the party system based on (1) literature on issue ownership and national party systems and (2) the long-term mean for a party in the manifesto item per605 (law and order) since 1978 if (1) the party has at least been present in four elections and (2) has not been coded as RPP. Changes in party names and mergers/splinters that have resulted in new parties have been taken into account.

Country	Party/Parties	Remarks
Austria	ÖVP	All years
Belgium	CD&V/CVP and predecessor/successors	All years; 2007: NVA data
Denmark	KF	All years
Finland	SKL	SKL: 1979–1999
	KD	KD: 2003–2015
France	UMP/RPR/Gaullists	All years
Germany	CDU	All years
Greece	New Democracy	All years
Ireland	FF	PD: 1987–2007
	PD	FF: 1978–1987
Italy	PLI	PLI (1979–1992)
	Forza Italia/Il Popolo della Libertà	FI/PdL (1994–2013)
Luxemburg	Demokratisch Partei	DP (1979–1989)
	Action Committee for Democracy	AR (1989–2013)
Netherlands	VVD	All years
Norway	Hoyre (Conservatives)	All years
Portugal	CDS (CDS/PP)	All years
Spain	PP (AP, PDP)	All years
Sweden	Moderaterna	All years
Switzerland	CVP	All years
United Kingdom	Conservative Party	All years

Used literature: Christensen *et al.*, 2015; Green and Jennings, 2017; Seeberg, 2016.

Chapter 12

The Radical Right in Power

A Comparative Analysis of Their Migration Policy Influence

Philipp Lutz

In December 2017 a new Austrian government, a coalition between the centre-right ÖVP and the radical right FPÖ, was sworn in. The electoral campaigns of both parties focused on the issue of immigration and on appearing tough in this realm. However, one of the first policy choices of the new government was to increase the immigration quota and to allow for the facilitated recruitment of workers from non-European countries by expanding the list of professions with labour shortages.[1] In other words, while the radical right cabinet has positioned itself as strongly anti-immigration, it has instead enacted a liberalization of immigration soon after taking office. This puzzle serves as an illustrative starting point for this chapter, which conducts a fine-grained analysis of the influence of radical right populist parties (RRPP) on migration policy when they gain government office. Do governments with the support of the radical right enact more migration policy changes? Do migration policies become more restrictive when the radical right takes government power?

Not just in Austria, but in most West European countries more broadly radical right populist parties have established themselves as a permanent feature of national party systems. In several countries they have joined coalition governments or provided support to minority governments (De Lange, 2012). The unifying feature of these parties is their opposition to immigration and multi-cultural societies (Mudde, 2013). However, despite the electoral mobilization of anti-immigration sentiments, European countries have overall become more open to immigration and expanded immigrant rights over the last three decades (De Haas et al., 2018; Helbling and Kalkum, 2017). Previous research provides mixed evidence for the policy influence of the radical right on migration policies and suggests that their influence is limited even when holding government office (Mudde, 2013; Muis and Immerzeel,

2017, 918). Scholars raise doubts on whether RRPPs are the cause behind restrictive reforms of migration policy. Money (1999), for instance, argues that governments before the emergence of RRPPs' influence have already enacted immigration restrictions, while others suggest that the preferences of mainstream-right parties, not the radical right, drive immigration restrictions (Akkerman, 2012; Duncan, 2010). The evidence is therefore inconclusive on whether and how RRPPs are able to use their policy-shaping capacity to further their migration policy agenda when they enter government coalitions.

This chapter analyses the migration policy output of RRPP-supported governments in Western Europe and tests the effect of the radical right on the quantity and quality of migration policy output. In so doing, I provide two main contributions to the literature. The first contribution is theoretical. I discuss how the policy attributes of admission, integration and control policies provide opportunities to and constraints on the radical right to shape government policies. The second contribution is empirical. I use a new large-N dataset of migration policies by governments across eighteen countries between 1990 and 2014. This chapter builds upon my previous analysis on the policy success of RRPP and expands it in scope and depth to assess the effect of government participation in more details (cf. Lutz, 2019).

THE RADICAL RIGHT AS POLICY-MAKER

Radical right populist parties are anti-immigration parties. Nativism is their definitional trait and their preference for more restrictive migration policies is their most salient issue preference (Arzheimer, 2009; Mudde, 2007; Rydgren, 2008). The central role that immigration plays in the policy agenda of RRPPs makes migration policy an important area to assess the performance of these parties as governors and policy-makers.

The influence of a party can be defined as a change in government policy that would not have occurred without the party's existence (see also Carvalho, 2013; Williams, 2006). In this contribution, I define the influence of RRPPs on migration policy as their capacity to enact policy restrictions (change-enabling) as well as their capacity to prevent policy liberalization (change-constraining) when compared to the migration policies of the counterfactual situation without RRPPs in government. This pathway of influence has been discussed as the direct policy influence of parties in contrast to the more indirect influence on government policies by exerting pressure on governments as an opposition party (Schain, 2006). The radical right has continuously expanded its policy-shaping capacity by entering governments as a junior partner or by providing support to minority governments in Austria, Switzerland, Netherlands, Denmark, Norway and Italy (De Lange, 2012;

Mudde, 2013). This chapter analyses the direct policy influence of RRPP as part of government coalitions while accounting for the pathway of an indirect influence.

Despite a burgeoning literature on the political consequences of the electoral success of RRPP, evidence on their policy influence after gaining government office is limited and inconclusive. Minkenberg (2001, 16) concludes that for the first radical right government participation in Austria in the year 2000 the centre-right coalition partner adopted a more restrictive stance on immigration when entering the coalition. In a similar vein, Zaslove (2004) concludes that in Austria and Italy, governing RRPP have been instrumental in passing more restrictive immigration policies. In studying the policy influence of the Lega Nord in Italy, Carvalho (2016) also finds a moderate influence on government policies. Others, however, find no evidence for a direct influence of RRPP on migration policies. Manatschal (2012) studies sub-national integration policies in Switzerland and finds no policy effect of the government participation of the Swiss People's Party, branded as the most successful RRPP in Western Europe. Reaching a similar conclusion, Zincone (2006) argues that the immigration policy of Italy is characterized by a remarkable continuity despite the participating role of the radical right in the government. For the Austrian case, Duncan (2010) concludes that restrictive reforms on immigration and integration during the time of radical right government participation do not deviate substantially from those of comparable cabinets. By comparing twenty-seven cabinets from nine European countries between 1996 and 2010, Akkerman (2012) shows that when the radical right gains governing power migration policies are restrictive but not more restrictive than those of mainstream-right cabinets. In a comparative analysis of RRPP influence in France, Italy and the UK, Carvalho (2013, 193) concludes that government participation is only weakly correlated with their policy influence. Overall, the review of previous evidence suggests that the radical right has limited influence on migration policies also when joining a government coalition (Mudde, 2013; Muis and Immerzeel, 2017).

Previous studies on the influence of RRPP on migration policies rely almost exclusively on qualitative case studies with a focus on specific parties. These studies provide detailed insights into particular RRPPs in different country-specific contexts. However, they often draw conflicting conclusions for the same empirical cases (Carvalho, 2016, 665). Furthermore, case studies grapple with assessing the counter-factual outcome: are the observed (restrictive) policies the result of the radical right or would they have also occurred in the absence of a RRPP as coalition partner? Scholars studying party competition stress that a move towards more restrictive positions on immigration is attractive for mainstream-right parties independent of whether they face electoral competition from the radical right (Akkerman, 2015; Alonso and da Fonseca, 2011). Restrictive migration policy changes may hence originate from the ideology or electoral strategy of mainstream-right parties instead of radical right pressure (e.g. Duncan, 2010; Money, 1999). As a result, it remains largely an open question whether RRPPs exert a significant influence on migration policies when winning government office.

THE SELECTIVE CO-OPTATION
OF THE RADICAL RIGHT

When RRPPs have gained a government office and therefore the capacity to shape policy, they have done so as junior partners of mainstream-right parties.[2] The resulting policy choices are therefore necessarily the result of a bargaining interaction between the mainstream-right and the radical right. Only when the mainstream-right party co-opts the more restrictive position of the radical right party we can expect a policy effect. Shifting their policy positions is electorally risky for parties. Such changes may alienate party voters, create internal divisions and undermine credibility in the public's perception. While policy inertia is generally the default option for parties, entering a coalition with the radical right provides mainstream-right parties the opportunity to gain a government office. Mainstream right parties co-opt the radical right most likely in those policy fields where ideological shifts are less costly and governing constraints lower. Following Akkerman (2015), I argue that this co-optation is likely to be selective in the case of a multi-dimensional policy such as immigration. I expect the decision of mainstream parties to co-opt or to oppose RRPPs to depend on the constraints and opportunities defined by the policy attributes of different sub-fields.

Although most scholars acknowledge the multidimensionality of migration policy, much of the relevant empirical research often does not explicitly take it into account. Based on an extensive literature on migration policy, I identify three sub-fields that differ in their policy attributes and in how conducive they are to influence from the radical right. Numerous scholars draw a main conceptual distinction between migration regulations and migration controls (Bjerre et al., 2015; De Haas et al., 2015; Helbling and Kalkum, 2017). Regulative policies can be further differentiated into the admission and integration of immigrants. RRPP position themselves as consistently anti-immigration with a preference for more restrictive policies on admission, integration and control (Zaslove, 2004). While the radical right exerts pressure for restrictive policies across all sub-fields, the actual policy choices of governments are likely to depend on contextual characteristics of these policies. Ample evidence has shown that these three sub-fields follow different empirical patterns (De Haas et al., 2018; Helbling and Kalkoum, 2017) and distinct political logics (Duncan and van Hecke, 2008; Givens and Luedtke, 2005; Money 1999). Many previous studies have treated migration policy as uniform, thereby not taking into account the variation of policy influence across different sub-fields. In the following, I discuss structural and ideological policy attributes that determine the opportunities and constraints of co-opting the radical right in admission, integration and control policies.

Admission policies contain all regulations about the entry and stay of immigrants. Although it is considered to be the sovereign right of nation states to decide whom to admit, states are severely limited in their policy choices due to structural constraints. Economic globalization and political internationalization have created latent pressures for liberalization and powerful constraints to restrictive admission policies (Hollifield, 2004). The structural dependency that compels a country to be open to immigration may motivate a government to shun restrictive reforms, since all governments are motivated to preserve the prosperity and competitiveness of the national economy. Over the last decades, the expansion of rights-based politics helped to expand immigrant rights across borders and create legal obligations that have reduced the space for discretionary admission policies (Joppke, 1998). Hence, global markets and individual rights severely limit the leeway of governing parties in admission policies. On the level of political ideology, admission policy is often described as a cross-cutting issue (e.g. Odmalm, 2011). Mainstream right parties are divided between cultural conservatism and economic liberalism. Mainstream left parties are divided between the protection of domestic workers and the universal principles of justice and equality. These internal divisions constrain the ideological mobility of parties and make the use of policy shifts to gain advantages in electoral competition less likely (Davis, 2012). Consequently, mainstream right parties share a moderate position on immigration in order to balance different constituents and internal factions with competing preferences. Co-opting the radical right's stance in admission policy may result in high electoral costs by alienating party members and constituents, as well as deepening internal tensions (Van Kersbergen and Krouwel, 2008). Both structural and ideological constraints create significant costs for the co-optation of more restrictive admission policies by mainstream-right parties.

Integration policies define the rights and freedoms of immigrants that are already admitted to the country. Such policies, mostly comprise domestic issues where international interdependencies and obligations are less of a constraint (Fitzgerald et al., 2014, 408). These policies regulate the terms of immigrants' incorporation into the host society and tend to follow different national models shaped by distinct understandings of the national community (Brubaker, 1992; Koopmans et al., 2012). Regarding political ideology, mainstream parties align along a socio-cultural divide with the left advocating liberal policies and the right advocating restrictive policies (Duncan and Van Hecke, 2008; Money, 1999). Liberal integration policies represent the left's ideology of social equality and is electorally deployed as a strategy to gain the votes of immigrants and ethnic minorities (Givens and Luedtke, 2005). Right-wing parties, on the other hand, tend to favour restrictive integration policies that represent their conservative values and national identity (Akkerman, 2012; Joppke, 2003). As a result, mainstream-right parties find themselves together with the radical right on the restrictive side of the integration policy continuum. Shifting to more restrictive policies on immigrant integration might therefore be an opportunity to find a common policy agenda with the radical right. Both structural and ideological factors provide substantive opportunities to mainstream-right parties for the co-optation of more restrictive integration policies.

Control policies focus on the implementation of immigration regulations by surveillance and law enforcement. Unlike regulations, they do not determine the formal openness of a country, but function as deterrence of unwanted migration, meaning despite and against the intentions of states (Guiraudon and Joppke, 2001). These policies address migration as an issue of sovereign border control and public safety. Although the effectiveness of immigration controls is often questioned, states are eagerly motivated to demonstrate control over immigration to claim their sovereignty and appease public anxieties (e.g. Wright, 2014). Furthermore, the capacities of states to control migration have increased over time, particularly by international cooperation (Lahav, 2004; Schain, 2009). Therefore, the area of control policies faces only limited structural constraints to actual policy choices. Regarding political ideology, mainstream right parties tend to have a stronger preference for law-and-order than mainstream-left parties (Akkerman, 2012; Joppke, 2003; Wenzelburger, 2015). Mainstream right parties find themselves together with the radical right on the restrictive side of the control policy continuum. We may therefore assume that the ideological costs of co-optation are limited. These policy attributes make control policies a likely case for RRPP policy influence.

Migration policies on admission, integration and control provide distinct structural and ideological opportunities and constraints for the co-optation of more restrictive policies by mainstream right parties. Such a co-optation of the radical right is most likely in the area of integration and control policy. These sub-fields offer a considerable policy space and allow for the integration into the mainstream-right ideology. Co-optation is, however, less likely in admission policy that offers a more limited policy space and collides with the economic liberalism of mainstream-right parties.

Finally, policy influence can be disaggregated into change-enabling or change-constraining effects. The government power of RRPPs can both enable additional restrictive reforms and prevent liberal reforms. Endowed with government power, RRPP have electoral incentives to demonstrate to their voters that they are capable of providing effective governance and are able to deliver promised policies, in particular when it comes to their core issue of immigration. The office success brings policy-making capacity providing RRPPs with additional leverage to pass their preferred restrictive reforms. As a result, I expect governments with RRPP support to enact more migration policy output and direct policy effects to be most likely change-enabling by prompting the government to pass additional restrictive reforms.

DATA AND METHOD

The direct influence of RRPP on migration policies is tested by a controlled comparison of cabinets with different ideologies. I use a large-N comparative design to analyse the migration policy output of governments across eighteen West European countries between 1990 and 2014. These are Austria, Belgium, Denmark, France, Finland, Germany, Greece, Iceland, Ireland, Italy, Luxembourg, the Netherlands, Norway, Portugal, Spain, Sweden, Switzerland and the UK. Radical right populism gained momentum in the 1990s and RRPP increasingly joined government coalitions in various European countries (De Lange, 2012). To ensure a sufficiently uniform context, the analysis is confined to Western Europe.

For both theoretical and methodological reasons, governments are the unit of analysis. Governmental terms are not only the main reference points for parties and voters, but also does the enactment of a policy agenda evolve over the whole office duration. The use of government units instead of the more common use of country-year observations allows for a more accurate attribution of policy outputs to the responsible government. Comparativists have demonstrated that using data based on government terms measures partisan influence most accurately (e.g. Schmitt, 2016). I define a cabinet as a government with the same party composition and the same head of government. A general election taking place, changes to the party composition of the government or a new person becoming the head of government refers to a new cabinet. The cabinet data is based on the Comparative Political Data Set by Armingeon et al. (2017a).[3]

As the dependent variable, I measure migration policy as the aggregated policy output that captures the directional change of whether policies became more liberal or more restrictive. I define migration policy outputs as all laws, regulations and policy measures enacted by national governments regarding the admission, integration and control of immigration. Following De Haas et al. (2015, 12), we can understand migration policy openness (restrictiveness) as the extent to which a policy measure expands (or limits) the rights and freedoms of immigrants. This definition is applicable to all three sub-fields of migration policy. In admission policy, it refers to the rights of immigrants regarding their entry and stay. In integration policy, it refers to the post-immigration rights of immigrant residents between a restrictive-assimilationist model and a liberal-multicultural model (see Lutz, 2017). In control policy, restrictiveness refers to the toughness of law-and-order rules. The data on migration policy changes is extracted from the DEMIG Policy dataset (De Haas et al., 2015) that measures the relevant policy output and offers sufficiently large coverage across time and space. For the purpose of this analysis, I assign each reform to the responsible government.[4] The aggregated policy output of a government is calculated as the number of liberalization minus the number of restrictions, with separate scores for each policy sub-field. To evaluate the different dimensions of policy influence, I use the numbers of liberalization and restrictions as separate variables as well as the sum of all policy changes enacted by a particular government.

The main explanatory variable is RRPP government participation. The classification of this party family follows the widely applied definition of Mudde (2007), which includes nativism as a core definitional element of their ideology. A government is coded as 'RRPP' if it hinges on the support of at least one radical right populist party, including both formal and informal coalitions. Based on these criteria, I classify eighteen cabinets across six West European countries as radical right.[5] The contrasting categories of government ideology, 'left', 'centre' and 'right', are integrated into a variable consisting of four categories. Right-wing cabinets serve as a reference category. This assignment allows for the estimation of the difference in policy output between mainstream-right and radical right governments. To control for an indirect influence of RRPP as opposition parties on government policies, I include the cumulative vote share of parties belonging to the RRPP party family at the last national election.

Based on the migration policy literature, the analysis includes a series of control variables that are likely to condition the postulated relationship. First, advanced capitalist economies are structurally dependent on continuous immigration and therefore face domestic demands for foreign labour (Hollifield, 2004). The higher the domestic labour demand, the more liberal policy changes we may expect. I include several factors to measure the latent economic liberalization pressure that results from such labour demand.[6] Trade openness serves as a proxy for economic globalization as a driver of structural labour needs due to economic integration. The unemployment rate that represents the business cycle accounts for the short-term labour demand. All controls are aggregated by government terms using the mean values across the years a government was in office.[7]

The second group of controls is related to the political and institutional context. Migration politics should be affected by the salience of the issue and the degree that public opinion is politically mobilized. I account for these dynamics by including the net migration rate and the RRPP vote share as determinants of immigration salience (Green-Pedersen and Otjes, 2017). The larger the ideological gap to the preceding cabinet, the more we could expect policy changes. The ideological distance between the incoming and the outgoing cabinet is included into the models. Following the veto player approach of Tsebelis (2002), the likelihood of a policy change hinges on the number of actors whose consent is necessary to change the status quo. Migration scholars stress that institutional veto players can restrict the influence of majoritarian sentiments on policy-making (e.g. Breunig and Luedtke, 2008). The number of veto players therefore serves as another institutional control (Database of Political Institutions, Cruz et al., 2016). The direction of policy changes may depend on the absolute level of policy openness that I measure with the IMPIC database (Helbling et al., 2017). To include such a policy baseline allows for the consideration of potential ceiling and level effects.[8] The use of governments as units of analysis requires adjustment for term duration measured by the number of days a government was in office. The more time a government spent in office, the more time it had to enact its legislative agenda. The compiled sample contains 134 governments clustered by eighteen countries. In admission and integration policy, there are more governments with a net liberalization than with a net restriction. In admission policy, seventy-five cabinets passed more liberalization whereas only nineteen cabinets passed more restrictions. For integration policy, this ratio is 66:27. Most cabinets, however, restricted control policies with a ration of seventeen cabinets with net liberalization to ninety-one cabinets with net restrictions. Hence, previous findings on policy trends are confirmed with admission and integration policies becoming more liberal and control policies becoming more restrictive over time. Finally, I use data from the Chapel Hill Expert Survey (CHES) to measure parties policy positions on immigration, integration and control policies (Bakker et al., 2015).[9] This analysis will allow for the evaluation of whether or not ideological differences are responsible for variations in policy influence or if contextual policy constraints prevent governing parties from implementing their preferred policies.

The large-N comparative sample allows me to assess the policy output of RRPP-supported governments in comparison with other governments. To model the migration policy output of governments, I estimate a series of panel regression models. Since the policy data contains variation across countries and time, I need to account for additional sources of heterogeneity. I do this by including country fixed effects and country-clustered standard errors. The fixed effects eliminate all time-invariant characteristics of countries such as most political institutions and other country-specific idiosyncrasies. There is no need to account for serial correlation since the policy outputs of cabinets are not strongly correlated over time.

Results

In a first step, I present the descriptive analysis of the migration policy output of RRPP-supported governments. All directional policy changes by radical right cabinets are shown in Figure 12.1. Despite the preference of RRPPs for more restrictive policies, we find liberalization across all three sub-fields, most pronounced in admission and the least in control. There are only seven governments that enacted more admission restrictions than liberalization, whereas this number increases to nine for integration and ten for control. The informal government coalitions enact slightly more restrictive policy output than formal coalitions with the radical right. Despite their anti-immigration agenda, when RRPPs join government coalitions, a substantive amount of policy liberalization happens.

To estimate the policy influence of RRPPs in a controlled setting, I run a series of panel regression models that take into account the clustering across countries, the varying cabinet duration and potential confounders of the relationship between government composition and migration policy output. The direct policy influence of RRPPs is estimated as the difference between RRPP-supported cabinets and mainstream-right cabinets without RRPP-support. The results are shown separately for admission, integration and control (see table 12.1). Model (1) on admission policy detects a small positive effect of RRPPs in government on policy openness, but the effect is not significant. This finding confirms the expectation of limited policy effects in policies of immigrant admission. In model (2) on integration policy, the effect of RRPPs' government power is negative, of substantial size and statistically significant. An RRPP cabinet shifts policy output on average more than two reforms into a more restrictive direction in comparison to mainstream-right cabinets. This finding confirms that integration policy is more conducive for RRPP influence. Finally, the direct policy effect of control policies in model (3) is just above zero and not significant. Unlike my theoretical expectations, this model finds no evidence that control policies become more restrictive with RRPPs in power. The three models confirm that there are substantial variations of policy influence across these three areas of migration policy.

The control variables have little explanation power. In particular, there is no evidence for indirect policy effect of RRPPs by their mere electoral strength. Regarding the general role of government ideology, there is also variation across the three policy fields. In admission and integration policy, left-wing and centre cabinets tend to be more liberal than right-wing cabinets,

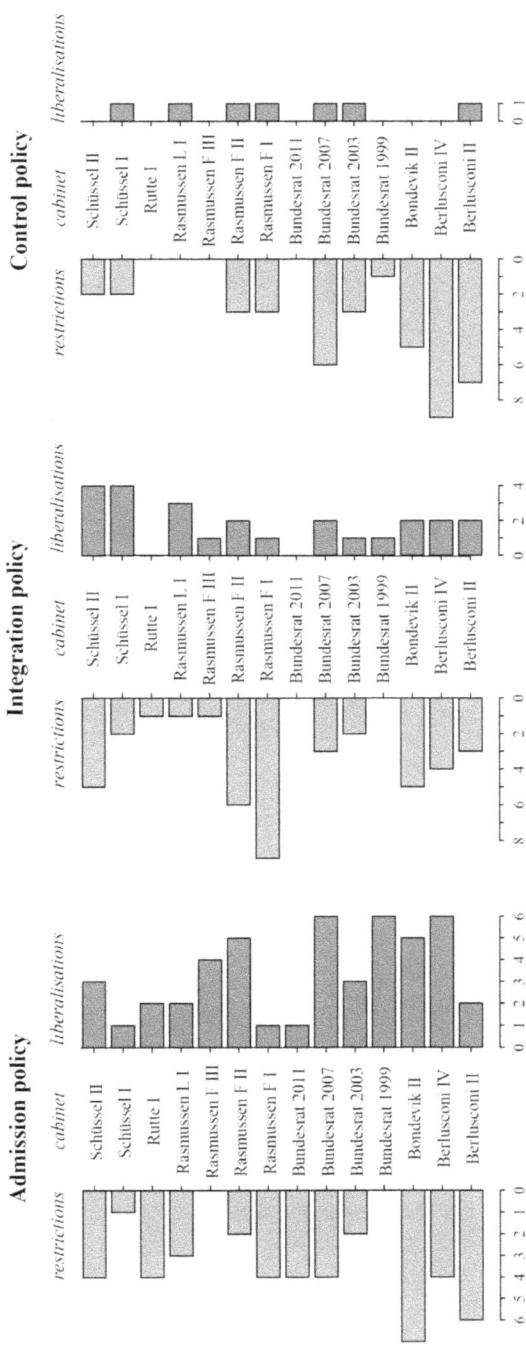

Admission policy

restrictions	cabinet	liberalisations
	Schüssel II	
	Schüssel I	
	Rutte I	
	Rasmussen L I	
	Rasmussen F III	
	Rasmussen F II	
	Rasmussen F I	
	Bundesrat 2011	
	Bundesrat 2007	
	Bundesrat 2003	
	Bundesrat 1999	
	Bondevik II	
	Berlusconi IV	
	Berlusconi II	

Integration policy

restrictions	cabinet	liberalisations

Control policy

restrictions	cabinet	liberalisations

Figure 12.1. Pyramid plots of migration policy changes by radical right cabinets.

Table 12.1. Determinants of migration policy changes

Predictors	Change in policy openness		
	Admission	*Integration*	*Control*
	(1)	*(2)*	*(3)*
Government ideology			
RRPP cabinet	0.40	**–2.19**	0.18
	(1.18)	**(0.99)**	(1.09)
Left cabinet	1.16	0.98	–0.23
	(0.95)	(0.79)	(0.88)
Centre cabinet	1.54	0.25	0.80
	(0.90)	(0.75)	(0.82)
Controls			
RRPP vote share	0.03	0.02	0.01
	(0.06)	(0.05)	(0.05)
Trade openness	**0.03**	0.02	0.00
	(0.01)	(0.01)	(0.02)
Net migration	–51.29	–6.15	–85.72
	(75.99)	(63.87)	(69.15)
Unemployment	**–0.29**	–0.06	0.05
	(0.13)	(0.11)	(0.12)
Veto players	–0.01	–0.00	0.19
	(0.39)	(0.33)	(0.35)
IMPIC score	5.84	1.27	-2.99
	(4.42)	(0.57)	(3.01)
Cabinet duration	0.00	**0.00**	**–0.00**
	(0.00)	**(0.00)**	**(0.00)**
Observations	134	134	134
Countries	18	18	18
Adjusted R^2	0.279	0.336	0.255

Note: All models are fixed effects panel regressions with country-clustered standard errors. Those coefficients that are statistically significant on the 95 per cent level are bolded.

but do not make a statistically significant difference. In control policies, cabinets appear similarly restrictive independent of their political ideology. Partisan effects are hence overall limited as is the policy influence of RRPP, with the exception of integration policy.

Economic controls play a relevant role only in admission policy where trade openness and lower levels of unemployment are significant predictors of policy openness. This suggests that admission policy changes are primarily determined by structural economic needs and business cycles. Net migration has a consistent negative effect on policy openness but does not reach statistical significance. The political and institutional controls also do not exert a significant influence on policy outputs. The effect of the ideological distance on the previous cabinet runs in the expected direction; that is, a shift to the left goes along with more liberal policy changes. A high number of veto players has a negative effect on openness in admission and integration but a positive one for controls. Policy changes are, furthermore, not dependent on the absolute level of policy restrictiveness measured by the IMPIC score. In the area of admission and integration a restrictive policy baseline is associated with more liberal reforms, whereas in the area of control a restrictive policy baseline is associated with even more restrictive reforms. Finally, the duration of a cabinet is a significant explanatory factor for the extent of liberalization in integration policy and the extent of restriction in control policies but is not significantly associated with admission policy changes.

In a next step, I analyse the influence of RRPPs on the quantity of policy output a government enacts. For that purpose, I compare the comparison of mainstream-right and radical right cabinets regarding their number of policy reforms. Governments with RRPP participation enact more policy changes across all three policy sub-fields. In substantive terms, the radical right cabinets enact on average approximately two more reforms in admission and integration and roughly one additional reform in control. Furthermore, the numbers vary across sub-fields with most reforms taking place on immigrant admission and the fewest in control policy.

Following this analysis of RRPP influence, I estimate a series of models using the numbers of reforms as the dependent variable. The higher salience of migration issues for RRPP should result in an overall higher number of policy outputs when they are governing. Figure 12.2 plots the estimates for radical right government participation. Across all three policy sub-fields, there are more policy reforms in RRPP-supported governments than in

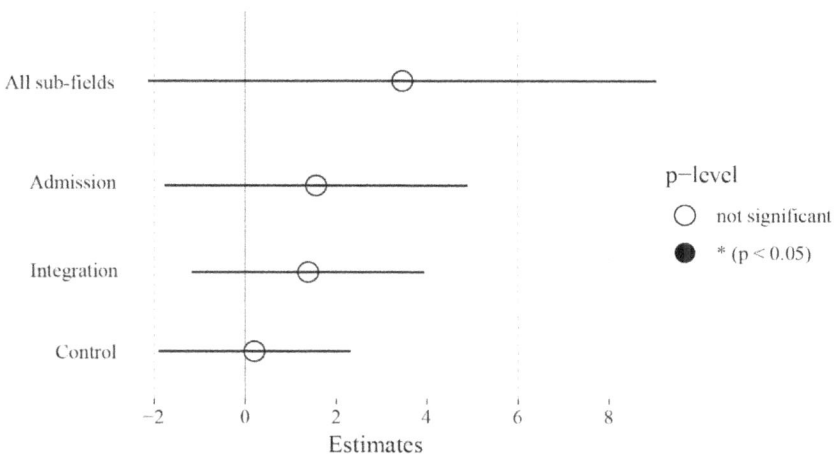

Figure 12.2. RRPPs' influence on the numbers of reforms.

comparable mainstream right cabinets. The difference, however, is only sub-stantial in admission and integration policy. In these policies the effects lie between one and two reforms but miss statistical significance. These results corroborate the finding of an overall limited policy influence. Despite the additional policy output when the radical right gains power, the difference to mainstream right cabinets is not significant.

To further assess whether the influence of RRPP on government policies is rather change-enabling or change-constraining, I run models separating liberalization and restrictions (see figure 12.3). The results suggest that in all three policy areas RRPPs mainly enable policy change. Compared with mainstream right cabinets, the enabling effect of RRPPs on additional restric-tive reforms is larger than the constraining effect of fewer liberal reforms. Moreover, governments with RRPP support enact more restrictions but also more liberalization in the external policy dimension of admission and control. Only in integration policy are changes consistently moving in a restrictive direction. The restrictive effect on integration policy is almost exclusively the result of additional restrictions that were enacted and to a much smaller extent by fewer liberalization. These findings show that when RRPPs gain government office, their only significant influence on migration policies is the passage of more restrictive reforms in integration policy.

To assess the robustness of the results, I conduct cross-validation tests by excluding single countries and governments from the sample. The results suggest that the main effects do not depend on a few influential observations or the specific case selection. Despite the small number of eighteen govern-ments with RRPP support, the pattern of policy influence is robust to classifi-cation or sampling choices. Separate estimations of policy effects for formal

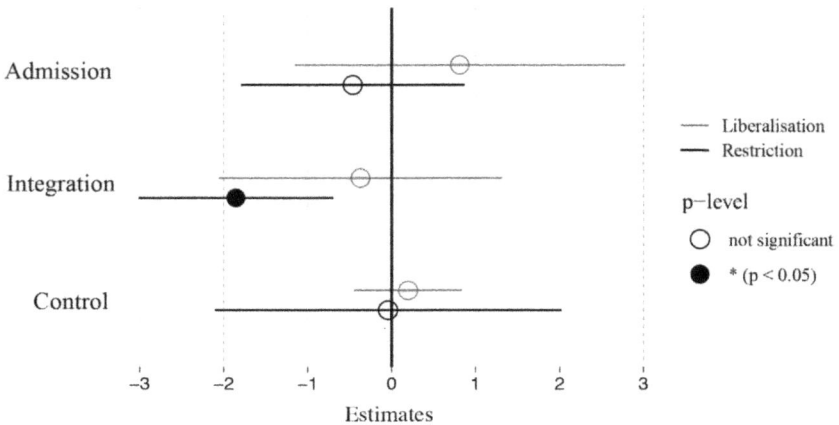

Figure 12.3.   Differentiated estimates of RRPPs' policy influence.

and informal coalitions with the radical right confirms the overall pattern of their influence. Their influence is stronger in the case of informal coalitions compared to formal coalitions both regarding the quantity and regarding the direction of policy output. While this suggests that providing support to mainstream-right governments is sufficient to exert policy influence, this conclusion is tentative due to the low number of six informal coalitions the estimates are based on. The cumulative results of resampling tests suggest that mainstream right parties do indeed selectively co-opt the radical right when they form a joint government coalition. Co-optation is found only for integration policy but not admission and control policies.

What drives the varying policy influence of RRPP government participation across the three sub-fields of migration policy? Which policy attributes are responsible for this variation? In the theoretical section, I discussed two potential drivers: varying ideological distance due to the different cleavage structure of the policy sub-fields and external constraints limiting the policy space of a government. Is the influence on integration policies the result of an ideological proximity between the radical right and the mainstream right in this policy area? I evaluate this with the policy positions of RRPP governments using data on the policy positions of the governing parties. Based on CHES data I compare expert evaluations of party positions on immigration, integration and control for six coalition governments between the radical right and the mainstream right.[10] All parties within these cabinets have a pronounced preference for restrictive migration policies across all three policy sub-fields. The position of the RRPP is systematically more restrictive than the position of their mainstream right coalition partner. Regarding the ideological distance there is little variation across the three policy sub-fields. On the 10-point positional scale, the average difference between the radical right and the mainstream right is 2.2 in admission, 2.6 in integration and 2.0 in control. This pattern suggests that the ideological distance between the radical right and their mainstream right coalition partners is very similar across the three policy sub-fields with the lowest distance in their control policy preference and the largest distance in integration policy. This systematic pattern across all cabinets excludes ideological distance as a plausible driving factor behind the selective co-optation of RRPPs. In turn, it is the attributes of policies themselves that shape the policy influence of RRPPs with different sets of governing constraints as the most likely driver of selective co-optation.

CONCLUSION

Radical right populist parties have risen to power in a number of West European countries since the 1990s. Does this increasing popularity mean that they can use their new role as governing parties to shape migration policies following their restrictive agenda? The previous evidence on this question remains inconclusive and tends to perceive RRPP policy success as limited. This contribution has analysed the direct policy influence of RRPPs by a controlled comparison of radical right with mainstream right governments. The results confirm that the influence of RRPPs on migration policies is limited. Only integration policies become more restrictive as the result of radical right government power, whereas no systematic effects are found for admission and control policies. As theorized, a restrictive turn is more likely in the field of immigrant integration than in admission where governments have limited leeway for discretionary policies. The absence of any effects on control policies runs, however, against the theoretical expectation. A plausible explanation for this finding is that the continuous trend of control policy restrictions and the virtual absence of control liberalization already represent a policy development that is preferred by the radical right. Therefore, when RRPP-supported cabinets enact control restrictions, their policies do not deviate from those of other governments as a result.

These findings suggest that the radical right uses its bargaining power inside a government coalition to shape the migration policy agenda of governments. Overall, governments with RRPP support enact a higher number of policy changes than comparable mainstream right governments. Their policy influence is therefore primarily due to the enacting of additional reforms in the preferred restrictive direction than via the veto power on policy liberalization. This interpretation is corroborated by the finding that the restrictive effect of RRPPs on integration policies is the result of a higher number of policy changes and restrictive reforms and not by their vetoing of liberal reforms. In contrast, the mere electoral success of RRPPs does not result in significant policy effects despite the electoral pressure on governing parties.

The finding that RRPPs use their government power to restrict the rights of already admitted immigrants corroborates the common expectations that RRPPs are a threat to minority rights in liberal democracies and the freedoms of those who are not considered part of the 'people' (e.g. Albertazzi and Mueller, 2013). The governing power of RRPPs may be in part an explanation of the backlash against multiculturalism and the extension of immigrant rights in Western Europe. This main finding can be reconnected to the example I depicted in the introduction of the Austrian radical right cabinet appointed in 2017 that liberalized immigration soon after taking office. This paradox can now be resolved following the argument and evidence of this chapter. The results have shown that the liberalization of immigrant admission is a common phenomenon among governments supported by the radical right. Instead, these governments opt for restrictive reforms in the domestic field of integration where governments are less constrained than in admission policy. The liberal reforms of the Austrian cabinet do indeed result from such constraints. The increase of the immigration quota was a requirement of EU law and the extension of the list of professions follows commitments of previous governments and the structural labour shortages of the country. At the same time, the government has taken a series of restrictive reforms in integration policy such as restricting social rights, restricting labour market access and banning headscarves in schools. This policy agenda of the ÖVP–FPÖ coalition government provides a more recent confirmation of my argument: When the radical right gains government power, the rights of immigrants are restricted but not immigration as such. The distinction between the external and internal dimension of migration policies demonstrates that the radical right is more likely to affect the rights of immigrants than the numbers of immigrants in a country.

NOTES

1. https://diepresse.com/home/innenpolitik/5351546/Regierung-erhoeht-Zuwan dererquote; https://diepresse.com/home/innenpolitik/5354524/Mangelberufe_Kurz-wirft-SPOe-Angstmache-vor (accessed 30 October 2018).

2. This only applies to Western Europe after the Second World War. An outlier is Switzerland, where the coalition government has included not only mainstream-right but also the Social Democratic Party.

3. When there is a reshuffle between elections without change in the head of government or the governing parties, no new government is counted. The cabinets of Switzerland, with its consociational government, are treated as an exception and four-year cabinets along electoral terms are coded despite the annual change in the head of government. The Swiss head of government does not have an equivalent power as in other European countries; rather it is a *primus inter pares* within the cabinet of seven members and it has no additional capacity to alter the migration policy agenda (Kriesi and Trechsel 2008, 75–76). Short-term cabinets of less than three months are excluded from the analysis.

4. One-third of the reforms in the sample occur in a year in which at least two cabinets were in office. The assignment of reforms to cabinets is based on the final political decision, e.g. approval by the parliament. The assignment was successful in over 99 per cent of reforms; only in the case of sixteen reforms was a clear assignment not possible.

5. The following eighteen cabinets are included: Schüssel I, Schüssel II (all AT), Berlusconi I, Berlusconi II, Berlusconi III, Berlusconi IV (all IT), Balkenende I, Rutte I (all NL), Bondevik II, Solberg (all NO), Bundesrat 1999, Bundesrat 2003, Bundesrat 2007, Bundesrat 2011 (all CH), Rasmussen F I, Rasmussen F II, Rasmussen F III, Rasmussen L I (all DK). The selection of cabinets largely follows the selection of previous studies (Akkerman 2012; De Lange 2012). Switzerland is a special case

with its government due to the consociational style of governance and its attendant 'magic formula'. All cabinets from 1999 onwards are coded RRPP-supported.

6. The data for trade openness, unemployment rate, GDP growth from the CPDS (Armingeon et al. 2017b), and net migration from the Quality of Government Standard Dataset (Teorell et al. 2018).

7. I base the calculation on 'year of influence'. The year of investiture is counted as the first year of influence, and additional years are included if the cabinet was in office at least for six months of the respective year.

8. A validation analysis shows that the DEMIG Policy dataset and the IMPIC dataset are comparable in their policy measurements over time (Schmid and Helbling, 2016). The use of fixed effects implies that the policy-baseline refers to the development over time but not across countries.

9. The CHES measures immigration policy positions of parties ranging from 0 = Fully opposed to a restrictive policy on immigration to 10 = Fully in favour of a restrictive policy on immigration. Integration policy positions are measured on a scale from 0 = Strongly favours multiculturalism to 10 = Strongly favours assimilation. Control policy positions are measured by parties' law and order preference ranging from 0 = strongly promotes civil liberties to 10 = strongly supports tough measures to fight crime.

10. Data for the following cabinets is available: Solberg I (NO), Rutte I (NL), Rasmussen F III (DK), Rasmussen L (DK), and Berlusconi IV (IT). I exclude the Swiss cabinets due to their distinct coalition-forming process in the country, which includes all major parties.

BIBLIOGRAPHY

Akkerman, Tjitske. 2012. Comparing radical right parties in government: Immigration and integration policies in nine countries (1996–2010). *West European Politics* 35, no. 3: 511–529.

Akkerman, Tjitske. 2015. Immigration policy and electoral competition in Western Europe: A finegrained analysis of party positions over the past two decades. *Party Politics* 21, no. 1: 54–67.

Albertazzi, Daniele and Sean Mueller. 2013. Populism and liberal democracy: Populists in government in Austria, Italy, Poland and Switzerland. *Government and Opposition* 48, no. 3: 343–371.

Alonso, Sonia and Saro Claro da Fonseca. 2011. Immigration, left and right. *Party Politics* 18, no. 6: 865–884.

Armingeon, Klaus, Virginia Wenger, Fiona Wiedemeier, Christian Isler, Laura Knöpfel and David Weisstanner. 2017a. Supplement to the Comparative Political Data Set. Government Composition 1960–2015.

Armingeon, Klaus, Virginia Wenger, Fiona Wiedemeier, Christian Isler, Laura Knöpfel and David Weisstanner. 2017b. Comparative Political Data Set 1960–2015.

Arzheimer, Kai. 2009. Contextual factors and the extreme right vote in Western Europe, 1980–2002. *American Journal of Political Science* 53, no. 2: 259–275.

Bakker, Ryan, Catherine de Vries, Erica Edwards, Liesbet Hooghe, Seth Jolly, Gary Marks, Jonathan Polk, Jan Rovny, Marco Steenbergen and Milada Anna Vachudova. 2015. Measuring party positions in Europe: The Chapel Hill expert survey trend file, 1999–2010. *Party Politics* 21, no. 1: 143–152.

Bjerre, Liv, Marc Helbling, Friederike Römer, and Malisa Zobel. 2015. Conceptualizing and measuring immigration policies: A comparative perspective. *International Migration Review* 49, no. 3: 555–600.

Breunig, Christian and Adam Luedtke. 2008. What motivates the gatekeepers? Explaining governing party preferences on immigration. *Governance* 21, no. 1: 123–146.

Brubaker, Roger. 1992. *Citizenship and Nationhood in France and Germany.* Cambridge, MA: Harvard University Press.

Carvalho, João. 2013. *Impact of Extreme Right Parties on Immigration Policy: Comparing Britain, France and Italy.* New York: Routledge.

Carvalho, João. 2016. The impact of extreme right parties on immigration policy in Italy and France in the early 2000s. *Comparative European Politics* 14, no. 5: 663–685.

Cruz, Cesi, Philip Keefer and Carlos Scartascini. 2016. Database of Political Institutions Codebook, 2015 Update (DPI2015). Inter-American Development Bank. Updated version of Thorsten Beck, George Clarke, Alberto Groff, Philip Keefer, and Patrick Walsh, 2001. New tools in comparative political economy: The database of political institutions. *World Bank Economic Review* 15, no. 1: 165–176.

Davis, Amber. 2012. The impact of anti-immigration parties on mainstream parties' immigration positions in the Netherlands, Flanders and the UK 1987–2010: Divided electorates, left-right politics and the pull towards restrictionism. PhD thesis, European University Institute.

De Haas, Hein, Katharina Natter, and Simona Vezzoli. 2015. Conceptualizing and measuring migration policy change. *Comparative Migration Studies* 3, no. 15: 1–21.

De Haas, H., Katharina Natter, and Simona Vezzoli. 2018. Growing restrictiveness or changing selection? The nature and evolution of migration policies. *International Migration Review* 52, no. 2: 324–367.

De Lange, Sarah. L. 2012. New alliances: Why mainstream parties govern with radical right-wing populist parties. *Political Studies* 60, no. 4: 899–918.

Duncan, Fraser. 2010. Immigration and integration policy and the Austrian radical right in office: The FPÖ/BZÖ, 2000–2006. *Contemporary Politics* 16, no. 4: 337–354.

Duncan, Fraser and Van Hecke, Steven. 2008. Immigration and the transnational European centre-right: A common programmatic response? *Journal of European Public Policy* 15, no. 3: 432–452.

Fitzgerald, Jennifer, David Leblang and Jessica C. Teets. 2014. Defying the law of gravity: The political economy of international migration. *World Politics* 66, no. 3: 406–445.

Givens, Terri and Adam Luedtke. 2005. European immigration policies in comparative perspective: Issue salience, partisanship and immigrant rights. *Comparative European Politics* 3, no. 1: 1–22.

Green-Pedersen, Christoffer and Simon Otjes. 2017. A hot topic? Immigration on the agenda in Western Europe. *Party Politics*: 1–11.

Guiraudon, Virginie and Christian Joppke. 2001. *Controlling a New Migration World*. London/New York: Routledge.

Heinisch, Reinhard. 2003. Success in opposition – failure in government: Explaining the performance of right-wing populist parties in public office. *West European Politics* 26, no. 3: 91–130.

Helbling, Marc, Liv Bjerre, Friederike Römer, and Malisa Zobel. 2017. Measuring immigration policies: The IMPIC database. *European Political Science* 16, no. 1: 79–98.

Helbling, Marc and Dorina Kalkum. 2017. Migration policy trends in OECD countries. *Journal of European Public Policy*: 1–19.

Hollifield, James F. 2004. The emerging migration state. *International Migration Review* 38, no. 3: 885–912.

Joppke, Christian. 1998. Why liberal states accept unwanted immigration. *World Politics* 50, no. 2: 266–293.

Joppke, Christian. 2003. Citizenship between de- and re-ethnicization. *European Journal of Sociology* 44, no. 3: 429–458.

Koopmans, Ruud, Ines Michalowski, and Stine Waibel. 2012. Citizenship rights for immigrants: National political processes and cross-national convergence in western Europe, 1980–2008. *American Journal of Sociology* 117, no. 4: 1202–1245.

Kriesi, Hanspeter, and Alexander H. Trechsel. 2008. *The Politics of Switzerland. Continuity and Change in a Consensus-Democracy*. Cambridge: Cambridge University Press.

Lahav, Gallya. 2004. *Immigration and Politics in the New Europe*. Cambridge: Cambridge University Press.

Lutz, Philipp. 2017. Two logics of policy intervention in immigrant integration: An institutionalized framework based on capabilities and aspirations. *Comparative Migration Studies* 5, no. 2: 1–19.

Lutz, Philipp. 2019. Variation in policy success: Radical right populism and migration policy. *West European Politics* 42, no. 3: 517–544.

Manatschal, Anita. 2012. Path-dependent or dynamic? Cantonal integration policies between regional citizenship traditions and right populist party politics. *Ethnic and Racial Studies* 35, no. 2: 281–97.

Minkenberg, Michael. 2001. The radical right in public office: Agenda-setting and policy effects. *West European Politics* 24, no. 4: 1–21.

Money, Jeanette. 1999. *Fences and Neighbours: The Political Geography of Immigration Control*. Ithaca, NY: Cornell University Press.

Mudde, Cas. 2007. *Populist Radical Right Parties in Europe*. Cambridge: Cambridge University Press.

Mudde, Cas. 2013. Three decades of populist radical right parties in Western Europe: So what? *European Journal of Political Research* 52, no. 1: 1–19.

Muis, Jasper and Tim Immerzeel. 2017. Causes and consequences of the rise of populist radical right parties and movements in Europe. *Current Sociology* 65, no. 6: 909–930.

Odmalm, Pontus. 2011. Political parties and 'the immigration issue': Issue ownership in Swedish parliamentary elections 1991–2010. *West European Politics* 34, no. 5: 1070–1091.

Rydgren, Jens. 2008. Immigration sceptics, xenophobes or racists? Radical right-wing voting in six West European countries. *European Journal of Political Research* 47, no. 6: 737–765.

Schain, Martin A. 2006. The extreme-right and immigration policy-making: Measuring direct and indirect effects. *West European Politics* 29, no. 2: 270–289.

Schain, Martin A. 2009. The state strikes back: Immigration policy in the European Union. *European Journal of International Law* 20, no. 1: 93–109.

Schmid, Samuel D. and Marc Helbling. 2016. Validating the immigration policies in comparison (IMPIC) dataset. WZB Discussion Paper.

Schmitt, Carina. 2016. Panel data analysis and partisan variables: How periodization does influence partisan effects. *Journal of European Public Policy* 23, no. 10: 1442–1459.

Teorell, Jan, Stefan Dahlberg, Sören Holmberg, Bo Rothstein, Natalia Alvarado Pachon and Richard Svensson. 2018. *The Quality of Government Standard Dataset*, version January 2018. University of Gothenburg: The Quality of Government Institute. http://www.qog.pol.gu.se doi:10.18157/QoGStdJan18.

Tsebelis, George. 2002. *Veto-Players: How Political Institutions Work*. Princeton, PA: Princeton University Press.

Van Kersbergen, Kees and André Krouwel. 2008. A double-edged sword! The Dutch centre-right and the foreigners issue. *Journal of European Public Policy* 15, no. 3: 398–414.

Wenzelburger, Georg. 2015. Parties, institutions and the politics of law and order: How political institutions and partisan ideologies shape law-and-order spending in twenty Western industrialized countries. *British Journal of Political Science* 45, no. 3: 663–687.

Williams, Michelle H. 2006. *The Impact of Radical Right-wing Parties in West European Democracies*. New York: Palgrave Macmillan.

Wright, Chris F. 2014. How do states implement liberal immigration policies? Control signals and skilled immigration reform in Australia. *Governance* 27, no. 3: 397–421.

Zaslove, Andrej. 2004. Closing the door? The ideology and impact of radical right populism on immigration policy in Austria and Italy. *Journal of Political Ideologies* 9, no. 1: 99–118.

Zincone, Giovanna. 2006. Italian immigrants and immigration policy-making: Structures, actors and practices. IMISCOE Working Paper.

Conclusion

Hans-Georg Betz and Laurent Bernhard

Over the past several decades, radical right populist parties (RRPP) have firmly established themselves in a large number of advanced liberal democracies. Once considered political pariahs by the established political parties and the media, and more often than not shunned, ostracised and 'quarantined' within the walls of a *cordon sanitaire*, RRPP have increasingly moved into the political mainstream. Whereas in the past, established parties on the centre-right and centre-left wanted nothing to do with them, more often than not they regard them as desirable potential coalition partners in many democracies nowadays.

The recent acceptance of some RRPP as potential coalition partners is to a significant extent a result of the growing fragmentation of party systems – due in particular to the dramatic loss of electoral support for traditional centre-right and centre-left parties, most recently seen in many West European countries and, arguably most dramatically, in Italy. As a result, it has increasingly become difficult to engage in coalition negotiations that rule out 'on principle' talking to the radical right. In fact, once mainstream parties abandoned the notion that they could permanently shut out the populist right from sharing power, they have proven more than eager to 'make a deal' with them, largely independent of political *couleur*. Prominent examples are the (by now dissolved) right-wing coalitions in Austria, Finland (until the breakup of the Finns in 2017) and Norway (re-elected in 2017, and headed by two women). The inclusion of RRPP in coalition negotiations raises a number of questions, to a large extent addressed in the chapters that constitute the main body of this volume.

This book aimed to study the influence of RRPP in terms of policies in contemporary Western Europe. To that end, the research question referred to the conditions under which this party family manages to leave its imprints on its core issues. In light of increased vote shares of RRPP, this edited volume has looked at the role played by party status. More specifically, the authors of the various chapters have investigated whether these parties are more likely to exert policy influence when they are in office than when they are outside power. The thematic focus was placed on immigration, law and order issues and European integration, since it is on these issues that RRPP claim to voice, represent and promote the views, desires and expectations of ordinary people. This means that once included in government, they are – or at least should be – expected to deliver, just like any other political party. Whether, if so, and to what degree this is the case is ultimately an empirical question this book has sought to address.

In order to be able to make a fair assessment, it is imperative to establish what distinguishes the radical right from its competitors in the electoral arena. In addition to authoritarian beliefs, contemporary radical right-wing populism is a composite of two ideational elements: *populism* and *nativism* (Mudde, 2007; Rooduijn, 2015; Rydgren, 2013). Populism is defined as a political doctrine that holds that society is divided into two antagonistic groups: the vast majority of ordinary people and corrupt elites that act in their own interest (Mudde, 2004). Populism is essentially about mobilising ordinary citizens around a common set of grievances and *ressentiments* that provide them with a sense of a shared identity as the genuine and authentic 'people' who are pitted against 'those above' held responsible for all their grievances. Populism aims to restore voice to the people and thus assure that politics once again becomes a true reflection and expression of the popular will, derived from the 'common sense' of ordinary people.

Nativism is informed by the notion that the sensibilities and needs of the 'native-born' should be accorded absolute priority over those of newcomers; the former should be given preference simply because they are 'native-born'. At the same time, nativism reflects a conscious attempt on the part of the 'indigenous' population to defend, maintain and revive the cherished heritage of their culture. Nativism has its origins in antebellum United States when the new country was confronted with a large wave of Western European immigrants, a majority of them from catholic Ireland (Betz, 2017). Their arrival provoked a vicious response on the part of large segments of the resident population, intent on defending the new country's Anglo-Saxon Protestant cultural heritage against the 'popish' threat. American nativists, such as the 'Know Nothings', held that Anglo-Saxon Protestantism undergirded the essential moral and intellectual qualities indispensable for democratic citizenship, which made American culture superior.

It is reasonable to suggest that the ideational construct underpinning RRPP's political claims and demands should inform the policy proposals advanced by these parties when in government. Like any other political party,

RRPP have an obligation to their voters to translate programmatic rhetoric (even if relatively vague, amorphous and lacking coherence) into concrete policies that not only respond to the expectations of their electoral base but are likely to benefit them. Support for RRPP is to a significant degree an expression of popular disenchantment with often arcane and opaque political processes negotiated among political elites without much input from the public, failure to deliver on their promises by parties that claim for themselves to reflect the 'popular will' can only but intensify sentiments of political powerlessness and disillusionment.

Whether RRPP entrusted with government responsibility manage to satisfy their supporters is one, albeit major, question addressed in this volume. Policy encompasses a broad range of fields and issues, not all pertaining to the radical right. Some are of particular importance to these parties, and they should be judged accordingly. RRPP, like any other relevant political party, have the opportunity to influence policy on several levels – local, regional and national – and in a number of ways – directly and/or indirectly, via framing the discourse on a particular issue, and/or via setting the agenda, to name but a few.

National politics certainly is the most visible arena where RRPP have increasingly been able to establish themselves. Equally important, however, at least in terms of potential policy impact, are lower levels of public administration, such as regions and local communities (see chapter 7 by Fred Paxton in this volume). Indeed, a growing number of these parties have seized the opportunities available, if only, as the Front national has done at local level, to translate political rhetoric into concrete measures on a relatively low level of governance serving both as 'laboratory' settings and 'showcases' for what the populist right can accomplish if in power. A particularly egregious example was the FPÖ's capture of the Austrian region of Carinthia under Jörg Haider (twice-elected governor) in the 1990s, who sought to make the region a showcase of populist governance. The results, however, proved to be disastrous, however.

A second question that follows from the first one is whether, and if so, to what degree, government responsibility has an impact on these parties. Experience suggests that new political parties – such as the Greens and related 'left-libertarian' parties a few decades ago – once poised to enter political office, have tended to moderate their demands as well as their image (most famously reflected in Marine Le Pen's strategy of *dédiabolisation*), if for no other reason than to broaden their electoral appeal beyond their core constituency. At the same time, broadening their appeal has meant watering down political demands, which, in turn, has only but intensified the political disenchantment of significant segments of these parties' core constituencies.

This raises a third important question. To what degree is engaging in government responsibility actually the best available strategy for RRPP to have a genuine, discernible impact on policy? Experience shows that not all of these parties have been particularly eager to shoulder government responsibility. The Belgian Vlaams Blok, for instance, in 1991 had the opportunity to fill a ministerial portfolio in the Flemish consociational government. It declined (Coffé, 2005, 211). And the Danish People's Party, one of Western Europe's politically most successful RRPP, seems to have been quite content supporting centre-right minority governments from the outside.

PEOPLE AGAINST THE ELITE

The contemporary radical right in advanced liberal democracies is an important part of the populist party family. Unfortunately, in recent years, with the adoption by the radical right of populism in rhetoric, style and strategy, populism has increasingly attained a negative connotation – a synonym for demagoguery and the cynical exploitation of paranoia and conspirationalism. From this perspective, the radical right's populist turn is nothing more than an expedient tool for scaremongering in the service of political manipulation, which should not be taken too seriously. In sharp contrast, RRPP themselves have generally claimed for themselves to be the only truly committed proponents and promoters of 'genuine democracy' – a democracy that listens to and respects the views and will of ordinary citizens and, in the process, accords them validation and dignity. Examples abound in the programmes, pamphlets and slogans produced by these parties, such as the well-known FN catchphrase *rendre la parole au peuple* (give people back their voice) and former FPÖ leader Jörg Haider's call for a genuine *Bürgerdemokratie* (i.e. a democracy for citizens rather than the established political elites).

These claims should not be dismissed as empty rhetoric, if for no other reason than that they resonate with widespread and often quite profound popular political disaffection, if not cynicism, coupled with an often profound sense of political powerlessness. Take the recent gains of the Alternative for Germany (AfD) in the eastern regions of the country that formerly made up the German Democratic Republic. Citizens from these regions, surveys indicate, still consider themselves 'second-class citizens' in post-unification Germany. It is this sense of humiliation stemming from a perceived lack of recognition, which to a significant extent explains why the AfD did particularly well in these parts, even in a relatively flourishing region such as Saxony (Betz and Habersack, forthcoming). Similar observations have been advanced by American analysts to explain the support Donald Trump garnered in 2016 in large parts of the upper Midwest (sometimes ridiculed and dismissed as part of America's 'flyover country').

These examples suggest that disenchantment with politics or, even worse, democratic distemper should not be underestimated as a driving motive for supporting RRPP. Support for these parties is, to a certain degree at least, an expression of a revolt against elites, their perceived arrogance and aloofness, and particularly their hold on the manipulation of symbols and imposition of meaning. It is hardly a coincidence, for instance, that virtually all RRPP have lined up against the 'ideology of gender' denounced as a left-wing ideological construct imposed by the elite against the common sense of the vast majority of ordinary people allegedly vested in traditional notions of the family. At the same time, however, these parties should be held responsible, particularly when in a position of power, for advancing concrete policies that not only empower ordinary people but substantially reduce the power – political and 'meta-political' (in terms of Gramsci's notion of 'cultural hegemony') – of the established political and cultural elite.

But the elite derive their privileged position not only from their hold on political and cultural power, but also from their disproportionate command of economic resources, resulting in ever-growing inequality. Studies on the various facets of inequality have shown that the combination of socio-economic and socio-cultural position exerts a strong influence on a number of trends – ranging from marriage/cohabition patterns (via 'assortative mating') to the probability the next generation will enrol in higher education – which, in turn, have a decisive influence on the perpetuation of inequality. Given the radical populist right's claims to promote the neglected interests of ordinary people, one would expect these parties to advance policy propositions that are likely to halt, if not reverse, inequality, for instance via the tax system (whether direct or indirect, both privileging the rich), limitations on executive compensation, or measures to curtail the structural power of the financial sector.

To be sure, RRPP have written into their programmes a panoply of policy measures that are supposed to shift power from the elite to ordinary citizens. Thus, virtually all of these parties call for the introduction and extension of various instruments of direct democracy, such as popular initiatives, referenda and the direct election of important political officials, such as mayors. It is also a fact that the radical right has consistently launched vicious and vitriolic diatribes against the 'ruling elite' and their hold on the 'mainstream' media of communication, by means of which the elite has been able to exercise their 'cultural hegemony' and enforce their version of 'political correctness'. At the same time, however, most of these parties have kept relatively mum on the question of socio-economic inequality, and this despite the fact that empirical studies have shown that anxiety and resentment in the face of mounting inequality (via the mechanism of 'positional deprivation') has played a significant role in the growing support for the populist radical right

(Burgoon et al., 2019; Gidron and Hall, 2017). Instead, the rhetoric of radical right-wing populist resentment has been primarily directed against the political and particularly the cultural elite.

The crucial question is not whether there is something to the radical right's narrative and rhetoric with respect to the elite. This is a highly charged question, subject to fundamental and heated ideological disagreement. Rather, it is whether and, if so, to what degree the radical right has offered concrete policies designed to empower ordinary people *and* concomitantly weaken if not 'disempower' the elite by depriving them of their privileged position with respect to the construction and enforcement of meaning (e.g. via the establishment of parameters circumscribing politically acceptable speech), the setting of the political agenda and the perpetuation of high levels of socio-economic inequality.

THE POLICY AGENDA

Much of contemporary literature on the radical populist right is focused on the question of immigration as the central issue embraced by these parties. RRPP not only 'own' this issue, their proven record on this question is also held to be the main reason for their success at the polls. It is therefore more than legitimate to scrutinize how these parties, once given the opportunity to share real power, have translated widespread popular uneasiness, if not outright hostility, with regard to immigration and certain ideas, such as multiculturalism, associated with it, into concrete policies.

As is reflected by the outline of this edited volume, the analysis of the success of RRPP has to a large extent focused on *culture* rather than economics in recent years. On this reading, the growing support for these parties is above all an expression of a backlash against secular processes of cultural homogenization and hybridization intricately linked to globalization. These processes appear to have engendered a growing awareness of cultural differences, which, in turn, have provoked a revived sensibility to the question of (national) identity and its recognition. RRPP have successfully promoted themselves as resolute defenders of both national as well as 'civilizational' identity and, somewhat ironically, as champions of Western liberal values.

Contemporary radical right-wing populist identity politics is almost exclusively targeting Islam, attacked and rejected as being fundamentally incompatible with Western values and the Western way of life. In policy terms, this means promoting measures that reaffirm, strengthen and reinforce the historical legacy of Western values and individual national identity. To be sure, the radical populist right has hardly a monopoly on cultural identity and its defence, as recent debates on what constitutes being British, Danish,

French, etc. and whether or not there should be a *Leitkultur* (culture of refer-ence) have demonstrated. Yet given the particular importance RRPP accord to this question, it is reasonable to expect that they push for concrete policies that affirm and safeguard cultural identity.

The defence of cultural identity is only one, albeit increasingly important, facet of contemporary radical right-wing ideology. A second facet is *wel-fare chauvinism*, the traditional vote-getter of the radical right. For RRPP, everything revolves around 'the own people first' (*eigen volk eerst*, as the Belgian Vlaams Blok used to put it on their pamphlets). In the past, this notion pertained particularly to jobs. With job opportunities for routine work-ers (especially if they do not speak the language of the host country) rapidly drying up in the wake of deindustrialization, delocalization and outsourcing, it is increasingly used to mobilize popular resentment with respect to the allocation of social benefits. This is a particularly important issue for RRPP. Outsourcing, technological innovation (such as automation and robotisation) and import competition from developing countries affect primarily 'ordinary workers', that is, persons who lack the necessary educational background and skills to take advantage of the new opportunities afforded by the Fourth Industrial Revolution. Over the past several decades, these parties have increasingly replaced the established social-democratic left as representatives of marginalized workers, voicing demands that were traditionally associated with socialism.

In terms of policy proposals, at least two foci suggest themselves: domesti-cally, measures that restrict the allocation of social benefits to (native-born) citizens in line with the well-known Front national notion of *préférence nationale* (national preference); in terms of international political economy, measures that shield ordinary workers from 'disloyal competition' from developing countries, via, for instance, economic protectionism; and mea-sures designed to 'keep money at home' particularly by substantially cutting development aid and halting contributions to the EU budget.

REALITY CHECK

Before an assessment is made of the radical right's impact on policy, a caveat is in order. As the preceding discussion suggests, theoretically at least, the opportunities for these parties to influence policy are potentially extensive and hardly limited to questions associated with immigration and its impact on society. The reality is significantly messier. The perhaps most egregious example is the Lega Nord. Ever since its inception in the early 1990s, the Lega had one central political objective – the transformation of Italy into a federal state, leaving the individual regions with extensive autonomy, particularly with respect to fiscal matters. The party's original leader, Umberto Bossi, would perennially threaten that if his demands were not met, the north (aka 'Padania' in Lega speak) would secede from the rest of the country. Yet after years of being a reliable junior partner in various Berlusconi governments, the Lega Nord had achieved little on the question of federalism, as is shown by the contribution of Christophe Bouillaud (chapter 6) in this volume. The next years will show whether the same will apply to the Lega under the leadership of Matteo Salvini.

In other cases, the populist right scored some initial policy success, only to see it watered down in subsequent stages. The Swiss People's Party (SVP), Western Europe's largest RRPP in terms of votes share, is a prominent case in point (Bernhard et al., 2015). In 2014, the party won a very slim majority (by roughly 19,500 votes) for its popular initiative 'against mass immigration', which was primarily directed against labour migration from EU countries. When the Swiss government failed to reach an agreement with the EU on migration limitations it 'caved in' and passed a law largely in line with the EU's intransigent position, a law which the SVP characterized as 'traitorous' representing nothing short of a 'capitulation before the EU'. Given the SVP's ultimate failure to limit the influx of EU labour migrants, it is not entirely coincidental that the SVP lost each and every subsequent popular initiative related to migration and national sovereignty, quite apart from the fact that the party now faces stronger resistance from civil society.

The latter example reveals that even with regard to the radical populist right's 'core competency' issue, that is, immigration, the translation of its rhetoric into concrete – and particularly enforceable – policy is subject to a considerable number of hurdles, constraints and veto points. This more often than not thwarts these parties' ambitious goals. João Carvalho makes a similar point in his chapter. The Front national, led by Marine Le Pen, for instance, officially stated that it would reduce legal immigration from annually 200,000 to 10,000 within five years (Libération, 2015). This might sound good to the party's core constituency; but even they are unlikely to believe in its realization.

Yet RRPP have continued to take credit for policies that restrict the scope of migrants', and particularly refugees', rights. In line with previous research (see Mudde, 2013 for an overview), the contributions to this volume clearly demonstrate that more often than not there is a large gap between their claims and aspirations and the reality 'on the ground' – particularly when the radical populist right is in a position of genuine power. The Lega Nord is perhaps the most emblematic case in point. While promoting itself in its pamphlets and speeches as an intransigent opponent of 'mass immigration', once in a position of power it oversaw what Christophe Bouillaud in his contribution characterizes as the most extensive 'regularisation' ever of immigrants in

Italy. The reason for this 'voter betrayal' was as mundane as it was obvious: Italy's industrial, agricultural and service sectors were looking for cheap and particularly submissive workers supposed, one might surmise, to help maintain Italy's international competitiveness.

The Italian case, as Philipp Lutz's comparative study in this volume demonstrates, is hardly unique. In general, despite all the rhetoric, RRPP seem to have had a relatively limited impact on immigration policy *sensu stricto*. As is suggested by coalition agreements between parties from the centre-right and the radical right (take for example most recent ÖVP/FPÖ coalition in Austria that Farid Hafez and Reinhard Heinisch address in this volume), this is primarily due to the needs of the labour market. In fact immigrants are literally sucked into Western Europe. Millions of them not only work in the fields, they also cook and serve the meals, build, repair and clean the houses, maintain the landscape and look after the children, the elderly, the sick and even the pets. This suggests that RRPP have relatively little direct impact on even those policy fields that they are said to 'own' – a finding already noted by Tijtske Akkerman some years ago (Akkerman, 2012). In fact, it seems that participation in government severely limits the policy impact of these parties, either because they choose to moderate their positions in order to be acceptable as coalition partners, or because they lack the political weight and/ or experience to prevail over powerful countervailing interests.

Yet this volume has shown that RRPP often do make a difference. The policy influence of RRPP has been found to be highly dependent on issues. RRPP have definitely left their mark on questions related to *integration*. The contributions by Juliana Chueri, Fred Paxton and Phlipp Lutz provide empirical evidence for this claim. Over the past several decades, most countries in Western Europe have adopted an increasingly restrictive immigration regime, often independently of the presence of RRPP in governments. At the same time, with the substantial presence of an increasingly visible and particularly vocal permanent population 'with a migration background', the question of how to integrate these minority groups has become increasingly urgent. For RRPP, the answer is simple: integration means full embracement of the host country's culture, traditions, norms and rules – in short, unconditional assimilation. This has moved the question of Islam to the centre of the radical populist right's 'identitarian' politics. It is here that these parties have had a significant impact on policy, both indirect and direct. A case of the latter was the adoption of the 'minaret initiative' in Switzerland in 2009, which represented a significant success for the SVP.

Policy impacts are also visible with respect to policies that target the material conditions of immigrants and particularly refugees. Integration, as Juliana Chueri notes, concerns not only immigrants' duty to make an effort to 'fit into' the host society, but also immigrants' and refugees' entitlements to social rights – to which RRPP vehemently object. In fact, virtually of all these parties have charged that immigrants and refugees are primarily attracted by what the Front national has called 'the suction pumps' (*pompes aspirantes*) of the welfare state. Consistent with their policy agenda, the radical populist right has advanced a range of policies designed to substantially curtail or out-right cut social benefits available to immigrants and refugees, particularly if immigrants happened to be illegally in the country – largely in line with the nativist evergreen of 'Own people first' (recently revived by Salvini's Lega in the form of the slogan *Prima gli italiani*). Our-own-people-first policies, however, are difficult to turn into reality, as the Lega Nord found out on the regional level: In 2017, the regional parliament of Veneto passed a law that would have restricted access to communal nursery schools to families who had been living and working in the region for at least fifteen years. The Lega defended the law, maintaining that it just followed 'common sense'. Common sense, however, did not prevail. In the following year, Italy's constitutional court declared it unconstitutional arguing that it violated the principle of equality and failed to present a reasonable link between long-term residence and need.

By contrast, several chapters have shown that RRPP obviously failed to deliver on their promises when it comes to European integration. The con-tributions by Christophe Bouillaud as well as by Farid Hafez and Reinhard Heinisch show that centre-right coalition partners are reluctant to make any substantial policy concessions in this field. This is hardly surprising after all. Indeed, the constraints to which EU member states are exposed and the fundamental ideological disagreements with the mainstream parties make it considerably more difficult for RRPP in cabinet to exert a direct policy influ-ence. Under these circumstances, the radical right can only hope that referen-dums are organized on the EU topic to achieve its desired policy outcome. As the Brexit vote suggests, direct democracy provides RRPP with an excellent opportunity to take full advantage of the pronounced division between cos-mopolitan elites and sovereigntist citizens that is currently available in West-ern Europe (Teney and Helbling, 2014). Beyond Euro-scepticism, evidence from Switzerland invites the conclusion that the radical right benefits much from referendums and popular initiatives on its core issues, as chapter 11 by Benjamin Biard on law and order suggests in this volume.

Taken together, the chapters in this volume suggest that the RRPP that are part of national governments only tended to exert a limited policy influ-ence. This is to a large degree attributable to the fact that the radical right in power has usually been the junior partner of mainstream parties in Western European cabinets so far. The opposite is the case when RRPP support centre-right minority governments from the outside. This strategy allows the radical right to exploit the fact that the government parties vitally depended on its goodwill, which made them vulnerable to 'blackmail' by the populist right. Indeed, no less than five contributions to this volume (i.e. those by Flemming Christiansen and colleagues, Nathalie Blanc-Noël, Juliana Chueri, Philipp Lutz as well as by Malisa Zobel and Michael Minkenberg) point out that this status leads to major policy influence. Arguably, the evidence presented here is highly driven by Denmark and the Danish People's Party. Hence, comparative researchers are well advised to carefully consider other instances of RRPP that tolerated centre-right cabinets in a recent past, especially the PVV in the Netherlands and the Freedom Party in Norway. We will return to the intriguing case of the Danish People's Party at the end of this conclusion.

Apart from that, many RRPP have been shown to exert an *indirect influence* throughout this volume. This applies to the Austrian Freedom Party as Farid Hafez and Reinhard Heinisch's chapter 8 demonstrates. The result has been a number of highly publicized restrictive policies targeting Muslim minorities, most prominently laws banning the burqa, and municipal measures (for instance via the manipulation of building and zoning codes) designed to impede the construction of new mosques. Another significant identitarian issue has been the defence of the 'visible' display of the crucifix in public spaces, particularly after the 2010 ruling of the European Court of Human Rights (regarding Italy) that the crucifix represented a reflection of majoritarian Catholic culture. In 2018, the Lega introduced a policy proposal in the Italian parliament mandating that crucifixes be visibly hung in public places such as schools, universities, prisons, public offices, consulates and embassies and ports.

Four other chapters have documented the occurrence of indirect policy effects in this volume. The quantitative analysis by Georg Wenzelburger and Pascal König suggests that it is the electoral threat that primarily leads right-wing governments to increase their spending on law and order policies. The chapters by Benjamin Biard (chapter 9) and João Carvalho (chapter 3) highlight that institutionally weak RRPP such as the Front national and RRPP that face a *cordon sanitaire* such as Vlaams Belang can under certain circumstances exert a disproportionate policy influence. Both qualitative studies show, among other things, that terrorist attacks played into the hands of the radical right, since governments in Belgium and France felt impelled to enact more restrictive measures on law and order issues and immigration as a result of these dramatic events. The contribution by Malisa Zobel and Michael Minkenberg (chapter 2) in this volume suggests that even marginal parties are able to exert a crucial influence on mainstream parties. Most tellingly, the German radical right decisively contributed to a right-wards shift in immigration policies long before the AfD made it to Parliament.

To summarize, all empirical chapters of this volume have found some direct or indirect policy influence of RRPP. In line with previous research, it has been shown that their influence is rather limited in most cases, however. We generally reject our party status hypothesis, given that the radical right in power does not clearly appear to be more successful than those outside power when it comes to shifting policies in their desired restrictive direction on their core issues. The assembled evidence here suggests that RRPP, even when in government, have been far less effective in exerting direct impact on policy than what the often rather hysterical coverage of these parties in the public media might suggest. RRPP are adept at hyperbole, but once in a position of power, hardly ever meet the emotions and expectations evoked among their voters. In fact, the prospect of sharing power seems to take the sting out of radical right-wing populism and 'domesticate' it, at least to a certain extent. This is nothing new. The Greens in Germany and elsewhere, once perceived as a radical affront to the establishment, have gone through a similar process.

Our results rather suggest that two nuances are in order. First, it appears that the influence of RRPP strongly depends on the issues at stake. We have established that this party family has been particularly successful with respect to integration policies. By contrast, it turns out that the influence has been very modest when it comes to European integration. Second, we have shown that RRPP that tolerate minority governments are very effective in influencing government policies. As is exemplified by the intriguing case of the Danish People's Party, several chapters suggest that exploiting the black-mail potential pays off much better than being part of government coalitions. Regarding the indirect influence of RRPP, this edited volume has found that this type of influence is quite pervasive. However, the causal mechanisms at work proved to be rather diverse. We thus invite scholars to deepen their understanding of the indirect policy influence of RRPP.

SOME FINAL THOUGHTS

Radical right-wing populism is currently among the most researched contemporary political phenomena. Until recently, much of this research focused on two questions: what accounts for the dramatic gains of these parties in recent years (i.e. the demand side) and what are these parties all about (i.e. the supply side). By now, these questions are largely resolved. We know who votes for these parties and why, and we also have a good sense of what these parties are all about. Strikingly, we know much less about the impact of these parties on concrete policies. We have focused on the core issues of RRPP, as questions of culture and identity derive their significance for the radical populist right from their symbolic value. They evoke considerable passions and emotions and thus lend themselves particularly to political mobilisation.

The chapters included in this volume suggest that the answer to this question is significantly less straightforward than what one might expect. To be sure, this edited volume had to reject the hypothesis about the positive effect of formal power on policy influence.

Against that, the Danish People's Party suggests that RRPP are politically most successful if they fully exploit their blackmail potential. The party appears to have been most successful at holding the other major parties to ransom, inducing them to adopt their radical policy propositions on migration and the question of Islam. Although the Danish People's Party has never taken part in any coalition government, it fundamentally shaped the country's immigration policy to the point that today, Denmark is among the least hospitable countries (both with respect of migrants and refugees) in Europe. Thus between 2015 and 2018, the country passed 'nearly 70 legal amendments tightening immigration laws' resulting in a precipitous decline in the number of recognised refugees (from 85 percent in 2015 to 36 percent in 2017). Many of the most egregious measures – such as the seizing of valuables from refugees, the invention of 'ghetto children' targeting Denmark's Muslim minority garnered international attention.

The Danish radical right populist's influence, however, has not been limited to government policy. The party has also been instrumental in fundamentally redirecting the programmatic course of the traditional Danish Social Democrats largely in line with the Danish People's Party's position on migration. The rapprochement between the two parties should come as no surprise, given the Danish People's Party's positions on socio-economic issues, which are very close to the Social Democrats. The result, however, has been disastrous for the party. After the Social Democrats did adopt much of its anti-immigrant positions, support for the Danish People's Party collapsed in the recent European and national elections, relegating it to the margins of Danish politics. This, however, has not been the case for other radical right-wing populist parties such as the Front national (recently renamed Rassemblement national) and the Sweden Democrats.

In the long run, however, the Danish case is likely to be of more momentous importance than the radical populist right's impact on policy. It is likely to send a strong signal to left-wing parties elsewhere in Europe (such as, for instance, the Austrian SPÖ) that the only way to regain the levers of power is to come to some kind of accommodation with the populist right, particularly if the latter espouse traditional left-wing positions with respect to social policy. Given the virtual collapse of a growing number of mainstream left-wing parties, accommodating the radical populist right presents an increasingly attractive option, if for no other reason than pure desperation. Given the virtual collapse of a growing number of mainstream left-wing parties (most prominently the German SPD), accommodating the radical populist right is bound to present an increasingly attractive option, particularly if it should continue to deflate support for the radical populist right.

In the literature on the radical right, the former *Front national* has generally been touted as the 'master case' of radical right-wing populism. The evidence presented in this volume suggests that it is time to revise this account. The Danish People's Party has been the radical right-wing populist party in Western Europe that has been most effective in translating its rhetoric into concrete policies. Migration, however, is only one, albeit increasingly important, issue area. The contributions of this volume suggest that despite their growing support at the polls, RRPP do not automatically exert a major influence on other policy areas. There is clearly a populist stance on social, economic and foreign policy that responds to the expectations and aspirations of ordinary people suffering from the negative impact of global economic and financial capitalism. Political parties that derive a considerable share of their support at the polls from routine manual and service workers not only have an obligation to push for policies that improve the latter's life chances but should also be held accountable for delivering concrete results.

BIBLIOGRAPHY

Akkerman, Tjitske. 2012. Comparing radical right parties in government: Immigration and integration policies in nine countries (1996–2010). *West European Politics* 35, no. 3: 511–529.

Bernhard, Laurent, Hanspeter Kriesi and Edward Weber. 2015. The populist discourse of the Swiss People's Party. In *European Populism in the Shadow of the Great Recession*, edited by Hanspeter Kriesi and Takis S. Pappas, 123–137. Colchester: ECPR Press.

Betz, Hans-Georg. 2017. Nativism across time and space. *Swiss Political Science Review* 23, no. 4: 335–353.

Betz, Hans-Georg, and Fabian Habersack. Forthcoming. Regional nativism in Eastern Germany: The AfD in former East Germany. In *Populism and Regionalism*, edited by Oscar Mazzoleni and Reinhard Heinisch. London: Routledge.

Burgoon, Brian, Sam von Noort, Matthijs Rooduijn and Geoffrey Underhill. Forthcoming. Radical right populism and the role of positional deprivation and inequality. *Economic Policy*.

Coffé, Hilde. 2005. The adaptation of the extreme right's discourse: The case of the Vlaams Blok. *Ethical Perspectives* 12, no. 2: 205–230.

Gidron, Noam and Peter A. Hill. 2017. The politics of social status: Economic and cultural roots of the populist right. *The British Journal of Sociology* 68, no. S1: S58–S84.

Libération. 2015. Le FN et la limitation à 10'000 immigrés, la grande imposture. Accessed 3 March 2019. https://www.liberation.fr/desintox/2015/11/05/le-fn-et-la-limitation-a-10-000-immigres-la-grande-imposture_1411376.

Mudde, Cas. 2004. The populist Zeitgeist. *Government and Opposition* 39, no. 4: 542–563.

Mudde, Cas. 2013. Three decades of populist right parties in Western Europe: So what. *European Journal of European Research* 52, no. 1: 1–19.

Mudde, Cas. 2007. *Populist Radical Right Parties in Europe*. Cambridge: Cambridge University Press.

Rooduijn, Matthijs. 2015. The rise of the populist radical right in Western Europe. *European View* 14, no. 1: 3–11.

Rydgren, Jens. 2013. *Class Politics and the Radical Right*. London: Routledge.

Teney, Céline and Marc Helbling. 2014. How denationalization divides elites and citizens. *Zeitschrift für Soziologie* 43, no. 4: 258–271.

Index

About the Contributors

João Miguel Duarte de Carvalho is a principal researcher of the research project entitled: Support and Opposition to Migration in Portugal at the Centre for Research and Studies in Sociology funded by the Portuguese Foundation for Science and Technology (PTDC/IVC-CPO/1069/2014). A second edition of his comparative monograph *Impact of Extreme Right Parties on Immigration Policy: Comparing Britain, France and Italy* was published by Routledge in 2016. He is the author of research articles published in high-ranking journals such as *Party Politics*, *Government and Opposition*, *Parliamentary Affairs*, *Comparative European Politics*, *Patterns of Prejudice* and *Ethnic and Racial Studies*.

Laurent Bernhard is a postdoctoral researcher at the Swiss Center of Expertise in the Social Sciences (FORS), which is hosted by the University of Lausanne (Switzerland). His main research interests include populism, direct democracy, political communication and asylum policies. He has published his academic work in *West European Politics*, the *Journal of Ethnic and Migration Studies and Electoral Studies* as well as with Palgrave Macmillan and Cambridge University Press.

Hans-Georg Betz is an adjunct professor in political science at the University of Zurich (Switzerland). Previously, he taught at York University, Toronto, Johns Hopkins University, Washington, DC, and Koç University, Istanbul. His most important contributions to the scholarly literature include *Radical Right-Wing Populism in Western Europe* (1994) as well as *The New Politics of the Right: New Populist Parties and Movements in Established Democracies* (1998).

Benjamin Biard is a FNRS research fellow in political science at the Catholic University of Louvain (Belgium). He is currently a visiting scholar at the University of Oxford. His research focuses on populism, public policy and democracy. He has published articles on the influence of radical right populist parties on policy-making in Europe in *Policy Studies and International Political Science Review*. He is also the co-editor of two books: On the state of political science in Belgium (2017) and the other one on the transformations of the state (2018).

Mikkel Bjerregaard, MA, political science (cand.scient.pol), is administrative officer at the Danish Ministry of Transport, Building, and Housing and former MA student at Aarhus University.

Nathalie Blanc-Noël is assistant professor in political science in Bordeaux University, France, and assistant director of the Montesquieu Research (IRM) Institute and of the Montesquieu Center for Political Research (CMRP). She founded the *Nordiques* journal.

Christophe Bouillaud is professor of political science at the Institut d'Etudes politiques de Grenoble (IEPG), and member since then of PACTE.

Juliana Chueri is a PhD candidate at the University of Geneva, Switzerland.

Flemming Juul Christiansen, PhD, is associate professor in the Department of Social Science and Business, Roskilde University.

Farid Hafez is currently Senior Researcher at University of Salzburg and Senior Research Fellow at Georgetown University's The Bridge Initiative. In 2017, he was Fulbright visiting professor at University of California, Berkeley, and in 2014, he was visiting scholar at Columbia University, New York. Since 2010, Hafez has been editor of the *Islamophobia Studies Yearbook*, and since 2015 co-editor of the annual *European Islamophobia Report*. He has received the Bruno Kreisky Award for the political book of the year, for his anthology *Islamophobia in Austria (*co-ed. with John Bunzl) and published more than 80 books and articles, including in high-ranking academic journals.

Reinhard Heinisch, PhD, is a professor, Chair of Comparative Austrian Politics, University of Salzburg, Austria. His research interests are comparative populism, Euroscepticism and democracy. He is the author of numerous publications, including most recently *Understanding Populist Organization: The West European Radical Right* (Palgrave 2016/coedited) and *Political Populism; A Handbook* (Nomos 2017/coedited). Other publication appeared in *West European Politics, Democratization, Comparative European Politics* and others. Currently, he is one of the project leaders of a European Union Horizon2020 project on populism and democracy.

Pascal D. König is a researcher at the Institute of Political Science at the Goethe-University Frankfurt, Germany. His research mainly deals with political communication, party competition, and policies regarding digital technologies. Recent work has appeared in *West European Politics, British Journal of Politics and International Relations, Review of Policy Research* and *Big Data & Society*.

Philipp Lutz is a PhD candidate and research assistant at the University of Bern, Switzerland.

Michael Minkenberg, PhD, holds the Chair of Comparative Politics at European University Viadrina in Frankfurt (Oder), Germany.

Fred Paxton is a PhD researcher at the European University Institute, Italy.

Jens Peter Frølund Thomsen, PhD, is associate professor in the Department of Political Science, Aarhus University.

Georg Wenzelburger is assistant professor (Juniorprofessor) of political science at the TU Kaiserslautern, Germany. His main research interests are in the field of Comparative Public Policy Analysis with a special focus on fiscal policies, social policies, law-and-order policies and welfare state reform policies. His most recent contributions have been published in the *British Journal of Political Science*, the *Journal of European Public Policy*, the *Journal of Public Policy* and *West European Politics*.

Malisa Zobel, PhD, is postdoctoral researcher at the Chair of Comparative Politics at European-University Viadrina in Frankfurt (Oder), Germany.